Careers in Law: A Guide for Students, Graduates and Professionals

Disclaimer We strongly advise that readers consult the organisations overseeing the career pathways they are interested in pursuing for up-to-date information on the structure of these careers. Whilst care has been exercised to present accurate information in this publication, errors may have found their way here. The editors, authors and publishers involved in producing this publication are not liable for any damages ensued as a result of following the advice discussed within.

Manda Raz • Erwin Loh • John Devereux
Editors

Careers in Law: A Guide for Students, Graduates and Professionals

Springer

Editors
Manda Raz
Department of Emergency Medicine
Monash Health
Clayton, VIC, Australia

Erwin Loh
St. Vincent's Hospital Melbourne
Fitzroy, VIC, Australia

John Devereux
Faculty of Law, The University of Queensland
Queensland, QLD, Australia

Reviewer
Dr Mina Miller

ISBN 978-981-15-3626-7 ISBN 978-981-15-3627-4 (eBook)
https://doi.org/10.1007/978-981-15-3627-4

This Springer imprint is published by the registered company Springer Nature Singapore Pte Ltd.
The registered company address is: 152 Beach Road, #21-01/04 Gateway East, Singapore 189721, Singapore

The law is our surest pathway through the clamor of irrationality into the peacefulness of truth

To all students and practitioners of law, you are agents of reason, virtue and change. MR
To my wife, Dr May Loh, and kids, Chloe, Charlotte and Christina Loh. EL
To my wife, Sarah Lai San Kam. JD

Preface

This book assists law students, graduates and young law professionals in deciding the area of legal practice to pursue as a career. The number of legal fields and sub-fields is over one hundred, making it virtually impossible for an upcoming lawyer to explore all of these career avenues. Many students finish law school with little understanding of what specific law careers involve, such as sports or space law.

Finding a law career that is a significant source of satisfaction is a function of serious thinking and active research, which the current university to legal practice journey may not always facilitate. This book is a practical guide for any student or current lawyer who is deciding and evaluating their future legal profession.

Clayton, VIC, Australia — Manda Raz
Fitzroy, VIC, Australia — Erwin Loh
Queensland, QLD, Australia — John Devereux

Contents

Contributors

Sayomi Ariyawansa Melbourne Law School, The University of Melbourne, Parkville, VIC, Australia

Sarah Bartholomeusz Hender Consulting, Adelaide, SA, Australia

Allison Berry The University of Melbourne, Melbourne, VIC, Australia

Matthew Burnham Victoria University, Melbourne, VIC, Australia

Sofia Cabral Monash University, Clayton, VIC, Australia

Joshua Ch'ng Monash University, Clayton, VIC, Australia

Tayla Crump Monash University, Clayton, VIC, Australia

John Devereux Faculty of Law, The University of Queensland, Brisbane, QLD, Australia

Lloyd England Victoria University, Melbourne, VIC, Australia

Ariella Gordon Monash University, Clayton, VIC, Australia

Ellen Leishman Monash University, Clayton, VIC, Australia

Jeremy Leith University of Sydney, Sydney, Australia
GradDipLegalPrac (College of Law), The Australian National University, Canberra, Australia

Cassandra Ludeman Monash University, Clayton, VIC, Australia

Vivek Mahadevan University of Wollongong, Wollongong, Australia
GradDipLegalPrac (College of Law), The Australian National University, Canberra, Australia

Ruth Morgan Hender Consulting, Adelaide, SA, Australia

Eliza Panckridge Monash University, Clayton, Melbourne, Australia

Sophie Ryan The University of Queensland, Brisbane, QLD, Australia

Edward Watson The University of Queensland, Brisbane, QLD, Australia

Chapter 1
Applying for Law

Eliza Panckridge

The vast majority of Australian universities offer tertiary studies in law, including:

Australian Capital Territory
- Australian National University
- University of Canberra

New South Wales
- University of Newcastle
- University of New South Wales
- University of Sydney
- University of Technology, Sydney
- Western Sydney University
- University of Wollongong
- Macquarie University
- University of New England
- University of Notre Dame
- Australian Catholic University
- Charles Sturt University
- Southern Cross University

Northern Territory
- Charles Darwin University

E. Panckridge (✉)
Monash University, Clayton, Melbourne, Australia

M. Raz et al. (eds.), *Careers in Law: A Guide for Students, Graduates and Professionals*, https://doi.org/10.1007/978-981-15-3627-4_1

Queensland

- Bond University
- Central Queensland University
- Queensland University of Technology
- University of Queensland
- University of Southern Queensland
- University of the Sunshine Coast
- James Cook University
- Griffith University
- Southern Cross University

South Australia

- University of Adelaide
- University of South Australia
- Flinders University

Tasmania

- University of Tasmania

Victoria

- Swinburne University of Technology
- Victoria University, Australia
- University of Melbourne
- RMIT University
- Monash University
- La Trobe University
- Deakin University
- Australian Catholic University

Western Australia

- University of Western Australia
- Curtin University
- Edith Cowan University
- Murdoch University
- University of Notre Dame

Types of Law Degrees

Tertiary law degrees can be structured in a variety of different ways. They may be single or combined with other degrees (for example Arts, Science or Commerce), undergraduate or postgraduate degrees. You may commence an undergraduate degree without having first obtained another tertiary qualification; postgraduate degrees, on the other hand, require you to have first completed an undergraduate degree.

Bachelor of Laws (LLB)

This degree is abbreviated to LLB (*Legem Baccalaureus* in Latin, meaning Bachelor of Laws). It typically takes four years of full-time study to complete. The LLB is an undergraduate degree, the first to be completed after secondary school studies. As such, it is open to secondary school leavers. It may also be open to current university students who wish to transfer into the LLB from another degree, but have not yet completed an undergraduate degree (university-specific criteria may apply).

Combined Degrees

A combined (or double) degree means the undertaking of two undergraduate degrees at the same time, such as a Bachelor of Laws and a Bachelor of Science. Whilst these degrees often take five or more years to complete, they are very popular for students who are unsure about pursuing a career in law, or want to gain knowledge in a second field to complement their future legal career. For example, a Bachelor of Arts would allow in-depth study of fields such as languages, history, politics or international studies, all of which can be highly valuable beyond tertiary study. The advantage of undertaking two degrees at once is that cross credit is obtained so that the combined degree takes, on average, five years, whereas if the degrees were undertaken separately, they would take in the order of seven years.

Optional Degrees

Many tertiary institutions also offer optional degrees (outside of a single or combined degree) that can be pursued alongside the LLB, such as a diploma. A diploma allows the study of a specific field outside that of the single or combined degree. For example, a student wishing to study a Bachelor of Laws may also wish to learn a language, but may not want to commit to a combined degree by also undertaking a Bachelor of Arts. Instead, they can enrol in a Diploma of Languages alongside their Bachelor of Laws. Diplomas usually take one year to complete and, depending on the tertiary intuition, are available in a wide variety of fields of study.

Juris Doctor (JD)

The Juris Doctor is the postgraduate equivalent of the LLB. However the JD, unlike the LLB, is only open to students who have already completed an undergraduate degree. The JD typically takes three years of full-time study to complete.

LLB or JD?

There are many things to consider when deciding whether to study law at an undergraduate or postgraduate level.

The LLB allows students to delve into law studies straight away, and takes less time to complete than an undergraduate degree followed by a JD. Thus, it is well suited to students who already know they want to study law. Government loan schemes such as HECS-HELP are also more widely available for undergraduate degrees, such as the LLB (criteria apply). However, ATAR entry scores for the LLB and combined undergraduate degrees are very high, and therefore entry into these courses can be competitive.

Conversely, the JD is an attractive option for students who may want to explore other fields of study in their undergraduate degree, or students who might not have been offered a place in an undergraduate law degree. However, depending on the undergraduate degree undertaken, this pathway often takes around six years to complete, and the JD can involve higher tuition fees, which may not be subject to financial assistance from the government.

The choice ultimately depends on your personal circumstances, areas of interest and academic performance.

Interpersonal Requirements

Law schools are not only interested in students with the relevant academic qualifications, but also those who demonstrate a varied range of skills and personal qualities. This list is by no means exhaustive, but intended to act as a guide on the qualities and skills that would be highly beneficial to law studies.

It is also important to remember that these skills can be nurtured and developed during study; you do not need to possess them all prior to commencing.

Communication Skills

Having good communication skills is an essential quality for law students and lawyers. Communication is key to most professions, and lawyers must learn to communicate with many different people in the community.

Verbal communication may involve taking instructions from a client, presenting a case in court or managing a mediation.

Written communication is also a vital skill for law students. You must be able to effectively communicate ideas and advice in assignments and exams, as well as understanding lectures and other written materials.

Legal writing must be clear, effective and very precise. Professionals often need to explain complex legal concepts to clients who are not familiar with the law. As such, students should learn to synthesise information in a way that is simple and easy to understand.

Students should also have excellent listening skills. At law school, students need to be able to listen to lecturers, tutors and other students effectively in order to extrapolate relevant information. As a legal professional, it is important to listen to clients, judges and other industry employees.

Communication skills also enable you to ask thoughtful, relevant questions to aid your understanding.

Research Skills

The skill of efficient legal research is taught and highly emphasised during law studies. More than just finding information, research includes verifying the validity of information, identifying its key points and accurately summarising large bodies of material.

Time Management and Organisation Skills

These skills are especially important to the study and practise of law. Students should determine what system works best for them, and use it to manage stress. Excellent time management and organisation skills will also make time spent studying or working more effective.

Technological Competence

As technology changes and develops, so does the law. Generally, students entering university should expect to encounter technology via online learning systems, online databases, the digitisation of library resources and computerised exams and more. Technological proficiency will continue to be essential in the practise of law. Law firms are increasingly using email, Skype and teleconferencing to communicate with clients and each other. Document processing, exchange and discovery is largely paperless; even proof-reading is becoming the domain of online systems, rather than human professionals. Many courts also use an online filing system in response to the development and application of technology to the law.

Resilience

The ability to accept and respond to constructive criticism is essential to success in law. Law students are often very high achievers and initially can find it difficult competing against a cohort of equally competent peers. Whilst it can be disheartening, try to use criticism as an opportunity to grow and learn.

Dedication

It takes many years of study and training to become a lawyer. On top of four or more years of study, you will also need to complete 'Practical Legal Training' and work experience before you can be admitted as a lawyer. It is a long process, so students must be dedicated and willing to commit a significant amount of time and effort to their studies.

Perseverance

Studying law is different to any other discipline and is often initially confusing and overwhelming. As such, it can take time to negotiate its intricacies. As well as being dedicated to studies, law students must be able to persevere in the face of unfamiliar and often challenging situations. This is particularly relevant to law students who are experiencing many new concepts for the first time.

Academic Requirements

Each law school in Australia sets its own requirements for entry into its law degrees.

Undergraduate Entry Requirements

Entry into university at an undergraduate level generally requires, as a minimum, "satisfactory completion of an Australian or overseas Year 12 program" (such as the Victorian Certificate of Education or the Higher School Certificate) and the satisfactory completion of some English study at a Year 12 level. This may include English, English literature or English as an Additional Language (EAL).

Law schools may also set additional requirements for entry into law, such as English language requirements.

Year 12 (or Equivalent) Subjects

A minimum score in a student's chosen English subject is common for entry into law. Most universities set a minimum study score of 30 (however this can vary, check the specific requirements of your chosen law degree).

Few law schools impose specific subject requirements other than English. However, there are many subjects that are particularly useful in preparing for later studies in law. For example, analytical subjects such as history and literature help develop transferrable skills such as communication, evaluative thinking and critical analysis. These subjects also develop students' essay writing skills.

Philosophy may also be beneficial because of its reflective and analytical nature. Law students, like philosophy students, should always question the world around them and consider the knowledge and behaviour of those around them.

International studies allow students to explore and dissect political, social and economic issues that are common and recurring themes in the study of law, particularly from a legal policy perspective.

Contrary to popular belief, Legal Studies is not a prerequisite to entry into law. It can, however, be a good general introduction to basic concepts, terms and language relating to the law. It may also provide an insight into whether you enjoy learning legal concepts and applying legal reasoning.

Ultimately subject choice in Year 12 should play to a student's strengths and interests to give them the best chance of success.

ATAR

ATAR stands for the Australian Tertiary Admission Rank. It is used to help universities rank applications for entry into particular courses. The ATAR is not a score, it is a ranking; a student's academic achievement compared to the rest of their cohort.

Students who satisfactorily complete their Year 12 studies receive an ATAR. Every state and territory in Australia uses the ATAR. In 2020, the ATAR came into use in Queensland, replacing the Overall Position ranking system.

For specific information about how the ATAR is calculated, see the Victorian University Admissions Centre and Universities Admissions Centre websites.

Minimum ATAR results for entry into undergraduate law are generally very high. However, this is greatly dependent on the university and specific course being applied to, as well as the year of entry and the popularity of the particular course.

ATAR requirements for specific courses can be found at the following websites:

State	Admissions centre	Website
New South Wales and Australian Capital Territory	Universities Admissions Centre (NSW and ACT)	http://www.uac.edu.au/
Northern Territory	South Australian Tertiary Admissions Centre	http://www.satac.edu.au/
Queensland	Queensland Tertiary Admissions Centre	https://www.qtac.edu.au/
South Australia	South Australian Tertiary Admissions Centre	http://www.satac.edu.au/
Tasmania	No specific admissions centre. Applications to the University of Tasmania are made directly to the University.	www.utas.edu.au/
Victoria	Victorian Tertiary Admissions Centre	http://www.vtac.edu.au/
Western Australia	Tertiary Institutions Service Centre	https://www.tisc.edu.au/

University Grades

Your marks at University can be an important factor in determining if you will be admitted to a postgraduate degree or allowed to transfer courses.

GPA

GPA stands for Grade Point Average. The GPA is an internationally recognised average of all the grades attained in a degree. It can be considered by universities when students want to go on exchange, change courses or study postgraduate degrees; it can also be considered by employers.

In most universities, the GPA is calculated on a 4.0 scale, meaning that a GPA of 4.0 is equivalent to a high distinction, 3.0 being equivalent to a distinction, 2.0 being a credit and 1.0 a pass. Universities offer a GPA calculator on their website for students to manually enter their grades, and most will actually do the calculation automatically for each student. The GPA will appear on each student's academic record.

A student's GPA takes into account not only the score received for a unit, but also the amount that the unit counts towards the degree. For example, some law degrees stipulate that first year units are not weighted as heavily as other units.

However, some universities (for example, the University of Sydney and the University of Melbourne) do not use the GPA. These institutions use the WAM, which means Weighted Average Mark.

WAM

Similar to the GPA, it is a score or grade that indicates a student's academic performance. However, the WAM applies only to a single course (i.e. Bachelor of Laws), as opposed to the GPA, which applies to a whole degree (i.e. Bachelor of Laws/Bachelor of Arts).

The WAM is a score, set out as a percentage, and weighs units in the same way as the GPA.

Examination Requirements

STAT or LSAT?

STAT stands for Special Tertiary Admissions Test. The STAT is taken by non-Year 12 leavers, or mature age students, for entry into undergraduate law.

LSAT stands for Law Schools Admission Test. The LSAT is taken by undergraduate students for entry into postgraduate law.

STAT

The STAT is an aptitude test administered and marked by ACER, the Australian Council for Educational Research. The STAT can take two forms.

Multiple Choice

The multiple choice STAT contains 70 questions and lasts for 2 h, with 10 min reading time. The STAT tests students' "ability to read and interpret graphical displays of information and passages of writing, to use mathematical relationships and to apply reasoning to tables of data."

Written English

The written English STAT requires students to write two essays, testing their communication skills, and lasts for 1 h, with 5 min reading time.

Not all courses and institutions require students to take the STAT, and it is not commonly used as the sole basis for selection into a course. The STAT is not usually required for students applying to law from Year 12.

Each state's Tertiary or University Admissions Centre website will detail whether the STAT is required for a particular course, or for a particular university, and how to make a booking to take the test.

The STAT can only be taken a limited number of times, however many institutions accept test results that are up to three or four years old.

STAT sittings occur in May, October and November in a range of locations, both metropolitan and regional.

Further information about the STAT, including a free Candidate Information Booklet containing sample questions, can be found on the ACER website: https://stat.acer.edu.au/.

Applications to sit the STAT can also be made through the ACER website.

LSAT

The LSAT is an internationally recognised test, administered by the Law School Admission Council.

The LSAT is required by many Australian universities, predominantly for entry into the postgraduate JD program.

The LSAT is well suited to law school admissions because it does not test knowledge, rather the application of rules to specific situations. It measures "acquired reading and verbal reasoning skills that are essential for success in law school."

The LSAT is a standardised test comprised of six 35-min sections: five multiple-choice sections and a writing sample. The sections are randomly ordered, however, the writing sample always appears last.

- Multiple choice: reading comprehension.

These questions "measure the ability to read, with understanding and insight, examples of lengthy and complex materials similar to those commonly encountered in law school."

Students are required to read a set of passages and answer questions to test their ability to understand, summarise and analogise the information read.

- Multiple choice: analytic reasoning.

These questions "measure the ability to understand a structure of relationships and to draw logical conclusions about that structure."

A scenario is posed and students must follow a set of rules to answer questions.

- Multiple choice: logical reasoning.

These questions assess an individual's "ability to analyse, critically evaluate, and complete arguments as they occur in ordinary language."

Students read a short paragraph, before being asked to identify the strengths and weaknesses of the argument contained in that paragraph. Students may also be asked to articulate any assumptions made within the argument, or whether it could be strengthened by certain facts.

- Multiple choice: logical reasoning.

There are two sections containing logical reasoning questions, making up 50% of a student's LSAT score. It is therefore important that students familiarise themselves with these questions through resources such as practice exams.

- Multiple choice: experimental section.

This section comprises either reading comprehension, analytic reasoning or logical reading questions. The experimental section is not scored, but is used by the Law School Admissions Council to test new questions for future LSATs. Students are not told which section is experimental.

- Writing sample.

Students must respond to a prompt with a short essay. The prompt describes a fictional person's situation and poses two possible approaches to the problem. Students then describe the best course of action based on the situation and the fictional person's goals.

Whilst the writing sample is not scored, it is nonetheless sent for consideration to a student's chosen law school(s).

For a free set of sample LSAT questions (including a sample writing topic) and their answers, see https://www.lsac.org/free-sample-test/.

The LSAT is scored based on the number of correctly answered questions. There are no penalties for incorrect answers, and each question carries the same weight. Scores are communicated through a scale that ranges from 120 to 180, being the lowest and highest scores respectively. Each university has their own minimum score required for admission (as well as other criteria, such as undergraduate academic results), however the international average result for the test is 151. LSAT results are valid for 5 years and students can take the test three times in any two-year period. The LSAT costs US$180 to sit.

The test can be undertaken in June, September/October, December and February at one of the following locations around Australia:

- Adelaide, SA, LTC Testing;
- Brisbane, QLD, Queensland University of Technology;
- Canberra, ACT, University of Canberra;
- Darwin, NT, Darwin Examination Centre;
- Hobart, TAS, University of Tasmania;
- Melbourne, VIC, University of Melbourne;
- Melbourne, VIC, Monash University Clayton Campus;
- Perth, WA, University of Western Perth Examination Centre;
- Sydney, NSW, LTC Testing Centre.

LSAT tests cannot be taken in February for entry into law in the same year. It is recommended by the Law School Admissions Council that students sit the LSAT in February or June of the year before commencing study. This allows students to re-sit the test later in the year, should they be unhappy with their results from the first sitting. However, students should note that universities would have access to the results of all LSATs undertaken by that student.

Applications to sit the LSAT can be made through the Law School Admissions Council, at https://www.lsac.org/.

Preparing for Exams, the STAT or the LSAT

Both tests require dedicated study in order to get good results. It is important to remember that the tests are different to the General Achievement Test (undertaken by Victorian and New South Welsh secondary school students) or any type of undergraduate assessment.

Start Preparation Early

The University of Melbourne suggest that LSAT preparation should commence no later than 6 months before sitting the test. This allows students ample time to familiarise themselves with the test.

Try to study consistently throughout your preparation time, as opposed to random blocks of study lasting a number of hours. This is not only more effective preparation, but reduces stress.

Complete Practice Tests Under Test Conditions

Practice tests not only allow students to adjust to the timing and conditions of the test, but also to identify their own strengths and weaknesses.

Practice test questions can be found, and additional questions purchased, via the Australian Council for Educational Research and Law School Admissions Council websites:

- ACER: https://www.acer.org/;
- LSAC: https://www.lsac.org/.

Find Techniques That Work for You

There is no single prescribed way to approach the tests. It is therefore essential that students find techniques that suit their learning and test-taking styles.

Read about the tests online and take notes on recommended techniques for answering questions.

The Law School Admissions Council has a YouTube channel, "LSACvideos", which offers a set of four videos detailing each part of the test and offering tips on how best to prepare.

The Victorian Tertiary Admissions Centre website offers tips for completing the Multiple Choice section of the STAT. For example, students should be working through questions one at a time and eliminating incorrect answers first.

Test candidates can also speak to students who have already completed the test. These students can provide insight, support and advice about how they approached the test, and their preparation techniques.

Preparation Workshops

Both the STAT and LSAT tests are covered in various preparation workshops. Whilst workshops can sometimes be costly, they can also be extremely beneficial to students preparing for the tests. Workshops can help students to develop strategies for taking the tests, whilst easing the stress associated with preparation.

Specifically, the Law School Admissions Council has published *The Official LSAT Handbook*, which can be a helpful guide to the test. It offers "tips and strategies to practise specific skill types... a diagnostic test to identify your strengths and weaknesses so you know what questions to focus on in your preparation... [and] a preparation guide for the week of the test".

Be Prepared for the Day of the Test

Being prepared is essential for reducing nerves and stress related to the test. The following tips can ensure you don't feel overwhelmed on test day, so as to allow your preparation to be most effective:

- Make sure you are well rested.

Try not to do any preparation the night before, as this will only increase nerves and stress. Also try to avoid using electronic devices up to an hour before going to bed, as they emit blue light that can hinder sleep.

- Have a nutritious breakfast.

Try to avoid sugary cereals, and instead opt for slow-release carbohydrates and protein, such as oats or eggs. These keep you feeling full for longer.

- Stay hydrated.

Dehydration can lead to headaches, tiredness and reduced concentration. Make sure you take a water bottle into the test, and drink plenty the night before and morning of the test.

- Prepare your test kit.

Familiarise yourself with the rules of the test, and work out what you will need to bring on the day. For example, ensure you have the right type of pencil and/or pen and make sure you bring an eraser and pencil sharpener, if required.

Preparing your kit the night before will alleviate stress and prevent you forgetting anything on the day. This kit might include stationary, identification and any documentation required.

- Arrive early.

Plan to arrive early to the test centre, and allow time for traffic or public transport delays. This prevents you missing any writing time and adding unnecessary stress on the day.

Extracurricular Requirements

Some universities require a written application that details why the applicant wishes to study there. Whilst there are no official requirements for extracurricular activities, they are looked upon favourably by universities for a number of reasons.

Extracurricular activities demonstrate a student's involvement with the community at a school, university, local or even international level. Universities want students to be part of the legal community: it allows them to make friends, reduce stress, enjoy university and achieve better academic results.

Law schools are also interested in students who possess a wide range of personal qualities and skills; involvement in extracurricular activities is an excellent way for students to demonstrate this to prospective universities.

For example, being part of a sporting team during school or university means an applicant will have good communication skills. Working a part-time job around study demonstrates excellent time management and organisation skills. Even pursuing a hobby such as craft, music or writing shows passion and dedication to a particular interest.

Extracurricular activities may include:

- Playing in a sporting team, such as soccer, Ultimate Frisbee, swimming or football;
- Being a member of a social, academic or religious club, for example debating, theatre or a cultural club;
- Volunteering with an organisation, such as The Salvation Army or a local charity;
- Pursuing a hobby or interest, such as the piano, gardening or model trains;
- Working part-time.

Leadership positions within these extracurricular activities are especially favourable to prospective law students, because they demonstrate a high level of commitment, perseverance and success.

Remember that these extracurricular activities don't have to be related to law. Universities are more interested in these activities being able to teach students transferrable skills such as communication, organisation and time management.

The quality of a student's involvement in clubs, volunteering or part-time work is more important than the quantity of activities. It is more worthwhile to be regularly involved in, and perhaps part of the leadership of one or two clubs, than to simply be a member of multiple clubs.

Chapter 2
Inside Law School

Edward Watson and Sophie Ryan

Sometimes, life can feel like a box of Forrest Gump's chocolates – "you never know what you're gonna get".[1] Whether you end up with a job you absolutely love, whether you make a difference in this world, whether you end up Prime Minister, all turns, at the end of the day, on 'Forrest Gumpian' luck. You either have it or you don't.

This chapter challenges that mindset. While there is of course an element of luck behind the experiences we collect in law school and in life, luck is *not* the determinative factor in whether we achieve all we set out to achieve. 'Luck' can only take you so far; you have to have laid down the groundwork that enables you to seize opportunities with both hands when they do come your way. In fact doing the groundwork, in many cases, *is* what points those opportunities your way.

Therefore, in this chapter, we will seek to help you start laying down the groundwork – to reflect on your expectations and aspirations and make the right choices to eventually achieve them. We hope that what follows will help form a blueprint for your endeavours to make the most of law school. We will guide you through the academic, extracurricular and professional aspects of university life and provide you with useful tips about planning your own law school experience so that your hard work, talent and good fortune culminate in success thereafter.

The authors thank those mentors and peers who provided invaluable assistance for various sections of this chapter. In particular, we thank Jacqueline Lynagh, Educational Designer at the University of Queensland TC Beirne School of Law, Professor Lucy Reed, Professor of Law and Director of the Centre for International Law at the National University of Singapore, and fellow law students or recent graduates, Josephine Allan, Kate Cincotta, Michael Chen, Jessica Downing-Ide, Thomas Fairweather, Genevieve Feely, Ellie Hilston, Emily McClelland, Ryan Palfrey, and Claire Robertson.

[1] *Forrest Gump* (directed by Robert Zemeckis, Paramount Pictures, 1994).

E. Watson (✉) · S. Ryan
The University of Queensland, Brisbane, QLD, Australia

M. Raz et al. (eds.), *Careers in Law: A Guide for Students, Graduates and Professionals*, https://doi.org/10.1007/978-981-15-3627-4_2

Starting Law School: Managing Your Expectations and Goals

Expectations of Law School

University is more often than not an exercise in trial and error. If you are entering law school straight after graduating high school, it is likely that you do not have a very clear picture of what a career in the law might entail. It is probable that you are not quite sure what studying at university is supposed to be like. It is possible that you have taken a stab in the dark by choosing to pursue a law degree. All of this is perfectly normal.

As you begin your law school career (or even if you are well into it), it is therefore handy to remember three things you should expect or *not* expect from law school. *First*, you should definitely expect it to be difficult and challenging. The concepts you learn will be confusing and the workload required to understand and remember everything will be substantial. *Second*, you should not expect law school to offer you experiences and opportunities on a silver platter. There is a lot of self-managing required with both your studies and extracurricular activities – you need to take initiative and get involved. *Finally*, do not expect law school to define who you are. Oftentimes, law students get a bad rap for being cliquey, hypercompetitive or elitist. Whether this culture develops or affects you, however, is up to you. Choose to create a positive law school culture and identity by being kind, collegial and fair.

More important than anything is what you shouldn't expect from yourself. Don't expect yourself to know everything. Embrace the Socratic Paradox – that true wisdom comes in knowing just how much you don't know. Be open-minded, flexible and appreciate the value of tapping into the *shared* knowledge and expertise of those around you.

Common Concerns of a Law Student

As exciting as joining the pathway to the legal profession is, your high expectations about the legal industry may turn to concern over your time in law school. Starting with the elephant in the room, many find themselves wondering: are there too many law students? Countless naysayers have been quick to denounce legal education: "thousands of students are undertaking a degree that will result in broken dreams"[2]; "law school leaves many graduates in a far worse position than they started"[3]; and

---

[2] Frank Carrigan, 'Law schools sell graduates down the river', *Australian Financial Review* (online), 8 August 2016 http://www.afr.com/business/legal/the-law-schools-of-rapidly-diminishing-returns-20160808-gqnday#.

[3] Eric Fuchs, 'I consider Law School A Waste Of My Life And An Extraordinary Waste Of Money', *Business Insider* (online), 14 December 2013 http://www.businessinsider.com/is-law-school-worth-the-money-2013-12.

"churning out lawyers shows a lack of judgment".[4] Even former Prime Minister Malcolm Turnbull has warned graduates, despite being a lawyer himself, not to study law "unless they actually want to be lawyers".[5] The warnings are seemingly backed up by figures; while close to 15,000 students graduate from Australian law schools each year, the legal profession consists of only 66,000 solicitors.[6]

There is the further worry of whether a law degree will even adequately prepare you to be a successful lawyer. New law graduates are expected to be commercially-aware and flexible workers rather than traditional black-letter law experts.[7] Evolving technologies are resulting in law firms creating products and services which require less human input. Firms are also facing new challenges which cannot be solved by simply employing book-smart law graduates.[8] There is pressure to be proactive in future-proofing yourself for the legal work of tomorrow, for example by establishing a start-up to demonstrate your innovativeness.[9]

Finally, there is the daily question: am I good enough? There is an expectation that *you*, as a law student, need to be smart, social and involved in every aspect of university life to be 'successful'.

Having a Positive Professional Identity

It is easy to allow these anxieties to consume us. However, that would make for a miserable university experience. To counter these anxieties, let your motivations for studying law and aspirations thereafter guide you, and evolve, throughout

---

[4] Adam Creighton, 'Churning out lawyers shows a lack of judgment', *The Australian* (online), 5 February 2018 https://www.theaustralian.com.au/opinion/churning-out-lawyers-shows-a-lack-of-judgment/news-story/c97c1b4c63556b8310b3702391118164.

[5] Louise Yaxley, 'Don't study law unless you really want to be a lawyer', *ABC News* (online), 2 February 2018 http://www.abc.net.au/news/2018-02-02/malcolm-turnbull-says-too-many-kids-do-law/9387508.

[6] Tom McIlroy, '"Too many kids are doing law": Malcolm Turnbull warns against law degrees', *Australian Financial Review* (online) 2 February 2018 http://www.afr.com/news/too-many-kids-are-doing-law-malcolm-turnbull-warns-against-law-degrees-20180201-h0sc6h.

[7] Ruth Callaghan, 'Legal sector looks to new hires to help it ride out disruption', *Australian Financial Review* (online), 13 February 2018 https://www.afr.com/leadership/legal-sector-looks-to-new-hires-to-help-it-ride-out-disruption-20180104-h0d96z.

[8] Luke Misthos, 'Students left behind as legal industry takes off', *Australian Financial Review* (online), 30 November 2017 https://www.afr.com/business/legal/students-left-behind-as-legal-industry-takes-off-20171129-gzuygb.

[9] Marianna Papadakis and Edmund Tadros, 'The secret to getting a graduate job at a top-tier law firm', *Australian Financial Review* (online), 8 January 2016 https://www.afr.com/business/legal/the-secret-to-getting-a-graduate-job-at-a-top-tier-law-firm-20160126-gme3g7.

university. Make law school not only a university experience, but a process of building your professional identity.[10]

Doing so begins with understanding your motivations and aspirations. What type of lawyer do you want to be? In law school, you will be exposed to many professionals: academics, solicitors, barristers or otherwise. It is important to use those observations to find the right professional identity for you, for instance whether you are suited to become a "facilitator of transactions" or a "warrior advocate".[11] Beginning to form a professional identity avoids the notorious 'imposter syndrome' because you understand how you fit in the broader legal community. You also avoid creating an 'image-based identity' because you reflect on your personal values and find what's best for your personality, rather than pursuing superficial rewards.[12]

In fact, you should also go one step further and ask yourself: do I even want to be a lawyer? The reality is many law students don't. The aforementioned figure of '15,000 graduates per year' is not only inconsistent with the data reported by the Council of Australian Law Deans, which shows that in 2015 the total number of law graduates was 7583,[13] but also fails to acknowledge that not all law graduates go on to become lawyers.[14] Thinking about your professional identity therefore corrects the fear of too many law graduates and reframes how you look at law school: it is not a tournament to receive a coveted place in the legal profession.

In our experience, studying law is not limited to learning about the law; it teaches you how to *think*. Law graduates are able to think analytically, see beyond the detail to the bigger picture and evaluate it. These are skills which imbue law graduates with value transferable to any field, legal or otherwise. Couple these generic skills with enhanced communication skills and a deep understanding of government and the structures of society, and law school is useful not only professionally, but also simply in forming informed and critically-minded members of society.[15]

While some deem this view overly optimistic or a 'self-serving myth' circulated by law schools,[16] we believe it is well-founded in reality. As Chief Justice Kiefel stated in 2017:

---

[10] Rachael M. Field, James Duffy and Anna Huggins, *Lawyering and Positive Professional Identities* (2014, Lexis Nexis Butterworths).

[11] Ibid 11.

[12] Ibid 17.

[13] Council of Australian Law Deans, *Data regarding law school graduate numbers and outcomes* (November 2017) Council of Australian Law Deans https://cald.asn.au/wp-content/uploads/2017/11/Factsheet-Law_Students_in_Australia.pdf.

[14] See this piece by Lawyers Weekly and Neville Carter, CEO of College of Law: Emma Ryan, 'College of Law boss busts grad number "myth"', *Lawyers Weekly* (online), 16 March 2018 https://www.lawyersweekly.com.au/careers/22909-exclusive-college-of-law-boss-busts-grad-number-myth.

[15] John F Kennedy, 'An Address by the President of the United States Commemorating the Founding of the University: The Educated Citizen's Responsibility in an Age of Change' (1963) 17 *Vanderbilt Law Review* 171, 174.

[16] Frank Carrigan, 'Law schools sell graduates down the river', *Australian Financial Review* (online), 8 August 2016 http://www.afr.com/business/legal/the-law-schools-of-rapidly-diminishing-returns-20160808-gqnday# ('... their [law schools'] claim that the legal problems undertaken

> The study of law has been described as a "training in logic" and its methods of solution "processes of analogy, discrimination and deduction". It is this training which explains why law is the choice of so many students, both from Australia and overseas. It provides the best foundation for any number of different careers.[17]

You are able to, and should, form your own career pathway based on what you identify with professionally. Law school is not a conveyer belt. Law graduates are present in almost every field from parliament to big business. Robert Menzies, John Howard and Bob Hawke, Australia's three longest serving prime ministers, were all lawyers. Mahatma Gandhi and Nelson Mandela were also lawyers by training. Even John Cleese studied law! Whether you're out to start a revolution or want to bring the world the next Monty Python, remember that studying law should help, not hinder, those aspirations.

Goalsetting

Realising your professional identity is no easy task, however; law school is not something that you can meticulously plan out to ensure you land in one particular job. In his 2005 Stanford commencement speech,[18] Steve Jobs used a helpful analogy: life is a series of connected dots. We can only connect those dots with the benefit of hindsight. For Jobs, this meant that the greatest challenge, and the most important thing we can do, is *trust* that the dots will somehow connect in our future. Therefore, focus on plotting each dot as they come along. Law school presents you with the opportunity to plot many seemingly disconnected dots – do not overlook or turn away opportunities because you cannot see how they connect. Of course, have end goals and strive for the dots necessary to get you there. Beyond these dots, have faith that following your interests, working hard and grabbing opportunities as they come along will take you to where you are meant to be.

A mindset that we suggest will help you ensure that your dots connect in the *right* way is the 'start with why' mentality championed by Simon Sinek. Such a mindset aligns well with developing your professional identity because identifying your 'why' clarifies what ***choices*** you need to make throughout your degree in order to ultimately achieve your professional ambitions. Avoid blindly following a straight

in law tutorials are a platform for a generalist degree – that will see students who miss out on a job as a lawyer well placed to enter other high-paid spheres of the economy – is a self-serving myth').

[17] Chief Justice Susan Kiefel, 'Why the Study of Law is so Important' (Speech delivered at The Opening of the University of Queensland's T C Beirne School of Law's newly renovated West Wing of the Forgan Smith Building, The University of Queensland, 13 March 2017) http://www.hcourt.gov.au/assets/publications/speeches/current-justices/kiefelj/KiefelCJ13Mar2017.pdf; See also, Chief Justice Robert French, 'Legal Education in Australia — A Never Ending Story' (Speech delivered at the Australasian Law Teachers' Association Conference, Brisbane, 4 July 2011).

[18] Steve Jobs, 'Commencement address' (Speech delivered at Stanford University Commencement, Stanford University, 12 June 2005) https://news.stanford.edu/2005/06/14/jobs-061505/.

path towards a particular career, merely 'ticking the boxes' on the way. *Find* and *start* with your 'why' in mind. Identify why you are here. Why do you want to go through law school? What is it that draws you to it? What do you find exhilarating and when do you feel most fulfilled? Why does it matter how you fare in university? The answer to these questions should be the yardstick against which you measure yourself and everything you do and want to do.

To help you lay down the framework for plotting your law-school dots, Fig. 2.1 outlines some general practices and a timeline for their implementation to help you plot the dots[19]:

Seeking and Accepting Help

The idiom, 'it takes a village', applies just as much to law school as life. You get the most out of law school by surrounding yourself with the diverse group of people you meet there. To revisit the Socratic Paradox – that true wisdom comes in knowing just how much you don't know – law school is all about stepping into the abyss and learning how to search for and acquire knowledge, or at least navigate your lack of it. This journey is made easier and more likely successful when you *don't* do it alone. Sure, Lord Denning is a great mentor through paper but you need more. You need an army of mentors – people you can glean advice, guidance and support from – to help you manage your time at law school (and beyond!) effectively.

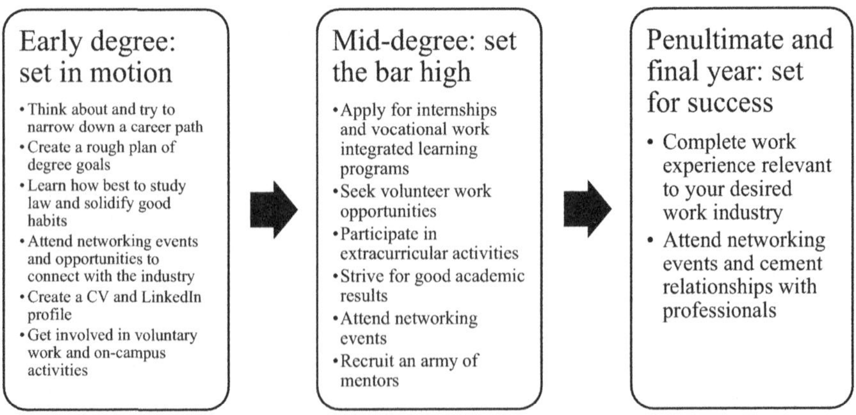

Fig. 2.1 Setting yourself up

[19] See, eg, BEL Student Employability Team, *Information for Students* (2017) University of Queensland Faculty of Business, Economics & Law https://bel.uq.edu.au/employability/information-students.

Law school presents the perfect opportunity to add to this army of mentors. It brings together some incredibly interesting, passionate and capable individuals who make great friends. Collaborate, rather than compete, with your peers. Show interest in your professors' subject areas and go to consultations to develop your classroom relationships into professional relationships. Everyone you meet at law school has something they can teach you, and will continue to be great contacts after you graduate, so get to know them!

Looking After Yourself

Law students and lawyers are 'notorious for living "unbalanced" lives'.[20] Many wear their lack of sleep and excessive study hours as badges of honour. However, research, experience and common sense all condemn this mindset – law students need to move towards smarter, rather than harder, work ethics. Law school and your career thereafter are a marathon, not a sprint.

Think about it strategically. Looking after yourself isn't just a matter of your own comfort, it ensures your success is sustainable. Take our former Foreign Minister, Julie Bishop, for example. Julie Bishop is renowned for carving out daily personal time despite working 20-h days. She insists on running every morning, no matter where she is. Why? She says that trying to keep fit and healthy allows her to *focus*.[21] Investing in her own wellbeing is investing in her productivity. She's not alone in thinking so. Ariana Huffington has said that "the success at the Huffington Post happened after I started taking care of myself".[22] Bill Gates stresses the importance of a good night's sleep: "I like to get seven hours of sleep at night because that's what I need to stay sharp and creative and upbeat".[23] Working towards *your* healthy 'balance' is a constant journey and it'll probably feel like you are never quite *there*. Nonetheless, consciously try to prioritise your wellbeing. In this section, we share ideas for other things you might consider when striving for that balance. For more in this space, you should also check out the Australian Law Students' Association's

[20] Ben Gibson, 'How Law Students Can Cope: A Students View' (2010) 60 *Journal of Legal Education* 140, 142.

[21] See, eg, Heather McNab, 'Foreign Minister or Super Woman' *Daily Mail* (online), 24 November 2014 http://www.dailymail.co.uk/news/article-2846740/Foreign-Minister-Super-Woman-Julie-Bishop-gets-just-60-minutes-morning-spends-half-jogging-works-20-hour-days-never-drinks-coffee.html.

[22] Ruth Umoh, 'Arianna Huffington says she became successful after she quit one common bad habit', *CNBC News* (online), 11 March 2018 https://www.cnbc.com/2018/03/11/arianna-huffington-became-successful-after-she-started-sleeping-well.html.

[23] Emmie Martin, 'Jeff Bezos, Sheryl Sandberg and 5 other business leaders all prioritize the same habit', *CNBC News* (online), 9 November 2017 https://www.cnbc.com/2017/11/09/jeff-bezos-sheryl-sandberg-and-other-leaders-who-prioritize-sleep.html.

Wellbeing Guide, a great document dedicated to helping you manage your wellbeing![24]

Health

How you care for your body affects how you perform. It can be easy to overlook yourself when trying to manage everything else in your life but the importance of managing your own health is much like the safety advice you receive on an airplane: "put your oxygen mask on first before assisting others". What this means is that to be successful in law school and after, you have to take care of yourself. We're not asking you for a full "Eat, Pray, Love" personal awakening here, just that you factor *you* into your time management. Start with the basics:

Sleep

People often feel like to get more out of the day they need to literally find more time in the day – sleeping less is the secret to success, they say. Fake news. While there are some people who don't need much sleep, most of us need a solid 7–9 h each night.[25] People who sleep less "are not as mentally sharp, as vigilant, as attentive or as patient as they would otherwise be".[26] In 2016–2017 there was an estimated 7.4 million Australian adults who did not get the sleep they need regularly.[27] Don't make this common mistake.

Eat

Eating healthily is an obvious but sometimes difficult 'right' decision. Like a car, we run better with good quality fuel. Acknowledge the power of 'brain foods' – foods like fish, berries, lean protein and nuts – and their power to help improve your concentration, recall and sharpness. Think also about how much coffee you drink and how it affects you.

---

[24] Australian Law Student Association, *2015 ALSA Wellbeing Guide* (18 May 2015) BeyondLaw https://beyondlaw.com.au/news/103-2015-alsa-wellbeing-guide.

[25] Sleep Health Foundation, *How much sleep do you really need?* (2011) https://www.sleephealthfoundation.org.au/public-information/fact-sheets-a-z/how-much-sleep-do-you-really-need.html.

[26] David Hillman quoted in Luke Cooper, 'Australia, We Have a Sleep Deprivation Problem' Huffington Post, 7 February 2017, https://www.huffingtonpost.com.au/2017/02/07/australia-we-have-a-sleep-deprivation-problem_a_21708513/.

[27] Sleep Health Foundation, *Asleep on the Job: Costs of Inadequate Sleep in Australia* (August 2017) https://www.sleephealthfoundation.org.au/files/Asleep_on_the_job/Asleep_on_the_Job_SHF_report-WEB_small.pdf.

Exercise

We all know it but whether we choose to do it is another thing – exercise is a necessary ingredient to good wellbeing. Exercise can be very effective at reducing stress and helping you maintain your 'mental fitness'. Physical activity produces endorphins which aids sleep and reduces stress. Even 5 min of exercise can help stimulate anti-anxiety effects! Think about exercise not as a burden but as a secret weapon to help you power through all those commitments. Business leader, Richard Branson, swears by the power of exercise to maximise efficiency: it "keeps the brain functioning well and I definitely can achieve twice as much in a day by keeping fit".[28]

Repeat

Remember that the point here is finding a balance and maintaining it! Establishing habits requires repetition – don't expect to become a health nut overnight. Accept your fallibility too; if you fall off the horse, remember that it's all about getting back on again.

Stress

Learning how to deal with stress now will not only help you weather the storms of law school, but also the storms that come after. Stress and the role it plays in your life cannot be separated from how you deal with everything else. Your study habits, time management techniques and approach to your physical health all play a role in your mental health. In this chapter we generally focus on managing stress in a big picture sense – how to gradually work towards the best 'you' and manage your time at law school in general. But how do you deal with stress when it overwhelms you in a single moment? Here's a couple of suggestions:

1. **Take breaks.** When stress starts impairing your productivity, recognise it and take a short (maybe 10-min) break to re-adjust. Some things you can do to re-centre include: exercising (even stretching can make a big difference); listening to music; watching inspirational YouTube videos; having a shower/bath; spending time with your pet; practising mindfulness; or smiling.
2. **Spend time with family and friends.** Always remember that you're not alone. Talking to others and immersing yourself in a community helps put things in perspective. Sometimes, law school can leave you feeling like you're all alone in the dark – your friends and family can help you, in these times, to find and turn on the light.

---

[28] Joe Polish, 'Richard Branson on Exercise and Productivity' (YouTube video, 00:00:51, March 2011) https://www.youtube.com/watch?v=QFjgMKwpz_k.

3. **Find and maintain hobbies.** Do something just because you love doing it, whether that be reading for pleasure, baking or arts and crafts. Doing something that isn't law can renew your attention and motivation.
4. **Ask for help**. Lean on those around you and seek help if you need it. It takes courage to recognise when you need help and to pursue it. Check out your university counselling and other support services and do not be afraid to use them. Outside university, there are numerous resources to help you, such as Beyond Blue, the Black Dog Institute, Smiling Mind and Headspace.

Fulfilling Your Academic Expectations and Goals

Assessment can often be seen as an unwanted but unavoidable part of university study. It can be difficult to rationalise how memorising and regurgitating 12 weeks of content would be useful when you become a lawyer. However, treating assessment as a chore overlooks the important skills you learn through them in law school: new knowledge; an ethical disposition to legal problems; critical thinking skills; research skills; an ability to communicate and collaborate; and self-management.[29]

This section will discuss how you can think about your learning and studying when it comes to exam preparation and assignment writing and offer some possible techniques you can use to improve your approach.

Exams

With exam preparation, an ideal study process can be roughly divided into four parts: *first*, the 'acquisition' phase; *second*, the 'resource-building' phase; *third*, the 'application' phase; and *fourth*, the 'feedback' phase.

However, it must be emphasised at the outset that every student will approach studying differently. Studying is a life-long skill you will use throughout your career to learn new skills and concepts. Everyone learns in their own unique way. This 'way' may be shaped by factors such as your previous knowledge; self-confidence; how you conceive of knowledge and learning; your approach to learning and studying; and your learning expectations.[30]

Thinking about how you best learn (and study) is therefore not only valuable to excelling at exam preparation, but also to becoming an excellent lawyer. The first thing you should consider when determining how to approach your learning is your

[29] Rachael Field, Mark Israel and Sally Kift, 'Drafting standards for the Bachelor of Laws' (2010) 37(10) *BRIEF* 32, 32.

[30] Diana Laurillard, *Teaching as a Design Science: Building Pedagogical Patterns for Learning and Technology* (Routledge, 2012) 27.

'why'.[31] Having a why, such as a career objective or the purely extrinsic goal of good grades (which is perfectly normal![32]), helps justify the hours you spend on difficult topics.[33] As we said in sections "Having a positive professional identity" and "Goalsetting", have a positive professional identity and set realistic goals.

Acquisition

The 'acquisition' phase is the first, and therefore fundamental, part to learning something new. It encompasses 'acquiring' the new knowledge. Importantly, acquiring is not limited to reading the course material for the first time, but also understanding it and being able to think critically about it. Keep the following tips in mind.

Be an Active Learner

Foremost, learning requires you to be active. Reading lecture slides and textbooks repeatedly does little to assist deeper understanding.[34]

A simple and easy way of making sure you 'understand' certain concepts is to try and process the knowledge you are trying to acquire. For instance, you could summarise your notes in your own words, or try and explain the topic to a friend who is not familiar with the ideas. As Seneca said, "while we teach, we learn". Discussing the ideas with your classmates is also an effective way of finding gaps in your knowledge or identifying information you had not noticed before. Having a study group is therefore very useful, as is visiting lecturers or tutors during consultation and going through the same process.

Some students find breaking their learning into various discrete stages beneficial. For example, you could first type your lecture notes and fill gaps using a textbook or the reading material referenced by the lecturer. You can then compile these notes into a single document and structure it so that it logically flows. Then, you might want to include a third stage: researching further and making your notes more comprehensive. At this stage, the key is to delve deeper into 'why?' questions – Why is the law the way it is? Why is this the underlying principle? Why are these the policy considerations? – provides some direction for further research.[35] By inquiring, you

---

[31] Ibid 29.

[32] Massimiliano Tani and Prue Vines, 'Law Students' Attitudes to Education: Pointers to Depression in the Legal Academy and the Profession?' (2009) 19 *Legal Education Review* 3.

[33] Wendy Larcombe 'Law Students' Motivations, Expectations and Levels of Psychological Distress: Evidence of Connections' (2012) 22 *Legal Education Review* 1.

[34] Adam M. Persky and Shelby L. Hudson, 'A snapshot of student study strategies across a professional pharmacy curriculum: Are students using evidence-based practice?' (2016) 8(2) *Currents in Pharmacy Teaching and Learning* 141.

[35] Diana Laurillard, *Teaching as a Design Science: Building Pedagogical Patterns for Learning and Technology* (Routledge, 2012) 29.

develop and construct your own ideas, thereby processing the information. This helps you commit the concepts to memory while also understanding those concepts' rationale and how they fit within the 'broader picture'.

Identify Strengths and Weaknesses

It goes without saying that your learning techniques need to adapt to your strengths and weaknesses. Time spent perfecting something you are already proficient at instead of working on something you struggle with is time wasted. Likewise, be smart about getting around your weaknesses. For example, if you have trouble understanding cases and distilling their ratio, then rely on academic articles or seek help from your tutor to get better at it.

If your university has distinct styles of questions, such as essay-style and advice-style questions, assess your abilities regarding these as well. For instance, if you struggle with essay-style questions, spend some time in the 'acquisition' phase reading academic commentary to get an idea of what the contentious issues and areas of reform are. By contrast, if you struggle with advice-style questions, which demand a broad knowledge of the law in a practical sense, then spend less time researching issues in the 'acquisition' phase and more time practising questions in the 'application' phase (which will be discussed later).

To illustrate, a contracts advice-problem may require you to understand all bases upon which a contract may be ended and ask you to provide advice on which option the client should pursue. Such a question would not require pages of reasoning about *why* a person can terminate a contract, but rather application of the technical rules of termination and judgement of the most appropriate termination method for the client in the circumstances. A deep knowledge of the law due to extensive research of underlying concepts would not help you succeed in such a question.

Managing Your Time

"But I have promises to keep, and miles to go before I sleep, and miles to go before I sleep." Robert Frost was not alone in lamenting how much he had left to do before he could sleep each night. There are only 24 h in a day within which you need to eat, sleep, socialise and study. Doing well in law school also requires maximising the amount of time spent doing effective study. That is already a lot of balls to juggle at once. The key, however, is not extra time but managing the time you have. Time management can be learnt, though not overnight. It takes perseverence and practice.[36]

The first step to effective time management is accepting the need for balance. Unfortunately, as Ben Gibson notes,

[36] See, for a generalist overview of research on the psychology of time management: Christine P. Bartholomew, 'Time: An Empirical Analysis of Law Student Time Management Deficiencies' (2013) 81 *University of Cincinnati Law Review* 897, 913–917.

> [l]aw students are notorious for living "unbalanced" lives and many take great pride that law school consumes such a great deal of their time. Especially in the first year, this attitude is not viewed as the beginning states of burn out but simply as the signs of a hard worker.[37]

The problem with this mindset is that it is not sustainable and results in 'time famine' – you physically cannot accomplish everything that you should be doing, like study, in the time you have.[38] Be realistic about how many activities you can undertake at once. Then, time management will naturally become achievable because you won't be stretched beyond your capacity.

The next step is to *plan* how you will spend your time when studying. When making schedules, consider the following four tips.

1. **Ensure you have time – underestimate your speed; overestimate your breaks**

   It has been said that 'you never know what you have to do until you do it' – often, it isn't until we actually *do* something that we fully understand what it requires. Underestimating what is necessary can therefore quickly lead to your well-laid study plans unravelling. To avoid this happening:

   - consciously evaluate how long a task will take (look to the number of readings you have to do, etc.);
   - know your attention span and factor this into your scheduling – set aside more time than you think you need to complete tasks;
   - start early to give yourself a buffer when you inevitably lose time later.

2. **Get through it all – know how to cut your losses and prioritise**

   Once you begin studying, it can be difficult to know when to stop and easy to find yourself lost in rabbit holes. As Justice Windeyer purportedly once said, you need to swathe a path through the forest, not stop to examine every leaf. Knowing when to move on is key to getting through everything you need to. When do you move on? For many, the temptation is to remain on a topic until you know it inside out. If so, your time management must be precise or you risk only knowing half the course content in time for the exam.

   Managing these difficulties requires knowing yourself and your needs. Invest time, therefore, in reflecting on your own study practices so that you can more precisely manage your time throughout the semester. More practical ways to ensure you don't let your time get out of control include:

   - keeping a calendar with precise timelines (including short-term and long-term goals), down to the hour where feasible, to complete topics;
   - implementing smart note taking practices in class (and *attending* classes) to ensure foundational knowledge is acquired;

---

[37] Ben Gibson, 'How Law Students Can Cope: A Students View' (2010) 60 *Journal of Legal Education* 140, 142.

[38] Christine P. Bartholomew, 'Time: An Empirical Analysis of Law Student Time Management Deficiencies' (2013) 81 *University of Cincinnati Law Review* 897, 900 adopting the definition of 'time famine' from Timo Anttila et al., 'Predictors of Time Famine Among Finnish Employees – Work, Family, or Leisure?' (2009) 6 Int'l J. Time Use Res. 73, 74–75.

- having daily action lists and *starting* with the hardest tasks;
- using timers or alarms to hold yourself to the study times you allocate;
- reading smartly – for example, read everything in three quick stages – skim read the first time so you roughly know what is going on, then focus on reading the relevant content properly the second time and finally, read for understanding particularly challenging aspects the third time; and
- reflecting on your time management regularly.

3. **Get through it all *in time* – schedule with deadlines, not tasks**

   While we can manage big tasks by breaking them down into smaller, more manageable tasks, don't let completing these tasks govern your scheduling. Rather, work according to deadlines to complete these tasks. This approach fosters time awareness and makes it easier to 'cut your losses' when necessary. In apportioning time, think about how much you have to cover, which depends on the subject's difficulty and the amount of learning left, and how much time you have until the hard deadline.

   The hard deadline will always be the exam date but you should try to have various soft deadlines before then. For example, if you have two exams and they are 2 days apart, you cannot focus on the first subject until the first deadline (date of first exam) and then move to your second subject for the remaining 2 days. This is even more problematic if your second subject is your weaker subject. In this instance, it is more effective to have a soft deadline 3–4 days before the first exam. Once you reach that soft deadline, you stop studying the first subject and concentrate on learning the second subject for 3 days.

4. **Have specific study goals and final products**

   This final tip ties into the next phase: 'resource-building'. When crafting your schedules, avoid broad and ambiguous goals such as 'I will summarise topic x' or 'I will learn the methods of contractual termination'. These goals offer you no guidance about what to complete by your set deadline, and can lead to a sense that you are not achieving what you set out to in your schedule. Instead, aim to have a final product which you can tangibly see is complete – create flashcards, flowcharts or a dot point summary.

Resource-Building

Once a working understanding of course content is acquired, you need to consolidate that understanding with additional resources. For some students, resource-building overlaps with the final stages of the acquisition phase because they deepen their understanding of, and retain, concepts by rearranging them into exam notes, flashcards or concept maps. However, avoid jumping the gun and preparing resources before you have at least passed your eyes over all of the course content. Doing so robs you of focus, leading to over-inclusion and a lack of understanding of which topics are the most challenging.

Have an Objective

The type of resources you need to consolidate the knowledge you have acquired depends on your objective. For example, for an open-book exam, the resources you need will be comprehensive and easily-searchable notes. If your exam requires issue-spotting, you might want to have short examples of each issue which are easily accessible. Additionally, you could prepare 'skeleton structures' of each type of issue to help prevent getting caught up in unrelated issues. On the other hand, for a closed-book exam, you may need flashcards or other memorising techniques. Your main resource in closed-book exams is your memory.

Another important resource-building objective is managing multiple subjects in a short timeframe. As suggested above, have soft deadlines for your various subjects. Then, ensure that you convert the information you have acquired from your first subject into something tangible that will jog your memory later, like flashcards.

Be Realistic

When you look around in open book exams, it is not uncommon to see binders full of paper. Unsurprisingly, too many notes is countereffective. Your exam notes are supposed to supplement your knowledge, not replace it. Although it may be comforting to have all your notes on standby, they are largely useless in a time-pressured situation. For this reason, keep your notes short and leave some time to familiarise yourself with navigating through them. A handy way to do this is to use them in the 'application phase', such as when doing past papers under exam conditions.

Similarly for closed book exams, having your resources in manageable sizes makes it easier to review them in their entirety and makes you less reliant on them, forcing you to remember larger chunks of information.

Application

The application phase is when you practise applying the content you have learned. Time constraints may make this phase the first you want to cut from your study schedule. This temptation is natural. Students tend to feel a false sense of security as soon as they finish their exam notes or memorise content. However, the application phase is critical because it links your understanding of content with the course coordinator and exam markers' expectations. You will not receive marks simply for understanding the content – you have to communicate that understanding effectively to the marker.

The most common method of practising application is through pre-made questions, usually tutorial questions, past exams or questions in textbooks. Of these, students tend to focus most on past exams. While completing past exams is useful, also be mindful of its limitations. It is unlikely (if not impossible) that exam questions will be repeated, and focusing on past papers only tests your understanding of a few select topics.

In order to gain the benefits of completing past exams, you need to use them intelligently. Some students use past exams as a resource in and of itself during their resource-building phase. They prepare short structure-style answers to the exam, then use the feedback to see if their notes are comprehensive enough. The past exam then dictates where further study and research should be directed. Other students may use past exams only at the very end of the study schedule, to 'check' their level of understanding under exam conditions.

Your ability to apply your understanding also benefits significantly from openly communicating with the course coordinator about their expectations. This prevents a mismatch of expectations, where students complain that they studied hard and knew all of the content but were 'marked harshly'. By attending lecturer consultations, you may discover that the course is more focussed on your original thoughts rather than regurgitating case law or academic commentary. In response, you can adjust your study habits to incorporate more discussions with other students rather than research and memorisation. Other courses may seek the contrary. In that instance, remembering key cases and academic articles may boost your marks.

Feedback

The feedback phase occurs at two critical points in your learning cycle. *First*, you should aim to 'relearn' after you have tried applying your knowledge. Don't leave past papers until the last minute. Since you will inevitably find gaps in your knowledge, it might be wise to do a past paper before you are confident in your knowledge, to redirect your learning. This ensures longer-term retention.[39] *Second*, after you receive exam marks, reflect on what went well and what didn't. Take time to figure out what type of 'learner' you are and think carefully about how you manage your time between the various phases of learning.

Assignments

Assignments are difficult to approach because they engage two challenging tasks: research and legal writing. This section will detail tips for each.

---

[39] See, eg, Rawson, K. A. and Dunlosky, J, 'When is Practice Testing Most Effective for Improving the Durability and Efficiency of Student Learning?' (2012) 24 *Educational Psychology Review* 419.

Research

The ability to effectively research is essential for both the study and practice of law. Often, a distinction is drawn between the academic and practising lawyer's use of legal research. The former, it is said, seeks more to understand the law, how it works, why it is the way it is and how it might evolve. The research skill of being able to confidently identify and exhaust all relevant sources is thus critical. Practising lawyers, in contrast, are often less interested in why the law is the way it is – what matters is the law itself and how it might be instrumentalised to fit the client's needs. The cost of the practising lawyer's time further requires sophisticated legal research skills that allow identification of the answer to a legal question in the most time-efficient way possible while also being sure all relevant sources have been canvassed. You can see how this might apply to your assignment as well; identify what type of question you are being asked (for example, is it a reform question or a client advice?) and determine your research strategy accordingly.

Research Strategy

One way to strategise your approach to legal research is to understand it as a three-fold process[40]:

1. Plan
2. Find
3. Apply

Fleshing out this process results in various sub-steps as summarised in Fig. 2.2:

Your initial analysis of the legal problem and identification of the relevant legal issues will help elucidate how you should approach research (and the plan for doing so). This plan will also help you identify which sources to look into and decide the order in which you work through those sources (Fig. 2.2).

Practical Tips and Tricks

You can implement your research strategy effectively by doing the following:

1. **Keep a literature review document**
   Start a document or a handwritten journal where you take notes from each source. Always identify: (a) the source; (b) the page number of the source; and (c) whether your notes are a direct quote or not. If you are taking notes by hand, a helpful practice is to only write on one side of each page so that you can use the opposite page for your own notes, thoughts and commentary on the source.

---

[40] Inspired by that provided for in University of Queensland *Legal Research Guide* accessed at http://guides.library.uq.edu.au/legal-research-guide. Consult your university's research guide or the law librarian to find out more about effective research strategies.

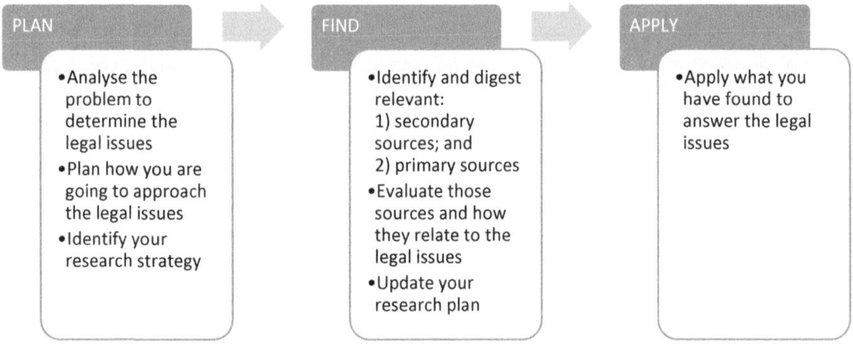

Fig. 2.2 Research strategy

2. **Separate legal issues into 'research documents'**

   If you find that your research uncovers multiple potentially pertinent legal issues, start individual documents for each topic. A helpful structure for such documents is this:

> **Topic:**
>
> Who's written on the point:
> Main schools of thought and their differences:
> Do I find this interesting? *this is more relevant for when you are directing your topic
> How does this topic relate to the central topic? Is it critical, supportive or irrelevant?

3. **Keep a record of your research plan and how you are progressing through it**

   Be sure to keep track of how you have approached research. For example, what databases you have used and in what order, which sources you have reviewed or have partly reviewed and whether they were helpful. Doing so will help you avoid looking at the same sources multiple times or overlooking important sources.

4. **Have a working bibliography**

   Create a bibliography at the outset containing sources you think will be relevant. Do not wait to add sources to the list only once you have read them – add 'to-read' sources to the bibliography and also use this document to keep track of whether you have indeed reviewed sources. A way to do so may simply be colour coding. For instance, in the excerpt of a research bibliography below,[41] sources are categorised by sub-topic and coloured black if they have been reviewed and red if they are yet to be reviewed.

[41] The actual sources in this excerpt are irrelevant, as is the topic of research. It is used only to illustrate the potential format of a research bibliography.

[...]

A. Systemic Implications of the Arbitral Mandate?

Reisman, W. Michael, 'Case Specific Mandates' versus 'Systemic Implications': How Should Investment Tribunals Decide? (2013) 29 *Arbitration International* 131

Schill, Stephan W., 'International Arbitrators as System-Builders' (2012) 106 *American Society of International Law* 295

Schill, Stephan W., 'System-Building in Investment Treaty Arbitration and Lawmaking' (2011) 12 *German Law Journal* 1083

B. Empirical Analyses of Precedent Usage in ISA

Commission, Jeffrey P, 'Precedent in Investment Treaty Arbitration: A Citation Analysis of a Developing Jurisprudence' (2007) 24(2) Journal of International Arbitration 129

Fauchald, Ole Kristian, 'The Legal Reasoning of ICSID Tribunals – An Empirical Analysis' (2008) 19 *European Journal of International Law* 301

[...] 5. **Know and use your library services**

Many law students do not fully comprehend or utilise the services available to them through their university. Make it a priority to learn what and how to use the services your library offers. Consider your librarians as research gurus and yourself their humble apprentice – soak up as much of their expertise as possible in your time at university. Often, university librarians offer 'how-to' or assistance sessions for legal research and writing. When you graduate law school these services may no longer be at your disposal – use them while you can.

Legal Writing

Legal writing, if it can be given its own category of writing, is no science and there are no hard and fast rules to excelling at it. Indeed, excellence in legal writing requires you to develop your own style over time. Like a musical instrument, beautiful writing takes time and practice. Thus, what follows are only suggestions that might assist you in refining the music you hope to play through your pen.

Approaching Your Assignment

Well-written assignments do not appear out of thin air – they require time and careful thought. The process for arriving at a desirable destination involves the following:

1. **Having a plan**

Both for assignments and exams, having a plan for your response immediately elevates your work by giving it structure. Having a pre-planned skeleton to your answer also helps you determine whether your response covers all relevant material. Your high school English teacher taught you the 'TEEL' structure (topic sentence, evidence, elaborate, link) for a reason. Planning your answer with structures like this helps you to convey your ideas effectively and ensures that you include the right information in the right order.

2. **Being ready to write**

Before you start writing, ensure that you are fully equipped to do so. If it is a research-heavy paper, try not start writing until you have done the necessary research. If it is a client advice question you are answering, do not start until you are sure you have all of the relevant law at your fingertips and you know how to apply it. To return to the instrument analogy, how can you expect to play a song if you do not know the tune? Effective legal writing requires substantive preparation.

The other sense of necessary preparation is mental. While dramatic, think of yourself as an artist or a great performer – your best work will come when you are in the best headspace. When you have assignments that you can do in your own time, be discerning with which time you spend on them. For most people, the mind is most acute in the morning when you start your day – find the time of day that works best for you and consciously reserve some of that time for the most difficult parts of your assignments. Try to be inspired and excited when you write. It will come across in your work.

3. **Get started and 'get it on the page'**

However, there comes a time when you simply have to put words on paper. Allowing writer's block or lack of research to prevent you from starting leaves you at risk of creating a badly presented and unclear piece of writing. Legal writing thus requires discipline in balancing between 'getting ready' and 'just starting'.

Additionally, writer's block may be caused by being overwhelmed by the number of possible directions to take or by having too many ideas to organise into a coherent argument. In both instances, the simple but by no means easy solution to your problem is to start. Write dot points and sentences which come to mind at random. Stop trying to make your assignment perfect from the get-go and get your ideas down on paper. Come back to sculpt it and make it pretty later. A practical tip that might make you more at ease in this process is using tools like parentheses to simply note which sections you feel need 'sculpting' or perhaps even axing later. [For example, if you find yourself questioning an idea, jot it down like this, mark it with parentheses, and revisit it later!].

Another problem law students often have is managing relevant information that comes up sporadically. For example, what do you do if you are writing a section on the doctrine of contract formation and, as you are reading a source, you find an excellent quote that is not directly relevant to the section, but you want to include it *somewhere* in your assignment? One answer is to start a 'Parking Lot' document or section at the end of your assignment where you 'park' the extra information that you aren't sure how or whether to incorporate yet. This will save you time (both presently, allowing you to concentrate on the section you're already working on and later, when you inevitably want to revisit 'that quote' but can't remember where it is from) and will also equip you with content to add 'icing to the cake'.

4. **Refine**

When scheduling your writing plan, leave enough time to *refine* your work. Whether it is having the time to put aside a written assignment for a few days and come back to it fresh-minded to evaluate its content, or having time in an exam to proof-read your work and make necessary adjustments, time to refine is a luxury few law students get to experience. Those who do, however, are uniquely positioned to improve the quality of their work. Strive to equip yourself with this opportunity by establishing good study habits and time management skills early in law school. Even if short on time, it is always helpful to print out your assignments and proof read them in hard copy before submitting them. At this stage, put on your 'Grammar Police' hat and get critical.

A tip that might assist you in the refining stage is one of structure. If you find yourself questioning where the best place is to include a section, or what order for your sections is best amongst a couple of competing approaches, go old school and print out your assignment, *cut it up with a pair of scissors,* find yourself a wall or a floor with enough space for each page and try out the different orders you are contemplating.

Illustrating the Process: "madman", "architect", "carpenter", "judge"

A more visual approach to the writing process is that devised by Dr. Betty Flowers, a Law Prose professor at the University of Texas. The approach breaks down the writing process and delineates the writing 'energies' into competing roles. The Madman is the part of you that "is full of ideas, writes crazily and perhaps rather sloppily, gets carried away by enthusiasm or anger, and if really let loose, could turn out ten pages an hour."[42] Anathema to the Madman, however, is the Judge:

> He's been educated and knows a sentence fragment when he sees one. He peers over your shoulder and says, 'That's trash!' with such authority that the madman loses his crazy confidence and shrivels up. You know the judge is right; after all, he speaks with the voice of an English teacher. But for all his sharpness of eye, he can't create anything.[43]

While you are stuck with the Judge haranguing the Madman, you also have the Architect and the Carpenter battling it out. The Architect is ridiculing chunks of your essay as irrelevant and unnecessary to the whole, while the Carpenter admires the elegance of those sections, but also critiques the finishings of other sections that the Architect says are foundational. This is where you get stuck: the "competing energies are locked horn to horn, pushing against each other" and no one gets

---

[42] Betty S. Flowers, 'Madman, Architect, Carpenter, Judge: Roles and the Writing Process' (Speech delivered at the 1979 Conference of College Teachers of English of Texas, Texas, September 1979) http://www.ut-ie.com/b/b_flowers.html cited in Bryan A. Garner, *Garner on Language and Writing* (American Bar Association, 2009) 4–5.

[43] Ibid.

anything done.[44] The trick to moving forward, Dr. Flowers says, is separating out these energies and giving them clearly delineated roles:

1. Begin by letting the Madman loose – let your raw passion flow onto the page, "[t]alk on paper, page after page, and don't stop to judge or correct sentences".
2. Next, let the Architect take over. Let her "read the wild scribblings saved from the night before and pick out maybe a tenth of the jottings as relevant or interesting". The Architect's mandate is identifying your best building blocks and arranging them to be structurally sound. It is a big picture job, looking at the paragraph level rather than getting bogged down in sentence structure or word choice.
3. Then, swap out the Architect for the Carpenter. Left with an essay stripped back to the building blocks, let the carpenter "nail" together your ideas "in a logical sequence, making sure each sentence is clearly written, contributes to the argument of the paragraph, and leads logically and gracefully to the next sentence".
4. Finally, let your Judge return to the courtroom, inspect the detail and make it 'perfect'.

Each of your alter-egos needs time alone on the essay – keep them separate and there'll be no brawls. Allow them to each contribute their part and your writing will be all the better for it!

Characteristics of Excellent Legal Writing

Mastering the process of writing your assignment should leave you with an assignment which is well thought and structured. The following general characteristics of excellent legal writing can help elevate the quality of that product. Excellent legal writing:

1. **Leads with the conclusion**

   Jean Kalicki, one of the world's top arbitrators, states: "In both written and oral advocacy, you should lead with your conclusion, starting with the most important point".[45] As another prominent international lawyer once advised, grown-up lawyers don't have the time nor patience to wait for your conclusion – so lead with it. Effective arguments begin with the conclusion and a brief summary of why it is warranted before proceeding to a nuanced and detailed construction of the argument. It then ends with a reiteration of the conclusion and why it is the preferred outcome.

[44] Ibid.

[45] Jean Kalicki quoted in Thomas K Sprange, 'Written Advocacy' in Stephen Jagusch QC and Philippe Pinsolle (eds), *The Guide to Advocacy* (Global Arbitration Review, 2016) https://globalarbitrationreview.com/chapter/1073034/written-advocacy.

Unfortunately, many students (and lawyers) fall into a trap of constructing their arguments through a 'build-up' method much like building a house, "where one lays the foundation before adding the upper floors and finally the roof".[46] Unlike house-building, in legal writing, "[t]he constraints of attention and time often interfere with the build-up method, and there is nothing worse than having a powerful conclusion that you never get effectively to deliver".[47] Make your conclusion the first thing your reader sees.

2. **Clear presentation**

A simple yet effective way to boost the impression of your writing is to respect the power of presentation. Messy presentation gives the impression of a messy mind. Therefore, even if you have a clean and precise legal argument, if it is presented in a way that makes it difficult to read, that difficulty can carry across to the reader's view of its content. Recognise the value of having space on your page. Use easy to read fonts, with generous line spacing and headings. Think about how you can help convey your clarity of mind to the reader.

3. **Simple and concise**

Good legal writing is concise. As Jan Paulsson says: "Less can be much, much more".[48] Don't think that more words mean more substance. Indeed, many judges have noted that "good lawyers often come in far below the page limits – and that bad lawyers almost never do".[49] This is because, as the late Justice Scalia of the U.S. Supreme Court and Bryan Gardner argue, "[l]iterary elegance, crudition, sophistication or expression – these and all other qualities must be sacrificed if they detract from clarity".[50]

To achieve clarity and conciseness, stick to one to two ideas per sentence, avoid using unnecessary words and stay in the active voice. A practical tip for identifying passive voice is reviewing whether you overcomplicate sentences with the proposition 'of'. For example, take the phrase 'the launch of the event'. It can be reduced to 'the event's launch' by reconsidering 'of' as a word choice. Also prioritise word choice at a higher level: excellent legal writers discern the *right* words to accurately convey what they want to say. Scalia and Gardner's words here ring true: "Lawyers possess only one tool to convey their thoughts: language. They must acquire and hone the finest, most effective version of that tool available. They must love words and use them exactly".[51]

---

[46] Ibid.

[47] Ibid.

[48] Jan Paulsson quoted in Thomas K Sprange, 'Written Advocacy' in Stephen Jagusch QC and Philippe Pinsolle (eds), *The Guide to Advocacy* (Global Arbitration Review, 2016) https://globalarbitrationreview.com/chapter/1073034/written-advocacy.

[49] Scalia and Garner, *Making Your Case: The Art of Persuading Judges* (Thomson and West, 2008) 98.

[50] Ibid 107.

[51] Ibid 61.

4. **Uses adjectives sparingly, if at all**

One way to imbue your writing with persuasive force is with adjectives. However, too many adjectives has the opposite effect. If everything is built up through adjectives, when you really mean it when you say something is 'strong' or 'compelling' or even 'determinative', those words have no effect. Save your favourite adjectives for when they matter most. Doing so adds impact.

Relatedly, when you choose to use an adverb, ask yourself whether it is necessary to convey the meaning you desire. For example, a common phrase students like to employ is that something is 'absolutely', 'really' or 'completely' unique. The word 'unique', by definition, means that something is the 'only one of its kind' or is 'unlike anything else'.[52] None of these adverbs add to this meaning. Being aware of the futility of such phrases can aid language simplification and, as an added side bonus, cut words if you are over the word-limit.

5. **Never overstates facts or law**

The ultimate impression you want to convey through your writing is a mastery of the law and its application. Conveying this impression is severely compromised when a crucial fact is omitted, (even if it does not assist your argument) and critically so if fact or law is misstated, overstated or mispresented. While it may sound better on the page, you are ultimately shooting yourself in the foot: excellent legal writers and advocates deal with inconvenient facts and law and can explain why they are inconsequential to their argument.

Long Term Improvement of Your Legal Writing

If you are wanting to improve your legal writing *style* – that unique but elusive characteristic of great legal writings – make sure to *read*. Supplement your assigned readings with personal reading of intelligent and stylish writers. Over time, wide reading increases your vocabulary and the variety of sentence structures at your disposal. If you want to accelerate this process, read with a focus on how model writers communicate. An extreme example is Robert Louis Stevenson, who was famous for taking a passage from an esteemed writer, reading it through twice and then trying to replicate word-for-word what he had read.[53] Over time, this practice allowed Stevenson to replicate artful sentence structures and master a broad vocabulary in his own work. Stevenson went on to write novels including *Treasure Island* and the *Strange Case of Dr Jekyll and Mr Hyde* and is acclaimed for his ability to "pick the right word up on the point of his pen, like a man playing spillikins".[54]

---

[52] *Macquarie Dictionary* (Pan Macmillan, 7th ed, 2017).

[53] Bryan A. Garner, *Garner on Language and Writing* (American Bar Association, 2009) 15.

[54] Gilbert Keith Chesterton, *The Victorian Age in Literature* (Holt, 1913) 246.

Referencing

Learn to love referencing. It is an aspect of legal writing and research that requires little, if any, thinking to excel. Make sure you identify what referencing system is applicable to you as early as possible (most likely the *Australian Guide to Legal Citation* ('AGLC')) and quickly familiarise yourself with it. Your approach to referencing and the AGLC is a classic example of a 'glass half full or empty' opportunity – while this guide is complicated in the number of variations it details for accurate referencing, this detail means that the guide will almost always have instructions on how to reference a tricky source. Think of it like the Room of Requirement in the Harry Potter series – "if you have to ask, you'll never know. If you know, you need only ask".[55] You have at your disposal the answer to your referencing problems in the AGLC and for those answers, you "need only ask" (or in our case, Ctrl+F) and it will appear.

Generally, it works best to reference sources as you go. This avoids the situation where you cannot remember what source you intended to reference and also helps obviate plagiarism risks. From a time management perspective, referencing as you go also prevents last minute referencing panic!

Group Work

While in some law schools, group assignments are rare if not non-existent forms of assessment, in others group assignments are on the rise, or at the least the recognition that group work is a source of great value. Don't shrink back from this reality! Learning how to work well in groups is pivotal for life after law school. So regardless of how often group assignments frequent your workload, knowing how to approach them is a must. Keep in mind the following seven tips:

1. if you can, choose your group wisely based on diverse skill sets;
2. make your expectations clear at the outset so that there is no conflict later;
3. have a plan of attack and delineate roles from the get-go so that everyone knows what they are supposed to do and can be held accountable;
4. check-in with your group members regularly to see how tasks are progressing;
5. pull your weight;
6. be honest, but considerate of others' opinions and feelings; and
7. leave time before submission to deal with unexpected issues.

[55] *Harry Potter and the Deathly Hallows, Part 2* (Directed by David Yates, Heyday Films, 2011).

Scholarships, Prizes, Awards and Medals (SPAMs)

While SPAMs serve as affirmation of your hard work in law school, their real value lies in their power to propel you forward further. SPAMs lend tremendous strength and credibility to your CV by proving you have learnt certain skills to a very high standard. Although receiving SPAMs is difficult, as Babe Ruth once said, "never let the fear of striking out keep you from playing the game". Put yourself out there and have a go; if you are unsuccessful, it is a good opportunity to reflect on how you can improve.

There are numerous SPAMs available to you – the trick is looking for and seizing those that are within reach. So how might you find those that are within your reach? Figure 2.3 provides some guidance.

Table 2.1 lists some local, national and international SPAMs you might be interested in.

Getting Experience Beyond the Classroom

Learning is not limited to the classroom and continues throughout your career. Even as a law student, there are many opportunities to learn practical and useful skills. Extracurricular activities provide one such opportunity to learn, practise and

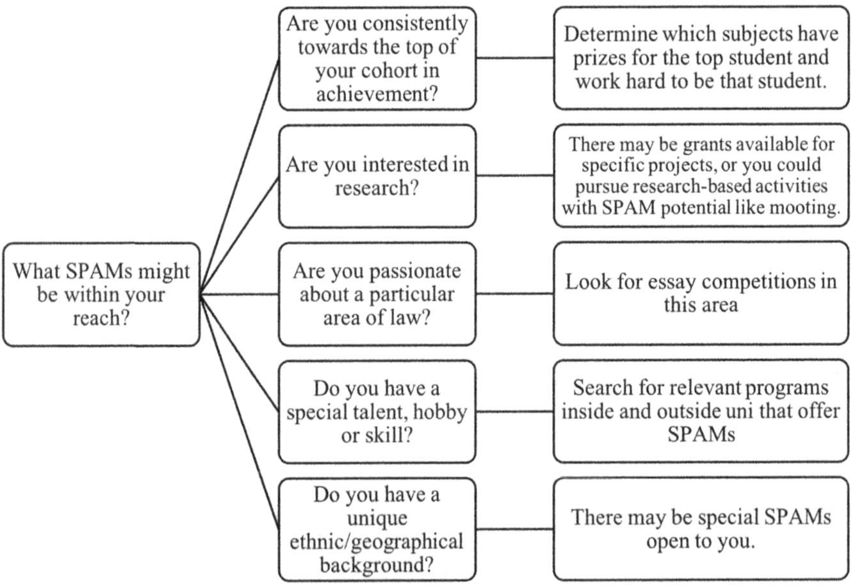

Fig. 2.3 Approaching SPAMs

Table 2.1 Possible SPAMs to pursue

SPAM	Offering entity	Further info
University-based prizes and scholarships	Specific universities	Look for a university-specific scholarships page, as well as a law-school specific page.
Law Council of Australia Business Law Section scholarships	Law Council of Australia	Various business-based scholarships on offer for essays
Australian Legal History Essay Competition	Francis Forbes Society for Australian Legal History	Essay competition on legal history
NELA Environmental Law Essay Competition	National Environmental Law Assocation	Essay competition
Global Mobility Immigration Lawyers Scholarship	Global Mobility Immigration Lawyers	Prize for essay on a specific topic
Undergraduate Awards	The Undergraduate Awards	Submission of outstanding coursework
Law Student of the Year	Lawyers Weekly	Recognises academic, community and legal achievements.
Westpac Asian Exchange Scholarship	Westpac Bicentennial Foundation	Supports undergraduates who are interested in Asia – for study at an Asian University
New Colombo Plan Scholarships	Australian Department of Foreign Affairs and Trade	For undergraduate study and internships in the Indo-Pacific
Frank Knox Memorial Fellowships	Harvard University	Awarded to students from Australia for graduate study at Harvard
Sir John Monash Scholarships	General Sir John Monash Foundation	Postgraduate scholarships to study overseas
Gates Cambridge Scholarships	Bill and Melinda Gates Foundation	Postgraduate study at the University of Cambridge
Schwarzman Scholarship	Stephen A. Schwarzman	Special postgraduate leadership study at Tsinghua University in Beijing
Rhodes Scholarship	Rhodes Trust	To pursue postgraduate studies at the University of Oxford

demonstrate your legal skills to your peers and the profession. Notwithstanding these benefits, **do not overcommit**. As we said in the previous section on time management, law students are notorious for overcommitting.[56] University should not be an exercise in box-ticking or resume-padding. Make sure to account for downtime, don't sign up for too many activities at once (giving them all substandard attention) and don't underestimate the importance of having a positive university experience.

[56] Misa Han and Edmund Tadros, 'Law students spend 'multiple years' building CV for clerkship', *Australian Financial Review* (online), 13 July 2017 https://www.afr.com/business/legal/law-students-spend-multiple-years-building-cv-for-clerkship-20170625-gwy9h3.

On the flip side, if you are already time poor, for instance because you need to undertake paid work to pay for rent and utilities, don't let this dissuade you from getting involved in extracurricular activities. You can be strategic in planning your degree by reducing your study load or shifting some of the burden to a summer semester.

Exchange

One way to gain experience outside the classroom is to incorporate a semester abroad into your degree. For most university students, exchange is on the agenda from day one. A semester overseas, with options to travel, where the grades from the host university (in most cases) don't carry across to your home academic transcript? It seems a no brainer. Yet, for many law students, the equation is a little more complex. Most law schools are strict about minimum requirements for completed courses, pushing the possibility of exchange back to the final years of the degree when most law students are focusing on solidifying their career path. Some law students are also dissuaded by the concern that using law credit on foreign law courses is a waste.

These perceived cons need not outweigh the pros. Exchange can actively contribute to and even *define* your law school story. Correctly utilised, your exchange experience can be both fun *and* professionally enriching. From an employer perspective, living in a foreign country demonstrates your capability to represent an employer abroad, adapt to different contexts and conduct business outside of the ordinary 'Australian way'.[57]

So how can you rig the exchange equation so that it adds to your law school experience? It depends, of course, on what your ambitions are. Nevertheless, consider these next three points when planning your exchange.

Choose Your Time for Exchange Wisely

The timing of exchange may in large part be out of your hands, but you may have some flexibility, especially if you study a dual degree. You can either use subjects from your non-law degree or restructure your program plan to align law electives with a semester abroad. However, there is also no harm in going on exchange in your penultimate and final years. The most interesting courses at a partner law school are often advanced electives, which may require you to have completed all foundation courses. From a professional viewpoint, going on exchange once you are

[57] Australian Industry Group and Asialink, *Engaging Asia: Getting it right for Australian business* (March 2011) Asialink Business https://asialinkbusiness.com.au/research-resources/essay-engaging-asia-getting-it-right 19.

well established within your law degree also maximises your prospects of securing an internship or work experience abroad.

Don't forget to also consider how exchange might impact your studies more broadly, such as whether it will delay graduation, prevent or impact clerkships, financially burden you, or hinder your GPA.

If you can't fit exchange into your degree, an equally appealing alternative may be to pursue **short-term programs**. Many universities offer opportunities to undertake courses at overseas universities or learning institutes over a summer or winter break for credit. Beyond your university's offerings, you can also look directly to overseas universities, find the program you want and then work backwards!

Be selective as to Where You Study

Resist the temptation of making holiday potential the determining factor in your decision of where to study. Think about which places and universities will add the most weight and credibility to your CV and bolster your career narrative. Check the ranking of universities in law. Look into the global standing of the host location you are thinking of and what its status is in the region. Frame these inquiries against your desired career trajectory. The point is simple: think bigger than 'fun' – think about how an exchange might add to your professional identity.

Look for Opportunities to Distinguish Your Exchange Studies from Your Peers'

Look for opportunities to add to the general advantages of a semester abroad so that it becomes something that sets you apart from the crowd. Some ways to do so include:

- organising an internship or work experience unavailable back home;
- undertaking a specialised research project (and ideally publishing it) or placement with your host university;
- studying courses unique to your host university that add to your skillset;
- learning a language;
- volunteering or completing pro bono work;
- doing things that add to your life experience; and
- extending your ability to do these things with the support of a scholarship like the New Colombo Plan or the Westpac Asian Exchange Scholarship (both of which provide recipients with funds and unique opportunities to immerse themselves in the Asia region).

Conferences, Seminars, Presentations, Personal Development

There are inifinite opportunities to enhance your law school experience with professional development events. The benefits of these events are both academic and social: you have direct access to professionals and like-minded peers that provide you with opportunities to grow your network. Conferences, seminars and the like can also introduce you to new areas of interest. They also demonstrate your interest in particular areas and commitment to those areas beyond the classroom – you can, for instance, bolster discussion in a job interview when talking about a topic like law and technology by premising a thought with "I realised when I attended the Annual Conference on Law and Technology that…".

There are lots of options available to you and their uptake will often turn on you seeking them out in the first place. Examples of events open to you include:

- your law student society's events (be sure you're on the mailing list and keep up with their social media page to know what's on);
- your university and law school's conferences, seminars and leadership programs;
- events facilitated by the Australian Law Students' Association (ALSA);
- specific workshops and conferences run by specialty organisations and associations; and
- annual conferences run by specific legal organisations and associations (e.g. the annual conference of the Australian and New Zealand Society of International Law).

The final two examples are professional conferences and therefore, may have steep registration fees. If that is a barrier to you, see if you can receive a grant to attend or if there are any volunteer opportunities to assist with the running of the conference. Also don't overlook non-law-specific opportunities, such as Model United Nations conferences or student leadership conferences.

When you do attend conferences and similar events, your participation should have two objectives: learning and networking. Learning entails absorbing information; networking entails absorbing opportunities. Both require you to be proactive. Have a notebook to take notes and research speakers and topics in advance. Most importantly, revisit your own goals, projects and ideas and consider which speakers might be able to further those – if you identify an alignment with a speaker, *talk* to them and ask for advice.

Volunteering

Volunteering and pro bono legal work can be greatly enriching experiences. If the term 'pro bono' is new to you, its meaning is simple – "for the common good".[58] As a law student, pro bono work usually involves providing services to disadvantaged

[58] See Australian Pro Bono Centre, *For Law Students* (2017) https://www.probonocentre.org.au/provide-pro-bono/law-student/.

people to increase their access to justice, or assisting not-for-profits, and doing so without any kind of reimbursement (or academic credit). Pro bono work can be deeply rewarding because it ensures disadvantaged people can secure access to justice, and introduces you to a community of like-minded people. Having such an outlet, for many law students, provides focus and clarity to their law degree.

Pro bono work also offers a unique opportunity to work directly for clients and equips you with practical skills that will aid you in most career paths. If you are passionate about justice, it will add meaning to your words if you can demonstrate how you have contributed to the wider community.

There are numerous ways to get involved in pro bono work. Many law schools have pro bono centres which provide opportunities for their students to volunteer their services. Your university may also have a clinical legal education program that allows you to undertake a placement with a legal service provider, such as a community legal centre, and gain course credit towards your law degree.[59] The Australian Pro Bono Centre also maintains a 'Social Justice Opportunities' page that describes a number of potential pro bono opportunities open to law students.[60]

Student Societies

To first year students, student societies can initially appear foreign and unwelcoming. Many student law societies are huge organisations with large executives. However, that should not discourage you from getting involved. In fact, large student societies offer an unparalleled opportunity to improve your communication, teamwork and time management skills – and are more than happy to get new students involved!

Student society executives plan and execute various events throughout the year. There are huge coordination issues which need to constantly be resolved – for example, how do you get a group of volunteer students to find a venue for, cater and adequately market an upcoming event? It requires both initiative and leadership from everyone involved.

Furthermore, student societies are one of the best forums through which you can build not only your student social network, but also your professional network. Your fellow students eventually become your fellow colleagues after all. Society

---

[59] For the difference between pro bono and clinical legal education see: National Pro Bono Resources Centre, *Information Paper: Pro bono and clinical legal education programs in Australian law schools* (August 2004) Australian Pro Bono Centre https://probonocentre.org.au/wp-content/uploads/2015/09/ProbonoandCLEs.pdf. Kingsford Legal Centre has published a guide on clinical legal education programs available at Australian Universities, see Kingsford Legal Centre, *Clinical Legal Education Guide* (2014) University of New South Wales http://www.klc.unsw.edu.au/sites/klc.unsw.edu.au/files/55386_clinical_legal_education_guide_web.pdf.

[60] Australian Pro Bono Centre, *Latest Opportunities* (2017) Social Justice Opportunities: A Career Guide for Law Students & New Lawyers https://www.sjopps.net.au.

participation also brings unique opportunities to connect with interstate law students through the Australian Law Student Association.

The easiest way to join a student society executive is to be an active member of the society. Attend events and try to find smaller opportunities to make yourself known to other members, such as by volunteering your time to help set up events. It can be easy to discount executive elections as a popularity contest – an exercise in vanity. That misses the point. Being an active member who volunteers time to make sure other law students can enjoy their university experience is something to be proud of. Becoming known is a positive side-effect and will help you gain election to the executive, where you can implement your own ideas and learn invaluable skills.

Competitions

Law competitions are both a fantastic learning experience and a way to demonstrate your legal research and communication skills. Sometimes, students question the wisdom of dedicating significant amounts of time to competitions when that time could be spent working on their GPA. The response, and defence for competitions, is simple: it is not time spent, it is time *invested.*

Each competition is modelled off of a particular scenario which you may be faced with as a legal professional. Namely:

- client interviewing mirrors the first meeting between a lawyer and their client;
- negotiation is based on discussions solicitors will have with each other on behalf of their clients in order to reach some form of an agreement;
- witness examination is modelled on cross examination during trial.
- paper presentation is similar to a conference presentation or thesis reading; and
- mooting simulates a court dispute, generally in an appellate setting.

Most law schools offer multiple platforms to get involved in these competitions. Some competitions, like mooting, may be a compulsory part of your law curriculum. Others will likely be offered internally by your student law society. Your law school will also likely offer opportunities to represent the university in external competitions. Starting early in internal competitions is ideal for gaining experience, practice and confidence. You can then work your way towards participating in domestic or international competitions. However, don't let inexperience deter you from applying for higher level opportunities. If you are confident you are capable of taking on a competition, go for it.

Finally, while this chapter will focus on law competitions, that should not dissuade you from participating in the various other competitions which are offered to university students. There are countless competitions which give a taste of working as, inter alia, investment bankers, management consultants, or policy writers.

The following sections will briefly describe how common types of law competitions are held.

Negotiation

Negotiation involves a pair of students representing their client in discussions with an opposing party. Depending on the factual scenario given, it may mirror a negotiation which occurs in transactional ('front-end') work or may be modelled off a settlement negotiation in a dispute ('back end' work). Notwithstanding the variety of situations which may arise, the competition essentially calls for you to think critically about both your client *and* your opponent's client's interests and strategise about how to achieve the best outcome which satisfies all interests.[61]

The competition's format involves the two opposing teams receiving an identical set of 'common facts' and unique 'confidential facts' – the latter generally includes instructions from the client. The negotiation then goes for 50 min during which time the competitors must set and follow an agenda and reach an agreed outcome that is beneficial to their clients. A 10-min reflection is then held for both teams and the judges are invited to ask questions about their strategy and how they would approach the same negotiation next time.

Negotiation teaches you how to be creative and flexible under pressure. You enter the negotiation with certain constraints imposed by your client's interests. Although preparation is essential, you will then be forced to reassess your approach once you begin to discover the opposing team's own constraints. The 10-min reflection is an excellent opportunity to critically evaluate your performance and help yourself improve for the next round.

Client Interviewing

Client interviewing involves a team of two students and a client, emulating a new client's first appointment at a firm of solicitors. The student pair will receive a brief overview of what the client is seeking assistance for. The pair of students must then gather as much information from the client as possible in the time available. At the conclusion of the appointment, the students should advise the client as to the next steps they should take.

Client interviewing requires quick and critical thinking. In contrast to preparation-heavy competitions such as mooting, client interviewing focusses more on thinking about the information needed to appropriately advise a client and how to ascertain that information through questioning. Commonly, the client will be reluctant to disclose all of the relevant facts. The competition therefore tests your ability to identify gaps in the client's narrative and ask pointed questions.

Client interviewing also introduces you to the realities of navigating a solicitor-client relationship. There are questions of ethics – to what extent should you trust your client and what should you do if they are not being honest? How do you deal

---

[61] For more on this, see Roger Fisher, William Ury and Bruce Patton (ed), *Getting to Yes: Negotiating agreement without giving in* (2011, 3rd ed, Penguin).

with an aggressive or grieving client? What avenues does a guilty client have? Providing general advice to your client also requires you to understand basic legal procedure. In some cases, you will need to make a judgement between advising your client to pursue litigation and explaining alternative dispute resolution options. For example, if your client wishes to keep their financial position confidential, then litigation would be detrimental to their interests. Understanding this strategic aspect of the law is a useful skill to learn while at university.

Witness Examination

Witness examination follows the structure of a real trial: the two competitors each represent either the plaintiff/prosecution or defendant/defence and seek to establish their client's case. Each competitor first makes their opening statement to set out their case theory – the narrative which explains the events in a way beneficial to their client.[62] They then proceed to examine their witness to admit relevant evidence and cross-examine the opponent's witness in order to point out inconsistencies in their case theory.

The competition is an incredible way to develop trial advocacy skills. There is often minimal preparation time for each round as the facts are only provided an hour prior to commencement of the mock trial. Competitors find their creativity and communication skills are tested, particularly when establishing a case theory. This competition is worth participating in if you are interested in becoming a barrister and wish to experience trial work.

Paper Presentation

The paper presentation competition involves students writing an academic article on a topic (usually of their own choice, but occasionally in response to a topic or stimulus) and presenting it before a panel of judges. The length of your article will vary with each competition, generally ranging between 2500 and 5000 words. Your presentation will usually be 15 min long and includes questions from the judges about the argument you put forward.

This competition is particularly helpful if you are interested in postgraduate studies and academia – it is an opportunity to engage in extensive research on an interesting and niche topic. Further, it tests your knowledge and understanding of the law and policy considerations surrounding your topic before qualified judges. Additionally, like witness examination, this competition is unique in that you compete individually. You test your individual ability to research and refine legal arguments. As such, it is better to view the competition as complementing your study

[62] For more on this, see Marcus Stone, *Cross-Examination in Criminal Trials* (2009, 3rd ed, Butterworths).

with an opportunity to gain both a broad and deep understanding of a particular area of law.

Mooting

Most students are fairly familiar with the basics of mooting. A simple yet succinct definition is provided by Cassimatis and Billings:

> A "moot" is a mock court, tribunal or arbitral hearing in which, generally, two teams of students present opposing oral and written legal arguments (or "submissions"), based on a moot topic, before a judge, arbitrator or tribunal member.[63]

Although mooting is considerably more preparation-heavy than other competitions, students often cite it as the best and most valuable experience in their degree. Foremost, it is a fun way to learn about a very niche area of law. To those who might discount such niche knowledge as "not worth" the time investment, consider Hugo Grotius, one of the founding fathers of international law. Sentenced to life imprisonment, Grotius was allowed to receive (strictly unnecessary) books in his cell every week. In 1621, Grotius escaped prison – in a book chest.[64] While the knowledge you gain through mooting may never be needed for a prison break, our point is this: you never know where new and interesting knowledge may take you, including potentially new and exciting career paths.[65]

There are a various other reasons why mooting is particularly useful:

1. **Oral and written advocacy**
   The very point of mooting is to provide you with an opportunity to practice your oral and written advocacy in a forum closer to reality than the classroom. The objective in any moot is to convince the judge that your submissions preset the most logical and favourable solutions to the dispute. That requires not only an intimate understanding of the constituent elements of your case and how they interact, but also an ability to convey that knowledge to someone who may only have a general understanding of the particular area of the law. Orally, moots demand that student advocates learn how to present their entire case in a short period of time and think quickly on their feet to answer questions from judges.

2. **Refined research skills**
   Moots require you to look beyond your textbooks, beyond the main cases in the area of law, to find not only *a* answer, but the *best* possible answer to a specific and complex legal question. While the degree of research required in a moot will vary and often internal moots don't require further research beyond the cases provided, most external moots are excellent opportunities to hone your research abilities.

---

[63] Anthony E Cassimatis and Peter Billings, *Thomson Reuters Guide to Mooting* (Thomson Reuters, 2016) 2 [1.20].

[64] Arthur Nassbaum, *A Concise History of the Law of Nations* (Macmillan 1950), 99–100.

[65] See our discussions in section "Internships" regarding internships.

3. **Time management**

   Participation in a moot during semester requires conscientious time management. Students often say that mooting is a subject of its own – to perform well in both your written submissions and oral rounds of you need to prioritise your commitments and leave sufficient time to research, draft and practice.

4. **Teamwork**

   One of the greatest gifts of mooting is your team. Law school provides few opportunities to truly be immersed in a team environment, which is unfortunate considering how central teamwork is to practicing law. Success in mooting requires teammates to challenge one another's ideas and refine them accordingly. Working in this setting exposes you to other ways of legal writing and public speaking, and therefore is an opportunity to improve your own advocacy.

5. **Confidence and composure**

   The ability to hone both your written and oral advocacy skills in a high-pressure environment like mooting instills you with greater confidence when approaching stressful situations later. Mooting is an opportunity to put yourself outside your comfort zone and in so, bring its constitutive elements – including public speaking – *within* your comfort zone.

Paid Work

Why Undertake Paid Work?

Paid work gives you both experience and money, two things which become increasingly important the closer you get to graduation. However, contrary to popular belief, you do not need to have paid work to gain experience in the legal industry. Instead, what is important is that you have a long-term role, responsibilities attached to that role and a hierarchy within which you are held accountable. It just so happens that paid work fulfils these three criteria.

Having a long-term role ensures that you develop relationships within your workplace and learn how to communicate and interact with colleagues appropriately. You learn a surprising amount of behaviour from simply observing other people and this latent knowledge can help you fit in when you begin a full-time role after graduation. Carrying responsibilities in your role is equally important because it builds up your capacity to communicate with supervisors, manage deadlines and fulfil expectations. Being held accountable may seem frightening but is an important lesson to have before it 'really matters'.

How to Gain Paid Work?

Finding paid work requires both luck and perseverance, as well as an open mind to trying different opportunities. Universities generally have a careers counsellor or employability team which alerts students to upcoming opportunities. Similarly, university societies may advertise paid roles. Subscribing to alerts from job seeking web sites such as Seek.com is also an easy way of staying informed about available opportunities.

While the process of finding suitable paid work that aligns with your university schedule is difficult, applying and successfully gaining the role is even more challenging. Often paid work will require a certain level of experience, which can be difficult to demonstrate if you are in your earlier years of university. If you have no prior working experience, keep an open mind and apply widely. Build up your experience by involving yourself in other extracurricular activities first.

When you gain experience, be sure to update your resume. Attending employability seminars and workshops hosted by your university is an excellent way to gain more information about resume and cover letter writing and interview techniques. Keeping specific records of your experience will also help you during the application process for clerkships or internships. Having a detailed narrative about what experiences you have had will make your cover letter and interview answers more convincing.

When looking for work, keep in mind that the more flexible your employer is, the better. Even if you cannot find flexible work, inform your employer that you are a student and be open about your university commitments.

Connecting with the Legal Profession

Even as a student, building your professional profile and making yourself known to professionals in the industry you aspire to be in is imperative. The predominant objective of having a well-managed professional profile is to create a positive reputation, which makes you appealing to future employers and colleagues. Being an appealing employee is key to receiving interesting work from supervisors, building relationships with clients and discovering new directions in which to take your career. There is nothing wrong with giving yourself some practice as a student. In fact, being able to manage a professional profile as a student will give you an advantage when it comes to applying for clerkships, internships and eventually, graduate roles.

Managing your professional profile requires two things: creating relationships through networking; and maintaining these relationships through effective professional communication.

Networking

Networking is an important skill to have as a law student. Unfortunately, the term is often thrown around as a buzzword and makes little sense in the abstract – everyone has a differing opinion on how it is best executed. If you have attended networking events, then you will also know firsthand the daunting experience of walking up to strangers and trying to engage in a normal conversation. 'Networking' as a concept therefore tends to take on a life of its own.

However, at its core, networking can be defined as simply creating relationships with other people in your profession and beyond. There is no metric for how *well* you network, nor is there any need for overstating its utility. At the end of the day, networking is not substantially different from our daily socialising, whether that be making new friends at university or starting a conversation with the barista at your local café. Professionals are people too and perhaps one of the easiest ways to be memorable as a student contact is to just form a genuine human connection.

What, then, makes networking appear so difficult? Beyond the awkwardness of forced interactions with strangers, it is hard to quantify the benefits of networking in a tangible way. The uncertainty of measuring the success of a networking event may lead you to rely on proxies such as how many attendees you spoke to, how many new LinkedIn connections you have, or (at its most extreme) whether you left the night with a job. Doing so results in you placing unnecessary pressure on yourself to perform at networking events.

The reality is that networking is a means to an end. Understand the two key purposes of networking. *First*, it is an information gathering exercise. As a student who is unlikely to have worked in a law firm, you probably know very little about the profession. Take every opportunity you can to ask questions which have been sitting around in your mind. For example, you may be interested to know what type of work a corporate transactions lawyer engages in, as opposed to an insurance lawyer. By asking questions, you learn a lot about the profession and can make better decisions about whether you want to pursue particular careers.

Second, it is a useful way to gain access to opportunities otherwise unavailable. As will become clear as you progress through your law degree, not all opportunities are widely advertised. Often, a lawyer or academic will have a task which they need completed and will turn to students they have met recently to ask if they are interested in undertaking the task. Alternatively, they might alert you to an opportunity you had not previously realised you could apply for.

With these two purposes in mind, here are some tips that you can employ to make the most out of networking events:

1. **Be genuine**

   No one enjoys talking to someone who has an agenda. It is uncomfortable, and being on the receiving end feels like you are being used for an ulterior purpose. Recruiters can tell when you are cosying up to them. Be respectful, be humble, and try to leave a good impression like you would with any other interaction. The encounter will be less awkward when you treat it as a conversation, not an interview.

2. **Make sure to research and prepare**

That being said, you should avoid being overly casual or unprepared. Professionals will be taking time out of their (often extremely) busy schedules to meet with students and talk to them about what they do. Researching ahead of time allows you to have conversations that are constructive for both you and the person you are talking to. Have questions prepared so that you are not left speechless and reliant on the professional to lead the conversation. This also makes the conversation more meaningful: researching what you can about a particular firm allows you to go straight to the point. Focus on talking about things that cannot be found from a google search. For example, you may like to ask for the professional's opinion on what might develop in their profession in a few years' time, or why they personally chose to work at the particular firm.

3. **Show respect to your peers**

It is a terrible look to try and dominate the conversation and only talk about yourself. Show interest in others and try to involve your peers in the conversation, especially where they are making an effort to join in. This makes the evening pleasant for everyone involved and reflects well on your own personality.

A Practical Approach to Networking: Learning How to Drink

A few helpful networking tips and tricks can also be thought of those related to 'drinks' – be those drinks actual liquid beverages, or just the conversations that occur under the pretense of sharing such beverages.

The Strategic Coffee

Whether you drink coffee, tea, hot chocolate or anything in between (it's not actually about the drink, the point is taking a break to consolidate contacts and make new ones), one of the greatest networking tricks is to 'go for coffee' with a professional you want to talk to. A casual coffee meeting can also be a godsend for more introverted personalities who shy away from more formal networking events.

While plucking up the courage to ask a professional you admire to meet at a local café can be daunting, don't let that phase you. Take concrete steps to make it as comfortable as possible. For instance, you might try to meet them first at a networking event rather than contact them out of the blue or arrange for an introduction through a mutual contact. When you meet people over coffee, be sure to make it worth their time – know your desired outcome, plan how you're going to connect, ask quality questions and be sure to follow-up. It is effective to leave the conversation on a positive note about a topic that you can then easily return to via email, such as a project they are currently working on.

When There's Alcohol Involved

A lot of formal networking events occur over drinks. Therefore, learning how to navigate your way around this atmosphere is important. A couple of tips:

1. *Know your limits* – never get drunk at a networking event. This is not the type of 'memorable' you want to be for a potential employer. Know yourself and don't feel pressured into keeping pace with other attendees.
2. *Hold your glass in your left hand* – an easy one that will help you avoid awkwardness. By holding your glass in your left hand, you're free to shake people's hands with your right without doing the awkward glass and wet/cold hand shuffle.
3. *Know basic information about types of wine, liquor and beer* – you're likely, at some point, to find yourself in a professional situation where someone offers to get you a drink. It's painful for everyone when you're asked what type of wine you'd like and all you can give in response is a blank look. Know what you will order and be aware of what that drink choice might say about you![66]
4. *Use 'getting a drink' at an event as a way to talk to strangers.* While it can be hard to strike up a conversation with complete strangers, this is the point of networking. One way to consciously ease some of the difficulty is through lines, either for food or drinks, at networking events. You can make a comment to someone in the line with you about how long the line is, how great the food is, *anything* … it is a way to get the conversation started (and also an out if things spiral out of control – get your drink and get out of there if you have to!).

Professional Communication

Once you have connected with professionals, either in person or online (or in-line!), it becomes incumbent on you to progress that relationship. This may be less daunting than initially breaking the ice, but is still difficult. You may have already experienced the stress of agonising over minute phrases and words when drafting emails to lawyers and HR contacts you have met. This is understandable and a good sign that you are treating professional communication with the requisite seriousness.

There are three main ways to undertake professional communication: online (ie, Linkedin or email), phone and in person. The most common method is email. It is unlikely that you will be calling or meeting with any professionals without first connecting via email. Even if you are not able to draft emails quickly, be sure to draft them carefully. Be courteous and respectful with your word choice; avoid slang and colloquialisms. Use reader's logic rather than writer's logic by placing important

[66] A lot of drinks are accompanied by social stereotypes. See, e.g., Bel Booker, 'What Your Choice of Networking Drink Says About You' on *Eventbrite* (10 November 2015) https://www.eventbrite.co.uk/blog/what-your-choice-of-networking-drink-says-about-you-ds00/.

information first before explaining the story behind it. Lawyers are busy people so make your emails concise and direct. Finally, always have a purpose: do you want to set a time for a coffee and catch up? Are you asking a specific question about their job? Do you just want to provide them with an update on how you are progressing at university? This makes it easier for the recipient to know how to respond.

In person and over the phone etiquette is less complicated but allows for less planning. Rather than attempting to script your conversation, have a few basic rules which you can follow naturally. For instance, if you are having a conversation with a professional, you may have a rule to speak about yourself for 30 s before asking the other person a question. This could avoid situations where you speak for too long or have difficulties moving the conversation along. There are other simpler rules: maintaining eye contact, using polite language, having clear articulation and speaking up to name a few.

Remember, softer skills are as important as your academic abilities if you aspire to work in team environments since your interaction with colleagues has a real impact on them. For this reason, treat in-person professional communication seriously and use it as an opportunity to demonstrate your best behaviour. If you are not a naturally sociable person, don't worry – being polite and respectful is more important than appearing extroverted.

Realising Your Professional Identity – Clerkships, Internships and Research Assistants

Completing a clerkship or internship, or becoming a research assistant for an academic or barrister, are all ways in which you can experience particular legal professions and hone in on the career path you want to pursue. The best time to start *thinking* about your career opportunities is in your first year. It is a strong internal motivation to do well and become involved in interesting extracurricular activities. It goes without saying that competing in legal competitions, attending networking events and volunteering or doing paid work are all activities which, to an extent, help you to secure a clerkship, internship or research assistant position.

This section describes what you can generally expect in these roles and offers some words of advice for approaching them. Before doing so, however, a few words on fitting these practical encounters into your bigger picture. For better or for worse, many law students feel acute pressure to complete clerkships, and clerkships with top tier firms. Clerkships provide security. Having completed clerkships is a way to illustrate your competence. Clerkships also provide the security of a clear career trajectory towards a graduate role. Yet, this security may be misplaced. What we seek to stress here is this:

1. See clerkships as just one work experience option of many. Clerkships are not a necessary component of your law degree. If you have no interest in a clerkship, think carefully about how it fits into your desired career trajectory. If you are

satisfied that it is the best way to gain practical and transferrable skills, then absolutely pursue it. If not, don't stress over it. Similarly, the clerkship pathway is not the only one to a job with a commercial law firm – indeed, many lawyers at the firms offering clerkships will tell you that they ended up there after pursuing a different pathway.
2. Do your due diligence. Before applying for and accepting clerkship or internship positions, assess whether the experience will satisfy your interests and priorities. If not, seek out the best and apply for those. As the Chief Operating Officer of Facebook, Sheryl Sandberg, says: "What would you do if you weren't afraid?"

Clerkships

Notwithstanding the warning above, undertaking a clerkship has several benefits. Most obviously, it is the most direct pathway to graduate employment at a firm (whether that be top-tier, mid-tier or boutique). Beyond that, clerkships can also provide insight into the reality of practising law in a firm environment and the differing firm workplace cultures. It is also excellent training experience that will teach you more about research, applying the law and working for clients.

There is an element of luck involved in gaining a clerkship role. Even the most intelligent students with extensive work experience or a fantastic GPA may not receive a clerkship offer from some firms. Equally, a low GPA does not preclude you from gaining a clerkship. What matters is whether you have an interest in law, an ability to work diligently in a team environment and demonstrated these two qualities throughout your degree (and application).

Chapter 3 on transitioning from law school to employment details how the application process is managed and offers advice on how best to approach it.

Internships

If you are interested in legal opportunities beyond law firms, or even outside of law altogether, being proactive is key. Graduate pathways in these areas can be difficult to discern depending on each industry and in some cases, gaining experience is even more competitive than clerkships. Generally, however, the hardest part is actually determining what experience you're after. Perhaps the greatest tip that we can give for overcoming this dilemma is to return to Steve Jobs' 'connecting the dots' analogy. Rather than focussing too much on plotting your dots to reach a specific end goal, follow what you are interested in more generally and keep your eyes peeled for any opportunities, even if they are in professions ancillary to those you are interested in. When you invest in topics of interest, it will be easier to tune into the right frequencies to hear about opportunities in the sector.

Another tip on this front is that if you're worried about securing a job on graduation, think carefully about where jobs will be. Make a conscious effort to learn and think about how the role of lawyers is changing. For example, as mentioned previously, there is an evolving intersection between law and technology. If you think you could one day be a gap-filler in this space, look for internships that relate to a law and technology topic! Is there scope for work experience with an institute researching the potential of disruptive technologies in the legal sphere? Is there an opportunity to attend a conference on law and technology? What are international institutions, like the United Nations, doing in this space? You'll find that as soon as you delve deeper into a specific issue or area of the law it is much easier to separate the forest from the trees.

Don't shy away from international internships either – they give you unique experiences and if the financials are tricky, various organisations, such as the Australian and New Zealand Society of International Law, provide financial support specifically for students undertaking internships abroad. Think about tying an internship in with exchange, or tailoring your degree program to allow for an internship - you may be able to get credit for one.

To help you navigate this murky area and get the creative juices flowing, we've listed some internship opportunities in addition to commercial clerkships in Table 2.2. There are also fantastic guides, issued by organisations such as the Law Society of New South Wales Young Lawyers,[67] which are worth consulting in detail. The key, however, is thinking outside of the box. Often, the best internship opportunities arise where there is no set internship program. Be proactive: follow your passions, build networks with like-minded people and immerse yourself in realising new opportunities.

Research Assistant

In addition to internships and clerkships, another work experience avenue is research assistance for an academic, barrister or judge. Being a research assistant is an excellent opportunity to find out about these areas of the legal profession and may precede a judge's associateships or postgraduate study, eventually leading to either academia or the bar.

There are several key differences between being a research assistant and undertaking a clerkship/internship (and there is no reason you cannot experience both). Being a research assistant does not necessarily smoothly lead to a postgraduate degree or work as an academic. Instead, it is an exercise in relationship building and skillset consolidation. Networking with researchers opens up new interest areas and contacts. Being a research assistant is also an opportunity to improve your research

[67] See, eg, Achinthi Vithanage (ed), *The International Law Internship Guide* (The Law Society of New South Wales(New South Wales Young Lawyers International Law Committee), 2nd ed, 2017).

Table 2.2 Ideas for internships

Internship provider	Place	Where to find more info
Australian Institute of International Affairs	Sydney, Melbourne, Canberra, Adelaide, Brisbane, Hobart	http://www.internationalaffairs.org.au/youth-and-community/internships/
The Aurora Project	Varies	http://auroraproject.com.au/legal
Australian Law Reform Commission	Brisbane	https://www.alrc.gov.au/internship-program
Canberra Community Law	Canberra	http://www.canberracommunitylaw.org.au/jobvolunteer-opportunities.html
Carnegie Endowment for International Peace	Various	https://carnegieendowment.applicantpro.com/jobs/709391.html
Department of Justice and Regulation Victoria	Melbourne	https://jobs.careers.vic.gov.au/jobs/VG-SO2775b
Environmental Justice Australia	Melbourne	https://www.envirojustice.org.au/get-involved/volunteer/
International Bar Association	London, The Hague, Washington DC	https://www.ibanet.org/Education_and_Internships/Legal_Internship_Programme.aspx
Lawyers for the Creative Arts	Chicago	https://law-arts.org/opportunities
North Australian Aboriginal Justice Agency	North Australia	http://www.naaja.org.au/get-involved/internship/
Oxfam Australia	Varies	https://www.oxfam.org.au/get-involved/volunteer-with-us/internship-vacancies/
United Nations	Varies	Check the UN Internship portal
The World Bank	Washington D.C.	http://www.worldbank.org/en/about/careers/programs-and-internships/internship and https://icsid.worldbank.org/en/Pages/about/Internships.aspx
World Trade Organisation	Various	https:// www. wto.org/english/thewto_e/vacan_e/iypp_e.htm#WTO_Internship

and legal writing skills. It is largely self-motivated – the emphasis is on completing tasks thoroughly, having attention to detail and being curious about deeper and more niche legal problems, rather than thinking commercially about providing client services.

It is possible to be a research assistant at any point in your degree. Your university may have a roster where you can advertise your availability. Commonly, academics will hire research assistants for discrete projects. Thus, your role might span from a few weeks to a few years, depending on the project and your performance. Importantly, these roles offer significant benefits because work can often be done from home or in between your classes. Consequently, research assistance is an ideal paid role to undertake alongside full time study.

If your university does not have a central mechanism through which to apply for assistant positions, the next best option is to directly approach academics. You should not be afraid to do so. Keep your eyes peeled as opportunities are much harder to spot than for formalised processes such as clerkships.

Making the Most of Your Experience

Do not be complacent once securing work experience opportunities: the real test of your skills and abilities begins once you start the role of clerk, intern or research assistant. Challenge yourself and demonstrate your full commitment and competence. There are four tips that you should always keep in mind:

1. **Be friendly**

In the early days of your role, set out to establish yourself as a friendly co-worker regardless of how big the team you are working in is. Focus on getting to know everyone – learn the names (especially pronunciation) and roles of those around you. This is useful for whenever you need a question answered or want some advice. Though it may be challenging to always be positive and smiling, treat everyone – especially support staff – with the same level of respect and kindness.

Further, learn the office protocol and administrative procedures early on. These will obviously be more established in a firm but the same advice applies to a research assistant role. Clarify firm routine. When do people have lunch? Is there a communal kitchen and what are the rules for using it? Do your colleagues and supervisors prefer to receive a message or email before you approach them in their office?

It is also critical to be visible, particularly in a clerkship or internship where you are one of several students in the office and need to demonstrate your suitability for a graduate role. This is achieved through small things, like saying hello to people you meet in the kitchen or in the lift. Do not be afraid to approach others in a more relaxed and sociable manner to find out more about what they like about their work and how you might fit in the firm.

2. **Demonstrate your interest**

Demonstrating your interest in what you are doing may be as easy as asking further questions about the context of the work you are being tasked, or following up how your task played into the overall project and how that project is progressing. Another simple way to demonstrate your interest is to ask for more work if you have available time to complete it. If you find yourself without something to do and unable to ask for more work, occupy yourself with tasks related to where you are working and with things that may help you down the track. When tasks are given to you, get started on them immediately – embrace the advice of Charles Dickens to "never do tomorrow what you can do today. Procrastination is the thief of time." This may mean staying back a little late one day to complete a task so it does not carry into later days.

3. **Demonstrate your ability**

Don't become complacent once you have submitted a resume in the application process. Employers not only look for students who are high-achievers, but also for students who continue to improve themselves. Therefore, make sure you put in your best effort for every task you are given, no matter how small it might be (without spending too much time on it of course; remember that your supervisor has time and budget constraints). Take every opportunity to demonstrate your abilities, whether it be black letter analysis of the law or thinking creatively about how to provide your product to your supervisor.

4. **Ask questions**

Don't be afraid to clarify things that you are unsure about. If you don't know something, don't pretend you do – it's easier to lose someone's trust than to gain it and these things have a way of catching up with you. It is also better to ask for clarification early on than to waste everyone's time doing something your supervisor did not intend for you to do.

5. **Take ownership of your work**

If you are given a task, respond as soon as you can that you are taking it on and give the supervisor an idea of how long it will take you. Then take ownership: provide your supervisor with updates, ask questions about how you might approach the task and try to look for areas where you can add your own value. For example, it is a good idea after you have been invited to attend a client meeting to take minutes during the meeting and to offer to undertake some of the simpler actionable items. Another very easy way to take ownership of the work you are given is to offer to proofread documents or to create a document which can easily be replicated to other similar tasks (such as marketing documents or presentations).

Conclusion

At the end of the day, law school is a melting pot of exciting and unexpected opportunities. Manage your expectations at the outset by beginning to craft a positive professional identity and setting goals. Think about who you are, what you want to be, and how the study of law can help get you there. Follow through by achieving well academically and applying yourself outside of the classroom. Finally, begin to create relationships with the industry you are interested in and pursue opportunities which put you on the path to realising your professional identity.

However, do not fret if you are uncertain about what career you wish to pursue. Whether your ideal career is a commercial lawyer, a barrister, an academic or is a profession that lies beyond the traditional legal sphere, law school presents many opportunities for you to test the waters. As you progress through your legal studies and meet more members of the profession, you will understand that there is no one correct pathway. There are barristers who used to be nurses, commercial lawyers who used to be athletes and academics who used to work as tradies. Likewise, there are commercial lawyers who become academics, criminal prosecutors, comedians – the list goes on. The common thread which joins these people is that they approached law school with a desire to challenge themselves and pursue a career which they find fulfilling.

You choose the chocolates that go in your law school box. Choose wisely!

Chapter 3
The Transition from Law School to Law Employment

Vivek Mahadevan and Jeremy Leith

The Final Year as a Law Student

Making it to the final year of a law degree is an achievement of itself. At this stage, it is important to plan your last year so that you can minimise stress, both in terms of your university studies and job applications, and enjoy the remainder of your degree. This chapter provides advice on your final year, and the transition from law school to employment, including the steps required to become a practising lawyer.

Electives

The final year of a law degree provides students with the opportunity to study elective units, which either build on core areas of the law or allow you to gain an overview of specialised fields. We have found the following considerations useful when selecting electives.

V. Mahadevan
University of Wollongong, Wollongong, Australia

GradDipLegalPrac (College of Law), The Australian National University, Canberra, Australia

J. Leith (✉)
University of Sydney, Sydney, Australia

GradDipLegalPrac (College of Law), The Australian National University, Canberra, Australia

M. Raz et al. (eds.), *Careers in Law: A Guide for Students, Graduates and Professionals*, https://doi.org/10.1007/978-981-15-3627-4_3

Course Content and Structure

If you have competing interests in different electives, consider requesting access to the course outline. This will provide you with information regarding the style of teaching, assessment methods and resources, so that you can align electives with your preferences. We also advise requesting information regarding electives that may be undertaken from outside the law faculty. Electives from other faculties can assist in providing background knowledge for your career. For example, a corporate finance elective in your university's business faculty will provide context as to how companies raise finance, which will be useful for a career in corporate law.

Another source of information when it comes to contemplating an elective is other final year students or recent graduates. An elective course may sound interesting on paper, but being actually involved in the elective could be a different experience. Consulting people who have undertaken the elective you are interested in may provide insight to help you better determine the most suitable elective for you.

Marks or Interest?

Electives are a great opportunity to explore areas of the law that you might find interesting. If you are unsure about which elective to choose, the best advice is to think broadly and select subjects that you would find interesting or a potential career path. If you are undecided as to what areas of law to practise in, consider the core subjects you have completed and choose electives similar to the core subjects that you have enjoyed. For example, if you enjoyed corporate law, securities regulation may be an appropriate elective for you to study.

However, we appreciate that there is also pressure to maintain or improve your grades in your final year, especially if you are looking to complete the degree with a particular average. A question invariably arises as to whether you should enrol in subjects that are perceived to be 'easier' in place of a subject that you might be interested in, but is considered to be difficult. While it may be tempting to pick the 'easier' subject, we recommend carefully considering this choice, because while obtaining high marks may be important, studying an elective that aligns with your interests will maximise your exposure to areas of law that could translate into your career. Further, having an interest or passion in a particular subject will likely motivate you to be attentive, producing better results.

Honours

Depending on your university, degree and grade average, you may be eligible to complete an honours program or independent research project in your final year of study.[1] This can be a valuable experience. As a self-guided research task, it will assist in developing your research skills and allow you to explore an area of law that you are passionate about. It will also provide you a showcase of your legal skills for future employers. Finally, an honours degree is often a prerequisite for completing further study – universities often require a first class honours degree for admission to postgraduate courses where that option was available in your undergraduate course, such as the University of Oxford's Bachelor of Civil Law program.

Making the Most of Your Final Year

The final year of law school may be your last opportunity to take advantage of the range of extra-curricular activities offered by your university. In addition, employers often seek well-rounded law graduates, and one way to round out your skillset is through extracurricular activities.

Examples of extracurricular activities include:

1. Volunteering

   Many universities have partnerships with community legal centres to complete volunteer internships. Alternatively, you may wish to be involved in on-campus activities, such as organising fundraising events.
2. Societies

   Each Australian law school has a student law society. Being involved in a governance position will provide you with management experience and the opportunity to make contacts (and hopefully friends). Your university will also have other student-organised societies that offer a variety of activities, ranging from debating to extreme sports. Regardless of your interest, there is likely to be a society or appreciation club that interests you.
3. Competitions

   Legal competitions are a great way to build legal skills outside of the classroom. Check Chap. 2 for details.

[1] Refer to your university guidelines to determine the grade point average or percentile cut-offs for the different honours classes.

Graduation

Overview

Graduation is an exciting time for students at the end of their degree. This section of the chapter will describe how a student becomes eligible for graduation, the application process and the ceremony itself. Graduation requirements will change over time, so we advise liaising with your university's graduation office for the correct application procedure.

Eligibility

To become eligible to graduate, you must have:

- completed all assessments and achieved the number of credit points required for your law degree. This includes any theses and practical components (even those on a pass/fail basis)[2]; and
- paid all outstanding fees, such as subject fees and library fines.

Application and Fees

Once you have satisfied the requirements to be eligible, the application process is generally in two stages – application and registration. The application is usually conducted online through your university portal. Key details to check are your name, course name and any applicable majors or minors. If your application is approved, then you will be required to register for a ceremony. There may be multiple dates to choose from, or you may be allocated a ceremony based on your degree and surname (i.e. you are already registered). Ceremonies are generally conducted twice a year. Many universities will conduct the actual ceremony 4–6 months after the graduation date. If you are likely to be away, you may wish to consider requesting to defer your graduation ceremony until you return.

Once a ceremony is chosen, you will be required to pay a fee for graduation. The fee will cover guest tickets, graduation programs, hall hire and presentation and post-graduation refreshments. For some universities, a hire of academic dress/regalia will also be included in the fee. If it is not included, make appropriate arrangements to purchase, hire or borrow the necessary regalia.

[2] If you are undertaking a double degree, check with your university as to the graduation procedure for each of the degrees, as you may be allowed to graduate from one degree before the other.

The Ceremony

There will be multiple ceremonies during a graduation day, so it is important to determine your ceremony time. Before the ceremony, make sure to bring photo identification and your student card to register for the ceremony, collect your tickets and (if applicable) your academic dress.

Applying for a Job

You will likely be considering graduate employment opportunities during your penultimate and final year of university. This section provides an overview of how to apply for a legal position, covering the application process through to interviews. There are different legal positions available to you, including:

- Law firms
  - Large
  - Boutique/mid-sized
  - Small
  - Rural
  - International
- In-house
  - Banks
  - Accounting firms
  - Consulting firms
  - Major corporations
- Public Sector
  - Government departments and agencies
  - Courts
- Not for profit sector
  - Community legal centres
  - Advocacy organisations

Structured Recruitment Programs

The appropriate time to apply for graduate employment will depend on the type of job you are interested in. As a general rule, you will be required to apply in your penultimate year for positions in large, boutique, international and mid-sized laws

Table 3.1 Regulation of seasonal clerkships

Jurisdiction	Professional body	Online application portal with participating firms?
Australian Capital Territory	Law Society of New South Wales (for the purposes of clerkships)	cvMail[a]
New South Wales	Law Society of New South Wales	cvMail
Northern Territory	Legal Practitioners Admission Board	No
Queensland	Queensland Law Society	cvMail
South Australia	The Law Society of South Australia	cvMail
Tasmania	Board of Legal Education	No
Victoria	Law Institute Victoria	cvMail
Western Australia	The Law Society of Western Australia (in conjunctions with universities)	cvMail

[a]cvMail is a centralised portal where participating firms list their seasonal clerkship and graduate offers

firms, as well as legal roles in banks, accounting and consulting firms. If successful, you will be offered a vacation clerkship or internship position for a period of 4–12 weeks, after which the organisation may extend a graduate offer to you. In contrast, small and regional law firms, not for profit centres and the public service will often expect applications in your final year. If successful, the organisation will extend a graduate offer without requiring a clerkship or internship.

For most graduate programs, your application will be made to the institution directly. In contrast, seasonal clerkships are regulated by each states' law society, set out in Table 3.1.

Your Application

The key elements of a legal job application are:

- Cover letter;
- Resume; and
- Selection criteria.

Why and How Are These Elements Used?

The abovementioned elements are used to assess a candidate against key attributes that the organisation would like to see in candidates who will be successful for the role. Taking the example of a graduate position, each hiring firm will have a theoretical 'assessment matrix', which describes what an employer will expect to see for any given candidate for a graduate position. For example, the following table sets out part of the criteria that could be used for a small/regional firm (Table 3.2):

Table 3.2 Example of assessment matrix

Traits	Demonstration of traits	Evidence	Comments
Strong academic legal record	High marks in law subjects In particular, high marks in property and tort law	Academic transcript Resume (including awards)	Good, 70 average Average
Ability to work independently	Works unsupervised Able to make decisions without supervision	Interview – when have you taken initiative to do something without any support? Referees – confirm example	Good answer Poorly told example, stumbled and not effective
Passion for property and tort law	Work experience in both areas Honours thesis in either area	Interview – what was your favourite subject at university and why?	Great prior work experience at small firm in property No honours, no thesis

Cover Letter

A cover letter is generally requested to accompany a resume. A cover letter should set out your experience and qualifications relevant to the position. Unless otherwise specified, you should generally aim for one page in length. When applying for legal roles in particular, you will be expected to demonstrate your interest in the position. Consider the following when drafting your cover letter:

Why are you interested in the relevant area of law?

Demonstrating an interest in the area of law that is the focus of the organisation (or particular position) is critical to demonstrating your interest. You can show this by describing relevant work experience in the same area of law and good marks in related law subjects.

Why this area of law over any others?

This is particularly relevant where you are applying for position in a particular area of law in a multi-practice firm. It is important not to come across as negative towards a particular area of law. Rather, you should simply emphasise your particular interest with an area of law above others (for example, your good marks in employment and labour relations may be your motivating factor to apply for a position with an employment law firm).

Why this particular organisation?

Showing an interest in the particular organisation is vital in a crowded legal market. Employers want to know what you think positively differentiates them from the rest of the competition. We advise researching the organisation in order to successfully address this question. Examples of points to include are:

- Recent successful projects or legal cases;
- Important clients to the firm, that have longstanding relationships;
- Volunteering causes supported by the organisation and their emphasis on pro bono work; or
- Any other particular issues they seem to focus on (e.g. ensuring flexible working arrangements or improving diversity in their workforce)

The following pages show an example of a good and bad cover letter followed by commentary on each.

Bad Cover Letter Example (Example 1)

XYZ Firm
Address
Dear Sir/Madam

I am writing to you to apply to *XYZ* Firm after reading your website. I think my experience and skills will be a good fit for your firm. Please find attached my resume for your consideration.

I am currently in my second to last year in my law degree. I believe my experiences at university show my passion to become a lawyer and the skills I have gained being a guitar teacher and an employee at Service Food Company will make me a productive member of your team, such as serving the client.

I hope you agree that I will make a beneficial impact to your firm. I look forward to hearing from you regarding my candidacy.

Good Cover Letter Example (Example 2)

Insert your name and address here
Sam Wintergarden
XYZ Firm
Address

Dear Mr. Wintergarden,

I am writing to apply for *XYZ Firm*'s 2018/2019 Vacation Clerkship Programme. I am in the penultimate year of the Bachelor of Laws at *ABC University*.

I am interested in the Vacation Clerkship Programme because I believe that *XYZ Firm* provides a challenging and rewarding environment for its employees. A highlight for me was *XYZ Firm*'s representation of IOP in their patent dispute with *JWR*. To me, this case showcases the high quality of work *XYZ Firm* engages in, and I feel that I would be able to flourish in this environment.

From my prior work experience, I have developed skills that will be beneficial as a clerk for *XYZ Firm*. During my legal studies, I have worked as a paralegal with *ERT Legal*. I currently co-ordinate the debt recovery practice of the firm. This role requires me to analyse complex problems and provide clients with commercially viable legal solutions. I have enjoyed the challenge of this role as it has allowed me to develop my ability to quickly evaluate information and draw accurate inferences, whilst also showcasing my communication and relationship building skills.

At university, I have displayed a high degree of knowledge and understanding of both legal and commercial concepts, as highlighted by my academic record. I have particularly enjoyed, and excelled in, my property and resources law courses, which I believe would prove useful given *XYZ Firm*'s focus on the mining sector. I have also developed client relationship and teamwork skills through my involvement in the *FGH Client Interviewing Competition*, for which I was a semi-finalist.

Thank you for considering my application. I would welcome the opportunity to discuss it with you in further detail.

Your name

Commentary

Length of cover letter

Your cover letter should not exceed one page (approximately 300 words). Make sure to use an appropriate sized font and page margins.

Personalisation

A key aspect of a cover letter is personalisation. Researching the appropriate contact person to send your application to demonstrates thoughtfulness. Generally, the appropriate contact will be the firm's human resources representative, graduate recruitment consultant or, if you are applying directly to a specific team in a smaller firm, a specific partner. Sometimes this will not be possible to find, in which case the generic Sir/Madam can be used.

As a general rule, if you can replace the name of the firm you are applying to with another competing firm and your new cover letter requires no further amendments, it is not sufficiently personalised. This is a clear difference between Examples 1 and 2. For reference, a good example of personalisation is shown in the second paragraph of Example 2, where the writer makes reference to a specific dispute conducted by the firm. It could be taken one step further if the writer did well in intellectual property law and could link an achievement in that subject, such as a good overall mark or individual assignment, to show their interest in that type of law.

Linking your achievements to your abilities

Practically, the cover letter is a document that allows you to link your skills and achievements to what a firm is looking for. It is crucial that you are able to show the reader you have the required skills for the job and demonstrate how you have developed or used those skills through an example. Example 1 does not have sufficient linking between the one skill it elaborates on and the role being applied for.

Breaking down a paragraph used in Example 2:

- From my prior work experience, I have developed skills that will be beneficial as a clerk for *XYZ Firm*. During my legal studies, I have worked as a paralegal with *ERT Legal*. I currently co-ordinate the debt recovery practice of the firm. **[introduce the role]**

- This role requires me to analyse complex problems and provide clients with commercially viable legal solutions. **[explain what the role requires]**
- I have enjoyed the challenge of this role as it has allowed me to develop my ability to quickly evaluate information and draw accurate inferences, whilst also showcasing my communication and relationship building skills. **[explain skills developed through the role]**

Resume

Your resume should concisely demonstrate that you meet the requirements of the position and the culture of the organisation, showcased through your skills and experiences.

What questions are you looking to answer with your resume?

As with your cover letter, there are certain criteria that the reader is looking for when reading a resume. This will vary depending on the position, but a targeted legal resume will provide the reader with an understanding of the following:

1. Work experience

The most relevant form of work experience is legal work experience. This includes work at a law firm (or with a sole practitioner) as a paralegal or otherwise, for a judicial officer or with a barrister, and other roles where the substance of your work involves the use of legal skills (for example, legal policy research for a government department or academic). Volunteering in the above roles or at, for example, a community legal centre, also demonstrates useful experience. Short of this, any form of employment should be listed, including less formal employment arrangements (e.g. tutoring), as having consistent work experience while also studying at university showcases your ability to balance life and work as well as to prioritise. Note that the organisation may focus on the duration of your previous positions. For any organisation, training staff (particularly if you are applying at a graduate or junior lawyer level) is a large initial cost. As such, employers will be looking to gauge your interest in building a career with the organisation.

2. Academics and languages

Your academic record will be a key consideration for graduate and junior legal positions. The focus here is twofold – strength of marks (i.e. how high) and consistency of achievement (i.e. how often). The ideal is to have a strong, consistent academic record, as this will signal to the reader that you have the ability to achieve and maintain high results.

As a general rule, a distinction average and above will be considered as passing the academic threshold for the majority of law firms. However, this is not to say those without a high average will not be considered and that those with a high average will always proceed to an interview – your application as a whole is what will be evaluated. If you cannot sell yourself on your marks, emphasise the other elements of your resume to contextualise your academic record in light of your other achievements.

Including reference to languages that you can read and write in other than English can be very useful, particularly for organisations with have international offices or an international focus. Your ability to match your secondary language to an organisation's overseas office can be a very important selling point on your resume.

3. Extracurriculars

Law firms are increasingly focusing on more than work experience and academic achievements when hiring graduates. The increasingly common view of employers is that candidates with a diverse set of interests are preferable (all other factors being equal), as it illustrates the ability of a candidate to balance work and social priorities. Having a variety of extra-curricular activities can showcase your abilities as a well-rounded applicant.

Extracurricular activities can take a variety of forms, including:

- Sports;
- Societies;
- Volunteering; and
- Enterprise (e.g. starting your own business or organisation).

4. Motivation

At the heart of your application, you should be demonstrating to the reader that you are motivated to work at the organisation that you have applied for. The more tailored your cover letter and resume, the more noticeable it is to readers that you have put thought and effort into your application.

Structure and Content

As a general rule, you should aim for your resume to be two pages (excluding references). However, there is no set page limit for a resume (the volume of experience and qualifications will determine this), but keep in mind that sometimes less is more – delivering information concisely is key to delivering your message effectively.

General rules you should keep in mind when drafting your resume are:

- Strengths first: make sure to emphasise your strengths throughout your resume. For example, if you have strong work experience, make sure to devote the appropriate amount of words to make this one of the focal points of your resume. Similarly, you should also ensure that the first page of your resume is also your strongest, as this will provide the reader with a good first impression.
- Spell check: your resume and cover letter are the reader's first impression as to your ability to communicate. In the legal field, attention to detail and written communication skills are vital to becoming a lawyer. Having spelling and grammatical mistakes in your resume will indicate to a reader that you have not been thorough in proofing your application, and will automatically cast doubt on your attention to detail.

The structure and content of a resume can vary, but a skeleton resume would include:

1. Contact details

Either placed at the top of the resume or within the header (or footer), you should include your name, current address, email and phone number. You can also include a link to your LinkedIn profile.

2. Personal statement (optional)

A personal statement is like an 'elevator pitch' for your resume. It is a paragraph summary of your resume that encapsulates who you are, what skills you have and what your goals are. It should be oriented towards what you can offer to the employer, just like your resume as a whole.

3. Key skills

You should include four to six key skills that emphasise your experience applicable to the position. If applicable, look to list out any skills that have been identified (or you have identified) as essential or desirable for the job, and link your experiences to these skills. For example, excellent verbal and written communication skills will be key to all entry-level legal roles, so examples from your work experience (e.g. employment as a paralegal) or your university work (through high marks in subjects) should be used to illustrate your achievement of the skill.

4. Education

You should list your current degree title and the institution you study at. You can also put down your high school, though this is optional. Depending on the strength of your academic record, you may also include your grade average with your education (e.g. distinction average over law degree), as well as any honours classifications. Generally, if you have academic achievements, such as academic awards or scholarships, they should be placed under this section. Include as many awards as you can that are relevant to your application. If you have many awards, select the best four or five that are relevant to the job being applied for or balance out your academic achievements.

5. Employment

You should list your employment history in reverse chronological order, listing the dates you were employed (month and year) and your title. If you do not have any employment history, you should substitute this with any work experience or internships you have completed.

For each job, you should illustrate:

- Your main responsibilities
- Key skills you developed (and how you have developed them – use examples);
- Key achievements in your role (particularly those which can be represented numerically, e.g. a 25% increase in sales)

6. Volunteering and Extracurriculars

Any volunteering or extracurricular activities should be listed in the same way as your employment history. It is important to distinguish between extracurriculars you participate in as a member compared to extracurriculars that you participate in as an executive. You can include both in this section, however you should prioritise experiences with executive positions, as you can elaborate further on responsibilities that you held in your position. However, this should be guided by relevance to the job being applied for.

7. Hobbies/Interests (optional, but recommended)

Traditionally, hobbies and interests would not form part of a resume. However, employers are increasingly relying on hobbies to seek out well-rounded applicants. In particular, your hobbies allow you to stand out and be memorable, showcase your diversified interests and show some form of personal achievement. You should limit your list to a maximum of three to four interests, and explain them in short form.

8. Referees and references

You should provide contact details for two referees on your resume that are willing to provide a positive reference for you. Ideally, one referee should be a professional referee (i.e. has worked with you as a supervisor/employer) and another in an academic capacity (i.e. a lecturer or tutor). However, your second reference can be personal as well. You may also withhold referees unless requested. We advise notifying your referees of the particular positions you have applied for, so that they have context for any requests for information that they may receive.

The following pages provide a sample resume that demonstrates the above points.

NAME
Address
Phone:
E-Mail:
Key Skills

- Excellent verbal and written communication skills developed through my employment as a paralegal and university studies.
- Ability to effectively work on multiple matters and communicate with team members, with a cross cultural sensitivity that allows me to work well people from a variety of backgrounds as shown through my time at university.
- Ability to work as an individual, while also being able to integrate successfully into differing workplaces, as highlighted by my paralegal role.
- A noted passion for the legal field highlighted by my results in my law degree.

Education
Bachelor of Laws ***Jan 2016–Present***

ABC University, expected to graduate November 2018.

- Distinction average (77).
- Achieved first place in Corporate Law.

Employment History

ERT Legal – Paralegal ***Jan 2017–Present***

- I am employed in the corporate team (working in mergers and acquisition) as a paralegal on a casual basis.
- My duties include researching procedural and legal issues, liaising with partners/counsel where required and creating documents related to business development and commercial awareness.
- These duties showcase my communication skills, my ability to work within limited time constraints and my commercial awareness, which helps tailor firm services to better suit the needs of our clients.

Peer Assisted Study Session Mentor (PASS) ***June 2016–Present***

- I am employed as a PASS Mentor on a casual basis.
- As a PASS Mentor, I am responsible for the co-ordination of mentoring sessions for Criminal Law and Law of Torts, both of which have failure rates above 20%.
- My sessions help reinforce key concepts of the two areas studied, which form a strong base of knowledge from which students can utilise in further law subjects. In my classes, 26% of my regular members achieved a Distinction or above in the subjects.
- This role required me to work, collaborate and communicate effectively with my peers, highlighting my teamwork and interpersonal skills.

Extracurriculars

ABC University Debating Society ***Jan 2016–Present***

- I am responsible for maintaining the membership list, expenditure invoices and writing end of year reports. This highlights my responsible nature and my excellent drafting skills.
- I have organised and participated in multiple events held by the Debating Society. I was awarded best speaker at *FGH* event.
- The position requires me to interact with students from a variety of backgrounds and engage with them in team-based scenarios, highlighting my strong ability to work well in teams.

Interests

- I am an active camper and hiker, having participated in and received a bronze Duke of Edinburgh award. The award also gave me further opportunity to volunteer with local community groups (e.g. Salvation Army).
- In my spare time, I am also taking lessons to learn German. I have a basic understanding of the language, but I am hoping to reach a conversational understanding by the end of my university degree.

Referees:

Mrs. X	Dr Y
XYZ Firm	*ABC University*
Partner	Lecturer, Faculty of Law
(02) 1234 5678	(02) 2345 6789

Academic Transcript

You will need to provide an original or certified academic transcript from your university when applying for positions. This will generally require making an application and paying a fee to your university's records office.

Selection Criteria

Selection criteria will be used in applications to supplement your resume and cover letter. In applications where specific questions are not asked, selection criteria are disclosed in the position description, which you must aim to satisfy in your resume and cover letter. Where specific questions are asked, you may be required to provide answers to the questions in a document separate to your resume and cover letter. The form of the questions will differ depending on the organisation, but as a general rule, they will be phrased as questions (e.g. why do you want to work in commercial law) or statements (e.g. the applicant will showcase good attention to detail).

At times, the organisation may delineate between essential and desirable criteria – this is more common for government positions. As is evident from its name, essential criteria must be satisfied by the applicant in order for an applicant to be considered. Desirable criteria are often used as a point of differentiation between candidates that satisfy the essential criteria and in effect make your application stronger.

Example 1 – selection criteria for a public institution (modified for a legal position):

- demonstrated capacity for effective communication;
- proven ability to work as part of a team;
- well developed customer service skills;
- sound level of knowledge about Administrative and Constitutional law;
- ability to learn localised Indigenous laws in remote Indigenous communities; and
- willingness to travel to remote communities.

Example 2 – selection criteria for a private institution:

- What attracts you to working at this firm and why?
- Why do you want to work in commercial law?
- What particular areas of law interest you, and why?
- Please list your university activities and achievements
- Please list your hobbies, interests and additional achievements relevant to your application.

Answering Selection Criteria

Answering selection criteria is a skill that you will develop as you gain experience in applying for jobs. We advise that you consider the following steps when answering selection criteria:

1. Understand the requirements of the selection criteria

The first step is to understand the parameters that your answer should follow. This includes, in particular, the word limits for each answer. If there are no specific word limits for each question, you will need to determine which questions require greater emphasis. If there are no word limits, this does not give you license to write as much as you can – by not setting a word limit, the organisation is testing whether you can concisely communicate your key skills in an appropriate word length.

2. Identify key words from the selection criteria and any additional criteria

The next stage is to break down the criteria by looking at key words. Using Example 1 above:

- The words *demonstrated* and *well developed* indicate that you should look to experiences where you have showcased the skills previously.
- Words like *thorough* indicate that you need to show an advanced skill level through your experiences.
- *Ability to learn* means that you must look to demonstrate your potential in learning the skill by looking to comparable tasks or experiences to show your capability.
- *Willingness* should be shown through actual experiences, but can be more of a general statement of intent rather than tied to a specific experience.

3. Match your experiences with each criterion

For each of the above criteria, look into your experiences over the last 2–3 years (in a professional or non-professional context, as required) and match these to the criterion above. Using Example 1, well-developed customer service skills could be shown through your customer-facing role at a fast food restaurant, and a sound level of knowledge about Administrative and Constitutional law could be shown through your strong marks in either/both subjects or your thesis topic.

4. Use the STAR method to elaborate on your experience

Once you have matched an experience (or more than one) to each criterion, you must then select a specific example to describe. Continuing the above example, your well-developed customer service skills were shown during your time at a fast food restaurant when your service team received a 100% rating by a mystery shopper. To structure and expand on your example, you can use the Situation-Task-Action-Result methodology (**STAR**).

- Situation – role as server, specifically at the drive through of XYZ restaurant.
- Task – needed to ensure high quality of service to customers, comprising of high quality front-end customer service and quick service of high quality food.
- Action – over 2 weeks, I initiated and trialled a 'two-minute drive' program (with my manager's approval) that aimed to get customers in the drive through and 'out the door' within 2 minutes of ordering. This required prompt attention from me (as the server) as well as co-operation with our cooks (to get the quality of food).
- Result – during the 2-week trial, we were visited by a mystery shopper who gave us a 100% rating. The shopper in particular singled out my efforts as a server, which contributed to the highest rating our store had ever received.

5. Review your answers

Once you have drafted an answer, review it to ensure that it complies with the requirements identified in step 1 above and to proofread it for spelling and grammar mistakes.

Using a Blind Test to Check Your Application

A useful method of ensuring that your application appropriately addresses the selection criteria is to provide to a mentor, friend or family member for review, without telling them which organisation it is for or what the selection criteria is. Once they have reviewed your application, ask them to identify the top three themes/skills they take from your application. Ideally, these skills should overlap with the skills listed in the essential criteria. At a basic level, the blind test should illustrate what a reader takes from your resume, which should guide any necessary amendments.

Next Stages

Testing

If you are successful in progressing to the next stage, you may be asked to do an online assessment. These assessments generally come in two forms – aptitude tests and a personality questionnaire.

Aptitude tests evaluate your comprehension, logic, reasoning and mathematical skills by a set of standardised tests. Note that generally:

- the assessments are timed (between 10 and 60 min);
- participants are all given the same form of test (that is, selected questions of the same difficulty from a test bank, although the order of the questions may change);
- the questions are multiple choice with a correct answer (e.g. true or false) and questions become more difficult as the test continues; and
- ranking is determined by the amount of correct answers.

Examples of aptitude tests include:

- abstract reasoning (e.g. 'continue the pattern' exercises);
- verbal (understand and manipulate words);
- numerical (manipulate figures and understand relationships between sets of data);
- perceptual (ability to correlate shapes and symbols); and
- spatial (ability to manipulate shapes and symbols in three dimensions).

Personality questionnaires seek to provide organisations with an insight into your behavioural style. Generally:

- the assessments are untimed;
- participants are given different questions based on their responses to previous questions;
- questions are multiple choice (with options from most likely to least likely) and there are no specific correct answers; and
- there are no rankings between candidates per se.

Networking Events

Many organisations host networking events as a way for applicants to find out more about the people and the overall culture of the organisation during the application process. The format of the event will vary depending on the organisation, however keep in mind:

- that unless expressly provided otherwise, formal business attire is required;
- you should aim to have a good understanding of the organisation before you attend;
- you will generally be allocated a buddy to assist in making introductions;
- you should speak to a wide variety of people at these events – this is your chance to find out how the organisation's culture operates; and
- you need to be responsible at these events – this is often your first impression at the firm, so don't overindulge in the alcohol!

Depending on how successful your applications are, you may have scheduling conflicts. If this occurs, you should let your human resources contact from each organisation know, without going into detail, that you have a conflict and that, if practicable, you will do your best to attend. If not, you may wish to choose one and stay at the entire event – the choice is personal. Although the networking events are generally not mandatory, we advise sending a courtesy email to your human resources contact beforehand, apologising and informing them that you cannot attend.

Assessment Day

Assessment days (also called 'assessment centres') are becoming more common, particularly in the public sector. Generally, an assessment centre runs from a half day to two full days and looks to test applicants through a variety of exercises conducted in person on the day. The composition of each organisation's assessment day will vary, but common exercises include:

- group exercises (generally with 3–10 group members, verbal or written);
- case studies (based on a real life scenario that you would encounter as a graduate);
- presentations (group or individual; sometimes based on your case study); and
- interviews.

The Interview

An interview is generally the final step in the recruitment process. It is an opportunity for the organisation to better understand your personality, abilities and overall suitability for the role and organisation. The most common interview formats are:

- one or two representatives;
- one or two representatives, with a human resources officer; or a
- panel interview (usually two to three representatives)

Organisations may hold two rounds of interviews. If so, we recommend recording notes of your initial interview, as you will likely be asked more targeted questions in the second interview that may be based on the feedback of your first interviewer(s). We recommend preparing for the interview by:

- Researching the organisation to understand the business, industry and current organisational developments, which can be used as discussion points. Consider particularly the organisation's values, purpose and history.
- Understanding who your interviewers are and their roles – this will assist in engaging with your interviewer.
- Memorising your application and have answers to common questions that may arise from your application.

Interview questions generally fall within three categories – motivational, behavioural and commercial awareness. Common questions include:

Common motivational questions

- Why this organisation?
- What can you tell me about yourself?
- What areas of our organisation do you have an interest in and why?
- Where do you see yourself in 5–10 years?

Common behavioural questions

- What is an example of how you have communicated or shared ideas with people from diverse cultural backgrounds?
- When have you instituted change or had to deal with change?
- When have you achieved a goal that you were proud of?

Common commercial awareness questions

- In your opinion, what are some of the key issues currently affecting our industry?
- How do you keep up to date with what is happening in our industry?

To answer the above forms of questions, you should rely on the experiences listed in the whole of your application for motivational questions, the STAR methodology for behavioural questions and your research for commercial awareness. Try to keep your answers to one to 2 minutes in length – being concise while conveying maximum detail is important.

Your role as the interviewee

As an interviewee, you can do more than answer the questions put to you by the interviewer. Often interviews are framed as formal 'chats' between you and the interviewer. If appropriate, we advise asking questions throughout the interview, so that it becomes more of a dialogue than a structured questioning session. At the end of the interview, your interviewer may ask if you have any questions for them. It is important to have questions prepared, which demonstrate your genuine interest in the organisation and the role.

Plan B

If you do not get your first choice of firm during the process, there are other options to consider. The most important thing to remember is that persistence will be key.

Gaining feedback for next time

If you were unsuccessful in the application or interview process, make sure to request feedback from the person who reviewed your application or interviewed you. Getting constructive feedback to take forward is key to being successful in the long run.

Graduate positions

If you are unable to secure a clerkship, consider investigating graduate positions that will be advertised in the coming year. A clerkship is not the only way to enter the legal profession.

Alternate pathways

As noted at the beginning of this chapter, there are a variety of organisations that can use lawyers or individuals with law degrees. A key benefit of a law degree is the development of critical thinking and communication skills, which are useful in many workplaces and different roles.

Practising as a Lawyer

Practising law in Australia requires admission as a lawyer to the Supreme Court of a State or Territory (**admission**) and obtaining certification with the law society or bar association of a State or Territory (**certification**). While admission and certification is regulated at the State and Territory level, the following section provides a general overview of the requirements for becoming a legal practitioner in Australia.

Admission as a Lawyer

Each Australian State and Territory has an admission board responsible for managing, in whole or in part, the application process and advising the relevant Supreme Court on whether an applicant is eligible and suitable for admission as a lawyer.[3] Information, including guidelines for the admission application process, can generally be found on your local admissions board, professional association or Supreme Court website. Although these guidelines are useful resources, we recommend that you also review the legislation relevant to your jurisdiction.[4]

[3] Note that in Tasmania, the Board of Legal Education provides a certificate to certify that the applicant has the relevant academic requirements. The Supreme Court of Tasmania does not receive advice on character requirements from the Board.

[4] *Legal Profession Act 2006* (ACT); *Court Procedures Act 2004* (ACT); *Court Procedure Rules 2006* (ACT); *Legal Profession Uniform Law Application Act 2014* (NSW); *Legal Profession Uniform Law* (NSW); *Legal Profession Uniform Admission Rules 2015* (NSW); *Legal Profession Act 2006* (NT); *Legal Profession Admission Rules* (NT); *Legal Profession Act 2007* (Qld); *Legal Profession Regulation 2017* (Qld); *Supreme Court (Admission) Rules 2004* (Qld); *Legal Practitioners Act 1981* (SA); *Legal Practitioners Education and Admission Council Rules 2018* (SA); *Uniform Civil Rules 2020* (SA); *Legal Profession Act 2007* (Tas); *Legal Profession (Board*

Eligibility and Suitability Requirements

The process of application varies across the Australian jurisdictions; however, the following are common eligibility and suitability requirements for admission as a lawyer.

1. Age

   To be eligible for admission, you must be aged 18 years or over.

2. Academic qualifications[5]

   There are three academic requirements for admission as a lawyer in Australia:

1. The completion of an approved academic course. It is most common for students to complete a Bachelor of Laws or Juris Doctor to satisfy this requirement, although alternative courses may also be available to you, such as the part-time Diploma in Law Course facilitated by the NSW Legal Profession Admission Board and University of Sydney Law Extension Committee.
2. The completion of a practical legal training program by an approved educational institution, which also requires you to undertake workplace experience under the supervision of a legal practitioner.[6] This workplace experience can generally be completed with a private law firm, government agency, judicial officer or legal aid service.
3. Sufficient knowledge of written and spoken English. Your admission board may require you to undertake an examination to demonstrate this, such as the International English Language Testing System. However, exemptions are generally provided if an Australian institution awarded your academic qualification in law.

A list of approved educational institutions and courses of study for the academic course are included in Chap. 1. A list of educational institutions offering practical legal training in Australian jurisdictions are included in Appendix 1.

of Legal Education) Rules 2010 (Tas); *Supreme Court Rules 2000* (Tas); *Supreme Court Forms Rules 2000* (Tas); *Legal Profession Uniform Law Application Act 2014* (Vic); *Legal Profession Uniform Admission Rules 2015* (Vic); *Legal Profession Act 2008* (WA); *Legal Profession (Admission) Rules 2009* (WA).

[5] Admissions Boards may have the discretion to exempt applicants from the academic course and practical legal training requirements if satisfied that he or she has sufficient academic qualifications or sufficient relevant experience in legal practice or relevant service with a government department or government agency.

[6] Note that in the Northern Territory, Victoria, Western Australia and Queensland, you may not be required to complete a practical legal training program if you complete articles or traineeship (supervised work experience).

3. Suitability requirements

Admission boards and Supreme Courts must also be satisfied that an applicant is a 'fit and proper person' to be admitted to the legal profession. You will be required to bring to the attention of your local admission board and Supreme Court matters relevant to your fitness for admission, and may be required to provide an affidavit or statutory declaration stating whether or not there are any matters that affect your suitability. You may also be required to consent to a police check or be medically examined. A failure to disclose a relevant matter may affect your application, or if discovered after admission, your ability to practise law.

In *Frugtniet v Board of Examiners*,[7] Pagone J considered the importance of honesty in admissions applications as reflecting a fundamental quality required of legal practitioners:

> *The requirement for admission to practice law that the applicant be a fit and proper person, means that the applicant must have the personal qualities of character which are necessary to discharge the important and grave responsibilities of being a barrister and solicitor. A legal practitioner, upon being admitted to practice, assumes duties to the courts, to fellow practitioners as well as to clients. At the heart of all of those duties is a commitment to honesty and, in those circumstances when it is required, to open candour and frankness, irrespective of self interest or embarrassment. The entire administration of justice in any community which is governed by law depends upon the honest working of legal practitioners who can be relied upon to meet high standards of honesty and ethical behaviour... The level and extent of trust placed in what legal practitioners say or do is necessarily high and the need for honesty is self evident and essential.*[8]

Matters considered by the admission boards and supreme courts are set out in the relevant legislation governing admission.[9] Depending on your jurisdiction, these may include whether you:

- are of 'good fame and character';
- have been bankrupt, or an officer of a company that has been wound up in insolvency or under administration;
- have been charged or convicted of an offence in Australia or a foreign country;
- have contravened a law about trust money or trust accounts, in Australia or a foreign country;
- have engaged in legal practice in Australia or in a foreign country when not permitted or in contravention of a condition of an Australian practising certificate;
- are currently the subject of a complaint, investigation, or charge under any Australian legal profession legislation or foreign laws;
- have been found to engage in academic dishonesty;

[7] [2002] VSC 140.

[8] [2002] VSC 140 at [10].

[9] See the legislation in your jurisdiction set out at footnote 4 for further details. For an analysis of the differences in approaches to the character requirements in NSW, Victoria and Queensland, see Francesca Bartlett and Linda Haller, 'Disclosing Lawyers: Questioning Law and Process in the Admission of Australian Lawyers', (2013) 41 (2) *Federal Law Review* 227–264. See also Gino Dal Pont, *Lawyers' Professional Responsibility* (Thomson Reuters, 6th ed., 2016).

- have had your right to engage in legal practice suspended or cancelled in Australia or a foreign country;
- have had a supervisor, manager or receiver, appointed in relation to any legal practice in engaged by you;
- have been removed from a local, interstate or foreign roll of lawyers;
- have been the subject of disciplinary action in another profession or occupation; and
- are currently unable to satisfactorily carry out the inherent requirements of practice as an Australian legal practitioner.

Admissions boards and Supreme Courts also have the discretion to consider other maters relevant to whether an applicant is a fit and proper person to be admitted, and may request further information regarding your application. The Law Admissions Consultative Committee's (**LACC**) *Disclosure Guidelines* advise for applicants to provide full accounts of relevant matters, rather than, for example, simply listing the criminal charges.[10] However, not all offences may need to be disclosed. The LACC also advise that court-ordered fines or administrative penalties, such as for traffic infringements, may need to be disclosed in circumstances where the "frequency or number of fines, or your failure to pay fines, could give rise to concern about your respect for the law." If you are concerned about whether a particular event in your past or medical condition may affect your suitability for admission, you may wish to apply to your admission board for an early assessment of your suitability.[11]

Application Forms and Documents

You will be required to complete application forms and may be required to provide:

- evidence of your academic qualifications;
- an affidavit or statutory declaration, in which you disclose to the admission board matters that may affect your fitness for admission; and
- references, which provide the admissions board with opinions of your character.

There will also be a fee associated with your application. If you are employed at the time of submitting your application, you should consider asking whether your employer will reimburse you for this expense.

---

[10] Law Admissions Consultative Committee, *Disclosure Guidelines for Applicants for Admission to the Legal Profession.* https://www.lawcouncil.asn.au/resources/law-admissions-consultative-committee/documents-about-present-admission-policies.

The Law Admissions Consultative Committee is a national body with representatives from the Australian admissions bodies, the Committee of Australian Law Deans, the Australasian Professional Legal Education Council and the Law Council of Australia, which makes recommendations on policies, procedures and other matters related to admission to the legal profession.

[11] In Tasmania, applications for early consideration are made to the Supreme Court of Tasmania.

The deadline for submitting your application in any given year will depend on the number of admission ceremonies to be held in your jurisdiction. Information on admission ceremony dates and application deadlines can be found on your admissions board website.

It is advisable that you keep a copy of your application form and any documents provided to the admissions board or Supreme Court as a personal record of your application. If not already a requirement, we recommend submitting the application form in person to ensure that all documents are properly received.

Admission Ceremony

If the admissions board and Supreme Court approve your application, the final step in becoming admitted is to attend a ceremony at the Supreme Court and sign the local roll of lawyers. Admission ceremonies generally comprise of a member of the legal profession requesting to the presiding judicial officer that your admission be granted, an Affirmation (or Oath) of Office, and a speech by the presiding judicial officer. A list of admissions boards in Australia is set out in the following table (Table 3.3).

Practising Certificate

Following admission as a lawyer, you must also obtain a 'practising certificate' to practise law in Australia.[12] Table 3.4 sets out the authorised professional associations within the Australian state and territories that issue, or facilitate the process of issuing, practising certificates. The requirements for practising certificates can be found in the legislation relevant to your jurisdiction,[13] and further information, including guidelines and policies, can be found on the website of your local professional association.

[12] There will also be a fee associated with your application. Like above, if employed at the time of submitting your application, you should consider asking whether your employer will reimburse you for this expense.

[13] *Legal Profession Act 2006* (ACT); *Legal Profession Regulation 2007* (ACT); *Legal Profession Uniform Law* (NSW); *Legal Profession Uniform General Rules 2015* (NSW); *Legal Profession Uniform Law Application Act 2014* (NSW); *Legal Profession Uniform Law Application Regulation 2015* (NSW); *Legal Profession Act 2006* (NT); *Legal Profession Regulations 2007* (NT); *Legal Profession Act 2007* (Qld); *Legal Profession Regulation 2017* (Qld); *Queensland Law Society Administration Rule 2005* (Qld); *Administration Rules of the Bar Association of Queensland* (Qld); *Legal Practitioners Act 1981* (SA); *Legal Practitioners Education and Admission Council Rules 2018* (SA); *Legal Profession Act 2007* (Tas); *Legal Profession Regulations 2018* (Tas); *Legal Profession (Barristers) Rules 2016* (Tas); *Legal Profession Uniform Law Application Act 2014* (Vic); *Legal Profession Uniform General Rules 2015* (Vic); *Legal Profession Act 2008* (WA); *Legal Profession Rules 2009* (WA).

Table 3.3 Admissions boards

Jurisdiction	Professional body
Australian Capital Territory	(ACT) Legal Practitioners Admission Board
New South Wales	(NSW) Legal Profession Admission Board
Northern Territory	(NT) Legal Practitioners Admission Board
Queensland	(Queensland) Legal Practitioners Admissions Board
South Australia	Legal Practitioners Education and Admission Council
Tasmania	Board of Legal Education
Victoria	Victorian Legal Admissions Board
Western Australia	Legal Practice Board of Western Australia

Table 3.4 Professional associations responsible for issuing practising certificates

Jurisdiction	Professional body[a]
Australian Capital Territory	ACT Law Society (S)
	ACT Bar Association (B)
New South Wales	Law Society of NSW (S)
	NSW Bar Association (B)
Northern Territory	Law Society of the Northern Territory (S/B)
Queensland	Queensland Law Society (S)
	Bar Association of Queensland (B)
South Australia	Law Society of South Australia (S/B)
Tasmania	Law Society of Tasmania (S/B)
Victoria	Victorian Legal Services Board (S/B)
Western Australia	Legal Practice Board of Western Australia (S/B)

[a](S) and (B) indicate the professional body with responsibility for issuing Practising Certificates for solicitors and barristers, respectively

Supervised Legal Practice

Chapter 7 describes the various law careers open to law graduates, including the differences between barristers and solicitors. Before applying for a practising certificate, you will need to decide whether you intend on working as a solicitor, solicitor and barrister in jurisdictions that have a fused legal profession, or solely as a barrister.

Several conditions are imposed on your certificate as a solicitor when you commence practice, including that you must only engage in supervised legal practice until you have completed the required period of supervised legal practice, which is between 18 months and 2 years, depending on the type of practical legal training undertaken. Supervised legal practise is generally undertaken in a law practice, or in-house for a corporation, government agency or community legal centre.

If you are interested in practising as a barrister, depending on your jurisdiction, you may be required to complete a further course focused on advocacy and a period of supervision and guidance from an experienced barrister or barristers. Before commencing the advocacy course and reading program, you may also be required to undertake and pass a set of bar examinations relevant to being an advocate, such as evidence, procedure, and ethics.

Suitability Requirements

Similarly to the admissions process, the professional associations may require you to disclose any matter relevant to your fitness for practice, which includes matters similar to those identified above. All professional associations require you to disclose any matter that is a "show cause event", and provide an explanation for why, despite the show cause event, you consider yourself a fit and proper person to hold a practising certificate. A show cause event may include:

- a bankruptcy-related event;
- a conviction for an indictable offence or tax offence, whether or not:
  - the offence was committed while you were engaging in legal practice as an Australian legal practitioner or was practising foreign law as an Australian-registered foreign lawyer; or
  - other persons are prohibited from disclosing the identity of the offender.[14]

The professional association may also request further information regarding your application, conduct an investigation into a disclosed matter, require you to provide a police check or be medically examined. Depending on the gravity of the matter, rather than refusing to grant a certificate, the professional association may decide to impose a discretionary condition on your practising certificate, such as requiring further legal education or restricting the type of legal practice that you may engage in.

Practising in the Federal Courts

To practise in the federal courts, your name must also be entered onto the Register of Practitioners.[15] This process is straightforward, requiring you to complete an application form and provide a copy of your Certificate of Admission and Practising Certificate to the Registry of the High Court of Australia.[16]

---

[14] See the legislation in your jurisdiction set out at footnote 13 for further details.

[15] *Judiciary Act 1903* (Cth) ss 55B–C.

[16] See further, High Court of Australia, *Register of Practitioners,* http://www.hcourt.gov.au/registry/register-of-practitioners

Mutual Recognition in Australia

In accordance with Part 3 of the *Mutual Recognition Act 1992* (Cth), Australian lawyers who are admitted in an Australian jurisdiction and hold a practising certificate are entitled to practise in another State or Territory, subject to certain requirements. Advice should be sought from the relevant professional body listed in Table 3.4 above.

The Junior Lawyer

Making the Transition There is a significant learning curve in transitioning from law school to practising as a junior lawyer. Having successfully graduated from law school, you will have a foundational understanding of the core areas of the law practised in Australia, modern research skills, and an ability to apply legal principles to limited factual scenarios. During your practical legal training course or articles training you will learn more about the application of the law.

We have found it useful to ask about the following when starting in a new team or organisation:

1. Document management – how documents and correspondence are filed, whose responsibility it is to manage documents, how often files need to be updated, and whether the team uses particular document management software programs;
2. Matter management – timeframes for tasks, how long common tasks are expected to take, who determines the priority of competing tasks, whether aspects of tasks should be delegated, and how your time is to be recorded for billing or project management purposes;
3. Context – who the intended recipient of your work is and how your tasks relate to the broader matter or project; and
4. Available resources – what legal databases and commentaries are available, and whether any internal guides or precedents have been created for completing particular tasks.

Having a Mentor Graduating from law school and entering the workforce can involve a steep learning curve. Finding a mentor who can guide you through the transition can be incredibly helpful. Generally, large organisations will have formal mentoring programs, pairing junior employees with more senior employees. Mentors outside of your immediate workplace, such as former university lecturers, are also valuable, as they can provide different perspectives and the opportunity to more openly discuss your career progression. If practising as a solicitor or barrister, we recommend that you contact your relevant professional association for information on available mentoring programs.[17]

[17] For example, the Law Society of New South Wales offers mentoring programs for final year law students and graduates, and newly-admitted solicitors. See further, the Law Society of New South Wales, *Mentoring Programs*, https://www.lawsociety.com.au/professional-development/mentoring

Beyond your First Year Once you have experienced and observed the practical application of the law for 12 months, it is worth reflecting on your professional goals and what you would like from a career in the law. Chapter 6 provides a useful overview of further educational opportunities if you would like to specialise in a particular field or enter academia.

Appendix: Accredited Practical Legal Training Providers[18]

Jurisdiction	Institution
ACT	Australian National University College of Law School of Legal Practice
	College of Law
NSW	College of Law
	University of Newcastle
	University of New South Wales
	University of Technology Sydney
Northern Territory	Australian National University College of Law School of Legal Practice
	College of Law
	Flinders University of South Australia
	University of Technology Sydney
	Queensland University of Technology
Queensland	Bond University
	College of Law
	Queensland University of Technology
South Australia	College of Law
	Flinders University of South Australia
	University of Adelaide
Tasmania	University of Tasmania Centre for Legal Studies
Victoria	Australian National University College of Law School of Legal Practice
	College of Law
	Leo Cussen Centre for Law
	Monash University
Western Australia	College of Law
	Leo Cussen Centre for Law
	The Piddington Society Inc. Curtin University

[18] Note that several of the practical legal training providers offer online courses, and reciprocal arrangements may allow a program approved in one jurisdiction to satisfy requirements in another. We advise consulting with your local admissions board to ensure the currency of this information.

Chapter 4
Advanced Law Training and Education

Sayomi Ariyawansa

Whether you have completed the Bachelor of Law (LL.B.) or Juris Doctor program (J.D.), obtaining a legal qualification is the culmination of a great deal of effort and hard work. Given this, the prospect of further advanced law training and education may be a daunting one.

For law graduates who intend to practise law, however, further advanced law training and education is a prerequisite to being admitted to practice as a legal practitioner. As outlined in Chap. 5, completing a practical legal training program by an approved educational institution is one of the academic requirements for admission as a lawyer. Thereafter, every Australian legal practitioner is required to undertake further professional development as a condition of maintaining their practising certificate.

This chapter covers further tertiary studies in law. Today, many law graduates decide to undertake further tertiary studies in law – most commonly, the Master of Law (LL.M.) or similar Masters-level programs. This chapter sets out some of the merits of undertaking further tertiary studies in law, and provides advice for choosing the right university and course, getting through the application process, and making the most of your experience.

Further Tertiary Studies in Law

There are many options for further tertiary studies in law. The most popular option is the LL.M., which is offered by many universities around the world. It is readily recognised as the "next step" after completing an LL.B. or J.D. However, there are also other types of advanced law training (Table 4.1).

S. Ariyawansa (✉)
Melbourne Law School, The University of Melbourne, Parkville, VIC, Australia

M. Raz et al. (eds.), *Careers in Law: A Guide for Students, Graduates and Professionals*, https://doi.org/10.1007/978-981-15-3627-4_4

Table 4.1 Examples of other types of advanced law training (non-exhaustive)

Institution	Course	Length (full-time)
University of Melbourne	Graduate Diploma in Legal Studies (other specialist options are also available)	6 months
Australian National University	Graduate Certificate in Australian Migration Law and Practice	6 months
Monash University	Graduate Diploma in Law	1 year
University of Oxford	Bachelor of Civil Law	9 months
University of Cambridge	Masters in Corporate Law	9 months

Additionally, there is the option to undertake a Doctor of Philosophy (Ph.D.) in Law, which is a highly advanced and specialised research degree, primarily designed for those who are interested in becoming a legal scholar or academic.

It is important to note there is also the possibility of undertaking further tertiary studies in an area other than in law, but with a view to supplementing your legal skills and/or transitioning to a legal role in a specific sector.

For example, law graduates may wish to undertake further studies in areas as diverse as:

- Criminology;
- Human Rights;
- Politics and Social Justice;
- Philosophy;
- Public Administration;
- International Studies;
- Public Health; and
- Development Studies.

For the remainder of this chapter, the discussion will focus on further tertiary studies in law at a Masters-degree level. However, many of the comments below also apply when determining whether to undertake further tertiary studies more generally.

Why Undertake Further Studies?

There are many reasons to undertake further tertiary studies in law. This section provides an overview of considerations to take into account when deciding whether further study is for you.

Developing a Specialisation

Developing a specialisation is one of the key reasons for undertaking further study.[1]

Many universities offer the option of taking a specialised Masters-degree level course. For example, at the University of Melbourne, you may enrol in the Master of Competition and Consumer Law, the Master of Construction Law, the Master of Health and Medical Law, etc.

If you do not wish to undertake a specialised Masters-degree level course, you can still tailor the course to specialise in a particular area of law, if you wish. Some universities, such as the University of Cambridge, allow a student to formally opt to specialise in an area of law and be designated as having specialised in that area.

In any event, completing further study allows you to focus closely on an area of law. For legal practitioners, this provides an opportunity to examine your field through a critical or academic lens, allowing you to obtain the type of invaluable insight which is rarely possible while practising, due to the pace of legal practice and the type of client-focused thinking it requires.

Moreover, completing further study allows you to change or develop a specialisation in a new area of law. It also provides you with access to a new network in this specialisation – through your professors, your peers and any relevant research centres. This may prove invaluable when attempting to access jobs in a new area of law.

In all cases where you are considering further study, the advice of Clara Solomon, Director of Counselling & Career Development at the School of Law, New York University, is sound: 'one way to decide whether an LL.M. is right for you is to talk to people with a job you would like to have and ask them for their opinion about the value of an LL.M. in their field.'[2]

Getting International Experience

Another reason for undertaking further study is to gain international experience:

> Studying international law allows students to develop insights into the global legal system and its influence on both national and international policies … In an era of tighter legal budgets and government cuts, specialist knowledge and flexibility are increasingly

[1] See, for example: V Wish, *7 Reasons Why Lawyers Do An LL.M.* (22 July 2011) https://llm-guide.com/articles/7-reasons-why-lawyers-do-an-llm-; Carla DeVelder, *LL.M. Factor: What to Consider When Deciding Whether to Pursue an LL.M. Degree* (1 November 2010) ABA for Law Students http://abaforlawstudents.com/2010/11/01/ll-m-factor-deciding-pursue-llm-degree/

[2] Ilana Kowarski, *Decide Whether an LL.M. Is Right for You* (26 January 2017) US News & World Report https://www.usnews.com/education/best-graduate-schools/top-law-schools/articles/2017-01-26/decide-whether-an-llm-is-right-for-you

demanded of lawyers. An awareness of international law is a strong advantage in today's globalised world.[3]

This experience can be gained from the course-work itself, by selecting courses with an international law or comparative law flavour. However, importantly, this experience is also gained by being involved with international research centres – such as the Sydney Centre for International Law based in the University of Sydney, or the Lauterpacht Centre for International Law based in the University of Cambridge – and engaging with your peers.

One of the most enriching parts of undertaking further study is the diversity of the student cohort. Many of the elite law schools pride themselves on the composition of the graduate student cohort. For example, the Harvard LL.M. class of 2016–2017 is composed of 182 students, 99% of whom are from outside the United States, from 71 different countries.[4]

Opportunity to Research and Publish

Masters-degree level programs can also provide research opportunities for students.

Some LL.M. programs are solely research-based, but most course-based LL.M. programs allow for a combination of the two. For example, a thesis may be submitted in lieu of sitting an examination, or a course may require the submission of a thesis in addition to other assessments.

In many cases, this work can be turned into a manuscript that can be submitted for publication. Some commentators have noted that a period of study is a good time to research and publish work,[5] something which is desirable for both those who wish to begin an academic career and also for those who wish to develop a public profile in their specialisation in law.

Finally, undertaking further studies in law can provide you the opportunity to join the editorial board of a student-run journal, and gain valuable experience in this process.

Moving into Academia

If you are considering a career in academia, undertaking a Masters-degree in law is a good way to see if this career path is right for you. A PhD is now regarded as the entry level requirement for a person wanting to be a legal academic.

---

[3]Yasmin Ahmed, 'Why Every Aspiring Lawyer Should Study International Law' *The Guardian*, 8 April 2015 https://www.theguardian.com/law/2015/apr/08/aspiring-lawyers-international-law

[4]Harvard Law School, 'LL.M. Class Profiles' http://hls.harvard.edu/dept/graduate-program/llm-profiles/

[5]See, for example: Gregory W Bowman, 'Law Career Blog: The Pros and Cons of LLMs' http://law-career.blogspot.com.au/2006/07/pros-and-cons-of-llms.html

As outlined above, you can take the opportunity to submit a thesis and in doing so, set out the roadmap for future doctoral research. If you choose to publish your thesis, you can also experience one of the key elements of academic life, and start building up your publications.

Moreover, you can use the opportunity to observe what academic life is like. As a Masters student, you are able to interact with professors during the course of your studies, however, you are also able to attend lectures, conferences and workshops, and see how academics work with each other and engage with the broader community. In some instances, you may also be able to participate in student-run research projects, or work as a research assistant.

Taking an Educational 'Gap Year'

In some cases, the best time to undertake further studies in law is after a period of practising law or otherwise working outside academia – i.e. in policy development or in government, for example (see below for a further discussion on when to undertake further study).

With that in mind, further studies in law can be thought of as an educational 'gap year'. While many of the full-time elite Masters-degree level courses are very demanding and require a great deal of hard work at the library, the return to an educational environment can provide an opportune time to reflect on your career and your professional goals.

One of the underrated elements of further study in law is the opportunity it provides for you to pause and consider important questions – such as what interests you, what you have learned from your practical experiences to date, what type of work you like to do, how you like to do your work, and what you would like to achieve. These are questions you may not have the opportunity to think about while working in a fast-paced and demanding environment, as law firms tend to be.

Networking and Job Opportunities

As a few commentators have noted,[6] undertaking further studies in law can provide significant networking opportunities.

Many elite universities hold job fairs or careers events specifically for LL.M. students, such as the New York University International Student Interview Program, or provide access to specific internships or other work-experience opportunities.[7] Some universities also offer 'externships' in community legal centres and legal

[6] Wish, above n 1; DeVelder, above n 1.

[7] Wish, above n 1.

clinics, government departments and agencies, or inter-government and non-government organisations.[8]

Finally, undertaking an LL.M. provides exposure to a larger network of academics, students and alumni.[9] This may prove invaluable, particularly if you are thinking of relocating abroad, or looking at careers in international organisations.

Indeed, Sandra Buteau, the Director of Graduate Career Services and Professional Development at Georgetown Law says that 'Networking is one of the most underrated reasons why the LL.M. degree is so useful in today's global legal environment.'[10]

'Upgrading' Your CV

Many commentators have noted[11] that undertaking an LL.M. at a well-known university is a way to add prestige to your CV; however they advise that this should not be the only reason for undertaking further studies in law. While adding a prestigious institution to your CV may show 'ambition and an upward career trajectory',[12] the monetary cost of undertaking an LL.M. can be very high, even if you secure some funding through a scholarship. Moreover, it is easy to overstate the value of an elite university on a CV. For many recruiters, a year of study does not necessarily equate to a year of practice. In fact, some recruiters have a practice of subtracting a year when calculating your PQE level, irrespective of where you studied.

In sum, you should not expect a payoff in your investment on a brand-recognition basis – you should have more substantial reasons for undertaking further studies, as outlined above.

Understanding Your 'Why'

Most importantly, you need to be able to articulate why further studies in law are appropriate for you at the particular stage of your career that you choose to embark on them. It is important for you to have a clear understanding of what you expect to get out of the experience. This is essential in the short term for preparing your applications for the particular postgraduate programs that you are interested in (as most universities will require you to submit some kind of statement of purpose) and in the

[8] *LL.M. Externships — Georgetown Law* https://www.law.georgetown.edu/academics/academic-programs/graduate-programs/externships/; *Externships* Columbia Law School http://www.law.columbia.edu/social-justice/students/classes-clinics-externships/externships; *One-Semester Clinics and Externships | NYU School of Law* http://www.law.nyu.edu/academics/clinics/semester

[9] Wish, above n 1.

[10] Ibid.

[11] Ibid; Bowman, above n 5.

[12] Wish, above n 1.

long term for helping you to be able to explain your decision in future job interviews. In the end, there is no "right" reason to undertake further studies in law – the right reason is the one that motivates you, and that you can justify in the future.

How to Choose the Right University for You

Deciding where to apply is based on many factors, including: your area of interest, whether you want to study full-time or part-time, funding opportunities, and whether you want to go overseas or not. Your university results to date are also important, as many well-known universities are highly competitive and in fact require that you have graduated with First Class Honours in your LL.B or J.D. For example, there are around 551 applicants for 90 places in the Bachelor of Civil Law program at the University of Oxford.[13]

Applications also involve a fee for administrative processing and require a considerable amount of time to complete – another reason to think strategically about where you apply.

Some matters – such as location, or whether you are able to study full-time or not – may be determined by circumstances outside your control. However, these are the considerations you should actively take into account when deciding where to apply.

Course Content and Structure

It is very important to do detailed research into the course content and structure of the programs you are considering. Most universities have a course 'handbook' that is available online.

The first question is whether you intend to do a Masters-degree by research or by coursework.

In general, a Masters-degree by research provides the best opportunity to lay the foundation for future doctoral research; however your primary teacher will be your academic supervisor. Unless you do so informally (i.e. by observing other classes, if allowed to do so), you will not necessarily be exposed to a variety of teachers, and you may not necessarily know or be able to choose your supervisor. However, a Masters-degree by research can often take 1 year off a doctoral program, if you think carefully about your topic.

A Masters-degree by coursework enables you to be taught by a variety of teachers, and also look at many different areas of law if you do not wish to specialise. The

[13] *Bachelor of Civil Law | University of Oxford* https://www.ox.ac.uk/admissions/graduate/courses/bachelor-civil-law?wssl=1

courses vary greatly in terms of how many courses you do, and how they are structured. For example, some Masters-degrees require you to take four subjects over the entire year. Other degree programs may require students to complete a certain number of units, and subjects may be worth a different number of units depending, allowing you to preference 'breadth' over 'depth' if you wish. It is also worth noting that many Masters-degrees by coursework also have an option of having a research component, if you would like to have this experience as well.

The second question concerns course content. You should consider whether the subjects offered cater to your interests. If you would like to specialise, you should consider whether a specialised LL.M. would be preferable to doing a general LL.M. degree instead.

As outlined in Chap. 5 regarding electives – the best advice is to select a degree program that you think will be interesting and engaging, and one which best suits your career objectives.

Prestige and Reputation

As noted above, for some people, undertaking further studies in law represents an opportunity to 'shop yourself up' and improve your alma mater. However, it was also noted that this should not be a primarily consideration in deciding whether to do further studies or not.

Nonetheless, when deciding *where* to apply – reputation is important.

This does not mean that you should apply to the top ten schools in the Times Higher Education World University Rankings. Of course, there are a few elite universities that one can reliably predict would provide you with an excellent learning experience across a broad range of specialisations. However, it is also worth considering other schools which may also be suited to your specific interests and which have a good reputation in those areas. You may also wish to consider an LL.M. program's job placement rates, if such information is available.[14]

Moreover, the top-ranked schools in the international rankings are not necessarily the most highly regarded universities within the Australian legal profession. Another tip is to do some research on the educational backgrounds of people you personally admire within the legal profession – such as judges or top barristers – to get some ideas on schools to consider.

Employer-Sponsored Study

Finally, it is worth noting that many law firms today sponsor their employees to undertake further studies in law on a part-time basis whilst working.

[14] Kowarski, above n 2.

This may limit the schools you apply to – as well as the courses or subjects you may choose – however, (lack of) funding can be one of the biggest barriers to undertaking further studies.

If you are interested in learning more about your current area of practice, this may be the ideal way forward. However, it is important to be clear about the expectations between you and your employer if you undertake employer-sponsored study. For example:

- whether your employer will contribute towards textbooks;
- the consequences of failing a subject (financially or otherwise);
- whether you will be granted study leave; and
- whether you are required to remain employed by the same employer for a minimum period (and what the consequences are if your employment ends, whether at your initiative or at your employer's initiative).

The Application Process

Timing

There is not necessarily a "right" time to undertake further studies in law.

However, there are matters you should consider when deciding when to return to further study. In some cases, there may be a negative perception if you go straight from an LL.B. or J.D. to further tertiary studies. For example, you may be perceived as avoiding or being unable to obtain practical job experience, or being uncertain about the direction of your career – and this is obviously something you would wish to avoid for future job interviews.

However, this certainly does not apply to everyone. You may wish to consider the following:

- Do you want to be an academic?

In some cases, this may mean that it is best for you to go straight into further study. You should speak to some academics working in the area of law you are considering and seek their views on the best way forward. For some areas, such as jurisprudence or legal history, practical experience in a legal environment may not be important. However, in other areas, practical experience may be an asset.

- Do you want to apply for a specific scholarship?

If so, then you may wish to apply for a scholarship as soon as you feel you fulfil any application eligibility and selection criteria, especially any age requirements. Also, if you are only intending on undertaking further study if you win a scholarship, it is less likely that you will face any negative perceptions for deciding to undertake further studies without first obtaining practical experience.

- Does your university have a 'dual degree pathway' or similar?

Some Australian universities have dual degree pathway programs which allow students to undertake 'combined' J.D./LL.M. or LL.B./LL.M. degrees with a partner institution, with an opportunity to win a scholarship to fund their studies at the partner institution – an excellent opportunity for high-achieving law students.[15]

This list of considerations is just a starting point. The most important thing is that you carefully consider your own career goals, and make sure you are able to justify why further studies in law are appropriate for you at the relevant stage of your career.

Be Organised

Managing multiple applications to different institutions – as well as multiple scholarship applications – can be very difficult. The first thing to do is to write a list of all applications you intend to make, and then set out the relevant dates in your calendar.

The application cycle generally begins in the latter half of the calendar year, in preparation for the year ahead. So, if you intend to apply for a place in the 2018/2019 program, you should be planning to submit applications in 2017 – at least a full year in advance.

Also, it is important to note the 'lead-in' times for various parts of the application process.

For example, you will need to contact your referees to give them ample time to submit a reference prior to the due date. This will be discussed further below.

For applications to LL.M. programs in the United States in particular, it is important to note that virtually all applications go through the centralised Law School Admissions Council – LLM Credential Assembly Service. This means you only need to supply your academic records once, and your referees need to supply a letter of recommendation once, and then these documents are distributed to multiple LL.M. programs. However, it also means that certain documents – such as your academic records – need to be submitted well in advance, so that they may be processed and authenticated before the application due date.

For these reasons, it is important to think ahead and carefully plan around due dates.

Application Forms

Most schools have an application form you are required to complete. While each form is different, they ask you to address similar questions such as:

[15] See, for example: *Degree Partnerships : Melbourne Law School* http://law.unimelb.edu.au/students/jd/enrichment/international-opportunities/degree-partnerships; *Monash-Cambridge Degree Pathway Opportunity – Faculty of Law* http://www.monash.edu/law/current-students/monash-cambridge-pathway

- your reasons for applying for the course;
- your research proposal (if applying for a degree by research);
- your career goals and future aspirations; and
- your personal statement (this is particularly relevant for scholarship applications).

When setting out your reasons for applying for the course, it is important to be specific. You should demonstrate that you have done some research about the school, and the course, and have a clear understanding of why you are a suitable candidate. It may, perhaps, be prudent to refer to the work of a particular research centre, or the content of particular subjects or modules, and why it interests you.

When setting out your research proposal, it is important to demonstrate that you are aware of the relevant literature in your area of interest. Depending on the word-limit, you may be required to provide a short summary of key texts before proceeding to outline your proposal. A research proposal should be engaging and capture the reader's interest. On that note, it is always interesting if you can provide a personal connection to your research proposal – perhaps your proposal has come from your work experiences, or is related to why you decided to study law.

When setting out your career goals and future aspirations, it is important to clearly set out your intended career path, and closely relate this to the course you are applying for. For example, you might identify a particular subject as being specifically relevant to your career goals.

Finally, when setting out your personal statement, it is important to address all key selection criteria that may be relevant to admission to the particular program (such as relevant experience and interests in the law) or to the award of a scholarship (such as demonstrated leadership skills and volunteer work). In doing so, it is important to build a narrative around your experiences to date (i.e. personal or work experiences that have challenged or shaped you), and what you hope to accomplish once you have completed the program you are applying for. You want to demonstrate that you are not only a well-suited as a candidate, but that you will use the knowledge you will gain during the program to further your career aspirations that you have been working towards.

In all cases, you should seek feedback and comments on your draft application form. You may ask your referees to provide their feedback (this is particularly important if you are submitting a research proposal), or you may ask people in your network to give their comments. If you can, it is always a good idea to ask previous Masters students to provide their feedback (especially those who have previously been admitted to the course you're applying for).

Academic Resume

Chapter 5 covers the relevant elements of a resume, and provides a good starting point. For applications for postgraduate study, however, your resume should be targeted to an academic audience. This means that you should re-frame your resume so it supports your desire to undertake further study and/or your specific research proposal. A few tips on how you can do this include:

- noting any research-projects you have been involved in, including if you have written an honours-thesis (even if you haven't done so in law);
- noting any work experiences (volunteer or otherwise) that support your research interests, or your desire to undertake further studies;
- ensuring your key skills are targeted for an academic audience by focusing on attributes that are key in an academic environment – such as, for example, critical reasoning skills, research and analytical skills, written and verbal communication skills;
- noting any publications (do not limit yourself to peer-reviewed publications if you have any other relevant publications, such as web articles or contributions to student-run journals, newsletters or magazines);
- noting any research experience (volunteer or otherwise); and
- if applying to a collegiate university (like the University of Cambridge or the University of Oxford), noting any extracurricular activities that are relevant to the college to which you intend to apply (i.e. sporting or musical interests).

Letters of Recommendation

Most applications require two or three letters of recommendation. Some applications specify whether 'academic' (i.e. a lecturer or tutor) or 'professional' (i.e. a person who has worked with you as a supervisor/employer) reference letters are required, so read these requirements very carefully.

Approaching people for a letter of recommendation can be daunting. However, it is always helpful to remember that many of these people – while more experienced than you – have nonetheless been through a similar process to you, and understand what it is like.

Some general tips for working with your referees:

- give them as much notice as possible – they are likely to be very busy people, and so would appreciate some lead-in time (at least 3–4 weeks, if possible);
- tell them how many schools you are applying for, and how many letters are required from them up-front, as a matter of courtesy;
- tell them how many scholarships you are applying for, and provide a summary of the key selection criteria for each scholarship as well;
- provide a copy of your resume, personal statement and/or research proposal;
- send a polite and friendly reminder a few days before each due date; and
- thank them for their time and always respond to their emails promptly.

Funding

For many applications, you are automatically considered for any available scholarships at the relevant institution if you submit a personal statement, as noted above. However, you should also be aware of any other internal scholarships that may require an additional application. If you are applying to a collegiate university (such as the University of Cambridge or the University of Oxford) you should also determine whether you are eligible for any college scholarships – this may also determine which colleges you select in your application.

Additionally, you should also be aware of any external funding sources that you are eligible to apply for. Certain funding sources are tied to a particular university (for example, the Rhodes Scholarship Program) or to a particular country (for example, the Fulbright Program). However, there are also scholarship programs that are more general (for example, the John Monash Scholarship or the Lionel Murphy Postgraduate Scholarship).

The critical thing is to do your research on funding opportunities for each university and course of study to which you apply. Most university websites set out the internal and external funding opportunities that are available for post-graduates; however, do not underestimate the time it takes to canvass all the funding opportunities for which you may be eligible.

Many scholarships are only awarded after a successful interview. Chapter 5 covers the important elements of an interview, and provides a helpful guide on how to prepare.

However, scholarship interviews can be very different from ordinary job interviews. Importantly, your interviewers are unlikely to be experts in your particular area of interest. Part of your role as an interviewee in a scholarship interview is to demonstrate why your area of interest is important, what impact your study is going to have on that area, and, more broadly, why you are worthy of the scholarship.

Interview questions generally fall within two categories – motivational and behavioural. Common questions include:

Common Motivational Questions

- Why have you applied to this school?
- Why have you applied to complete this course?
- What are your career aspirations?
- Why is your research important?
- Why are you interested in this area of study?

Common Behavioural Questions[16]

- When have you demonstrated leadership skills?
- When have you demonstrated original thinking?
- When have you solved a problem?
- When have you demonstrated excellence in your field?

---

[16] Note: These questions will be heavily influenced by the objectives of the scholarship organisation and the selection criteria for the specific scholarship.

Making the Most of the Experience

Once you have received an offer and have dealt with any funding issues, some of the hard work is well and truly behind you. Now you can focus on making the best of the experience ahead!

Volunteering

Many universities have opportunities to engaging in volunteer work – either by participating in community legal centres or legal clinics, or by being involved in student-run campus activities, such as fundraising activities or pro-bono legal research projects.

Societies

Many law schools have a graduate law student society that caters specifically for Masters-level students. You can join the committee and gain some management experience, or you can be involved by participating in the activities and events.

Many universities also have other student-run societies and associations and the larger universities, in particular, can cater to rather niche or unique interests – for example, there are Quidditch Clubs in universities across the United States and the United Kingdom.

Study Groups

At the post-graduate level, some of the most valuable learning opportunities come from your peers. As noted above, the diversity of the student body can be its best asset – not only based on country of origin, but also based on life and career experiences. Take advantage of this by creating or joining study groups and discussing what you've learned.

Diversify

Take the opportunity to leave your comfort zone. Go to events organised by other faculties, connect with networks outside the law. Look for opportunities for engaging in interdisciplinary conferences or workshops. As a student, particularly if you have a place at one of the elite universities, you have access to the world's best and brightest thinkers. Take full advantage of the opportunity to learn from them, and to broaden your horizons beyond the law.

Sayomi Ariyawansa is a Melbourne-based lawyer and Research Fellow at Melbourne Law School. She researches across the fields of labour migration, labour trafficking and labour law, with a focus on the use of migrant labour in the Australian agriculture industry. Prior to joining Melbourne Law School, she completed the Master of Law programme at the University of Cambridge, where she graduated with First Class Honours and was awarded the Kate Bertram Prize for Academic Excellence. She is also a former Editor of the Cambridge International Law Journal, and is a Forum Member of the Centre for the Study of Global Human Movement.

Chapter 5
Preparing Yourself for a Career in Law

Lloyd England

This is your career and there is only one you. Therefore, no two career pathways are going to be the same for different people, or would even be particularly appropriate. This is not a Chapter purporting to provide an extensive list of the plethora of opportunities available to law students. There are many such well-researched and formatted guides available,[1] with graduate voices and typical industry explanations, and they are well worth looking at to purview the range of traditional opportunities available to you once you have embarked upon the study of law.

I wish instead to challenge you further and highlight the fact you are fortunate and in an enviable position when supported by a legal education. I often provocatively ask potential students or audiences of non-lawyers for 'hands up' anyone who can mention an area, any area at all, of human endeavour, enterprise or activity not regulated by or impacted by the law. Usually no hands up. That's because no such endeavour, enterprise or activity really exists; the law is a human construct to govern the affairs of humans, all affairs. For fun, I then go on to unpack areas, which, at first glance, have nothing to do with the law, but when you drill down, you realise the law eventually impacts everything in some manner. For example, an adventurous audience member once retorted 'art and air': 'art' attracts copyright, moral rights, Indigenous appropriation regulation, the tort of passing off, law of bailment, torts to goods, etc., to name but a few; 'air' is protected by the tort of private

[1] E.G. *The Law Guide 2019–2020; Your Complete Guide to Careers with a Law Degree*, published by gradaustralia in partnership with the Law Society of New South Wales; see <https://gradaustralia.com.au/library/2019/sector-guide-law>.

L. England (✉)
Victoria University, Melbourne, VIC, Australia
e-mail: Lloyd.England@vu.edu.au

M. Raz et al. (eds.), *Careers in Law: A Guide for Students, Graduates and Professionals*, https://doi.org/10.1007/978-981-15-3627-4_5

nuisance and/or trespass to land privately, and by international climate treaties to a limited extent, publicly.[2] The law, and careers in it, are literally everywhere.

So really, you are uniquely fortunate to possess a legal education, as it opens the door to all endeavours, enterprise or activity, industry or field you may care to work in. This infinite variety and opportunity can, in itself, be overwhelming and lead to 'career freeze' and a bewilderment or FOMO resulting in career freeze. While faced with so many options, the vastness of potential opportunities also significantly increases the risk of simply taking the wrong career path for individual you. The trick then is how to deduce what specifically would be best for you, and then how to find a way into it to 'test it'. It is with this I wish to help you.

My goal in this chapter is to share with you the 3 Golden Keys of Successful Recruitment that I learnt working for an international financial recruitment consultancy. I hope to empower you with a paradigm of recruitment that is powerful and all encompassing, not mysterious and intuitive, instead practical and applicable. I wish then to marry this with my understanding of psychological well-being, gained over the past 14 years working at Monash University's Faculty of Law and Victoria University's First Year College in legal education and student experience, meeting thousands of law students attempting to enhance their well-being, encouraging individuals to thrive and most importantly to make terrific legal career decisions. I hope that by understanding factors contributing to your own wellbeing you will increase your likelihood of finding career satisfaction, fulfilment and happiness. With the experience gained as Co-Convenor of Legal Practice Programs at Monash Law, I then explain the critical importance of Clinical Legal Experience (work integrated learning or co-curricular legal 'work experience') in applying these 3 Golden Keys, with an eye on your wellbeing. I do this and identify for you 9 skill sets, so you can illuminate your career choices with personalised, first-hand knowledge, information and experience; what I term 'career informed consent'. This way you will then be armed with some practical tools to help you choose not just any law career, but your own law career, just for you.

Let's get into it.

Part I: The 3 Golden Keys of Successful Recruitment

Recruitment is essentially about managing risk when hiring new staff, specifically the risk that the person recruited into the role will be unsuccessful and managing the risk of how long they will stay in that role, so delaying replacement and subsequent recruitment and increased associated cost.

[2] Although with pollution face-mask sales even a thing, more work clearly (pun intended) needs to be done.

Early in my career, I worked as a financial recruitment consultant for Robert Half International, a US$5 billion professional services company.[3] Founded in the US in 1948, their claim to fame is they invented 'temps', i.e. strategic, flexible, temporary staffing. I worked on the temp-desk in Windsor, West London with clients such as British Airways, SAP and IBM. It would be fair to say they know what they are doing regarding recruitment.

I learnt at Robert Half that to secure a successful recruit, focus needed to be on three essential elements, what I will refer to as the '3 Golden Keys of Successful Recruitment'. Firstly, *can* the person do the job? Secondly, if the person can do the job, do they *want* to do the job? Thirdly, if the person can do the job, and wants to do the job, will they *fit* in? The magic of these 3 Golden Keys to Successful Recruitment is that every single aspect of the recruitment and selection process fits neatly into one of these 3 criteria. The advertisement or position description, your cover letter, your resume, your response to key selection criteria, even your responses at an interview all go to one of the 3 Golden Keys. Even your decision to accept an offer and then turn up at work fits. By having the 3 Golden Keys paradigm in your mind, you can better navigate the recruitment and selection process to better secure a suitable role, with the emphasis on its suitability to you as an individual. To illustrate, let's think about a typical recruitment and selection process and then apply the 3 Golden Keys so that you may understand them in action.

'Can You Do the Job?'

'*Can*' is an essential Golden Key to Successful Recruitment. Even if you absolutely want to do the job and will absolutely fit in; if you simply *cannot* do the job, you will not be a low-risk successful recruit.

A recruitment advertisement talks about key responsibilities and goals of the role and will usually include a position description. The advert is literally being proscriptive about the skills in the potential applicant, identifying and seeking the specific skills in the person in order to successfully do the role or job. This advertisement is essentially a public call (to whatever designated applicant pool it is published towards) attempting to appeal only to candidates who possess the pre-requisite skills required in their view to do the job and exclude all other candidates who do not have the skills. The position description specifically drills into the skills needed to be successful in the role in order to dissuade non-qualified applicants. It literally proscribes what you need to be successful in the role, often by further articulating key selection criteria. Luckily for us, there are arguably only 9 individual skill categories which you as a law student or graduate should be able to clearly articulate, and we will revisit these 9 skills for you later in the chapter. For now, if you have seen the advertisement and have the skills to do the job, you are a third of the way

[3] <https://www.roberthalf.com.au/corporate-info>.

to being an ideal recruit. You now simply need to communicate that fact to the recruiter.

You do this by responding to the advertisement by way of writing a cover letter or email and providing a resume and occasionally responding to individual Key Selection Criteria. You may decide to stand out from the 'written application crowd' by picking up the phone and calling the recruiter/hiring manager directly and introducing yourself. This commences the process of demonstrating your suitability as a candidate by gaining further clarification on the role during the call and contemporaneously articulating your suitability, thereby not only understanding the role beyond the advertisement, but also getting your name noted and advising them to be expecting your application. Whatever your approach, in all of these responses you will be demonstrating and attempting to prove that you as a candidate have enough of the skills for success; that you '*Can* do the job'.

During an interview, you then have a final opportunity to demonstrate (this time verbally) with further rich and fuller examples from your experience that you *Can* do the job. This is achieved by demonstrating your skills capacity by way of time-specific examples of using those skills in a previous situation. Some skills may be absolutely a pre-requisite (e.g. 'possesses a law degree, or rights to be admitted to practise as a Solicitor or Barrister') and these are the non-negotiable, 'must have' essential skills. If you do not have these skills, you simply cannot do the job. Lower priority are 'should have' skills, thereby further reducing the recruitment risk, which would usually be your demonstrated experience and success in a similar role, or a transferrable example of exhibiting skills doing something similar. Finally, 'ideally have' skills (or 'nice to have') would be ideal, in an ideal world with the ideal recruit. If you have the 'must have', 'should have', and 'ideally have' skills, then you are deemed the most less-risky recruit and most likely to succeed in the role. But, and here's the thing, it is not an ideal world and the organisation cannot have it all their way. It is important to see recruitment as a two-way street. Arguably, you are interviewing the organisation as much as they are interviewing you! This is hard when you are starting out in your career after commencing law school. This is hard as someone new to an industry, regardless of your age. This is even harder if you are young and entering the world of work, perhaps inexperienced and not particularly self-confident. Nonetheless, it is true; it is highly unlikely the organisation is going to find the ideal, perfect, totally minimum-risk recruit. This is terrific news for you, as it is therefore absolutely reasonable and thus open to negotiation once you are past the 'must have' skills or qualifications, and totally open for you to demonstrate you have enough 'should' or 'ideally' of what they are looking for to convince them to take the risk of hiring you. You may no doubt be stronger in demonstrating some skills than others, and that's OK as you can 'up-skill' any deficits reasonably rapidly, as long as you exhibit that you have the others in volume, then you are likely to prove you have the skills to success in the role, ie you *Can* do the job.

'Do You Want *to Do the Job?'*

'*Want*' is another essential Golden Key to successful recruitment. Even if you absolutely *Can* do the job and will absolutely *Fit* in; if you simply do not *Want* to do the job, you will (eventually) not be a successful recruit.

This is a very different question than '*Can* you do the job' which is an objective assessment of your abilities. Either you have a law degree or you do not. You can demonstrate teamwork or you cannot. Whether you *Want* to do a specific job or role is a subjective question, one all about your motivation to undertake the work. We are all motivated by different things, so this is essentially a personal and deeply intimate question. This is a values-based decision and one worthy of much deeper consideration. Getting this '*Want*' Golden Key right is, in my view, the fundamental crux to a satisfying, rewarding and healthy career. Ironically, this Golden Key is the one most often overlooked or just assumed, or based on 'decisions' we made at school when 16 years old and choosing a degree, or worse still, are based on someone else's wants or decisions.[4] We shall return to this values-based analysis later in this Chapter to help clarify your *Want* Golden Key.

The job advertisement will attempt to address and appeal to your *Wants* by providing an indication of salary range and other benefits in order to attract the best candidates from within the reduced pool of those who actually can do the role and would potentially fit. Employer of Choice awards will be spruiked. Flexible working conditions espoused. Tax efficient salary-sacrificing schemes promoted. Gym memberships and healthcare offered. Quality of opportunity, mission statements and broader contextual meanings explained. Perhaps travel and promotion opportunities will all be part of the advertisement, all attempting to make the job more attractive and appealing to lure in the 'best' (aka 'reduced risk') candidates and make them *Want* that particular employer, over and above their industry competitors.

For now, let's assume you either want the money, or that it is a role or industry you sincerely think you desire, and you do decide you *Want* to do the job. The effort involved in your application is your first demonstrable action signalling to the recruiter that you *Want* the role. Your overall attitude, professionalism, demeanour, energy and positivity all focussed on securing the role are also indications that you *Want* to do the job. Your working through the selection and interview process (assessment centres, aptitude testing, Seasonal Clerkships, etc) literally demonstrates you *Want* to do it. There may be further indications on your resume (similar work, volunteering, shadowing, gaining specific qualifications so that you *Can* do the work, etc.) which also point towards and provide evidence that you *Want* to do the job. Ultimately, accepting an employment offer and commencing work on your first day are further signals you *Want* to do it, thereafter turning up daily into the

[4] UNSW study found a significant number of law students chose to study law for someone else; see Tani, M and Vines, P, Law students' attitudes to education : pointers to depression in the legal academy and the profession? Legal Education Digest, Vol. 18, No. 2, July 2010: 41–46.

future and committing to quality work output is all really just 'wanting to do the job', in action.

So, if you have seen the advertisement and have the skills to do the job and have communicated the same and demonstrated you want to do the job, you are two-thirds of the way to being a successful recruit.

'Will You Fit *in?'*

Finally, '*Fit*' is the other essential Golden Key to successful recruitment. Even if you absolutely *Can* do the job and absolutely *Want* to do the job, if you simply do not *Fit* in the job or environment, you will (eventually) not be a successful recruit.

Organisational or role *Fit* is another values-based criteria, this one is both objective and subjective. There may be external indicators you do not fit in (e.g. wearing a *Legalise Marijuana* tee shirt whilst sporting dreadlocks during a corporate law firm interview) which you may be able to hide and disguise (pop on a suit and get a haircut for the corporate law firm interview). But it is important in life to be authentic as we shall learn below, and the organisation may simply conflict with your internal values and essentially not be a good fit. Tobacco manufacturing or dolphin-unfriendly tuna; whatever your clash, if you are not a good *Fit*, it will probably start to erode your *Want* or desire to do the job, so it becomes toxic and starts to erode the success of the recruit, which is why *Fit* is the other essential Golden Key to successful recruitment. You should not wish be a round peg in a square hole; better to find a hole that fits you, then you are more likely and naturally set-up for authentic success!

Fitting in is tricky business; there are laws against discrimination, racial vilification, union membership rights, Equal Opportunity legislation, etc., and rightly so. Applicants present very differently on paper than in person and we all have our idiosyncratic foibles. The '*Fit*' factor essentially boils down to, 'Can I work with you for 8 hrs a day?' or, 'Will you drive me nuts?' or, 'Can I put you in front of our clients and have you represent the firm?' This is why most recruitment and selection ultimately culminates in interviews, because we are humans, not machines. To check the 'Fit' whilst testing the Can and Want. Or, put another way; to ostensibly verbally test your claimed *Can* and *Want*, but really also checking out your *Fit*.[5]

So, if you have seen the advertisement, have the skills to do the job and have communicated the same and demonstrated you want to do the job, attended an interview and will fit in, then congratulations! You are an ideal potential successful recruit (ie a reduced-risk recruit). If you are the top-ranked of the reduced-risk recruits, you will be selected and will be offered the job. This is a good time to finally re-check your *Want* before accepting!

---

[5]This is probably not a two way street, as they are essentially checking out whether you fit with them, not them with you, as they will not change their entire culture to fit in with you.

Remember the 3 Golden Keys; they will serve you well. You now have a framework for everything that a recruiter asks you regarding an opportunity as it will always pertain to one or more of the 3 Golden Keys.

Part II: Self Determination Theory

Self-determination Theory suggests that there are certain ingredients or 'nutriments' to psychological wellbeing, positive mental health or thriving.[6] *Autonomy* is experienced when our actions, tasks and goals are self-selected, chosen by ourselves, i.e. authentic, rather than imposed upon us or controlled by others.[7] *Belonging with Relationships* refers to being accepted into a social group or organisation, and sharing positive interactions with others in the group where people feel mutually valued, respected and trusted.[8] *Competence* or *Mastery* is the ability to manage the interactions, tasks and challenges we face.[9] Self Determination Theory posits that individuals need all these nutriments to generate and sustain 'autonomous motivation',[10] a key driver of mental wellbeing.[11]

'What Makes Lawyers Happy?' published in 2015, is a significant U.S. study of over 6200 practicing lawyers and 120 judges by Clinical Professor Larry Krieger and Psychologist Professor Kennon Sheldon.[12] They measured what factors influenced well-being and positive affect of lawyers in the workplace. The study used 24 validated measures covering feelings of positive emotion like enthusiasm and strength; negative emotions like nervousness, guilt or fear; and overall life satisfaction to generate a measure of subjective wellbeing, aka 'happiness' or 'feeling good

---

[6] Deci, E.L., & Ryan, R.M. (2000). The "what" and "why" of goal pursuits: Human needs and the self-determination of behavior. *Psychological Inquiry, 11,* 319–338.

[7] Niemiec, C. P., Ryan, R. M., & Deci, E. L. (2010). Self-determination theory and the relation of autonomy to self-regulatory processes and personality development. In R.H Hoyle (Ed.) *Handbook of Personalty and Self-Regulation.* Pp 169–191. Wiley-Blackwell, Oxford, UK.

[8] Cockshaw, W. D., & Shochet, I. (2010). The link between belongingness and depressive symptoms: An exploration in the workplace interpersonal context. *Australian Psychologist, 45*(4), 283–289.

[9] Seligman, M. E. (2012). Chapter 1: What is well-being? *Flourish: A Visionary New Understanding of Happiness and Well-being* (pp.5–29). New York: Simon & Schuster. In his section titled "The elements of wellbeing" (pp. 15–18), Seligman outlines his own five-dimensional model of wellbeing. The model is called PERMA, which is an acronym for the five dimensions: Positive emotion, Engagement, Relationships, Meaning, and Accomplishment. These last three approximate the three psychological needs in SDT (relatedness, autonomy, and competence, respectively).

[10] Ryan, R. M., & Deci, E. L. (2000b). Self-determination theory and the facilitation of intrinsic motivation, social development, and wellbeing. *American psychologist, 55*(1), 68.

[11] Ryan, R. M., & Deci, E. L. (2000a). Intrinsic and extrinsic motivations: Classic definitions and new directions. *Contemporary Educational Psychology, 25,* 54–67.

[12] What makes Lawyers Happy?: A Data-Driven Prescription to Redefine Professional Success. 83 *GEO. WASH.L.REV.* 554 (2015).

about life'. This measure was then tested against various factors and information concerning lawyers' lives, like salary or making partner. The study calculates 'R Values' on the power of association, relation and prediction between two items and generates a number between zero and one. For our purposes, a number above 0.5 suggests associations are very powerful.

'Data from several thousand lawyers in four states show striking patterns, repeatedly indicating that common priorities on law school campuses and among lawyers are confused or misplaced. Factors typically afforded most attention and concern, those relating to prestige and money (income, law school debt, class rank, law review, and USNWR law school ranking) showed zero to small correlations with lawyer well-being. Conversely, factors marginalized in law school and seen in previous research to erode in law students (psychological needs and motivation) were the very strongest predictors of lawyer happiness and satisfaction. Lawyers were grouped by practice type and setting to further test these findings. The group with the lowest incomes and grades in law school, public service lawyers, had stronger autonomy and purpose and were happier than those in the most prestigious positions and with the highest grades and incomes.'

Four items came in at over 0.55 suggesting significant associations with 'happiness' or thriving. *Autonomy*, a feeling of agency over one's life; *Relatedness*, strong relationships to community members, and a sense of *Belonging*; *Competence*, a feeling of being good at something or having mastery over it; and *Internal Motivation*, related to autonomy, in that one is acting consistently with internal drivers or values. The results then drop right down to 0.19, a very weak association, between lawyer income and law school debt and impact on happiness. Marks at university and class rank were even lower at 0.12. Making partner had 0.0, zero, association with a sense of subjective well-being in the surveyed lawyers and judges.

The results are striking and perhaps surprising to some, but less so for proponents of Self Determination Theory. So, what does this mean for us, reading this Chapter, Choosing a Law Career?

It is essential for our mental health, overall wellbeing and to thrive at this one chance at a career that we do things that we genuinely want to do or choose to do, rather than doing things which we think others want us to do. Our wellbeing literally depends on it. Autonomous motivations are thwarted and wellbeing is undermined when we feel pressured to act or we feel controlled by others. Trying to impress or please others, or chasing money or prestige, all 'extrinsic motivators' is simply not psychologically nurturing; we are not 'being ourselves' and acting in accordance with our internal values and interests. This is harmful and can create 'cognitive dissonance' between our outward actions or situation and our inward desires or wants.[13] Essentially, if you want to save dolphins then practicing corporate law probably will not scratch this itch. If you do not like children, do not be a school teacher. Making

[13] Harmon-Jones, E. E., & Mills, J. E. (1999). Cognitive dissonance: Progress on a pivotal theory in social psychology. In *Scientific Conferences Program, 1997, U Texas, Arlington, TX, US; This volume is based on papers presented at a 2-day conference at the University of Texas at Arlington, winter 1997.* American Psychological Association.

money or law firm partner are extrinsic motivators, so is attempting not to disappoint a parent or loved-one, and as Krieger & Sheldon showed, has little to do with your sense of happiness or subjective life-satisfaction you will get from your career. 'Not being yourself' is not psychologically nurturing. Likewise, Autonomous Motivation is also blunted and undermined when we feel we are not capable of doing the task at hand (no Competency or Mastery) and our actions have no effect, making us feel impotent. Instead, Autonomous motivation is sustained and reliant upon regular experiences of *competence*, *autonomy* and *relatedness*.[14] We need to be and feel competent and able in an environment of our own choosing, with people and a culture that we value, trust and 'fit' with, where we can build meaningful relationships and thus belong and relate to it.

What is of joyful note for us here when Choosing a Law Career, is the almost carbon-copy overlap between Self-Determination Theory's *Competence*, *Autonomy* and *Relatedness* and the *Can, Want & Fit* of the 3 Golden Keys to Successful Recruitment! Our 60 year-old, tried-and-tested Global Recruitment Consultancy Method is underpinned by a robust, empirically supported, evidence-based modern theory of psychological wellbeing! That is fortunate indeed.

Can you do the job goes to your *Competence* or Mastery Key, with your skills being utilised appropriately and for the best, allowing you to psychologically thrive. Do you *Want* to do the job goes to your motivators, your Autonomous drivers and desires Key (and if you focus on your intrinsic motivators, your internal desires and values, you will find a psychologically rewarding role – forget the extrinsic, external pressures). Finally the *Fit* key talks directly to your *Relatedness* to a community, where you are valued and respected and may build deep and meaningful relationships, based on care, trust and mutual understanding and respect; finally finding your work-tribe!

So now we understand that the 3 Golden Keys are fully endorsed by a comprehensive theory of psychological wellbeing, helping us to find a career which is supportive of our mental health, allowing us to be the best authentic versions of our professional selves we can be and to thrive and succeed in the workplace! That is good news indeed.

Let's now think about where then to choose a workplace or industry or endeavour to direct your full attention to, and make yourself happy in the endeavour.

[14]Vansteenkiste, M., Lens, W., & Deci, E. L. (2006). Intrinsic versus extrinsic goal contents in self-determination theory: Another look at the quality of academic motivation. *Educational psychologist*, *41*(1), 19–31.

Informing Can, Want & Fit (or Competency, Autonomy & Relatedness)

You have chosen to undertake a law degree; this is a professional, vocational degree leading to Admission to Practise law in a given legal jurisdiction. You are mandated to study the Priestly 11,[15] key subjects granting a broad comprehension of the legal system and key doctrinal understanding. You also must complete some 'quasi-compulsory' subjects in order to meet the professional accreditation requirements of the profession in your particular jurisdiction. Finally, you have a few 'electives' left in the degree course to explore other areas of interest which are not compulsory but add a uniqueness to your qualification. Here you may 'deep dive' and specialise on an area on interest (e.g. Advanced Evidence, Trail Practice & Advocacy for an aspiring criminal lawyer) or broaden your understanding of a variety of legal practice areas (e.g. IP Law, Family, etc.). Electives you literally elect to take, and are thus the first 'choice' an undergraduate law student will make. Some of us knew instinctively what we were drawn to, and so explored this. For example, an interest in 'people' may have suggested Employment or Family law, or natural justice may peak an interest in exploring Human Rights, Native Title or Animal Law. Others focussed on 'corporate law' electives, perhaps to enhance competitiveness for the Big Law firm corporate law opportunities, or to specialise early in industries they already had exposure to.[16] Others still may have chosen electives complimentary to their double degree discipline, such as Construction Law for the Law & Engineering students, International Law for Arts students majoring in Politics or International Relations, Law & Medicine or Bioethics for the Law & Medicine students, etc. Others amongst us may have purely intellectual pursuits in mind, such as the study of Jurisprudence or Legal History. All of this is fine, but can now your choices can be informed and enhanced (and validated) by your understanding of SDT and the 3 Keys.

Successful study of an area is your first indication that you *can* do the specific area of law, such as Employment Law for example. You have displayed Competency in the understanding of Employment Law. This in turn may inform your *Want*, or Autonomous decision to peruse a career in an Employment Law Practice. This is all good information to have and to test your thinking on whether, in this example, you want to be an Employment Lawyer, or more broadly work in the field of Industrial Relations (eg IR Consultant, Human Resources Manager, etc).

In fact, all of your subjects on the LLB are the beginning of your understanding about and deepening comprehension of specific fields or areas of legal practise.

[15] https://www.lawadmissions.vic.gov.au/qualifications-and-training/academic; Criminal Law and Procedure; Torts; Contracts; Property; Equity (including Trusts); Company Law; Administrative law; Federal and State Constitutional law; Civil Dispute Procedure; Evidence; and Ethics and Professional Responsibility.

[16] Many Universities now offer Juris Doctor post-graduate degrees, often to 'mature age' post-graduate students, already immersed or experienced in an industry, profession or discipline.

They provide a window into the sorts of matters, issues and transactions a given area of law is concerned about, and an overview of the theories, goals, policies and regulatory framework of that area. They are a great starting point to informing your *Can* and *Want*, your *Competency* and *Autonomy*, starting to provide direction and potential for your career aspirations. The more you enjoy studying an area of law, reading about it and immersing yourself in the area, and perhaps being rewarded with higher marks in that subject, the more you are informed about your own interests and motivators regarding areas to think about pursuing a career in. They are a great 'intellectual' *Can & Want, Competency and Autonomy* sanity checks or tests, and provide good insight into your unique interests and drivers and may be useful proof of your competence later on when you apply for a job.

Based on your academic understanding and perceived (and rewarded) competence in an area,[17] you think you might like to work in it. For a real understanding of the area of practise though, there is simply no substitute for experience; it is my strong recommendation to, as soon as you are able, apply for a part-time job, an internship, go volunteering, shadowing, and ideally within the curriculum as Work Integrated Learning, finding practical legal work-experience opportunities. It is never too soon for you to seek work experience within the law in an area or field you think you might be interested in pursuing. There are a number of reasons why this is important.

Part III: The Importance of Clinical Legal Experience (Work Integrated Learning or Co-Curricular Work Experience)

Thinking you want something is often different to the actual practical realities of it. You may be 'intellectually interested' in an area of practise after completing a Unit of study, but it may play out entirely differently than you thought 'in practice.' I would strongly encourage you to get out into a practice and 'try before you buy'. You reasonably test drive a car, lie on a mattress, or try on your clothes or shoes before committing to purchase. Your career deserves the same test run, the same 'trying it on' before committing, and there are many different ways to achieve this. What may help you here is an understanding of the fundamental 'Jobs versus Industries' paradigm.

[17] Presuming you Pass.

'Jobs Versus Industries' Paradigm

You may not be able to get work experience as a brain surgeon whilst unqualified, but you can be the Trolley Porter in the health care industry working at a Neurosurgery ward of a hospital. Separate Jobs from Industries, and then try to secure experience, even at an entry-level job or indeed regardless of the job, in an Industry you wish to explore to better understand more deeply the Job or role you aspire to.

Once you have Industry experience, it is much easier to move up or across the jobs ladder within that industry, as you have gained relevant and niche industry-specific experience and knowledge. You are a reduced-risk recruit as you have the exactly relevant 'Industry experience', and you are more likely 'to be in the right place at the right time' to secure that opportunity, ideally before it is advertised to the wider pool of candidates (ie the world) and becomes more competitive thus less likely to secure.

Let us imagine for example someone who 'really wants to work in radio', perhaps as a presenter. They apply for a 'Runner' job[18] at a radio station and, regardless of not having any radio experience, they get the role because they have the skills to do the job; because they are bright, keen and positive. They work hard, understand the goals and drivers of the industry, they learn the equipment, watch the professionals, and become friendly with the team. They may stay late and hone the art of radio when all have gone home, or just do so at home. One day a presenter fails to turn up for a shift and so our Runner volunteers to take the gig, and there is nobody else available and they know the gig inside out, so they get given the opportunity to host the radio show! Voila, they are a Radio Presenter! Some would say, 'that is just luck' but you can really see that they actually created their own luck, by being ready, willing and able. But also by being in the right place at the right time; that was not an accident, because remember, they really wanted to 'work in radio' and were doing so in any capacity. So we can see from this example that *any* industry experience (regardless of the role) is important and helpful, and that when trying or thinking about breaking into an industry, we should be more focussed on the industry than the specific role or job; that can come later.

Alternately, once you have mastered or qualified in (or simply chosen) a job or role, you can do the same job across many different industries, as you have the exactly relevant job experience and knowledge, and are simply applying this in an alternate industry setting. So for example, a post-room clerk in an international Big Law city firm is a very low risk recruit for a post-room clerk in a television production company, or a local suburban law firm, and visa versa. A lawyer at a firm can simply choose to move firm, or be an 'in house' lawyer at a corporation, and this is low risk recruitment, as they have already proven their abilities in the job, albeit in a different industry setting.

The things to note here are these. It is easiest (read 'most reduced recruitment risk') to secure the *same* job in the *same* industry you have already experience in;

[18] 'Gofer' or helper.

you are simply changing employer. Next less-easiest (with slightly more recruitment risk) is to change jobs in the same industry; you at least have relevant Industry experience. You are also more likely to be in the right place at the right time and access the 'hidden job market',[19] getting an opportunity that never even becomes advertised and generating a public call of mass applicants. Likewise, it is relatively easy to change Industry in the same job; you have the relevant job or role experience. By far the hardest job move in the world, is to *change job and industry* at the same time; it's almost impossible, as you have no relevant job or relevant industry experience! This is indeed a high-risk recruit! It might work out, but there is no evidence to support this being likely, thus most recruiters will not entertain the risk.

We can take this 'Jobs versus Industries' paradigm and apply this to our work experience strategy; it becomes more about the Industry we want to gain experience in rather than the job title. I am consistently amazed at bright, capable law students who work part-time serving drinks in hospitality; it is simply the wrong industry for them to be spending time in. Other than earning money and displaying a few 'transferrable skills' it is not the best use of their precious time.[20] They would be infinitely better off in any business or organisation trying to 'get near the legal' in that organisation. All businesses deal with contracts and suppliers, sale of goods and services, etc.

Alternatively, just step back, and take any job or opportunity to penetrate a law firm, of any description. Ideally one that practises in the area you were 'intellectually interested in' as per above, and then road test that area of legal practise and see what it practically is all about. Shadow a lawyer or Barrister. Work a day per week in a law firm as 'work experience'. Or even better still, apply for or arrange a Clinical Legal Placement within your LLB Degree Curriculum, Legal Placement at an employer, or secure work experience as a co-curricular activity. Ideally, securing a part-time paralegal job with a law firm so you can pay your bills whilst investigating an area of practise to inform your career decisions.

Here's the thing to remember though with this – your first firm is the hardest to get into. That's because you have no Industry or role experience. Once you have one firm on your resume, via work experience, shadowing, WIL Placement or even volunteering, the next firm is exponentially easier to secure a role in, because at least you now have directly comparable relevant industry experience.

---

[19] Anecdotally, 7 out of 10 jobs are unadvertised, hence 'hidden'. Contacts, networks, referrals, etc. all feed into this hidden job market; thus the importance of a well-polished, professional and up to date LinkedIn profile and a relentless networking attitude and practice. See Levinson, J. C., & Perry, D. E. (2011). *Guerrilla marketing for job hunters 3.0: How to stand out from the crowd and tap into the hidden job market using social media and 999 other tactics today*. John Wiley & Sons.

[20] For an urgent self-review of the passing of your life and the importance of your limited time, see https://waitbutwhy.com/2014/05/life-weeks.html

'Grouping Your Career Arrows'

Now you understand the Job versus Industry paradigm, you can clearly see the value in 'grouping your career arrows' in or around a particular Industry or Role. Why would you waste time flitting between different industries or different roles, cluttering your resume with untargeted experiences?

Consider a law student supporting themselves, working part-time through a five and a half year double degree, working various different jobs in hospitality, accounts payable, call centres or sales, retail and manufacturing. Compare this to if they had worked five and a half years, part-time whilst studying, as a receptionist at a Personal Injury firm, proof reader at a corporate Big Law firm, volunteering at a Community Legal Centre or a local Conveyancing firm. Eventually they may end up in a part-time paralegal role in a legal department of a corporate head office, or of a bank, or ideally a paralegal at a law firm in an area of law they wish to practise! What a very different experience the same student would have, whilst earning similar money. Think about all the information, context and content they would have learnt about various and distinct areas of practise, from plaintiff litigation and TAC claims, to intense unrepresented litigants seeking assistance with criminal and family law matters, both urgent and serious, to high street firms dealing with property matters, etc. Insight into corporate affairs and marketing issues, to Initial Public Offerings, or regulatory affairs in high finance. Think about all the networking opportunities in their chosen discipline of law they would have been exposed to; all the people they would have met, worked for, or liaised with, all the good will generated by good work, a good attitude and good attendance and diligence. All just by simply 'grouping their career arrows' in one particular industry, namely legal. Don't even worry that it is not the role for you (reception, post-room, gofer, paralegal, administration assistant), or that the area of law is 'not quite what I think I want to do', just get experience and exposure to the legal industry at every opportunity you can manage. The experience would have also concurrently shaped their knowledge around areas of law that held genuine interest for them, thus would have informed their choice of electives. It is for this reason alone it is never too early in your legal career or educational journey to engage in securing experience of legal practise. Group your career arrows; it all informs your Informed Career Consent.

'Informed Career Consent'

The notion of 'informed consent' in a legal context is based upon the premise that you have enough information in order to provide you the opportunity to give truly informed, appropriately adequate, real consent. Inadequate information vitiates and voids the appropriateness and applicability and alters the nature of the consent as it was given based on incomplete, inaccurate, or misunderstood information. Whilst Co-Convenor of Legal Practice Programs for the Faculty of Law at Monash,

Australia's largest University, I witnessed and observed law student experiences leading me to unequivocally argue that Work Integrated Learning, the experience of working in the clinical setting of the Legal Industry, is literally essential in providing true and *Informed Career Consent*. Whether it is formally embedded in your degree curriculum, or self-sourced and secured outside your fomal legal education so 'co-curricular', I have seen practical legal experience become truly 'transformational' for law students, often hearing that Practical Placements in law firms or legal departments have been literally 'the highlight of my degree'.

I submit that true and real informed consent cannot be adequately given by a law student to a given area or practise or future career unless they have first-hand experience of that real legal practice and how it plays out. It cannot be truly 'informed' consent if they do not have the first hand 'information' to make that decision, to give that consent. Television, media and Netflix shows do not paint an accurate picture of legal practice reality; they are sensationalised and dramatized to make them engaging and are quite simply unrealistic.[21] The practise of law is best observed during the genuine practice of law and anything less will miss the mark.

What is transformational about practical legal experience, however secured, is that for a law student there is literally no such thing as a bad experience. Remember, you are 'trying before you buy'. If it is good, then great. Usually and overwhelmingly students report affirming experiences, reconfirming their 'intellectual *Want*' by witnessing practical application of the theory in practise. They emerge from work integrated learning or work-experience with renewed focus and vigour towards a specific area of practise. If it was not good, then that's still great; for the few who report it was not quite what they thought, or they did not enjoy the work or culture, there is significant benefit in understanding this as a student rather than on your first month on the job in practice. How much better to have a negative, unenjoyable time in a firm or practice or area of law whilst you are a student; even if to simply better inform what it is you definitely do *not* want to do, rather than finding out after graduation and during your first day at work in a real graduate job.

It is also worthy as a law student of deep consideration to unpack what it was specifically that you found positive and negative about any work situated placement. Dig deeper; try to uncover specifically what and why you enjoyed it or not, in order to identify themes and patterns, to better understand your own unique drivers, skills or talents. There is a big difference for example in corporate culture between a Big Law City Firm and a sole practitioner in the suburbs or regional remote country areas, or in a Department of a large firm, verses a boutique law firm specialising in the same work. Size, scope, work and location are all significant variables when considering a legal workplace, and really you need to have experienced some, and ideally as many as you can, in order to give yourself the benefit of Informed Career Consent.

[21] The author has watched all seasons of 'Suits' to date, ostensibly about legal practice and deals, but noting there is virtually no law mentioned whatsoever. It is dramatic though, and what is the thing with Lewis..?

Better to get all the information you can, on many areas of practise you think you are 'intellectually interested in' and try this out in as many different environments, to better inform your career consent, so that you are truly aware and know what you are getting into. How else can you talk to your '*Want*' or Autonomous motivation at interview when trying to secure an opportunity? We have all heard the phrase, 'Be careful what you wish for.' I have been amazed at how many law students are stressing about marks and grades for a corporate law job, who do not even know what a corporate lawyer does! The irony. This is not 'informed career consent', far from it; this is un-researched, ill-informed 'career hearsay' and it is unsurprising that so many law students who make it into competitive Big Law are not there 5 years later. They simply lacked informed career consent.

Think More Widely than Just Law Firms to Secure Legal Experience

Many corporates have a legal department; if not they have a law firm that assists them, or more than one. Many government departments have a legal division. Many Councils have legal departments. Even Universities have an Office of General Council. The Courts, Consumer Affairs, watchdogs, ombudsman, etc. The point here is to think more broadly about where you can secure practical legal experience and then try to network your way in.[22]

One Caveat with Volunteering…

Be aware, volunteering must be a mutually beneficial endeavour. This is another two way street. Initially the host will probably be putting in more effort and getting little return, as they 'bring you up to speed', you learn systems, methods of working, etc. All the while you are getting your experience. At some point, you will start generating work product or output that starts to add value to the host, and their input and management of you will reduce and the scales will tip, so that they are benefitting from having you there and creating valuable output. All the while you are experiencing, so that is good, and once you are 'up to speed' and 'working', the experience is really valid. After a while (insert variable time here), the benefit you get from the experience 'expires' and is no longer worth your time; you have got all the experience you need or want, and it is time to 'get off' the ride. 'Voluntexploiation' is where you stay on volunteering for too long, whereby the balance is tipped too far back towards the host's benefit, far outweighing the initial investment they spent in

[22] <https://www.monash.edu/career-connect/jobs/find-a-job/networking>.

on-boarding you, so you are simply being exploited.[23] You are generating work product for no remuneration, in breach of the Fair Work Act, not paid a minimal wage or the EBA rate, and the benefit of the experience for you is now being overshadowed and outweighed by the burdensome time commitment from you. You need to judge this correctly to avoid exploitation. It is right to 'pay back' the inconvenience of initially managing you and getting you up to speed, but when this is achieved, it is time to move on and look for alternate experiences. If you have reached an objectively reasonably fair status quo, you should value your own time enough not to give it away free, which you are essentially doing once the value of the experience for you has passed. Do not undervalue your worth, regardless of your skill level or experience.

Part IV: Confirming Competence (Can), Autonomy (Want), Belonging (Fit) Whilst Gaining Practical Legal Experience

We have learnt that we need all 3 of these facets of job suitability to be a good and lasting recruit and reduce risk when we are being hired, therefore increasing the chances of securing a role. We have also learnt that getting these 3 things right also significantly increase our chances of feeling 'happy' or experiencing subjective positive effect, and bolstering our mental health and wellbeing and allowing us to thrive.

With annual leave at 4 weeks per annum, and the other 48 weeks working on average 40 h, you will spend many of your waking hours working. Do not think this is insignificant. You thriving in your working environment is important for your overall mental health and wellbeing. You can hopefully see that a happy, fulfilled, relaxed, secure confident worker is much more likely to be a happy, fulfilled, relaxed and confident friend, or partner or parent; it will spill over into the rest of your life. Conversely, get this wrong and be frustrated, unfulfilled, worried, insecure, vulnerable, unhappy and troubled worker, and this will probably spill over into your personal life, maybe making you more likely to be a frustrated, worried, unhappy friend, partner or parent. Furthermore, just unhappy in yourself. So to avoid this, let's refocus on what you can do to get this right and increase your chances of choosing the *right* law career for you. Below are a skills framework to frame your employability, which you can road-test whist experiencing industry based learning or work-experience.

[23] For example, see <http://www.abc.net.au/news/2018-05-03/what-job-ads-reveal-about-the-rising-internship-culture/9713918>.

9 Employability Skills to Illustrate Your Can/Competency

Some competency-based requirements may talk to certain qualifications, such as the LLB and a Post Graduate Diploma in Legal Practice in order to qualify as a lawyer. These are non-negotiable, must have, pre-requisites to entry into the profession, threshold qualifications you must have obtained before you can enter into the profession.

All other 'non qualifications' employability competencies can be summarised by the 9 Employability Skills outlined below. Student Futures,[24] an award winning careers platform[25] developed by Monash University, researched skills mapping across 32 significant industry, government and commercial organisations to land on 9 'Universal' Employability Skills.

If you reflect and develop these skills whilst you are at university and record examples of when you have exhibited these skills, you will be well placed when you apply for a job or role. Even better would be to practice, enhance, develop and note these skills in action during a Work Integrated Learning placement or Co-Curricular work experience activity. Then, when you apply for a role, you can cite legal industry-specific examples of you possessing these 9 Employability skills, which is superior applicability and illustration of your experience to the legal role you are applying for. This in turn reduces the risk of your recruit, as you are not asking the hiring manager to 'link' or connect these 'transferrable skills' secured whilst being a waiter for example, to the legal role at hand. This again is why it is both important and helpful to 'group your career arrows', as outlined above. Let's explore 9 Key Employability Skills to help us scaffold our decision of choosing a law career and check your *Can* or *Competency* ability.

Communication

Communication is the ability to effectively exchange information across various mediums, and to different audience. Having good communication skills in the workplace allows you to convey information to others clearly and simply in order to be understood and get the job done. Some key communication-related tasks might include, transmitting and receiving messages, reading your audience appropriately, giving and receiving instructions, making requests or submissions or presentations and asking questions in order to obtain information.[26]

---

24 <https://www.monash.edu/student-futures>.

25 <https://www.atem.org.au/awards/2017-best-practice-awards_ESS Global Award for Excellence in Innovation>.

26 https://www.monash.edu/student-futures; Ways in which you might demonstrate *Communication* skills you acquired during a Legal Work Experience or WIL Placement might include:

- Building Rapport and interacting with others;
- Listen, understand and providing constructive feedback to others;

This is a critical skill in law. Think about the importance of this skill when taking instructions from a client, researching a problem, applying the law to the facts and communicating this to the client, or providing options to a colleague. Alternatively, the importance of communication when preparing a letter explaining potential outcomes and consequences, or summarising a position to brief a barrister or manager. Accurate, efficient and persuasive communication is essential in any legal or quasi-legal industry.

You may be a natural communicator, or it may be you need to invest in developing your communication skills in one or more of the areas outlined here. The point is that your 'Can' or Competency is measured against this key skill when you are seeking employment. It is also good to measure your own abilities in this space, recognising your strengths and weaknesses, and recording instances when you have had opportunity to practice these skills in the workplace, so you have things to talk to at interview or mention in your written application, or responses to Key Selection Criteria. And to self-reflect and be honest; if this is your 'top skill' and you love it, then explore what this gift and ability opens up for you. Written legal communication may lead you into academia, where the mantra is literally 'publish or perish', or legal publishing, or libraries, or digital databases of legal resources. Offer your skills as a Research Assistant to a lecturer, or undertake optional written assignments. Consider writing an Honours Thesis, or further study via Higher Degrees by Research (HDR) at Masters level, or really dive in and write your PhD.

Obviously the verbal mastery of this skill may suggest a legal career in advocacy, such as a barrister, articulating persuasive arguments to the court, but needing to communicate in writing when providing written opinions. Shadowing a Barrister would test this intellectual *Want* and clarify the true '*Can*' skills or competency necessary to succeed in this career space, furthering your 'informed career consent' and clarifying future directions. Alternate use of verbal communication dexterity would be in legal reporting in the media, sales roles, External Relations or charitable fund-raising causes; any career needs communication skills, but some roles simply depend on it. Allow truthful self-reflection to inform your reasonable career choices in this regard.

- Recognise and work with differences and manage conflict;
- Evaluate, exchange and express information and ideas concisely and clearly;
- Speak clearly and directly to a variety of individuals or groups;
- Demonstrate and effectively convey a high level of understanding;
- Logically summarise legal or factual information or data;
- Read, synthesise and explain in a way that is comprehensible and relevant to a range of others;
- Use numeracy to convey ideas or arguments;
- Recognise communication protocol and etiquette;
- Communicating Professionally and Ethically;
- Establish relationships and networks.

Creativity and Innovation

Creativity and Innovation is about thinking creatively, working creatively with others, developing or designing novel products or processes, and implementing innovations. It relates to applying and recognising the value of new ideas to develop new products and strategies and deliver benefits. It involves the capacity to challenge perceptions of how things are, and how they might be, and to recognise a potential opportunity.[27]

This is another critical skill in law, although at first glance many may think the law is not particularly creative. Think about the importance of this skill when undertaking statutory interpretation, seeing how the law will affect or regulate the conduct of your client. Or the arguments to make regarding whether a particular conduct is bound by the laws of precedent of a case, or whether you can argue your case should be distinguished out from under the binding judgement, and therefore not be bound. Novel and new arguments are intrinsic to the development of the common law, and is the very nature of its plasticity and ability to evolve with society. Think about the recent digital revolution and disruption in law;[28] for example the arrival of blockchain,[29] artificial intelligence,[30] and open source, CopyLeft intellectual property regimes,[31] the challenges and opportunities the internet affords society, biotechnology, and all the innovations of the twenty-first century. These evolving technologies all need governing and managing by the law and other regulatory mechanisms, so creativity and innovation have never been more critical skill for a modern worker to embrace, or at the very least be aware of and conversant in.

Legal practice is facing significant disruption.[32] Digital technologies and the Internet of Things are breaking down traditional structures, boarders, jurisdictions and opening up significant opportunities. The legal profession is already starting to

---

[27] https://www.monash.edu/student-futures; Ways in which you might demonstrate C*reativity and Innovation* skills you acquired during a Legal Work Experience or WIL Placement might include:

- Improve or develop existing practices or processes through creative and critical analysis;
- Synthesise and apply established and new knowledge and skills to situations;
- Creative innovative solutions to current and anticipated problems;
- Develop or design novel products, processes or strategies;
- Challenge or extend perceptions of how things are, and might be, and inclusively generate new ideas.

[28] Richard Susskind, Tomorrow's Lawyers (Oxford University Press, 2013); Richard and Daniel Susskind, The Future of the Professions (Oxford University Press, 2015).

[29] See <https://www.digitaltrends.com/computing/what-is-a-blockchain/>.

[30] E.G. Martin Ford, Rise of the Robots (Basic Books, 2015); Tim Dunlop, Why the future is WORKLESS (NewSouth2016); David H Autor, 'Why are there still so many jobs? The history and future of workplace automation', (2015) 29(3) Journal of Economic Perspectives 3; Eric Brynjolfsson and Andrew McAfee, The Second machine Age: Work, progress and prosperity in a time of brilliant technologies (Norton & Company, 2014).

[31] See <https://www.gnu.org/licenses/copyleft.en.html>.

[32] George Beaton and Imme Kaschner, Remaking Law Firms: Why & how? (ABA Book Publishing, 2016); Alec Ross, Industries of the future (Simon & Schuster, 2016).

look and feel significantly different to that of only a generation ago, and many predict even further, radical and fundamental change.[33] Advertisements are now looking for 'Legal Architects', 'Legal Solutions Manager', 'Legal Content Manager', 'Legal Project Manager' rather than just 'lawyers' and the silos of traditional legal practise are being opened up, allowing off shore resourcing and the breaking up of traditional legal work and distribution of the parts; the gig economy meets legal practise.

Creativity and innovation are important skills for us all to embrace and you may find evidence of these skills in other areas of your professional or personal life. Embrace change and always question the status-quo, attempting to find efficiencies and better ways of doing things. Work Integrated Learning gives you the chance to enter an organisation with a 'fresh pair of eyes', bringing your unique perspective. You need not revolutionise their business, but focussing on adding value, you are better placed than those deep within the business of 'seeing the wood for the trees.' At the very least, practical experience will enhance your understanding of the professional and business environment, dynamics, drivers and market of the area of practise or quasi-legal environment that you may work in; soaking up the environment is critical and your openness to change and innovation an important, modern skill you would want to exhibit awareness and examples of.

Initiative and Enterprise

Initiative and Enterprise is about learning to think strategically and to invest energy and resources into solutions. It is about translating ideas into actions, improving processes and systems and taking the lead in the approach to tasks or situations. It also relates to being able to identify and capitalise on new opportunities.[34]

There is some overlap here with *Creativity*, but this skill is more about mobilizing and activating initiatives. It also talks to your attitude. I learnt early in my legal career at U.S. corporate law firm Shearman & Sterling, was I to be 'part of the problem or part of the solution?' and it was simply up to me to choose. Make this fundamental decision daily before you step into your workplace and it will literally inform every subsequent decision you make all day long and frame your choices furthering the mission or enterprise, finding solutions and exhibiting a bias for action.[35]

---

[33] Richard Susskind, Tomorrow's Lawyers (Oxford University Press, 2013).

[34] <https://www.monash.edu/student-futures>.

[35] https://www.monash.edu/student-futures; Ways in which you might demonstrate *Initiative and Enterprise* skills you acquired during a Legal Work Experience or WIL Placement might include:

- Generate a range of options to address a situation;
- Think flexibly and independently;
- Adapt to a range of situations to achieve desired outcomes;
- Work autonomously, take the initiative and be self-directed in undertaking and achieving tasks;
- Initiate innovative solutions;

Intercultural Competence

Intercultural Competence is an ability to communicate effectively and appropriately with people of other cultures. Intercultural competence is composed of several key skill sets including the ability to recognise multiple perspectives, to recognise one's own cultural values and those of others, and to work effectively within and across different cultural groups. Inter-culturally competent people are able to engage in a globalised world. They demonstrate an outward focus and commitment to community and to social and cultural inclusion.[36]

This is a critical skill for any legal work environment. Australia is built on migration and nothing is surer in your work day that you will interact with people from different cultural, religious, ethnic and SES backgrounds. Objectivity is a critical legal skill so you need to manage your subjective responses and reactions to others and work with people, clients and colleagues alike, from a diverse range of backgrounds and cultural contexts. Mutual respect and understanding is the cornerstone of any civilized society, and you should strive to be a living exemplar of these values in the workplace, for your own benefit and for the benefit of the whole community.

Planning and Organisation

Planning and Organisation is about identifying and completing the steps needed to undertake tasks and manage workloads. This involves the capacity to prioritise, make decisions, establish clear goals, identify and manage resources and plan for contingencies.[37]

- Identify opportunities not obvious to others;
- Thrive through transition and change and adapt and be an early adopter in new situations;
- Develop strategic, creative, short and long term visions;
- Liaise with a range of stakeholders and sponsors to develop an innovative outcome.

[36] https://www.monash.edu/student-futures; Ways in which you might demonstrate *Intercultural Competence* skills you acquired during a Legal Work Experience or WIL Placement might include:

- Strive for and commit to social and cultural inclusion and diversity;
- Effectively engage in a globalized world through understanding of and participation in productive relationships across nations and cultures;
- Understanding and navigating and effectively interacting with a culture different from your own;
- Manage personal reactions to difference and work with difference in others;
- Demonstrate actions which show commitment to social and cultural inclusion;
- Respond sensitively and appropriately to the needs of different stakeholders and consumers;
- Recognise and respect diverse beliefs and opinions to achieve goals.
- Draw on diverse ideas and opinions to achieve goals;
- Work effectively with people of different ages, gender, race, religion or political persuasion;
- Demonstrate an outward focus and commitment to local and/or global community.

[37] https://www.monash.edu/student-futures; Ways in which you might demonstrate *planning and organization* skills you acquired during a Legal Work Experience or WIL Placement might include:

You need to be organized and on top of your work and obligations in any role, but none more so in a legal or quasi-legal role. 'Justice delayed is Justice denied'[38] – don't let this be because of you!

Deadlines, filing dates, lodging dates, response times, statutes of limitations, etc., all point to being highly organized in order to be successful in a legally accurate environment. 'Fail to Plan then you Plan to Fail' is a well-known management mantra, and planning really is your best friend enabling completion of projects on time and on budget.

'To arrive early is to be on-time, to arrive on-time is to be late, and to arrive late is unacceptable!' is another common workplace mantra; being late is disrespectful of others' time and speaks volumes as to your work ethos and skills in this space; get organized, be early and start kicking goals. Let deadlines, calendars and plans be your tool.

Problem Identification and Solution

Problem Identification and Solution is about identifying and addressing routine and non-routine problems in order to reach positive and productive outcomes. It involves the capacity to anticipate potential issues and to utilise a range of resources to develop solutions, design contingencies and reflect on the process. It takes good listening skills to get to the significant part of the matter and separate the non-material information.[39]

- Work autonomously and with others to develop a vision and proactive plan to achieve it;
- Apply research analysis processes to a range of situations;
- Plan and organize workload commitments;
- Establish clear project goals and deliverables;
- Participate in improvement and planning processes;
- Manage time and priorities, including setting timelines and coordinate tasks for self and others;
- Manage resources and plan for contingencies;
- Take the initiative to make decisions.

[38] Conflicting accounts of who first noted the phrase. According to *Respectfully Quoted: A Dictionary of Quotations*, it is attributable to William Ewart Gladstone, but such attribution was not verifiable (*Respectfully Quoted: A Dictionary of Quotations Requested from the Congressional Research Service*. Library of Congress, 1989 – Laurence J. Peter, *Peter's Quotations*, p. 276 (1977). Alternatively, it may be attributed to William Penn in the form "to delay Justice is Injustice"; Penn, William (1693), *Some Fruits of Solitude*, Headley, 1905, p. 86.

[39] https://www.monash.edu/student-futures; Ways in which you might demonstrate *problem identification and solution* skills you acquired during a Legal Work Experience or WIL Placement might include:

- Discover and analyse information, critique synthesise and evaluate views;
- Take the initiative and make decisions to contribute to productive outcomes;
- Identify and address routine an non-routine problems in order to achieve objectives;
- Engage with knowledge which is not restricted to traditional boundaries;
- Consider data and circumstances in order to test assumptions;
- Make connections and propose creative solutions;

Professionalism

Professionalism is about understanding and working within workplace protocols, roles and responsibilities. It is about navigating various work contexts, reflecting upon and managing your own behavior and learning, and making career-related choices. Demonstration of professionalism also involves the capacity to identify and manage responsibilities, and to work honestly, ethically and transparently.[40]

Nowhere is this more important than in the law; lawyers are officers of the court and have a duty towards the court and the profession to act ethically at all times and not bring the profession into disrepute. Lawyer's ethical duties are an integral part of practise; any legal or quasi-legal role carries with it a huge responsibility to behave professionally.

Teamwork

Teamwork is about working effectively as part of a team and forming productive working relationships. Successful team players interact effectively with others and are able to work with a range of people. They are able to acknowledge and respect different opinions and points of view. They encourage contributions and are comfortable seeking feedback and ideas from others. Team players demonstrate an ability to understand individual responsibilities as well as group objectives.

Nature abhors a vacuum, and it is highly unlikely you will end up working in a 'lone-wolf' capacity not needing the assistance of a team of some sort to deliver the work place outcome product or service. Teamwork skills are essential in the

---

- Develop practical and effective solutions;
- Apply problem-solving processes and strategies;
- Creatively and critically reflect on and learn from own actions and actions of others;
- Recognise and work with complexity.

[40] https://www.monash.edu/student-futures; Ways in which you might demonstrate creativity and innovation skills you acquired during a Legal Work Experience or WIL Placement might include:

- Demonstrate an awareness of ethical considerations and consequences of different approaches;
- Work honestly, transparently and openly within a role and organization;
- Recognise and understand explicit and implicit rules, rights and culture of organization;
- Demonstrate academic integrity in the search for new insight and knowledge;
- Take responsibility for one's own professional learning and development within a role;
- Make decisions about when and how to align behaviors with organizational culture and protocol;
- Research, discover, evaluate and effectively and ethically use information;
- Clarify and negotiate work roles and responsibilities;
- Understand how tasks and responsibilities contribute to roles and work of others;
- Take responsibility for one's own actions;
- Demonstrate social responsibility in relation to organizational operations.

workplace, and your ability to maximize team outputs may in turn define your individual success.[41]

Use of Tools and Technology

Use of Tools and Technology relates to the application of relevant tools and technologies and digital systems to locate, evaluate, organise and use information to effectively complete tasks and achieve goals. This includes understanding current technological trends and developments, and their relevance to the job. Competence in this skill area also involves the utilisation of tools and technology to manage and improve processes, as well as a willingness and capacity to learn new skills and use tools appropriate to the workplace and tasks required.

Darwin's Theory of Natural selection is often misquoted as 'survival of the fittest'; his main thesis was actually 'survival of the most adaptive', namely he felt the ability to adapt and respond to an environment was the key determination of survival.[42] Nowhere is this more important in the workplace in being able to adapt to new tools and technology, to enhance efficiencies and enable you to produce and thrive.[43]

---

[41] https://www.monash.edu/student-futures; Ways in which you might demonstrate creativity and innovation skills you acquired during a Legal Work Experience or WIL Placement might include:

- Work collaborately and inclusively with others to achieve a common vision or outcome;
- Defend a particular position but be able to willingly change or re-evaluate that position if necessary.
- Identify and work with strengths and limitations of team members and self;
- Treat team members with equal respect and foster positive positive working relationships;
- Coach, mentor, motivate and provide support to others;
- Contribute to and share information, ideas, expertise and resources;
- Participate enthusiastically and persuasively without dominating others;
- Be comfortable and work positively with disagreement amongst team members;
- Recognize your and others' roles in a team.
- Demonstrate leadership, or work with direction as appropriate.

[42] Charles Darwin, "On the Origin of Species by Means of Natural Selection, or the Preservation of Favoured Races in the Struggle for Life," 1859.

[43] https://www.monash.edu/student-futures; Ways in which you might demonstrate creativity and innovation skills you acquired during a Legal Work Experience or WIL Placement might include:

- Recognise and use skills, information and communication technology relevant to a role;
- Understand workplace specific information management systems and protocols and effectively manage information overload; work with current developments in technology;
- Select and use tools, equipment and applications to promote efficiency and productivity;
- Use equipment, technology and systems to connect with others, access, organize and present information, manage risk and achieve outcomes;
- Locate, evaluate and organize information using appropriate systems and tools.

A Framework for Analysing Your Want/Autonomy/ Intrinsic Motivations

Whether you *Want* to do a particular job, what motivates you internally, is a personal decision and no book or friend or colleague can even start to purport to give you individual advice on what it is you should *want* to do. Instead this is your task to deep dive and think about what is important to you and then to prioritise these facets so you get an insight and understanding on what specifically drives, motivates and pushes you towards wanting some things above others. Often these Wants or drivers are conflicting and by definition you can't always get what you want; choosing a law career you *Want* then, is a question of compromise. It is certainly worth considering deeply and below is a framework of Drivers for this.[44]

Personal Drivers

Your personal drivers include Identity, Self-Esteem, Passion, Achieving your Potential and Life Meaning. These are unique to you and allow you to live a fulfilling life. This in turn changes over time, so your dreams as a child or later may be different to now as your frames of reference develop as your knowledge grows. We need to be satisfied by these Personal Drivers, and fear of death makes all of them seem important and urgent. Notwithstanding this, Personal Drivers are often overlooked by the other Drivers below, and may explain why some highly successful people are unhappy and feel they succeeded in the wrong field. People who study law are often bright and had the marks at school to 'get in' to law school or medicine, and may have felt it a 'waste' (or somebody else did) not to put their early evidence of intellectual capacity to 'good use'.

Social Drivers

Our social Drivers include Status, Inclusion, Respect, Power, Fame and Appreciation. Some of these Drivers are primitive and wanting (*sic* needing) acceptance by the tribe and deeply held fear of embarrassment or disapproval.[45] Your Ego also needs to be satisfied, ideally admired and at the very least appreciated. Some have a very strong Social Driver to please someone else who has psychological power over them, perhaps a parent. Some people study law because they are drawn to the status and prestige of a lawyer and the respect and power that may come with that role.

[44] I have adapted this 'Drivers' section from Tim Urban's 'Yearning Octopus' of wants in his Blog Post, 'How to Pick a Career (That Actually Fits You)'. See <https://waitbutwhy.com/2018/04/picking-career.html>.

[45] The Social Survival Mammoth, see <https://waitbutwhy.com/2014/06/taming-mammoth-let-peoples-opinions-run-life.html>.

Lifestyle Drivers

Our Lifestyle Drivers include Freedom, Balance, Flexibility, Comfort, Ease and Means. We all want to have a nice, relaxing, calm and happy time. We want to have choices about what we do and how we do it, ideally in the warmth with as little headaches or frustration as possible. These drivers are particularly conflicting, as the driver to relax, meditate, and find balance holds us back from working hard to build wealth to buy time, space and luxury. Stress-free is at odds with entrepreneurialism. Some people study law thinking it will equate to money and a luxurious lifestyle, sports cars and mansions, perhaps overlooking the hours needed to succeed in the profession.

Moral Drivers

Our Moral Drivers want us to Reduce Suffering, have Impact, enhancing Social Justice, promote Fairness, Protect the Vulnerable and make the World a Better Place. Many people study law wanting to contribute and enable this Moral Driver, allowing them to literally affect positive change and make a difference to society. These Moral Drivers are often at odds with our other, self-centred Drivers and can generate real internal conflict.

Practical Drivers

Security, Housing, Food, and Clothing all have to be secured, and your Practical Drivers are concerned with paying the rent so you can sleep somewhere and being warm enough to sleep soundly. We must avoid financial ruin by living beyond our means and incurring perpetual debt. The majority of us who need to generate an income from our career to support ourselves are acutely aware of this Practical Driver when choosing a career.

We may have more Drivers than this, but for now when choosing a career, you need to invest some time to 'sit on a rock' and unpack these Drivers in your subconscious. Really think about what legal career appeals to you, then unpack what Driver is behind that choice.

For example, I have met Law Students who simply want to be rich. If you are attracted to Corporate Big Law Partnership and Money, what is really, personally for you motivating and driving that desire? Is it a yearning for Security from your Practical Driver? Or is it not really about Security but a want of luxury for your Lifestyle Driver or Social Driver? By examining honestly your own Drivers, some will become clearer in your mind in terms of importance, and you can start to understand your own hierarchy of Drivers that are fuelling your career decisions.

The next step is then to challenge your Drivers you have identified as the strongest, and check that they are your authentic, personal drivers, and not those imposed on you by someone else during your childhood, or by the dominant surrounding social culture. You ask why you want the Drivers and why they are important to you to check they are self-generated, not imposed on you by others. Check the authenticity of your Wants. Ask why do you *Want* this Driver? Some Drivers you will find are independently yours, whilst other fears or desires you have taken on-board and are unhelpful for you to live your authentic self in the here and now. If you want to choose a career, then you need to discard external Drivers and discover what your own Drivers are. Only then will you know what it is you really Want.

A Values Framework for Analysing Your Fit/Belonging *to a Culture*

By immersing yourself in a Work Integrated Learning or Work Experience opportunity, you can literally 'try before you buy'. This is shown to be far better predictor of better choices than 'going with your gut instinct', with research in the science of decision making collected over several decades suggesting our intuitions are often misleading and only work in certain circumstances.[46]

Better to check personal fit by experience and providing evidence that a particular culture, role, environment, or organisation is right for you, by securing 'informed career consent' in situ.

It has been shown above that Self Determination Theory posits a sense of belonging to a culture or community is essential for psychological wellbeing. We need to be aligned with our employers' values in order to fully contribute to them in a way that does not cause us cognitive-dissonance, or unhappiness.

The Australian legal academic and philosopher Professor Jonathan Crowe has argued that human flourishing depends on certain forms of life that are inherently good for humans by virtue of our nature; a plurality of basic goods that humans characteristically value and pursue in life. Building on the work of jurisprudence scholar John Finnis, Crowe argues for a framework of wellbeing grounded on the importance of 9 broad categories of fundamental human values, positing human flourishing involves participating in these values in a balanced and integrated way.[47] I wish to re-purpose those 9 categories below, to provide a values-based framework as a practical tool for us to measure our personal Fit or Belonging to a given career culture or organisation.

1. The *Good of Life* captures the value of bringing about, nurturing and protecting the possibility of human flourishing. The Universal Declaration of Human Rights[48] was a watershed global document attempting to embody this value. All human rights based legal work is driven by enabling human flourishing and

[46] <https://80000hours.org/articles/dont-go-with-your-gut-instinct/>.

[47] Crowe, Jonathan, 'What is Wellness? The Role of Human Values', Keynote Paper at the National Wellness for Law Forum, Do No Harm 15–16 February, 2018 Bond University, Gold Coast.

[48] <http://www.un.org/en/universal-declaration-human-rights/index.html>.

working for the *Good of Life*. A vast array of legal work is grounded in this value; access to justice depends upon people motivated to enable people's equal treatment before the law and appropriate legal representation and fair due process. Much of the work of Community Legal Centres, the courts and criminal justice system, international treaties, War Tribunals, Royal Commissions, tribunals and protective services are all underpinned by this value. Fair Trade Coffee, Chocolate and Tea all embody this value, as do anti-slavery laws and the Trespass to the Person torts,[49] for examples. The global 'Black Lives Matter' protests are in direct response to deaths caused by police brutality contravening this Good. An organisation's view or attitude, output or practices towards the Good of Life are a useful measure of your cultural fit, or otherwise. Does the organisation's products or services enhance or diminish this value? It is a useful way for you to benchmark what the goals, drivers and outputs of the organisation are and how they align with your view of this fundamental value.

2. The *Good of Health* reflects the value of physical and mental wellbeing. Does the organisation's products or services enhance or diminish this value? What about the employment or business practices employed to generate the goods and services? Does the organisation value mental and physical health? In Australia, we have the Tristan Jepson Memorial Foundation dedicated to supporting a safe and healthy legal workplace.[50] TJMF responded to increasing awareness of poor mental and physical health outcomes in the legal profession, including anxiety, depression, substance abuse and suicide,[51] by raising awareness and commissioning research[52] to uncover the prevalence of the issue. They developed phsycho-social employer's Workplace Wellbeing: Best Practice Guidelines,[53] identifying 13 workplace factors contributing to the mental health or otherwise of an organisation's employees. Over 150 legal organisations in Australia and beyond are signatories to the guidelines,[54] pledging awareness and attention to the mental health and wellbeing of their employees. It is not only the organisation but the conditions and expectations of the organisational culture that can inform the true measure of this value. Long hours where gym access is limited can be quantified against this value; 6 day working weeks can be measured

[49] The common law torts of Assault, Battery and False Imprisonment.

[50] <http://www.tjmf.org.au/>.

[51] Krill P.R. Johnson R. Albert L. (2016) The Prevalence of Substance Use and Other Mental Health Concerns Among American Attorneys Journal of Addict Med. 2016 Feb; 10(1): 46–52. <http://www.ncbi.nlm.nih.gov/pmc/articles/PMC4736291/>.

Clarke B.S. (2015) Coming Out in the Classroom: Law Professors, Law Students and Depression. Journal of Legal Education, Volume 64, Number 3 (February 2015) http://jle.aals.org/cgi/viewcontent.cgi?article=1029&context=home

[52] Kelk N. Luscombe G. Medlow S. Hickie I. (2009) Courting the Blues: Attitudes towards depression in Australian law students and lawyers <http://www.cald.asn.au/docs/Law%20Report%20Website%20version%204%20May%2009.pdf>.

[53] <http://www.tjmf.org.au/the-guidelines/>.

[54] <http://www.tjmf.org.au/the-guidelines/signatories-to-the-guidelines/#list>.

against this value; 'all-nighters' in the office can be yard-sticked against this value, regardless what the HR or marketing departments say of their conditions, or whether they are signatories to Best Practice Guidelines or not. Many firms, businesses and organisations pay gym memberships, have Employee Assistance Providers (counselling, etc.), generous sick leave, mental health days, RU OK Day,[55] etc. By immersing yourself in this culture during work experience and talking to current employees and really 'walking the talk' in a firm organisation and living it day to day, in a short while you will recognise their alignment or otherwise to this value. You may then make your Fit and Belonging decisions accordingly, depending upon your prioritisation of this value.

3. The *Good of Pleasure* captures the value of experiencing positive effect. Does the organisation's products or services enhance or diminish this value, or are they indifferent? As an employee do you experience positive effect by the outcomes, and what of the effect on others and clients? Tobacco corporations might argue they are devoted to this Value initially,[56] but we all agree they would score very poorly on The *Good of Health* above. Some areas of law are more obviously devoted to this value, such as defamation law protecting our reputations, or Trespass to Land protecting our exclusive possession of land, and Private Nuisance protecting our peaceful enjoyment of our land. The criminal justice system is driven by this value, and arguably, most legal regimes are around the goals of protecting and keeping the peace, attempting to regulate the affairs of citizens for the benefit of an orderly society and to reduce conflict and distress. This is a good value to measure the importance of your work in an organisation or overarching goals of it, and in turn any deviation or otherwise from this value will need reconciling with your own prioritisation of the value. For example, if an abattoir slaughters animals for providing meat for the pleasure of its consumers, you might not be able to tolerate the suffering in that environment to justify the end result; the end does not justify the means. You may alternately take the view that you wholeheartedly support the work of the abattoir to provide meat to the end consumer, and that the end does justify the means, and that is ok with you. So in your workplace, this *Good of Pleasure* is a great measure of what you do and for what reasons in an organisation or business sector,[57] and whether that aligns with you and whether you fit there.
4. The *Good of Friendship* reflects the importance of social connectedness and a mutually supportive community. This is a great value to measure an organisation by when thinking about your Fit or Belonging. Obviously when you work some-

---

[55] <https://www.ruok.org.au/>.

[56] Also eventually, potentially not much pleasure in dying of emphysema.

[57] Securitisation was a terrific practice for business and law firms in the 1990s, divesting and hiving off debts from corporations and then raising capital in the markets on the back of the shell corporation left with just the shiny assets; less so later contributing to the 2007-8 Global Financial Crisis. Selling sub-prime loans to over-extended consumers was terrific business for banks, until defaults left them with over-valued security on the loans, also contributing to the global meltdown of financial markets.

where you are not all neccesarily going to be friends, as a collective you have been assembled to perform a variety of functions, so the accounts personnel and IT staff will have very different skill sets and probably different personality types than the sales team or the lawyer. But you can all be friendly colleagues. Within the role however in a funny way you are all grouped and brought together to carry out the same or similar function simply by 'coincidence of your CVs', so we all completed an LLB to be a lawyer, for example. Just like you probably weren't great friends with everyone at Uni, you are not going to be great friends with everyone in your firm, but a culture is in place in any organisation and this is usually set by the management team and senior personnel, either positively and respectfully, or otherwise.[58] If during a work integrated learning opportunity your read of the staff and culture is not positive, then you may well not fit in there. If you walk away after a week or two and think you could not like your peers or management as friends, then it may well not be the culture for you. This probably embodies other values, as certain professions do attract certain character traits[59] so if these are at odds with you and your make up, then it is unlikely you will find connectivity or belonging with that group. Conscientious objectors during mandatory conscription wedded to passivism would not enjoy enduring friendships with napalm-delivering U.S. bomber pilots over Vietnam;[60] they simply have little in common and competing values. If you can't be friends with anyone in the organisation, it's probably not the organisation for you.

5. The *Good of Play* embodies the value of structured forms of achievement and recreation. This is important from a wellbeing perspective and organisations know this. Employers often promote team sports and activities to build teamwork and relationships, to foster the *Good of Friendship* and camaraderie amongst a team, for enhanced results and outputs. Some see their role as a sort of game they wish to win; the adversarial paradigm in law can facilitate this mindset, litigation teams with tactics wanting to 'win' for their client, at the very least prosecute their client's agenda and objectives and maximise their benefit. Legal academics 'play the game' of trying to secure publications in the best Journals, Law firms 'play the game' of attracting and retaining the best clients, Barristers 'play the game' of being briefed on the best cases, then 'play the game' of winning it in court, etc. This needs to align with your own value of this; many think you find your recreation predominantly outside of work, but a more holistic view would see creativity and freedom how to accomplish your goals in the workplace as an embodiment of this value, and so is worth thinking about when assessing your fit or belonging to a community or culture. If you just can-

[58] 'A fish rots form the head'; a greedy, careless, ambivalent, ruthless, disdainful management team will have a different organisational culture and impact than a generous, caring, empathetic, gracious and concerned management; you will feel it!

[59] Extroverts do well at sales; introverts with attention to detail in accounts, for example.

[60] 388,000 tons of napalm was dropped in Vietnam during 1963–1973 period <https://thevietnamwar.info/napalm-vietnam-war/>.

not stand 'playing the game' of a particular business or industry, then you will have trouble authentically belonging.

6. The *Good of Appreciation* captures the value of aesthetic experience and the sense of wonder, satisfaction or delight it invokes in us. Some people sell airplanes, boats or Ferraris because they love airplanes, boats or Ferraris. Most lawyers appreciate accuracy and a certain sense of order around documents.[61] The more you know yourself, the easier this value is to align with a workplace. Again, the value of work experience or work integrated learning to experience an environment is priceless to see how you align with this value and in turn how the organisation or type of organisation aligns with you.
7. The *Good of Understanding* expresses the human quest to know our nature and environment. Literally whole industries of research and development are founded on this value, in order to then capitalise on this understanding. This value literally drives innovation regardless of industry; pharmaceutical, medical, engineering, biotech, IT. It is a driver in all industries. Lawyers constantly seek to understand in order to apply or innovate the law; to regulate and modify behaviour; and to resolve disputes and facilitate commerce and industry. Our own learning journey since we were born is fuelled by this value.[62] An organisation that tries to understand its clients and environments is agile and adaptive, thus more likely to be successful and hence more attractive to belong to.
8. The *Good of Meaning* reflects the role of commitments, projects and relationships providing our lives a sense of purpose. What is your vocational meaning? What are you trying to achieve, or achieving in your role? What is the organisation trying to achieve? This value is a great way to yardstick your values against an organisation or industry or role. It is important for your wellbeing to be clear on the 'Why' to justify the day-to-day 'What'. As above, the 'End must justify the Means,' otherwise something is out of balance. Seeing the big picture stops us getting overwhelmed with the detail. A mountain is climbed one step at a time. The *Good of Meaning* value is powerful in checking our career is on track and going in the right direction; it is also powerful in checking organisational fit and whether you wish to belong and buy into the mission statement of the organisation.
9. The *Good of Reasonableness* involves connecting our actions with our deeper goals and values, and is a useful reminder for us that purpose drives practice. It is important to self-reflect and use our reason to justify our actions and sanity-check our actions are aligned with our goals and aspirations, values and motivators. The law is a manifestation of the values of a society, and the area we spend

[61] For example, I disproportionately dislike an unevenly folded or soiled, crumpled or ripped document; I much prefer the aesthetic of a clean, crisp and neatly folded document in an envelope. Am I overtly fussy? Probably, but I literally cannot help how I feel about an ugly, misaligned, wonky and dirty letter leaving my office, and I simply will not allow it; it confronts my *Good of Appreciation* too much.

[62] Ancora Imparo is the Monash University motto; 'We are still learning' <https://www.monash.edu/about/who/history/sir-john-monash>.

our individual time, energy and effort must be individually meaningful to us in a reasonable manner to avoid cognitive dissonance and instead facilitate a sense of personal fulfilment. Are you happy to be an ambassador of the organisation and its goals and would you be a proud proactive member of the community? This is an important value to measure your career against as we only have one life to make a broader contribution to society; what will yours reasonably be?

Part IV: Conclusions

One mistake is to think that your next job or role will define what you do for the rest of your working life; the data suggests this will not be the case and it is more likely you will have 17 jobs over 5 distinct careers.[63] Steve Jobs compared life to connecting dots, pointing out that it's easy to look at your past and see how the dots connected to lead you to where you are but that it is impossible in life to connect the dots forwards.[64] Seeing your career as a series of dots or jobs to move forward is accurate, but also helps you realise you only need to focus on the next dot on your path. Do not worry about 3, 4 or 5 dots away, chances are you will have changed,[65] your Wants and drivers will have changed,[66] the job market would have changed[67] and you will know yourself and your skills better. You will have also experienced more work places, cultures, and environments to again better inform your next career move and your network of people in those industries would have grown.

I once met a Tibetan Buddhist Lama at a meditation session and he reflected that Westerners are very 'flighty' with their careers, often flitting between one job or career to the next, 'like a butterfly'. He laughed as he explained they would often work incredibly hard with devotion to rise in a particular field or discipline, then throw it all away and start again at the bottom of a new, entirely different field or discipline, wasting precious time. 'Throwing the baby out with the bath water!' he chuckled. He observed this practice would be ridiculous in Tibetan culture. 'Better then,' the Lama continued, 'to slightly bend or gently change path in order to take a new direction, rather than break and start again all the way back down the bottom.' This reminded me of Confucius' quote, 'The green reed which bends in the wind is

---

[63] 'the national average tenure in a job is 3.3 years (3 years and 4 months), based on voluntary turnover of around 15% per annum….assuming they start their working life aged 18 (in a part-time role) and are retired from all work by 75, they will have 17 different employers in their lifetime. Based on 3 jobs before upskilling or career changing, this means that they will also have 5 separate careers in their lifetime.' <https://mccrindle.com.au/insights/blog/job-mobility-australia/>.

[64] <https://www.youtube.com/watch?reload=9&v=UF8uR6Z6KLc>.

[65] <https://80000hours.org/2015/02/we-change-more-than-we-expect-so-keep-your-options-open/>.

[66] <https://80000hours.org/career-guide/personal-fit/>.

[67] E.G. see <https://www.jobs.gov.au/news/australian-jobs-2017-highlights-changing-workforce, and https://www.qt.com.au/news/how-every-job-australia-going-change/3205427/>.

stronger than the mighty oak which breaks in a storm.'[68] I also liken this to 'Grouping your Career Arrows' we explored above; if you study law and find you do not particularly wish to be a lawyer, and think you might like to be a teacher, then the Lama would say start teaching law! If you liked research skills, be a Legal researcher, in either a firm or a university, in government or industry. If you liked the learning and teaching of skills in the law, be a Learning Skills Advisor in a law library. If you like writing, be a legal writer, in newspapers, blogs, online publishing, etc. Bend, don't break! By 'Grouping your Career Arrows' and slightly bending your career trajectory, your jumps between job dots or roles are more natural, congruent, less risky and you bring with it your knowledge, experience, skills and abilities, i.e. your ever-increasing Competency. You can fine-tune your Wants and internal Motivators, honouring your Autonomy, all the while checking your Belonging and Connectedness to an organisation or cause, by aligning it to a values based paradigm of successful recruitment, enhancing your wellbeing and allowing you to thrive in your career. Your unique career, tailor-made just for you.

[68] <https://www.goodreads.com/quotes/210361-the-green-reed-which-bends-in-the-wind-is-stronger>.

Chapter 6
Choosing a Law Career

Ruth Morgan and Sarah Bartholomeusz

A career in the law is no longer as guaranteed as it once was, and graduates are increasingly concerned about employment opportunities in the legal industry.

This downturn is due in part to a variety of factors, not the least of which is that the legal industry is still experiencing somewhat of a hangover from the global financial crisis, which resulted in many firms exercising caution about taking on too many graduates. While 2016 saw a significant improvement on increased graduate numbers, it may be a while before we see peak graduate placements again.

An even larger contributor is disruption to the legal industry in the form of applications and automated contract documents and the continuing 'professionalisation' of paralegals performing many of the tasks that were once delegated to graduates and junior lawyers.

Clients are expressing dissatisfaction with current billing practices. In addition to demanding fixed fee work, they are questioning the value of time spent by junior lawyers on their files when precedent software has done half the work.

This is a difficult issue to address, as junior lawyers find it increasingly difficult to build up knowledge and key skills that they require to advance their career.

Graduate Careers Australia provides a breakdown of employment and salary outcomes for law graduates every year. In 2015, 74.1% of graduates were in full time employment, 10.6% were unemployed and 15.3% were working part-time or casually while seeking full-time employment.[1]

There are many things law students can do to leverage themselves and their skills to stand out from the crowd, but perhaps one of the most constructive options is to play the long game. A law degree can take you many places other than the

[1] Graduate Careers Australia, *Employment and Salary Outcomes of Recent Higher Education Graduates*, December 2015.

R. Morgan (✉) · S. Bartholomeusz
Hender Consulting, Adelaide, SA, Australia
e-mail: ruth.morgan@hender.com.au

M. Raz et al. (eds.), *Careers in Law: A Guide for Students, Graduates and Professionals*, https://doi.org/10.1007/978-981-15-3627-4_6

traditional partnership with a mahogany desk and large leather backed chair. Statistics indicate that the number of solicitors holding practicing certificates peak in the 30–34 year age bracket (17.1%), with a significant and continuing decline over the following years:

- 13.7% at 35–39 years
- 12.4% at 40–44 years
- 9.5% at 45–49 years.[2]

So where are all the lawyers going? In this chapter we are going to explore some of the options you may wish to consider to augment your law career.

Teaching & Academia

In years gone by, securing a part time position as a tutor was a popular and valuable way to augment your income, particularly for newly minted barristers who are working on building up their practice and reputation.

In today's marketplace, tutoring and lecturing roles are no longer a 'supplementary' activity, but an increasingly professionalized and competitive career choice. Lecturer positions are still predominantly part time positions, with only 65.1% engaged full time.[3]

In addition to the ambition to teach law, post graduate qualifications with a history of quality published research papers are crucial to secure a role as an academic.

If you have the ambition to teach law, you should begin with a *research focused* LLM and create opportunities to get your work published. If you are ultimately seeking a permanent full time lectureship, you will undoubtedly need a Ph.D.

Being an academic is not just about writing papers and collecting degrees. The pieces you publish will demonstrate your analytical and interpretation skills. They will exhibit your expertise in a specific area of the law and demonstrate a wider understanding of the law at play.

Experience teaching and tutoring will strengthen your position in the marketplace, but ultimately, it will be your publications that lead you to a successful placement in academia.

If you are interested in a career in academia, you should take some time to review some job descriptions. They often read like this:

To be successful in this role you will have:

- *A PhD or equivalent postgraduate qualification with expertise in [insert specific area of law here]*
- *A successful research publications record*

---

[2] Law Society of New South Wales, *2014 Law Society National Profile, Final Report*, April 2015.

[3] http://joboutlook.gov.au/occupation.aspx?code=2421&search=alpha&Tab=prospects (8 March 2017).

- *Experience in teaching at a tertiary level preferred, but must demonstrate the ability and an interest in teaching and the development of innovative teaching methods*
- *Strong interpersonal skills, including a demonstrated ability to work collaboratively.*

Consulting

A consultant is simply defined as 'someone who provides expert advice' or an 'independent professional'. Consulting may not be the answer for everyone, but it is an increasingly popular approach offering greater control, flexibility and more diversity than being an employee.

The rise of consulting is a significant consequence of the deconstruction of 'traditional' law firms driven by client demands. In world where tailored contracts can be electronically generated from a template on the internet, "full-service law firm" holds less value than it once did. Costs add up quickly when you have a team of four lawyers charging you in 6 min blocks, and clients are increasingly demanding to know *who exactly* is working on their file and what all those 6-min phone calls are. Many of them are choosing instead to hire a consultant to work with them on a specific task or project for a flat or pre-agreed rate.

Similarly, many lawyers reach a point in their career when they no longer wish to account for their 14-h day in 6 min lots.

0800–0806: Phone call with Mr. Joe Bloggs
0800–0812: Phone call with Solicitor for the other side
0800–0824: Drafting email to Client
0800–0830: Phone call with regulator
0800–0845: Amending application form
0800–0851: Drafting email to regulator
0800–0910: Teleconference with witness

And it's only just 9 am.

Consulting can have many faces and there are opportunities to consult in some unexpected places.

International Law Firms

Globalization means many international law firms are seeking experts qualified in other jurisdictions. You may not be registered to practice law in that jurisdiction, but you can certainly consult as an Australian Law Consultant. As Australasia takes its place on the international stage, particularly in the resources sector, there are many opportunities to travel and live as an expat.

Local Law Firms

As law firms adjust to the current disruption in the marketplace, they are seeking to reduce their overheads. This often means not engaging full time employees in areas of law where they may not be able to support or create full-time work flow. A more flexible solution is to engage a consultant to work with them on specific projects to service their client's needs as and when they arise.

This can be particularly lucrative if you practice a unique or less widely practiced area of law, think Maritime and Aviation Law, Tax Law and Intellectual Property Law.

Corporate Clients

Corporate clients would comprise the largest category of consulting opportunities. Corporate clients are increasingly moving away from full service firms and seeking the 'in-house counsel' experience. They want someone who understands business, or more importantly, who understands ***their*** business. They have reviewed enough contracts to put together a standard document but want a specialist pair of eyes to review and advise. They are savvy enough to negotiate a small acquisition but want someone on their side of the table to manage their risk and due diligence. The board is slipping and they want someone to come in and review board practices and put together a session on governance and director's duties.

As you build a reputation and develop relationships with your clients you may find that you become less a 'consultant' and more an independent in-house counsel and trusted advisor. These types of relationships can be quite lucrative, but more importantly, they are highly rewarding.

An advantage of moving into Corporate Law Consulting is that is can open doors to Governance positions.

Non-Executive Director (NED)

Non-Executive Directors, otherwise known as a NED, is a career option that is perhaps suited to its own section in this Chapter. We have however chosen to include it here in Consulting for two reasons.

Firstly, becoming a NED is often a natural progression from Corporate Consulting, and secondly, while you will have a different title, capacity and responsibilities, NEDs are usually engaged for their capacity to provide consultation on matters within their expertise.

Non-Executive Directors fulfil a very specific role on boards by bringing an independent perspective to the company decision making. They are generally appointed for their expertise and knowledge in specific fields, such as law. You will not be a consultant, but the board will consult you on legal matters.

Multi-disciplinary Consulting

We are certain there are quite a few of you who have chosen to forgo straight up black letter law and undertake a double degree. If you are still wrestling with the choice of which area to specialize in, take heart – you may find yourself in the prized position of being able to combine both your study areas as a multi-disciplinary consultant.

Some combination degrees may offer more opportunity and flexibility than others but you have already carved out your niche expertise before even beginning your career. Whether you have chosen engineering and law, science and law, technology and law or business and law (to name but a few), you can choose to brand yourself as a legal consultant with industry knowledge, or an industry consultant with legal knowledge. Either way, if you position yourself in the market skillfully, you may be able to develop a highly sought after consulting practice.

Alternative Dispute Resolution and Mediation

Mediation is a process that promotes the self-determination of participants and in which participants, with the support of a mediator:

(a) *communicate with each other, exchange information and seek understanding*
(b) *identify, clarify and explore interests, issues and underlying needs*
(c) *consider their alternatives*
(d) *generate and evaluate options*
(e) *negotiate with each other; and*
(f) *reach and make their own decisions.*

A mediator does not evaluate or advise on the merits of, or determine the outcome of, disputes.[4]

Alternative Dispute Resolution ("ADR") and Mediation are becoming increasingly professionalized, not just in areas of Family Law but also within commercial settings where negotiation has failed and parties are seeking to reduce the costs of

[4] National Mediator Accreditation System (NMAS), Clause 2.

litigation and resolve matters more efficiently. Courts have increasing powers to refer parties to mediation[5] and a study by Justice Bergin suggested a settlement rate as high as 46% for matters referred from the New South Wales Supreme Court to mediation over a 3-year period.[6]

Mediation offers some significant benefits to parties involved in disputes. It is comparatively cheaper than litigation and allows the parties to retain some degree of control over the potential outcome, thereby avoiding the uncertainty of a third-party decision. Mediation is conducted with complete confidentiality and undertaken 'without prejudice', that is, whatever allowances are made during the process are not admissible in court.

Mediation is also voluntary, meaning the parties can withdraw at time and agreements are non-binding until such time as they are registered as consent orders with the Court or drafted and executed as an enforceable contract between the parties.

Mediation requires an understanding of complex personal and legal relationships and is fast becoming an essential part of legal practice. Most law schools now include compulsory ADR subjects as part of their course requirements.

Mediators come from all professional backgrounds, from therapists and counsellors, to engineers and of course lawyers.

Being a lawyer and a mediator has some challenges. It requires you, in most situations, to leave your legal hat at the door, refrain from giving legal advice and focus on assisting the parties to reach an agreement.

Being a lawyer however can also offer distinct advantages. Lawyers are trained to quickly identify the issue at the heart of a dispute, evaluate the relevant facts at play and stay focused on the specific problems that need resolution.

The professional standards of conduct, confidentiality and conflicts of interest required of a mediator are well known to lawyers. The National Mediator Accreditation System ("NMAS") is the organization which accredits mediators and sets out the minimum standards of training, conduct and assessment required to comply with the Approval and Practice Standards which are part of the National Mediator Accreditation System.[7]

The NMAS requires that anyone seeking to become a qualified mediator must, '*be of good character and possess appropriate personal qualities and experience to conduct a mediation process independently, competently and professionally*'.[8]

---

[5] Civil Law (Wrongs) Act 2002, section 195(1) (ACT); Civil Procedure Act 1970 (NSW), section 26(1); Supreme Court Rules (NT), section 103 J; Supreme Court Act 1935 (SA), section 65(1); Supreme Court Rules (Vic), Chapter I, Rule 50.07 and Rules of the Supreme Court 1971 (WA), Order 29.2(q) – (ra). 2 See "The Objectives, Scope and Focus of Mediation Legislation in Australia".

[6] "The Objectives, Scope and Focus of Mediation Legislation in Australia", paper delivered by Justice P A Bergin, 11 May 2012, page 14.

[7] https://www.msb.org.au/mediator-standards/national-mediator-accreditation-system-nmas (22/02/2017).

[8] National Mediator Accreditation System (NMAS), Clause 2.1.

To qualify, a mediator must complete a minimum of 38 h training by a mediator sufficiently qualified to be 'coach'[9] followed by an assessment involving, among other things, simulated mediation and observation over a period of time.[10] In order to become an accredited NMAS Mediator, you must complete at least 25 h of mediation and undertake CPD ("Continuing Professional Development") of at least 25 h per year.[11]

The NMAS also sets out minimum practice standards, which include guidelines relating to:

(a) Conducting a preliminary conference or intake
(b) Conducting the mediation meeting
(c) Suspending or terminating mediation
(d) Power and safety of parties
(e) Procedural fairness and impartiality
(f) Ethical conduct and professional relations
(g) Confidentiality

Mediators are held to professional standard as high (if not higher) than lawyers. They must demonstrate competence, integrity and accountability, impartiality including avoiding conflicts of interest.

Mediators are also responsible for ensuring the safety of parties and procedural fairness of the mediation process and comply with their confidentiality and reporting obligations.

Mediation courses are offered through a variety of course providers. When choosing one, make sure you refer to the Mediator Standards Board, the Australian Mediation Association and the Law Society in your State or Territory.

Entrepreneurship

You may have been told throughout your degree and early law career that lawyers do not make good entrepreneurs. Like any career choice there are challenges that may be more suited to some than others, but simply "being a lawyer" does not preclude entrepreneurship.

Many lawyers have launched successful business, Peter Thiel and David Sacks were the co-founder and CEO of PayPal. Both have gone on to engage in other business ventures including Facebook and Yammer. Malcom Turnbull, a lawyer turned politician and founder of OzEmail is the wealthiest Prime Minister in Australian history. Elizabeth Holloway Marsten was a lawyer who went on to develop what we now know as the modern polygraph test, and the list goes on.

[9] ibid at 2.3.

[10] ibid at 2.4.

[11] ibid at 3.

Whether you are studying a double degree in law and business, or a straight up black letter law degree, you are in the process of developing skills and qualities that will serve you well in the world of entrepreneurship.

Tenacity is a common attribute amongst law students. The drive to achieve, which sees you fall down, get up and try again. Every melee with a concept of the exception to the exception of the rule of section 3653 subsection 455 of (insert name of Act here) that makes Leo Tolstoy's War and Peace look like a children's bedtime story, sets you up to be an entrepreneur.

This single-minded obsession that drives you to succeed, when combined with passion for something you believe in, are the ingredients for a successful venture – whether that is within the law, or whether you ultimately discover your passion lies elsewhere.

Resourcefulness. A lawyer who tells their client "we can't do that" may quickly be replaced by a lawyer who can. The best lawyers are those who find a way to meet their client's needs, and entrepreneurs are no different. Often working within a limited framework, financially or otherwise, being resourceful will enable you to find solutions to problems you didn't know you had.

Negotiation Skills. The skills you learn in law school and eventually legal practice will stand you in good stead to negotiate contracts, question assumptions and probe for the information necessary to make the deal, whatever that may be, the best one.

It won't be an easy path, very little that is truly great ever is. Some of the challenges that lawyers face include perfection and risk aversion.

Entrepreneurship is, by its very nature, the practice of taking risks, something that most lawyers are uncomfortable with. Lawyers are also often perfectionists by nature, while entrepreneurship requires you to move quickly, change direction and accept 'good enough', lest you drown in increasing piles of drafts and proposals while your business peters out.

Lawyers who want to become entrepreneurs can enhance their skill set in a variety of ways.

Undertake an MBA, business degree or other commercially focused study. Learning commercial acumen and risk management (as opposed to risk aversion) will strengthen your business perspicacity.

Take a position as in-house counsel. In-house counsel are often required to resolve a broad range of legal issues having regard to their commercial outcomes, rather than purely legal consequences. This practice will leverage the skills you built in law and develop your ability to take risks and make hard decisions.

Going to the Bar

For many students, the only bar they may consider would be the one that serves beer & cocktails. For some of you however, taking the bar (this expression is not all that well known in parts of Australia) may be your ultimate goal.

There are those who suggest that you can take the bar straight out of law school. It is of course possible, but most experienced barristers would recommend working for a few years as a solicitor first. Taking a few years to practice will allow you to find your niche area of law, develop your experience and understanding of the law in practice, as well as learning from mentors in a law firm environment.

This however, is not the only reason… barristers are self-employed. The success of your practice will depend heavily on your connections, relationships and most importantly, your reputation among your colleagues.

Your fellow law students and colleagues during your first few years practicing as a solicitor will become your briefing solicitors when you take the bar.

In addition to a passion for advocacy and a thorough knowledge of your chosen practice area, you should add networking to your list of necessary skills. Stay connected with your friends and fellows from law school, get engaged in young lawyer's societies and participate in events that will build your reputation.

When you are ready to take the leap, you will need to complete the Bar Practice Course and Exams.

Bar Practice Course

The Bar Practice Course and exams will all take a different structure depending on which state you are in, so it is worth visiting the bar Association website for your State.[12]

The Course runs for 4–8 weeks (depending on which state you are in) and each course has different assessment approach. *All* courses are delivered in intensive mode, so be prepared to put every other distraction aside.

The Victorian Bar Practice website provides a good outline of what you can expect during the course:

- *Oral Advocacy, including interactive workshops and mock trials (moots) held in real court rooms.*
- *Written advocacy, including drafting exercised for pleadings, affidavits and outlines of submissions.*
- *Effective communications, including workshops from trained actors and sessions with the Bar's most entertaining and engaging advocates,*

[12] https://www.vicbar.com.au/home
https://www.qldbar.asn.au/
http://www.nswbar.asn.au/
http://www.tasmanianbar.com.au/
https://www.wabar.asn.au/
http://www.sabar.org.au/

- *Forensic decision making, including lectures and workshops on exercising good judgement, reasoning to avoid bad judgement and a session on detecting deception.*
- *Ethics and conduct, including sessions from community organizations and senior barristers who approach topical issues such as direct briefs, risk management and dealing with difficult clients.*
- *Practice development, including advice from expert marketers, clerks, and one-on-one sessions with a business coach.*
- *Court and justice facilities, including excursions to corrections centre and the courts*[13]

Assessment and Admission

As mentioned above, assessment varies from state to state. Victoria for example runs several moots (mock trials) throughout the course which will be assessed on pass/fail basis. Other states run a series of exams, or a single final exam. For more information on the course relevant to your state, please see your bar association website.

Once you have passed your assessment, you will be admitted as a Trainee Barrister, or 'Reader', for 12 months. This will often be referred to as your 'reading year'. You will be assigned a senior Barrister to be your tutor whose role it will be to ensure that obtain the maximum benefit of your reading year.

Chambers

The first 1–2 years as a barrister can be a financial challenge. Not only must you pay for the Bar Practice Course and exam, but you will also need to pay for your professional indemnity insurance, practicing certificate and Bar Associations Fees. On top of those immediate outgoings, you will also need to rent Chambers.

Chambers are essentially a series of offices for Barristers, preferably close the to the Courthouse.

It is possible to work from home as a newly minter Barrister, especially if you already have substantial support network and potential briefing solicitors. You may however find that a significant portion of your first briefs will come by way of referral from other Barristers in your Chambers. More importantly, if you are working

[13] https://www.vicbar.com.au/about-us/how-to-become-a-barrister/readers146-course (8 March 2017).

from home, you will miss the significant benefit of contact and coaching with your Tutor, not to mention travel time lost between your home and the Court.

Some Chambers will have a Readers Room available for free or for a significantly reduced fee. Other options for newly minted barristers are to share rooms. This is a very popular option for Readers, but will require the consent of the floor. Also with consent of the floor, you may 'float' from one vacant office to the next. Going on circuit to the suburban courts is also a popular option, particularly if you have an interest in criminal law.

Pay Day

It is important to remember, that while you are sitting the Bar Practice Course you are not being paid. You may also not get a paying brief on your first day off the starting block.

You should ensure that you have financial reserves to support yourself and pay your practice expenses for at least the first 6–12 months of practice.

Get Started Now

Taking the bar, for most barristers, not something you stumble upon, it is a calling.

For those of you who head the call, it's never too early to get started. Get networking and start building up your advocacy skills.

While you are still at university, you should seek out moot courts and participate in advocacy events.

Approach your local Bar Association and attend some information evenings and events for students. There are sometimes opportunities to volunteer as a 'witness' for the mock trials during the bar practice course.

Judges Associateship

A very beneficial early career move for aspiring Barristers is a Judges Associateship. An associateship tends to be a 1 year contract acting as a Judges Assistant, although they are sometimes extended by a year.

The definition of Judges Associate is an elusive one and it is often said that no two Associates have the same experience. This is due in part to the nature of the different Courts. The role of an Associate in the Family Court is significantly different than perhaps an Associate at the Federal Court or the Administrative Appeals Tribunal.

The other reason is that the role involves a close working relationship between the Judge and Associate and each relationship will be unique. Each Judge will have a different way of managing their work, drafting, researching, and as an Associate, your role is to be both a personal and professional confidential aide. Your duties could include (but are not limited to):

- Legal research
- Liaising with court staff, legal representatives, members of the public, professional associations, media and other government bodies.
- Administration, including filing, recording of orders, listing matters, proofreading, custody of files and any other court matters.

Associateships provide unique and in depth insight into the Court, its processes and procedures. You will gain a fundamental understanding of relationships, both with the Judges, as well as legal representatives, and you will get first class seats to advocacy in action.

The Law Council of Australia publishes a guide for Judges Associateships every year. It covers a wide range of crucial information including which Judges in the High Court have vacancies, how to apply including addresses and email addresses, tips and hints for preparing your application and how to address Judges.

It also has some invaluable pieces written by current Associates, busting myths about what they do and offering a window view into the life of Associate.

Public Service & Politics

Public Service positions are often forgotten in the race to the top corporate law firms, perhaps due in part to misconception among law students that the best and brightest end up in Top Tier Corporate Firms, with a 'filter down' effect which ends with public service roles. This could not be further from the truth.

9.6% of solicitors work in government roles[14] and there are many incredibly talented public service lawyers and high profile lawyers in leadership positions. Candidate selection criteria to secure most roles can be incredibly tight. A career in the public service can be fulfilling and rewarding, particularly if you are passionate about the role the organization plays.

Public Service positions can also lead to political careers. Almost half of Australia's Prime Ministers have been lawyers, Sir William McMahon, Harold Holt, Sir Robert Menzies, Gough Whitlam, Bob Hawke, John Howard, Tony Abbot, Julia Gillard and Malcom Turnbull to name a few. A significant number of cabinet ministers also have legal backgrounds.

There is no clear path from law school to Prime Minister. Each person who has held the office has taken a different course, but one thing they all have in common

[14] Law Society of New South Wales, *2014 Law Society National Profile, Final Report*, April 2015.

is that they have followed their passion, served in a variety of public service roles and engaged in politics early in their career.

Every arm of the government has some need for a lawyer – some more than others. You can specialize in anything from Environment Law, Health, Education, Immigration, Public Safety, Corporate Law, Transport Law, National Defence and Criminal Law. The possibilities are endless. *Do* choose something you are passionate about. Taking on a role with the finance regulator APRA may ultimately be soul destroying if you are not passionate or remotely interested in banking and finance legislation (they exist – truly they do!).

So, join the Young Liberal/Labor/Greens party (or establish your own independent party, like former South Australian lawyer, Nick Xenophon has), and while you are waiting the Top Job, there are plenty of rewarding Public Service positions available for talented passionate lawyers.

Starting Your Own Law Firm

Many a young lawyer has dreamt of hanging out a shingle and building their own practice, but starting a law firm is not for the faint hearted.

You will need to create a robust business plan and have sufficient financial backing to get you from start-up to cash flow.

While the industry is continuously working towards a national body to regulate the legal profession we are not there yet and the rules will vary from state to state. The relevant Law Society for each state all have extensive "How-to" guides.

Before you can hang your shingle, you will need to complete the practice requirements, including the Practice Management Course and obtaining a Principle Practicing Certificate.

Practice Management Course

Every state will also require you to complete a practice management course. Practice management courses can be done directly through your Law Society, or through private education institutions such as the College of Law or FMRC.

Principal Practicing Certificate

Before you even consider starting your own practice, you will need to meet the minimum requirements of being a sole practitioner or principal.

Depending on your admission path, and the State in which you practice, this can vary from 1 to 2 years.

Section 49(1) of the Legal Profession Uniform Law (NSW) provides that it is a statutory condition of an Australian practicing certificate granted in New South Wales that the holder must in New South Wales engage in supervised legal practice only, until the holder has completed;

(a) *if the holder completed practical legal training principally under the supervision of an Australian lawyer to qualify for admission to the Australian legal profession-a period or periods equivalent to 18 months of supervised legal practice; or*
(b) *if the holder completed other practical legal training to qualify for admission to the Australian legal profession-a period or periods equivalent to 2 years of supervised legal practice. If you completed a practical legal*

Once you have, or can, complete the practice requirements you will need to consider everything related to running a practice, from creating a business plan and budgeting for chairs to professional indemnity insurance and failsafe policies and procedures relating to document management and client correspondence.

Structure of Your Practice

There are several structures available to operate your practice, depending on the number of principle practitioners (partners) and how you would like your assets protected.

(a) **Sole Practitioner**

Simplest structure with lowest overheads offering full control, and therefore responsibility, for the practice.

(b) **Partnership**

Two or more principle practitioners who share resources, experience and spread responsibilities and liability.

(c) **Incorporated Legal Practices** must have at least one principle legal practitioner who is a director of the practice. ILP's have additional legislative requirements under the Corporations Act 2001 (Cth) and the Legal Professional Rules in your state, including notice requirements. Although the regulatory requirements are more burdensome, they offer protection of assets, greater flexibility for capital raising and some tax advantages.

(d) **Multi-Disciplinary Practice**

Must have at least one principle legal practitioner partner and at least one non-legal partner. MDPs also have regulatory notice requirements and can give rise to ethical and commercial conflicts of interest

Each option requires you make sure the relevant documents are in pace. Partnership Agreements, Constitution, Shareholders Agreements etc.

Funding

Funding for law practices vary depending on your chosen structure. If you are establishing a partnership, this usually consists of partner equity loans.

Incorporated Legal Practices may seek external funding in the source of bank loans and lines of credit. You should seek advice from your accountant when deciding on the structure and financing of your practice.

Your cash flow will be one of the most important factors in setting up a new business. You should have very carefully calculated how long you can support the practice without a client. It is also essential to factor the time between your first client engagement and cash in the bank.

You must have a system (or accountant/bookkeeper) to ensure that you have a clear ongoing snapshot of your practice cash-flow.

Registration

Once you have drafted your business plan and established your structure you will need to register your business.

Firstly, with the Law Society. Each state has different requirements, but all of them require notices to be provided to the Law Society indicating your intention to set up your own practice and complying with all the requirements of the Act of in your State.

You must also register your business with Australian Securities and Investment Commission ('ASIC') and obtain an Australian Company Number ('ACN').

You will need to register with the Australian Taxation Office ('ATO') and obtain an ABN for GST purposes. If you have staff you will need to register for payroll tax and set up superannuation.

You will also need to have compliance processes in place to ensure that you meet all the requirements of each organization.

Finally, you will need to register any trademarks and trading names.

Insurance

Insurance will be one of the biggest expenses of your legal practice. At a bare minimum, you will be required to hold the legislated level of professional indemnity insurance through your Law Society.

Review your insurance carefully and buy private top-up insurance through private insurers for extra protection.

Depending on the size, structure and location of your practice, as well as your personal circumstances, you may also need additional insurances.

- Life and disability insurance can be particularly important if you are supporting a family.
- If you have employees you will need to have a workers compensation insurance policy.
- If you invite clients into your office or property you may need to consider Public Liability Insurance.
- Building Insurance
- Loss of Profit Insurance can offer protection for loss of profit, staff wages and even an alternative office if your property is damaged.
- Trade debtor insurance for protection against bad debts
- If you have established an ILP or MDP, consider Directors and Officers insurance.

Risk Management

Your insurance will take some of the risk out of running you firm, but there are some risks you simply cannot insure and you should undertake a complete and thorough risk assessment of the issues that may affect you and your business. That is not to say that we give up because you find (and you *will* find) that the risks are great and many. Most lawyers are by nature risk averse, but the key to Risk is to management, and we cannot manage something we have not identified.

Here are a few of the most significant risks faced in every business, but you should consider every single aspect of your practice:

- Financial Risk including cash flow, bad debts, no clients.
- Regulatory Risk – how will you respond to changes in the legislation? How to you monitor your requirements?
- Security risk, including hard copy and electronic files, accounting records and valuable documents?
- Employee risk? Will you take on employees? How will you manage loss of key employees? How will you manage workplace health and safety conditions? How will you manage performance concerns?
- Potential threats to your working environment, through development, fire flood?

Bank Accounts

Setting up your business bank account can be straight forward process, particularly if you have liquid assets to support you. If however you require a line of credit or loan to establish your practice, you will also need to have a water tight business plan and collateral to secure the loan, remembering that there are restrictions on borrowing for some practice structures.

Depending on which area of law you are planning to practice, you may need a trust account. Trust accounts are necessary if you are practicing conveyancing law as you will need to hold deposit and purchase funds on behalf of your clients, and even other parties. If you practice in Wills and Estates you will need a trust account. As a general rule, Family law firms will also operate a trust account to isolate funds per agreement between the parties or on the Order of the Court.

Trust Accounts come with a distinct and very strict set of rules. You must complete the training course on Trust Accounting, register your trust account with the Law Society, comply strictly with the requirements of holding funds in trust and engage an Auditor to audit your Trust transactions annually.

Failure to comply with the law relating to trust accounts has very serious consequences. Negligence or recklessness will result in loss of your practitioner's license and fraud or dishonesty can have criminal consequences.

Premises

One of the biggest decisions you make will be your premises. The last few years has seen a significant shift in the legal industry, with clients demanding better value for money and technology changing the way we interact with our clients.

It is becoming less necessary to have an office on the 'high street' so to speak, but exercise caution: the physical location of your office, if indeed you have one, will influence the clients you attract. If you are planning on practicing commercial and corporate law, you may need to be where the clients are, that is, in the city. If, however you want to practice personal law such as wills and estates, conveyancing and small business related matters then a suburban office or a shingle on your garden gate may be sufficient.

Whatever you choose you will need to invest in the premises, whether that be a corporate office or a comfortable well lit room in your home to welcome clients.

You will also have to consider safe custody documents. Last Will and Testaments, passports in Family Court matters, cheques, money orders and other documents with cash value, guarantees, loan documents, and other original and/or irreplaceable documents with inherent value to your client are all examples of things you may be asked to hold in safe custody. Not all firms offer this service due in part to the nature of their service but also due to the cost of buying a fireproof safe.

Marketing & Business Development

As with any business, your marketing and business development strategy will form one of the most important aspects of starting your own legal practice. You may you spend just as much, if not more, time building your practice than practicing law – especially in the early years.

One of your first steps will be to build your personal brand. Become the expert in your chosen area of law and carve out your niche.

If you are a one-person firm, building alliances and corporative practices with other firms in which you can refer business can significantly strengthen your position.

A website alone is not enough to generate new business. You will need to be creative to reach potential clients, build rapport and trust.

An effective marketing strategy should include several key steps:

1. Identify your clients. Are they corporate? Private? Community or social organizations?
2. What is the best medium to reach those clients? Traditional advertising like radio and newspapers? Podcasts and blogs? Corporate networking events?
3. What are you trying to communicate? Raise awareness, get referrals?
4. Create the message. Prepare the contents structure and format. Be clear and concise.
5. Measure the results. Has your marketing campaign generated new clients or opportunities?
6. Rinse and repeat.

Managing Your Practice

It is one thing to set up a practice, but you need to be diligent about its ongoing management and processes, for everything from file notes and client communication to billing and continuing professional development for both you and your staff.

When it comes to running a law practice, the devil is often in the detail. Your practice will be audited by an assessor to ensure that it is organized, structured, and complies with all requirements of the Law Society (and your insurers!). Let's take file notes for example. You have a telephone conversation with a client: – Are your files notes legible and do they make sense? Are they stored within the file? Does it record the date, time and duration of the call? Does it accurately record who you spoke to and what about? Does it contain a record of page numbers?

Under the heading Managing your practice comes, Billing. Like everything else in your practice, there are rules relating to your billing practices. Most of this will be covered when you complete the Practice Management Course. Each Law Society has also published a Guide to Costs and Billing.

Your firm should have a billing policy that includes, among other things: -

(a) How you calculate estimates;
(b) Whether you receive money on account;
(c) Whether you bill for work in progress or on completion of the matter; and
(d) How the invoices are itemized so that the client understands precisely what the charges are.

Conflicts of Interest

You will need to ensure that your practice has a policy on identifying and managing conflicts of interest. This includes a current register of clients that is accessible to all lawyers and a process that ensure conflict checks are undertaken prior to confirming instructions to your client.

It is essential that all staff are trained in recognizing a conflict and understand clearly what process must be followed if you do identify a conflict.

Managing Your Matters

Before you take on any new matter, you should satisfy yourself that you are not working outside your area of expertise. Family Law for example is a very specialized area of law. A complicated divorce and child care arrangement is perhaps not the best matter for a seasoned Banking and Finance Lawyer. Similarly, if you are a Family Lawyer you may wish to decline providing litigation advice on a trademark infringement. This is where alliances and referrals become a key business development strategy! On this note, it is also important to ensure that your professional indemnity insurance covers you for the areas of law you intend to practice, and that you don't practice outside the scope of your insurance.

Managing your matters entails that you have appropriate diary systems in place to record and remind you of all deadlines, limitation periods, cooling off periods, court dates, conferences, file reviews, settlements and any other meeting or event relating to the matter.

You should implement a policy to ensure draft documents are checked before being provided to your client and particularly any other party.

You must keep up to date and accurate files for each matter and a have a clear process for document management. Files should be regularly and systematically reviewed and kept for a minimum of 7 years.

When a matter is closed, the client should be informed in writing including any future actions that may need to be taken by the client.

Managing Your Clients

Communication with your clients is the most essential key to a successful practice and the best way to prevent malpractice claims. Win-Win!

You should always start a new matter by confirming the client's instructions and making a record of what their expectations are in the matter. You should provide your client with an outline of the process or necessary steps required to be undertaken and continue to communicate with them throughout the process.

Lawyers running their own practice need to be versed in more than just the law. You should be skilled in providing an empathetic explanation and professional advice in the legal matter at hand. You will need to be skilled at responding to complaints, and astute enough to review and follow through on all 'near misses' that occur in your practice.

Work Environment

A law degree is a great foundational skill set to have whether you are embarking on a career in law or commerce. Many lawyers upon graduating will follow the usual course of action and start applying to law firms. This is often a very competitive process with hundreds of graduates applying for a limited number of opportunities available to join law firms. It can be a good place to start your career as law firms usually provide excellent continuing professional development and are a great training ground to learn from more experienced lawyers. They also give you exposure to a wide variety of clients which helps to expand your knowledge in a given area of law. However over the past 5–6 years law firms have started to reduce the number of graduate positions available as a result of a non-buoyant economy. They are now running leaner and taking a more conservative approach to recruiting staff. It is therefore good to know that there are a range of other career options available to graduate lawyers to follow to help launch their career other than this traditional path.

Another aspect to consider when deciding which career path to take includes thinking about what you actually enjoy doing. If you can stop and think about this at the start of your career rather than going into the area that you think might pay a better salary or because it's perceived as being more interesting, it may save you reinventing yourself in years to come. You spend a lot of time at work, and people perform better when they are happy in their job. A legal career offers many options so it is worth speaking with a number of people in various legal positions to gain some insights into what their role involves on a daily basis and to see whether you would find that job rewarding. Sometimes approaching people to have these types of career conversations can actually lead to a job opportunity as it increases your network and demonstrates your interest in what they do. You may enjoy researching and solving problems, or you may be more of a 'people person' and enjoy speaking to and potentially providing advice to people, or are you competitive and enjoy a good argument in which case litigation may be for you. If you are very black and white about things, and like everything to be 100% accurate compliance might be for you. You spend a lot of time at work so it's worth reflecting on which areas of your studies you have enjoyed the most, and potentially excelled at, as that is usually a good indication as to which career path to follow. There are a range of personality profiling tests available through career consultancies which may help you identify the type of job that will best suit you, and the type of environment.

Outlined in the pages that follow are a range of career paths open to lawyers either at the start of your career, or to consider branching into later on in your career.

Government – Federal and State

There are three levels of government in Australia: Federal, State and Local Government. Most legal opportunities exist within the Federal and State Government (otherwise known as the public sector) so that's what we will cover in this section.

The Federal Government comprises both Australian Public Service (APS) agencies and non-APS agencies. The APS refers to Australian Government departments and agencies where staff members are employed under the Public Service Act 1999. Australian Government agencies usually advertise graduate employment opportunities between February and June each year.

The APS provides the support the Government needs to undertake its roles and responsibilities. It does this by providing policy advice and managing and facilitating the delivery of programs, enforcing regulations and providing services agreed by the government. The APS consists of a large number of organisations that provide information, services and support to almost every part of Australian life. Government departments form a large part of the workforce and are one of the largest employers. Opportunities within Government can offer interesting career opportunities as the scope of services is usually fairly broad and there is always change occurring.

Some of the Government Departments offering legal careers include:

Government Regulators and Policy:

- The Australian Competition and Consumer Commission
- Australian Human Rights Commission
- Australian Prudential Regulation Authority
- Australian Securities and Investment Commission
- Department of Attorney-General and Justice
- Department of Prime Minister and Cabinet
- Fair Work Ombudsmen
- The Law Reform Commission
- Reserve Bank of Australia
- Productivity Commission
- Public Defenders Office

- Various Ombudsmen Offices

Justice, Prosecution and Associateships:

- Judge's Associate
- High Court of Australia
- Federal Courts and Supreme Courts
- Australian Government Solicitor
- Administrative Appeals Tribunal
- Office of Parliamentary Council
- Department of Public Prosecution

Law Reform and Social Justice:

- Community Legal Centres
- Law Internships
- Australian Law Reform Commission
- Aboriginal Legal Service
- Public Interest Advocacy Service

There are lots of career paths you can pursue within the government, or the public sector. The Government sector can give you exposure to a wide range of legal issues providing you with transferable skills which can be attractive in the private sector if you choose to make a move later in your career. For example, if you work in an agency developing policies impacting the community, your experience could easily translate into a non for profit organisation operating in the human services space. Roles within Government can be focussed on litigation, legislative interpretation, investigation, implementation, advisory, policy making, legal compliance and regulatory enforcement.

All agencies require legal staff for their operation, and qualified professionals are in high demand. Legal staff provide advice, prepare and draft legal documents, conduct negotiations, plead cases in court and tribunals, hear legal and other matters in court and tribunals, and interpret, analyse, administer and review the law.

Some of the benefits of working in the Australian Public Service include:

- diversity of work
- flexible work practices and conditions
- multiple career paths
- relative job security.

There is an extensive range of work on offer either within the personal human rights arena: Family Law, Criminal Law, Child Support, Migration Law and General Civil Law and outreach services (Court & Tribunal work), at the Civil and Administrative Tribunal, the Administrative Appeals Tribunal, the Youth Court, Family Court and the criminal divisions of the Magistrates, District and Supreme Courts in South Australia.

Another starting point for many graduates is to commence as Judge's Associate which allows you to get some experience on your resume and then move across into other areas within the public sector. By being employed in the public sector, you are then eligible to apply for other positions which are only open to Government Employees. A Judge's Associate will generally act as some combination of personal assistant, research assistant and/or Court assistant to a specific Judge.

Judge's Associate positions are very rewarding and highly sought after, and offer a considerable amount of variety. The exact responsibilities will vary from Judge to Judge, however typically they become very familiar with court documents, proceedings, processes and procedures which can be an attractive background when applying for your next position.

Non for Profit

Non for Profit organisations exist to provide services to their clients, who can often include the vulnerable or minority groups in the community. They generate income, and receive funding, to enable them to provide services to, or provide support to, their clients at a subsidised rate. They don't exist to earn a financial profit to benefit the owners or shareholders. As such they can have complex structures and need to be compliant with a range of laws and regulations around legal, operating and reporting models which can make it necessary to have an in-house lawyer. This sector can also be subject to considerable policy or legislative changes and in the current market, they are becoming increasingly impacted by competition which can activate merger and acquisition activity.

The Non for Profit sector can to be a great way to find a career that aligns with your values and interests and typically attracts people who are passionate about the cause or mission of the organisation. These roles will mainly take on an advisory compliance function. With many non for profit organisations also representing minority groups across different sectors such as aged care and disability services, they often take on an advocacy role for the sector they represent and make recommendations for policy changes.

International opportunities also exist within the non for profit sector with organisations such as Amnesty International, The Australian Delegation to the United Nations, The Human Rights Watch, International Fund for Agricultural Development, UN High Commission for Refugees to name a few. Therefore working in the non for profit sector can give you international experience which is quite unique.

As non for profits are usually run on very strict budgets they look to employ people who are versatile and happy to do more purely what's on their job description. They will employ fewer staff with broader skill sets. This can give you a great deal of job satisfaction because you are contributing to a worthwhile cause.

It is perceived that jobs within the non for profit sector don't pay as well as within the commercial sector however there are tax and salary sacrificing opportunities which can elevate the net worth to the individual to bring it close to commercial market rates. Quite often though people tend to work in this sector because they want to make a difference or give back to the community rather than being attracted to it for high paying roles.

Private Practice

The decision to enter into private practice remains a carer pathway that is full of opportunity. Prior to the GFC (global financial crisis) employment rates were far higher than they are now but interestingly the quality of the experience that an entry level lawyer receives now is higher and more engaging. No longer are there groups of 15–20 clerks sharing the work but more like 5–10, allowing each graduate more exposure to the spread of issues, processes and legal and commercial considerations that come into play when providing legal advice to a client.

This will be the most likely career path many graduates start to look at prior to graduating, which makes it a highly competitive process to secure a position, and the application process is quite ruthless. How do you stand out from the crowd? Certainly strong academic results are a good place to start, however firms are recruiting more laterally these days to ensure they also get the right cultural fit for their firm. Some of the other factors you might like to consider including in your resume are certainly your sporting commitments as this demonstrates teamwork and possibly a competitive drive. Any part time jobs you have had during your studies. They don't have to be related to law, but what it tells an employer is that you can manage your time effectively between study and work, that you are motivated and that you've had experience following instructions. If you have interests in social media that may be another skill that could be adapted to marketing activities. As well as indicating a potential skill set which may be beneficial to the firm, it goes towards your character which can help determine cultural fit.

Many graduates will start by sending through an application consisting of a letter, resume and their academics and wait to see if they hear anything. So what can you do differently to the majority?

From talking to the Human Resource Managers who handle the graduate intake process it is impressive if a graduate has made a call to the firm to introduce themselves and find out what they look for when recruiting graduates, and get the details of their process and what's required. A few weeks after you have submitted an application, if you've not heard anything, it is a good idea to follow up with a phone call and check at what stage the process is up to and the timeframe until you hear whether you have secured an interview or not. If you are unsuccessful, it is worth phoning up to ask for some feedback to see what you could have done differently. Once the process has been completed, it is still a good idea to stay in touch with the Human Resources Manager from time to time (say every 3 months) to see if there are any other opportunities due to become available. Timing can be everything. This also demonstrates an interest in working for that firm and demonstrates your enthusiasm and determination. It will also be beneficial to set your profile up on LinkedIn with a professional photo, as many recruiters will look at your online profile.

The law firm of today is not the law firm of the future. Future career paths are not known, the linear career path is no longer what many lawyers seek. Partnership is not the driver for many who are in private practice. Some law firms don't accept this, others embrace it as there have always been bottlenecks for people trying to progress to partner level.

Roles within law firms are typically broken down into areas of specialisation such as corporate law, civil law, environmental law, employment law, insurance law, tax law, family law and criminal law. Lawyers spend a great deal of time on research and paperwork for specific cases or providing advice to clients. They draft legal documents, offer legal advice, facilitate meetings and negotiations and represent clients in court. When you work within a law firm you are required to keep account of your time in 6 min units so that clients can be billed accurately. As you progress in a law firm there are also obligations to meet a budget that is allocated to you based on your salary and hourly rate.

Many law firms employ new law school graduates as law clerks. The legal field also provides careers in legal support, court clerks and administrators, jury consultants and many other roles. Law firms start by offering summer clerkship positions and it's the perfect opportunity to understand how a commercial law firm operates and may be the stepping stone into a graduate position. Clerkships are paid 4 week placements over December, January and February. It will depend on the size of the firm as to how many positions they offer, usually medium to large firms will offer 6 students 4 week blocks. Depending on the performance of summer clerks, many firms offer graduate positions at the end of the clerkship, however there might only be 1 or 2 graduate positions available.

In terms of variety of work, while the clerkships certainly focus on ensuring variety and movement between practice groups, a graduate position will generally be placed in a specific team as that will be where the requirement is. This would be the case with most small-to-medium firms, as generally speaking these sized firms are not of a size to accommodate formal graduate programs and the rotation of graduates.

In relation to the recruitment process for clerkships /graduate positions, law firms look at a range of criteria including:

- Personal fit
- Academic results
- Other qualifications, in particular a second degree and the relevance of that degree
- Work experience, other legal experience, involvement in extracurricular activity at university (such as the student councils).

While it is fair to say that for many years commerce was the most relevant second degree for graduates seeking to work in a commercial law firm, that is certainly no longer the case. Firms are very keen to talk to candidates with qualifications in computer science, medical science, engineering, IP etc. The interest in second degrees that are a bit "outside the square" is still increasing. Even beyond study, some people of course have work experience outside commercial business and that too is relevant.

Career progression in most law firms is still pretty traditional. Graduates enter as a law clerk pre-admission, then Graduate, Lawyer, Associate, Senior Associate, Special Counsel, Partner. The research however supports that graduates are not necessarily looking along that complete path when taking a graduate position. It certainly used to be the case that every Lawyer wanted some day to be a Partner. That is no longer the case.

Working in a law firm offers considerable variety and exposure into a range of organisations which helps you build both depth and breadth of experience. There are also law firms recognising that some practitioners prefer to remain delivering the law and not progress into partnership where there are leadership and business development responsibilities. In some law firms new structures are forming where those with leadership and business development skills are identified and progressed into managerial roles and those are have strong technical expertise don't step into the traditional leadership role. Entry level lawyers in some firms are now provided the opportunity to work directly with business development on client strategies including client attraction, retention, thought leadership, social media and event design. Professional development opportunities extend to supported volunteering, advocacy positions and roles on committees and boards which in years gone by were held for those above Senior Associate level. From day one firms want to know what else interests you and how can they use those skills to engage you.

It is always advisable that if there is any chance you will, at some point in your career, wish to seek a career in private practice, you should do your Graduate Diploma in Legal Practice (GDLP), undertake clerkships and go directly to private practice. It is very difficult to come back in to private practice otherwise. Having said that, if unsuccessful in securing a graduate role in private practice, it is advisable to apply to government agencies and be prepared to move. It is quite commonly acknowledged in private practice that the training and structure provided in government (particularly Commonwealth) is highly regarded. So to do a 1–2 year government internship is probably the next best thing to private practice.

In terms of professional development, it is considered that private practice can often provide a very thorough program comprised of internal sessions (both technical and soft skills) and external continuing legal education through the Law Society and other providers. Law firms are also supportive of post graduate study and financially support lawyers with their Masters of Law, and also industry specific post graduate qualifications.

There are several areas to choose from within private practice. It is part of a lawyer's job to be a representative and advisor for businesses and individuals on legal issues and matters. It is their job to know the law and be able to research current laws, rules and regulations in order to support their client's case. Within larger law firms positions will tend to specialise in the following areas: corporate/commercial advisory, commercial litigation, insurance law, property law, tax law. Criminal and Family law firms typically sit separately from commercial firms.

At a small firm, the environment may be much different than at a larger firm. The practice may be more general overall and the firm may not have a formal training program. Instead, new graduates are likely to have more client contact and more hands-on experience from the start. Some small firms are classified as 'boutique' and focus on one specific area of law. Smaller firms quite often have fewer resources compared to larger firms that may offer a law library and paralegals to assist with research. The benefit of working for a smaller firm is that you typically gain wide ranging, hands on experience a lot faster.

Working in private practice also offers the opportunity to undertake secondments into a client's workplace. This is a great opportunity to broaden your experience and see whether you enjoy working in-house. If not, it will certainly enhance your ability to relate to clients once the secondment has finished and you are back in private practice. It gives you a real insight into how legal provides advice to all areas of a business, working in partnership with them to achieve the organisation's strategic objectives.

Starting in private practice does also give you the opportunity further in your career to open your own practice or partnership. Once you have built a reputation in the marketplace and are starting to get business referred to you, you may feel that you want the autonomy of operating your own practice.

Corporate or In House

The Corporate, or private sector, offers many career opportunities and these positions can often enable you to gain breadth of experience, as opposed to working in a law firm where you gain depth of experience in an area of specialisation. Private practice tends to see you focus on law alone, whereas in an in-house role you get to draw upon your legal competency, and also learn about the key drivers behind the business. Companies experience a range of commercial transactions which gives a lawyer a wide range of experience. It is not uncommon for a lawyer working in private practice to be recruited by one of their clients as they have developed knowledge of their business. One of the key differences working in house is that you get to truly partner with the business gaining a deeper understanding of what the business wants to achieve and see a process through from start to finish, rather than giving advice to an organisation and then moving onto the next client.

1. Legal counsel/In House Lawyer

Lawyers may be employed within a company or business to analyse legal issues, provide legal advice on transactions and business decisions and recommend internal policies and practices. Lawyers also have a strong focus on risk management and can save organisations thousands of dollars by identifying mistakes before they are made. Lawyers in private companies handle activities such as transferring properties, company mergers, setting up company structures, reporting and corporate taxation issues. Companies, such as financial institutions, are regularly impacted by legislative changes and need to review their terms and conditions and documentation to remain compliant which often drives the need for them to have an in-house lawyer with specialised expertise. With an increase in start up and smaller companies who look for investors, there are also opportunities within venture capital companies who source and then invest in these companies, and then oversee their performance. These type of investment companies also employer lawyers with a commercial knowledge.

These are highly sought after positions, working within a company as they offer the opportunity to advise an organisation on legal issues and to have full involvement and responsibility for managing a legal matter. These roles are mainly focussed on commercial advisory activities and then brief out to external solicitors when it comes to litigious work, however in house lawyers would be involved in research and preparation. As these roles mainly exist within larger organisations, and typically within the head office of a company, these positions are more available in the Eastern states. As they provide a lot of career satisfaction people don't frequently vacate these roles which means that opportunities don't arise as frequently as in other sectors.

2. Commercial Management/Contract Management

Commercial Management positions perform different tasks in different organisations, however typically they either call for a legal or accounting background as the foundational skill set. If they are open to a legal background then the role will primarily be involved in drawing up and reviewing commercial contracts. A more junior solicitor may commence in a contract management role and then progress into a more senior commercial management position which could encompass broader functions than pure legal responsibilities. These positions can provide a good career transition out of a straight legal role and can expand to take on an advisory role supporting commercial transactions within the company. Quite often Commercial Management can be a stepping stone into General Management or to become a Chief Executive Officer (CEO) of an organisation.

3. Industrial Relations specialist

Industrial relations expertise is sought by organisations who are seeking advice to avoid industrial action when making decisions impacting staffing, or organisational restructuring or in their dealings with unions, hence it can take on an advisory role. Otherwise an organisation may find itself seeking representation from an external specialist IR consultant if they are on the receiving end of an industrial claim from a staff member, in which case the role takes on a litigious focus.

This skill set can be combined within a Human Resources role in an organisation although as this field is becoming increasingly complex, and requiring a specialist skill set, companies seem to gain external specialist expertise. This area lends itself well to setting up an independent consulting practice and assisting a range of organisations when they require assistance.

4. Pathway to Corporate Services

Corporate Services is an area within an organisation which provides a range of support services across the business including finance, legal, IT, Human Resources and administration. These positions can have a strong focus on negotiating, drafting and managing contracts with external service providers, as well as taking on the drawing up employment contracts for staff.

5. Governance and compliance and Company Secretarial
   If you work for a publicly listed company there are considerable statutory reporting obligations to adhere to. The company is also responsible to it's shareholders and needs to have a high degree of transparency with it's reporting and decision making. These roles quite often have more of a compliance focus ensuring that the company is meeting these obligations, and also sits on the Board of the company to ensure corporate governance.

6. Insurance Companies
   Insurance companies employ high numbers of lawyers to manage claims, handle disputes, provide advice to companies and individuals and undertake litigation. So if you enjoy the field of insurance law this could certainly be a career option.

7. Insolvency and Litigation Support
   Specialist firms exist to undertake a range of forensic investigations to identify what has lead an organisation into bankruptcy and is part of the commercial litigation process. These firms employ both accountants and lawyers.

8. Board Appointments
   Later on in your career, once you have gained experience, there is the option to get involved with an organisation at Board level. Legal expertise is highly sought on Boards. Boards provide the strategic oversight to an organisation and ensure governance and having legal experience on a Board can also provide good risk management.

Work Type

Whether you look for full time, part time or casual/contract work depends on a number of factors, both personal and market based. You might look for contract or casual work to gain some work experience while you are completing your studies or to rapidly build a wide range of experience by working for a number of different organisations. It can also give you insights into which sector you would most enjoy working in. There may also be times in the market when there are very limited permanent opportunities available and you might need to take a contract until the market picks up. The more flexible you are around what type of opportunities you consider, the more opportunities for employment there will be for you.

Full Time Employment

Legal professionals typically work Mondays to Fridays during regular business hours however you may need to work additional hours researching and preparing for cases in order to meet deadlines. Typical working hours are 8.30 am to 5.30 pm with up to an hour for lunch however working in most environments, especially in private practice and the private sector, there is the need to be flexible depending on workload.

It is not uncommon for employment contracts to be for a 12 month renewable term which means that your job is renewed each 12 months. Most positions however are offered on a full time permanent basis which offers a higher level of job security. Organisations, especially law firms, can be impacted by economic conditions and in recent years we have seen many law firms downsizing their employee numbers but the current trend does seem to indicate that they are re-employing.

Part Time Employment

As it is very competitive for graduates to seek employment once they have graduated you may have a competitive advantage if you work and study part time during your last year. It's less of a financial investment for organisations to employ someone on a part time basis and it may position you well to move into a permanent role once you've graduated. It may mean that you have to spread your study out over a slightly extended period, however you will then be well positioned to transition your career from part time to full time within your current place of employment, or be a competitive applicant in the marketplace against other graduates without experience.

Part time opportunities work well when there is back up support in the office when the person isn't at work, for example, when you are part of a larger team. Job sharing can also work well, this is where two people work part time in the same job ie. one works Monday and Tuesday, and the other person works Wednesday, Thursday and Friday. These are rare opportunities and require strong communication between the two individuals job sharing and a willing employer. It also requires seemless communication with people within the organisation and with clients. The benefits to an employer is that if they employ well, they get two very motivated employees with different skills and knowledge for the price of one salary.

To make part time employment work well, you need to be highly organised so that you maximise your time, and therefore your output, at work. If there is urgent work that cannot wait until you are next back in the office, you will need to enlist the support of others, and there is a strong need to communicate expectations to others around timeframes for delivery of work.

Casual or Contract Employment

An interesting option to consider is casual or contract work. Taking on some casual work will help to give you experience and build your resume. It is a good way to get your foot in the door to a firm or an organisation as quite often contract roles can lead to a permanent position, so you could be in the right place at the right time. It's like a working interview, you have the opportunity to prove yourself on the job and it gives both parties a chance to 'try before you buy'. It can often lead to a longer term career path with that organisation because you have had an opportunity to ensure it is the right cultural fit before you commit.

With tighter recruitment budgets today, many organisations look to increase headcount by taking on lawyers on a contract basis. Law firms are slowly following suit. Contracts can be extended or made permanent, with some with fixed terms running as long as 2 years. These are becoming more widely accepted as a commercial reality so it is advisable to be open to the contract market.

Contract work also enables you to build your network and as a lot of recruitment is done off the back of a conversation where people ask their network "Who do you know?" the bigger your network, the more the potential for referalls.

When considering contract or casual work you will often be paid on an hourly rate basis. This rate however will be different to the hourly rate a lawyer would be charged out by a law firm at. It will be based on the annual salary equivalent if the role was a permanent position. When employed on a contract basis you don't attract annual leave or sick leave however in some longer fixed term contracts they will include those entitlements.

The legal industry often experiences peaks and troughs in work flow and is starting to embrace employing lawyers, especially more junior lawyers, on a contract basis when the workload increases. This can be a great way to gain breadth of experience very quickly and take a look inside different organisations (government, corporate or practice) and see which environment suits you best. It certainly can provide you with a lot of variety.

With office space costing a premium, there may be some contract legal work that can be undertaken at home, such as research or drafting of documents.

Contract work can also add value to your career as it then gives you referees you can list on your resume, which are essential when you are applying for work.

References

References for Section "Government – Federal and State"

The Legal Services Commission.

References for Section "Non for Profit"

The Legal Services Commission of South Australia.

References for Section "Private Practice"

Cowell Clarke Lawyers.
Piper Alderman Lawyers.

References for Section "Corporate or In House"

Beyondlaw.com.au
Apsjobs.com.au., http://www.lawyersweekly.com.au/careers/17449-students-urged-to-look-beyond-the-careers-fair

Chapter 7
Areas of Legal Practice

Allison Berry, Ariella Gordon, Cassandra Ludeman, Ellen Leishman, Joshua Ch'ng, Matthew Burnham, Sofia Cabral, and Tayla Crump

There are many preconceived ideas about what a career in the legal profession entails. In reality, one individual's career in law can bare no resemblance to another's. What determines the nature of your professional life is largely the speciality area you pursue, combined with where you work.

Types of Specialties

If you are unsure about what interests you, it is advisable to get as much experience as possible early in your career, including whilst you are a student. Look at whether you enjoy going to court and advocating in that setting; if so, you may consider a career in litigation. If you prefer negotiations and contract formation, perhaps transactional work is better for you. Many specialty areas will require a variety of skills across a number of settings. Finding a specialty area that allows you to use and emphasise your strengths is the first step toward building a successful career.

Where You Work

Lawyers work across a number of settings for various organisations and bodies. Throughout your career, you may find yourself moving between workplace settings, including but not limited to the broad examples listed below.

Beginning your career in one stream does not prevent you moving to another, and many workplaces encourage you to develop a portfolio of broad experiences. For example, many firms and government bodies offer secondments to community legal centres, clients' in-house teams, government departments and other workplaces. Lawyers will often work closely with colleagues from a variety of workplaces and other areas of legal practice, so the 'streams' are by no means exclusive.

A. Berry (✉)
The University of Melbourne, Melbourne, VIC, Australia

A. Gordon · C. Ludeman · E. Leishman · J. Ch'ng · S. Cabral · T. Crump
Monash University, Clayton, VIC, Australia

M. Burnham
Victoria University, Melbourne, VIC, Australia

M. Raz et al. (eds.), *Careers in Law: A Guide for Students, Graduates and Professionals*, https://doi.org/10.1007/978-981-15-3627-4_7

Animal Law

What is Animal Law?

Animal law regulates the interactions between humans and animals, including agricultural regulations.[1] It is an area which has experienced recent international growth, particularly in the United States.[2] In the past few decades, animal law concerns have spread throughout the globe as animal welfare movements have mobilised to bring greater awareness around issues of animal cruelty and inhumane treatment. Animal law has expanded not only as an academic, specialised area for study and research, but also in practice as governments issue regulations and legislate further into the area of animal law.[3] In Australia, animal cruelty is a criminal offence covered by various state and territory laws.[4] However, animal law and standards for the welfare of animals differ between jurisdictions.[5] No national legislation currently applies for animal law, and regulation is not uniform. This means that if you travel between states, you will find different laws about matters such as farming, registration of animals, keeping pets and regulations for animal breeders. Animal law also covers areas such as property law, veterinary malpractice, and liability for trespass by animals, as well as issues such as the eradication and prevention of animal diseases.

What are the Challenges and Rewards of Working in This Area?

Animal law is still a developing field and has great potential for further innovation and change. This is certainly a niche area, and animal rights lawyers often perform animal law work pro bono or work with not-for-profit animal welfare organisations. It is an area where you can use your legal education to make a real difference, and if you are passionate about the welfare of animals this is a great way to get involved in a worthwhile legal cause. Animal rights have gained more visibility and, more than ever, community standards are leaning towards increasing protections for animals and imposing duties on owners.

[1] Oxford University Press, *Australian Law Dictionary* (at 29 November 2017), 'Family Law'.

[2] Ibid.

[3] Ibid.

[4] *What Is The Australian Legislation Governing Animal Welfare? – RSPCA Australia Knowledgebase* (2017) Kb.rspca.org.au. http://kb.rspca.org.au/what-is-the-australian-legislation-governing-animal-welfare_264.html

[5] Ibid.

Recent Developments in Animal Law

One of the most recent significant developments in animal law is in regards to puppy farms in Victoria. Parliament introduced the Domestic Animals Amendment (Puppy Farm and Pet Shops) Bill in 2016, which resulted in several positive changes for our household pets.[6] There are now new limits on the number of fertile female dogs that breeders can keep, as well as a simplified animal permit system.[7] Pet shops also can no longer sell dogs and cats unless they are sourced from shelters, pounds or enrolled foster carers.[8] Further offences for non-compliance have also been added, along with other changes.[9] These reforms are largely a response to greater awareness of harm to domestic animals caused by puppy farms or similar operations, and the need for more regulation regarding the protection of animals being sold in pet shops.[10] It is hoped by many animal welfare organisations and activists that other states and territories will move in a similar direction. There are many other animal law issues that continue to be debated in Australia, and we can certainly expect further changes in the law to better protect animals.

Resources and Tips for Interested Students

Students interested in this area might consider volunteering for animal law organisations, which may involve activities such as administrative help, legal research, writing submissions or helping spread awareness of animal rights issues.[11] Pro bono and animal organisations very much appreciate the help of volunteers, and this is an excellent way to develop your legal and other, softer skills that employers value.[12] Many universities now offer animal law subjects, which will give you a real insight into the law, as well as the policy considerations behind why the law is the way it is, or perhaps allow you to explore how the law should adapt and change. Also have a look out for legal seminars and workshops on animal law issues, as this can be a great way to learn more about the field and get to know its experts.

---

[6] *Domestic Animal Legislation And Latest News, Registration, Legislation And Permits, Pets, Agriculture Victoria* (2017) Agriculture.vic.gov.au. http://agriculture.vic.gov.au/pets/registration-legislation-and-permits/domestic-animal-legislation-and-latest-news; *Domestic Animals Amendment (Puppy Farm and Pet Shops) Bill 2016* (Vic).

[7] Ibid.

[8] Ibid.

[9] Ibid.

[10] Ibid.

[11] *Your Legal Calling: Considering A Future In Animal Law?* (2017) Liv.asn.au. https://www.liv.asn.au/younglawyersblog/april-2013-(1)/your-legal-calling%2D%2Dconsidering-a-future-in-animal.

[12] Ibid.

Career Pathway

This is a great area to consider either in research, practice, volunteering or as a pro bono lawyer. Pro bono lawyers may represent animal rights groups and animal activists as they take on animal rights cases or seek to change the law in their state or territory. It can also be an area which involves international law through international treaties, along with import and export laws which are central to animal rights issues.[13]

Aviation Law

What is Aviation Law?

Internationally, air travel is the cornerstone of globalisation; it facilitates travel, trade, and even war. As such, aviation law is the one of the most heavily regulated industries in Australia and the world, providing a great variety of component parts for practitioners.[14] Various aviation regulatory authorities are responsible for creating, enforcing and implementing civil aviation laws, as well as ensuring the adherence of international laws and treaties. International law has an interactive relationship with domestic aviation law. Domestic aviation law addresses: the civil liability of air carriers and any available defences; any damage caused to passengers; cargo; third parties on the ground; and the choice of jurisdiction for any lawsuits.[15]

Legal professionals and firms working in aviation law will generally seek to be proficient in commercial and regulatory matters, as well as liability and insurance issues. This includes providing advice on various international treaties and pieces of domestic legislation, whilst also being capable of negotiating commercial contracts. Firms may also act for plaintiffs taking action against airlines and airports for various liability and cargo-related claims.

What are the Challenges and Rewards of Working in This Area?

International aviation law is largely based on domestic, bilateral and multilateral rules and regulations for global air transport. As such, there are various intertwined regulatory authorities and regimes over which aviation law experts must remain

[13] Deborah Cao and Steven William White, *Animal Law And Welfare* (Springer, 2016).

[14] Kirk Griffin, 'Aviation Law' (2013) 30(2), GPSolo 46–50.

[15] Brian F Havel, The Principles and Practice of International Aviation Law (Cambridge University Press, 2014).

abreast. However, international collaboration is also an advantage of this practice area, with modernisation in one area of the world presenting an opportunity for best-practice to be implemented globally. This cooperation also affords for a comprehensive approach to security to protect air travellers.

Technological advancements also present a dynamic challenge for aviation law practitioners, who are involved with due diligence and commerciality related not just to aircraft, but also air travel and airports.

Recent Developments in Aviation Law

Aviation law is becoming increasingly intertwined with environmental law, creating a rapidly expanding practice area: aviation environmental law. For example, the Kyoto Protocol points to emissions produced by international aviation as an area requiring separate consideration by the International Civil Aviation Organisation.[16]

Resources and Tips for Interested Students

Studying international law and aviation-specific subjects at university is a strong stepping stone for pursuing a career in aviation law, though by no means compulsory. As aviation law encompasses negotiation, litigation, employment issues, risk-management and an understanding of environmental law, there are various skills prospective practitioners can seek to develop in law school. Joining environmental groups, debating teams and mock-negotiation exercises will all serve to provide experience in areas relevant to aviation law. Mooting will serve as valuable experience for those hoping to be litigators and negotiators, as it requires participants to communicate clearly, think on their feet and perform under pressure. As with all specialty areas, work-experience is an ideal way of developing contacts in the profession whilst gaining practical knowledge. Applying for volunteer and work experience positions at firms with aviation specialty practices areas, or within aviation bodies, are great pathways for building careers in this area. More broadly, experience in international law and statutory interpretation would be relevant and valuable.

[16] See Kyoto Protocol to the United Nations Framework Convention on Climate Change, art. 2(2), opened for signature Dec. 11, 1997, 2303 U.N.T.S.

Career Pathway

Aviation law, particularly in Australia, is a particularly competitive and niche area, so seek as much experience and exposure as possible. If applying to firms for work experience, clerkships or graduate positions, look for those with leading Australian aviation lawyers; seeking exemplary mentors is a positive step to building a successful career in any area of the law. Keep in mind that many firms will only employ graduates who have undertaken a clerkship with them previously. If you're unsure where to start, look also for peer-based assessments of the leading aviation firms in Australia (or internationally, depending on where you wish to practice). Additionally, careers in aviation law will often stem from employment in aviation-focused bodies. For example, individuals interested in aviation law may look for careers in aviation authorities and academies, or as in-house counsel for airlines or airports. Experience in statutory implementation and showing an understanding of international treaties will assist in applying for aviation-specific positions.

Banking Law

What is Banking Law?

Banking law refers to the legal management of financial institutions. As a general aim, banking law seeks to ensure that Australia's banking sector and financial system is functioning effectively and fairly.[17] To achieve these aims, banking law seeks to balance consumer rights with the powers of financial institutions. Given these competing interests, there are several regulators associated with Australia's financial system. Two of the main regulators are the Australian Prudential Regulation Authority (APRA) and the Australian Securities and Investment Commission (ASIC).[18]

APRA seeks to ensure that organisations can meet their financial commitments.[19] More specifically, APRA focuses on mitigating risks that may threaten the stability of the financial sector.[20] Further, one of its objectives is ensuring competition and efficiency of various authorised deposit taking institutions, including banks and insurance and superannuation companies.[21]

ASIC has regulatory powers over financial institutions in promoting and protecting the rights of the consumer.[22] Further, State and Territory-based Fair Trade Bodies

[17] Mallesons Stephen Jaques, *Australian Finance Law* (Thompson Reuters, 6th ed., 2008), 2.

[18] Ibid.

[19] Ibid.

[20] Ibid.

[21] Australian Prudential Regulation Authority Act Cth (1998), Section 8(2).

[22] Jaques, above n 1, 5.

such as Consumer Affairs Victoria seek to offer similar protective mechanisms for consumers.[23]

What are the Challenges and Rewards of Working in This Area?

The Royal Commission was a substantial challenge for those working in the banking sector. There was extensive media coverage of submissions and depositions which were detrimental to financial institutions' reputations. The recommendations of the Commission exerted further pressure on financial institutions.

Further, banking lawyers must be able to understand the varied and complex relationships financial institutions have with their clients. Those practising in this area must have a strong working knowledge of the transactions in which a financial institution can engage. To elaborate, banks have reciprocal relationships with consumers, investors and other financial institutions. For this reason, banking law concerns many areas of practice, including consumer and corporate contracting, company law and property law.

Recent Developments in Banking Law

In late 2017, the Governor General of Australia announced a Royal Commission into misconduct in the banking, superannuation and financial services sector.[24] While this investigation was not borne from banking law, the recommendations it established are likely to cause significant legislation and policy change in the Australian banking sector. Specifically, the Royal Commission sought to determine whether financial institutions were engaging in misconduct or conduct which fell below community standards.[25] In making determinations, the Commission considered the corporate culture of institutions, the adequacy of existing laws and the effectiveness of self-regulation.[26] At its conclusion, the Royal Commission made recommendations that involved legislative amendments which substantially altered banking law practices.

---

[23] Ibid, 8.

[24] Commonwealth, Royal Commission into Misconduct in the Banking, Superannuation and Financial Services Industry, Letters Patent (2018), 2.

[25] Ibid.

[26] Ibid.

Resources and Tips for Interested Students

Students interested in banking law may seek to apply for graduate positions at major Australian banks. Many banks offer graduate programs for in-house legal teams.

Additionally, students in their penultimate year may apply to clerk at firms with strong banking practice groups or major banking clients.

Students may also wish to apply for graduate roles in one of the many regulators mentioned above.

Finally, students in pre-penultimate years of study may consider banking law electives or advanced property law units.

Bankruptcy or Insolvency Law

What is Insolvency Law?

An entity is insolvent when it can no longer pay its debts as they become due and payable.[27] In Australia, the area of insolvency law is typically separated into sub-categories based on the type of entity: personal insolvency or bankruptcy law for individuals, and corporate insolvency law for corporations. Insolvency law has a rich common law history, and both areas are strongly governed by statute: the former by the *Bankruptcy Act 1966* (Cth) and the latter by Chapter 5 of the *Corporations Act 2001* (Cth). Being a counter-cyclical industry (which booms when the economy enters a downturn), the 2008 global financial crisis (GFC) has recently put insolvency law back in the commercial law spotlight. With an ever-present need to balance the competing interests of debtors and creditors, there is also a multitude of policy factors influencing the development and reform of insolvency law.

What are the Challenges and Rewards of Working in This Area?

Insolvency law is an extremely diverse area of law with strong ties to property, contract and corporate laws, in addition to taxation, trusts, equitable duties, family law and employment law. Practitioners are not only lawyers, but also detectives of sorts. The ability to read and understand financial documents is integral to the role as the lawyer traces monies, for example, into potential assets for recovery or investigates fraudulent breaches of trust accounts.

Another common scenario in personal insolvencies involves the trustee in charge of the bankrupt debtor's estate attempting to recover or claw-back property to distribute to all of the debtors' creditors. The trustee might allege, for instance, that an

[27] Bankruptcy Act 1966 (Cth) s 5; Corporations Act 2011 (Cth) s 95A.

individual creditor received a payment of money, security or other property 'in preference' to other creditors, or that the transfer of property to a spouse or child occurred to defeat other creditors. In these cases, the insolvency lawyer becomes involved in negotiations, mediations, and possibly litigation.

In the realm of corporate insolvencies, administrations and liquidations, it is common for lawyers to also be involved in organising corporate restructures, such as with Centro, Ansett Airlines and Alinta. When dealing with clients of such scale, teams are multidisciplinary and therefore insolvency practitioners often work with other lawyers from litigation, banking and finance, and mergers and acquisitions. As commerce has become has become more globalised in the past decade, cross-border insolvency has also developed significantly and gives practitioners opportunities to add an international dimension to their work.

Recent Developments in Insolvency Law

The 1988 Harmer Report by the Australian Law Reform Commission[28] was probably the most impactful development in Australian insolvency law, influencing academic writings, case law and government legislative agendas. In light of the recent GFC, there have been calls for a similarly detailed report to further modernise insolvency law for the twenty-first century. The *Insolvency Law Reform Act 2016* (Cth) introduced significant changes to Australian personal and corporate insolvency law in an attempt to reduce red-tape and complexity and improve public confidence in the industry.[29]

Another recent trend is the increasing popularity of debt agreements. Although the number of individuals becoming personally insolvent increased by 2.1% in 2016–17, the number of debtors entering bankruptcy has decreased almost every year since 2009–10; over 2016–17, the number decreased by 5.1%.[30] Instead, debtors have been entering debt agreements with the creditors as an alternative to bankruptcy. This informal and inexpensive alternative, under Part IX of the *Bankruptcy Act*, was inserted in 1996 to allow low-income and low-debt debtors to avoid the stigma of bankruptcy, while also practically allowing a better return for creditors.[31]

[28] Australian Law Reform Commission, *Report No 45, General Insolvency Inquiry* (AGPS, 1988), (commonly referred to as the Harmer Report after its chair, the late Mr. Ron Harmer).

[29] Commonwealth, *Parliamentary Debates*, Senate, 3 December 2015, 14637–40 (Mitchell Hawke).

[30] Australian Financial Security Authority, Australian Government, *Personal Insolvency Statistics* (4 January 2018) https://www.afsa.gov.au/statistics/personal-insolvency-statistics-0; Australian Financial Security Authority, Australian Government, *Provisional annual personal insolvency statistics 2016–17*. https://www.afsa.gov.au/sites/g/files/net1601/f/afsa_quarterly-pi-statistics_201709.zip

[31] Explanatory Memorandum, Bankruptcy Legislation Amendment Bill 1996 (Cth) [45]; Commonwealth, *Parliamentary Debates*, Senate, 26 June 1996, 2825 (Daryl Williams).

Resources and Tips for Interested Students

As with any commercial practice area, it is important for students to stay up-to-date with business news and the economy. The Australian Financial Review is the go-to news source for the majority of practitioners and offers discounts to university students.

In addition, given the vast breadth of insolvency law, which is affected by many other practice areas such as employment law, taxation law, family law, property, contract and trusts, students should also avoid pigeon-holing themselves early in their degree and should instead expose themselves to a wide variety of legal disciplines.

Interested students can also seek further information online from the ASIC website, which focuses on corporate insolvency, and the Australian Financial Security Authority website, which focuses on personal insolvency. Any work experience in an insolvency and restructuring department of a law firm or accounting firm will likewise be invaluable for students wishing to enter the industry.

Career Pathway

It is common for students with accounting and finance backgrounds to enter the insolvency and restructuring practice area, but these backgrounds are not mandatory to become a practitioner. Many Australian universities offer post-graduate Master's courses, and the Australian Restructuring Insolvency and Turnaround Association (ARITA), which represents the majority of Australian insolvency practitioners, offers various courses for insolvency practitioners based on their knowledge level. New entrants into the industry, for example, can undertake the two-day 'Introduction to Insolvency Program', while more experienced practitioners can undertake short courses or seek ARITA membership by completing specialised study for an ARITA advanced certification.

Capital Markets or Securities Law

What is Capital Markets Law?

If a company requires money, be it for a substantial purchase of property, plant or equipment, or to expand their operations, the first answer may be to obtain a bank loan. However, when the amount of money required is large, in the tens or hundreds of millions or even billions, a company would be hard-pressed to find a bank willing to provide a loan without overwhelmingly stringent terms. The solution for such a company may lie in capital markets. These are financial markets where debt or equity (a term separate from the equity branch of law) instruments or 'securities' are traded. These securities include bonds (debt), company shares/stocks (equity), and derivatives. Sourcing finance by issuing these securities provides the company with greater flexibility compared to a bank loan, because the company is not locked into the fixed, bilateral loan terms. Meanwhile, purchasers of securities can easily sell their bonds or shares if the risk becomes too high, in contrast to the bank which cannot transfer its risk from a loan.

Capital markets law (also known as securities law) facilitates these transactions. For example, where a company wishes to issue equity securities, capital markets lawyers will often be required to assist with the contract drafting, disclosure requirements, due diligence, developing share purchase plans, and negotiations. This issue of equity securities can be in the form of an initial public offering (IPO), where a private company decides to become public and lists on a stock exchange, or a subsequent rights issue of fresh shares.

What are the Challenges and Rewards of Working in This Area?

Lawyers practising in the capital markets industry get to experience a more dynamic side of commercial law, as compared to the more academic focus of barristers in commercial litigation. The work in capital markets involve deals and transactions that almost always have a direct connection to the current developments in the financial markets and economy. In larger law firms, lawyers could open the newspaper and see reports of a transaction on which they worked.

While there are negotiations involved, the parties involved are usually trying to achieve the same thing – lawyers are there to facilitate the transaction. This means that the negotiations are comparatively less adversarial than litigation or other areas of commercial law, such as employment law.

The large sum of money involved and the complexity of the transactions means that this area of law is conceptually challenging and intellectually rigorous. In addition, as with all transactional law, the hours of work can fluctuate drastically because transactions are time-sensitive and often on strict, stressful deadlines.

However, capital markets work often involves international parties, which makes overseas travel a more realistic possibility than non-transactional fields such as family law, criminal law, or consumer law.

Recent Developments in Capital Markets Law

In recent years, the capital markets industry has been performing well. In 2017, for example, global IPO activity was at the highest levels since 2007 (pre-GFC) and, in the Asia-Pacific region, there was a 44% increase in IPOs from 2016.[32] At the same

[32] EY, *Global IPO trends: Q4 2017 A busy 2017 with more mega-IPOs on the horizon* (2017) EYGM Limited. http://www.ey.com/Publication/vwLUAssets/ey-global-ipo-trends-q4-2017/$FILE/ey-global-ipo-trends-q4-2017.pdf

time, since the GFC there has been a global trend toward increased regulation and scrutiny in the financial markets industry. These legal requirements create a substantial amount of compliance work and due diligence procedures for companies. These regulatory regimes include, in the United States, the Bank Secrecy Act for anti-money laundering issues, the Commodity Futures Trading Commission and the Dodd Frank Act, and in the European Union, the second Markets in Financial Instruments Directive regulatory framework and the European Market Infrastructure Regulation.

The Turnbull government also announced in its 2017–18 federal budget that a new regulatory body, the Australian Financial Complaints Authority, would be set up to replace the Financial Services Ombudsman, Credit and Investments Ombudsman and the Superannuation Complaints Tribunal to become a one-stop-shop for all financial complaints.[33]

Resources and Tips for Interested Students

Similar to students interested in a career in investment laws such as private equity, venture capital or hedge funds law, it is important for students to have a strong understanding of how financial markets work. Keeping up to date with current economic and market trends is necessary, and students should be comfortable discussing these topics in job interviews. Financial newspapers such as the business section of the Australian, the Australian Financial Review and Bloomberg are excellent sources of business news and market analysis. A commerce or finance degree is not necessary, but will help students with their financial literacy.

Another useful skill is the ability to explain complex concepts simply. The transactions involved can be very convoluted and are further coupled with rigorous regulatory requirements. Good lawyers will be able to provide clear legal advice that is understandable to clients without legal backgrounds.

Competition or Anti-Trust Law

What is Competition Law?

Australian competition or anti-trust law focuses on ensuring that markets function in a manner that does not detrimentally restrict competition between businesses or corporations.[34] In *Boral Besser Masonry v ACCC*, his Honour summated the

[33] The Treasury, *Australian Financial Complaints Authority* (2017) Australian Government. https://treasury.gov.au/consultation/c2017-232832/

[34] Stephen G. Corones, *Competition Law in Australia* (Thompson Reuters, 6th ed, 2014) 3.

purpose of this practice area: 'to promote competition, not to protect the private interests of particular persons or corporations'.[35]

On a macroeconomic level, competition between corporations is typically seen as a means of achieving economic efficiency and prosperity. Competition law thus aims to address market failures, restrictive practices and sub-optimal market structures.[36] In *QCMA and Defiance Holdings,* his Honour held that competition serves economic, social and political goals, further stating '[w]e must focus on its economic goal as a device for controlling the disposition of society's resources'.[37]

More specifically, competition law concerns the deterrence and regulation of anticompetitive conduct and market failures.[38] Broadly, anticompetitive conduct refers to detrimental competitive rivalry between corporations or businesses that may result in failures such as limited consumer choice and cartels.

Further, given that the government has the power to restrict corporations through regulation, competition law seeks to ensure that restraints are not unjust. The law that governs these regulations is the *Competition and Consumer Act 2010* (Cth), previously known as the *Trade Practices Act 1974* (Cth).

What are the Challenges and Rewards of Working in This Area?

A major challenge of working in competition law is the breadth of the practice area. A lawyer in this area would have to understand the consequences of a corporation's various plans, production and business processes to determine what actions are impermissible. To exemplify, competition or antitrust law extends beyond the internal management of an individual corporation. This area of law also regulates mergers between corporations.[39] Mergers that involve two or more parties contracting to create a cartel in the market are impermissible.[40] Cartel provisions vary, yet they typically strive to create a monopoly.

---

[35] (2003) 215 CLR 375, 411.

[36] Ibid.

[37] (1976) 25 FLR 169, 187.

[38] Corones, above n 1, 22.

[39] Corones, above n 1, 269.

[40] Ibid.

Recent Developments in Competition Law

In 2016, there was a major amendment to section 46 of the *Competition and Consumer Act* through the implementation of a controversial 'effects test' for misuse of market power.[41] An 'effects test' simply means that the law is focused on the effect of a corporation's actions and not so much their intent or desired outcome. This amendment was a result of a review, colloquially known as the Harper Review.[42] The Harper Review stated that section 46 of the act was not adequate to protect against anti-competitive conduct.[43] Prior to the amendment, the threshold in this test was low and vexed.[44] These amendments now prohibit corporations from using their substantial market power to damage a potential or actual competitor. In its amended form, section 46 prohibits corporations with substantial market power from engaging in conduct that 'has the purpose, or is likely to have the effect, of substantially lessening competition'.[45]

Resources and Tips for Interested Students

One pathway into competition or antitrust law is attempting to gain a graduate position at the Australian Competition and Consumer Commission (ACCC). The ACCC is the body that primarily regulates anticompetitive and associated behaviour.

Further, various firms have strong competition or antitrust practice areas. Penultimate students might wish to direct clerkship applications to such firms.

Students who are not yet in their penultimate year may wish to apply to a pre-penultimate program. Some firms offer 1–3 day programs that aim to give insight into commercial law and the clerkship process. Often these programs allow students to interact and build connections with lawyers and partners at the firm.

[41] Professor Ian Harper, Submission to Department of Treasury, *Competition Policy Review*, 31 March 2015, 335.

[42] Ibid, 1.

[43] Ibid.

[44] Commonwealth, *Parliamentary Debates*, House of Representatives, 29 March 2017, 2667 (Anne Ruston).

[45] *Competition and Consumer Act* (2010), Section 46.

Consumer Law

What is Consumer Law?

Consumer law involves the protection of consumers through the promotion of fair trading.[46] In Australia, this area of the law is largely focussed on misleading and deceptive conduct, misrepresentations which people have made and unfair contract terms.[47] Consumer law is tied to competition law, which generally regulates how the providers of goods and services interact so as to avoid unlawful collusion and monopolies. It is therefore also the foundation of marketing and advertising law, dictating what is and is not acceptable.

Many of the actions taken under consumer law provisions overlap with contract and torts law, though separate actions cannot be applied simultaneously.[48] As such, consumer law practitioners will often have a proficient or in-depth understanding of tort and contract law as well; this allows them to advise clients which area of the law is best to action. If an act is both criminal and in violation of consumer law, only the criminal conviction may be applied.[49]

What are the Challenges and Rewards of Working in This Area?

Consumer law, despite being heavily regulated, requires creativity and innovation from practitioners.[50] This is because consumer law must remain abreast of changing consumer and competition practices to best protect consumers. For example, the movement toward online marketplaces has spelt the need for new kinds of comprehensive consumer protections. Many lawyers working in consumer law describe a frustrating element of their careers to be that they are not able to assist some consumers who have been treated unfairly, especially where it is because the law cannot keep abreast of consumer practices. Conversely, one of the most rewarding elements of this area of law is being able to help other consumers and advocate for changes to the law so it affords up-to-date protections.

---

[46] Adrian Coorey, *Australian Consumer Law* (LexisNexis Butterworths, 1st ed., 2015), 2.

[47] Coorey, above n 1, V.

[48] Coorey, above n 1, 26.

[49] Coorey, above n 1, 26.

[50] Jaymes Carr, *Consumer Law Area of Practice* (2018) GradAustralia. https://gradaustralia.com.au/law/consumer-law-area-of-practice

Recent Developments in Consumer Law

Consumer law in Australia undertook major reforms in 2011, with the consolidation and replacement of a variety of national, state and territory laws in order to create one uniform national law: the Australian Consumer Law (ACL).[51] The ACL, amongst other things, ensures that there are universal definitions for key terms across all jurisdictions in Australia, as well as more comprehensive protections for consumers including national information standards for goods and services.[52] The ACL is also aimed at improving competition in Australian markets and reducing coalitionary cartel behaviours to promote robust economic competition. Nation-wide consumer laws have also provided a number of remedies, both criminal and civil, as well as enforcement powers for the ACCC.[53]

Resources and Tips for Interested Students

Interested students may consider studying consumer law and/or competition law subjects during their law degree. In addition, undertaking research into consumer law through an honours project or another academic pursuit will deepen your understanding of the area and may assist in finding future profession-related positions. Due to the litigation element of consumer law, mooting may be a valuable experience during law school; moots simulate a court experience, forcing participants to think on their feet and communicate a clear legal argument.

Interested students should also look to gain work or volunteer experience in firms or organisations with a consumer law or competition law practice. If looking for a graduate position, consider that many firms will hire graduates from their pool of clerks; as such, it is worth considering clerking in the penultimate year of your law degree and looking carefully at which firms can offer you the specialty areas in which you are interested. Similarly, consumer law bodies such as the ACCC offer summer internship programs.

Career Pathway

There are a number of different career paths available for those interested in consumer law: government bodies, independent consumer rights groups, firms with competition and consumer law practices, as well as in-house legal teams for specific companies. Each firm and body will have its own recruitment process.

[51] Coorey, above n 1, V.

[52] Coorey, above n 1, 3.

[53] Coorey, above n 1, 3.

In terms of government bodies, consumer law in Australia is monitored and enforced by the independent ACCC, as well as numerous Fair Trading Commissions within states and territories.[54] ASIC is responsible for protecting consumers where financial services and products are concerned.[55] Graduate or junior lawyer positions at the ACCC, ASIC or state/territory Fair Trading Commissions are a fantastic kick-start to a career in consumer law. Each of these bodies have their own recruitment processes, which can be found on their websites. Researching graduate recruitment processes early in your degree can mean you avoid missing deadlines in the future. For example, an application for the ACCC's graduate program should be made in the final year of your law degree, usually by early April.

Constitutional Law

What is Constitutional Law?

Australian constitutional law is the study of the federal Constitution and the constitutions of each Australian state as the foundational documents for state and federal law, which govern the interaction between the three arms of government; the legislature, the judiciary and the executive government.[56] The Constitution cannot be completely understood by looking at the text alone, therefore the practice of constitutional law involves study of the vast and continually developing case law and literature accompanying the Constitution.[57] Constitutional law involves judicial determination of whether Australian statutes conform to the federal Constitution, which involves an interpretation of the text.[58] However, this can prove a difficult task, as Callinan J noted in his dissent in *Workchoices*: 'there has been little sustained unanimity on the part of the 46 Justices who have constituted this Court during its 103 years of existence as to how the Constitution should be interpreted'.[59]

---

[54] Coorey, above n 1, 2.

[55] Coorey, above n 1, 3.

[56] Ray Finkelstein and David Hamer (eds), *LexisNexis Concise Australian Legal Dictionary* (LexisNexis, 5th ed., 2015) 132.

[57] John Quick and Robert Randolph Garran, *The Annotated Constitution of the Australian Commonwealth (Revised Edition)* (LexisNexis, 2015), xi.

[58] Sarah Joseph and Melissa Castan, *Federal Constitutional Law: A Contemporary View* (Lawbook, 4th ed., 2014) 36.

[59] Ibid 39; *New South Wales v Commonwealth* (2006) 229 CLR 1, 301.

What are the Challenges and Rewards of Working in This Area?

People who practice in this area have commented that the work is highly intellectually stimulating and rewarding.[60] However, to be successful in constitutional law you will need to be truly passionate, enthusiastic and willing to put in the work required.[61] Constitutional law requires a firm understanding of all High Court cases in constitutional law.[62]

Recent Developments in Constitutional Law

High Court constitutional law cases often attract media coverage, as the decisions may have far-reaching political repercussions.[63] An example of this is the case of *Re Canavan*,[64] handed down on 27 October 2017. In this case, the High Court held that, under s 44(i) of the Constitution, various members of Parliament were held to have been invalidly elected because they were citizens of a foreign power at the time of election.[65] Another example is the case of *Wilkie v The Commonwealth; Australian Marriage Equality Ltd v Minister for Finance* [2017] HCA 40, which concerned the executive government's capacity to fund the voluntary postal survey on same-sex marriage.[66] The public was so interested in the outcome of this particular case that the High Court's website crashed as a result of large number of people trying to access the judgment.[67]

[60] Law Society of New South Wales, *Young Lawyers: Careers Guide to Public Law and Government* (1 October 2009) 13. https://www.lawsociety.com.au/cs/groups/public/documents/internetyounglawyers/064359.pdf

[61] Ibid 10.

[62] Ibid 10.

[63] Joseph and Castan, above n 3, 36; 37.

[64] *Re Canavan; Re Ludlam; Re Waters; Re Roberts [No 2]; Re Joyce; Re Nash; Re Xenophon* [2017] HCA 45.

[65] Tony Blackshield, *Seven Little Australians* (30 October 2017) AUSPUBLAW. https://auspublaw.org/2017/10/seven-little-australians/

[66] Anne Twomey, *Wilkie v Commonwealth: A Retreat to Combat over the Bones of Pape, Williams, and Responsible Government* (27 November 2017) AUSPUBLAW. https://auspublaw.org/2017/11/wilkie-v-commonwealth/

[67] Ibid.

Resources and Tips for Interested Students

There are many essay competitions which may provide students with an avenue to hone their critical analysis skills in constitutional law. For example, the Governor General's Prize is an essay competition that is run each year by the Constitution Education Fund Australia.[68] It is open to all undergraduate students studying at an Australian university, and a justice of the High Court of Australia chairs the judging panel for the competition.[69] Another essay competition in constitutional, law open to all undergraduate and postgraduate law students, is the Sir Anthony Mason Constitutional Law Essay Competition.[70] There are also free public lectures involving issues in constitutional law available.[71] Attending these lectures may assist in building your knowledge of current constitutional law issues. Oral skills are important if you are looking at a future career at the bar. It may be useful to apply to be involved in a constitutional law moot, for example the Sir Harry Gibbs Constitutional Law Moot.[72] The moot problem has, in past years, been written by justices of the High Court (the Honourable Justice James Edelman in 2017 and the Honourable Justice Stephen Gageler in 2016).[73] The competitions mentioned are just some examples of the types of constitutional law competitions open to Australian law students.

Career Pathway

The federal Constitution is interpreted by the High Court.[74] Therefore, career pathways that lead to work that involves the matters being heard by the High Court may lead to a career in constitutional law; for example, working as a barrister. A career in academia may also involve the study of constitutional law. Positions in government may involve practice of constitutional law. For example, the job of the Solicitor-General of Australia involves advising the Commonwealth Government and appearing for the Commonwealth Government in mainly constitutional law cases before the High Court.[75]

---

[68] Constitution Education Fund Australia, *Governor-General's Prize*. http://www.cefa.org.au/governor-generals-prize

[69] Ibid.

[70] AUSPUBLAW, *Public Law Events Roundup July 2017* (3 July 2017). https://auspublaw.org/2017/07/public-law-events-roundup-july-2017/

[71] Ibid.

[72] Melbourne University Law Students' Society, *2017 Sir Harry Gibbs Constitutional Law Moot*. http://mulss.com/competitions/2015_sir_harry_gibbs_constitutional_law_moot

[73] Ibid.

[74] Joseph and Castan, above n 3, 36.

[75] Law Society of New South Wales, above n 5, 9.

There are also opportunities to research and practice in constitutional law as a law graduate, such as working as a Research Officer in the High Court library.[76] Work as a judge's associate may be another pathway to studying and practising in constitutional law. However, associateships are often highly competitive,[77] and therefore previous experience, such as employment in the law and/or experience in research and editing, may be useful to assist with a successful application. An associateship position is also a personal decision of the judge in question and therefore appointments may also be a matter of whether your personality is a good match to the particular judge to whom you are applying.[78]

Construction Law

What is Construction Law?

Construction law involves all areas of the law related to tangible projects; it concerns contracts, planning and approvals, employment law, torts, property law, dispute resolution, occupational health and safety, and knowledge of a variety of legislative requirements. Construction lawyers work with developers, contractors, engineers, architects, surveyors, insurers and investors.

This area of the law encompasses a broad spectrum of work from transactional (such as the drawing of contracts), to dispute resolution, to litigation where disputes arise. As such, construction lawyers generally have a diverse, well-rounded practice which ultimately allows for the development of broadly-applicable skills. It is a particularly client-centric field, focussing on the practical outcomes of delivering projects on time, in budget and of the desired quality.[79]

What are the Challenges and Rewards of Working in This Area?

Construction law in Australia requires practitioners to navigate the nine separate jurisdictions within Australia's federal system. Construction law is dictated by states rather than by federal law; it is therefore made up of nine sets of case law and nine sets of legislation. Whilst this can create confusing issues in relation to jurisdiction and prevailing laws, legal professionals involved in construction law can

[76] Law Society of New South Wales, above n 5, 13.

[77] Law Society of New South Wales, above n 5, 43.

[78] Law Society of New South Wales, above n 5, 42.

[79] Ian Bailey and Matthew Bell, *Construction Law in Australia* (Thomson Reuters, 3rd ed., 2011), xi.

often circumvent these issues by creating well-drafted contracts and agreements during negotiations and the early stages of project-management.

Recent Developments in Construction Law

Practitioners in construction law have an increasing amount of exposure to dispute resolution tools outside of the court system. There has been a movement amongst the various jurisdictions within Australia toward expanding the role and powers of adjudicators and arbitrators in relation to construction industry disputes. This serves to not only lighten the burden of court systems, but also reduce costs for parties and, in some circumstances, encourage more open dialogue. Commercial arbitration legislation in Australia is relatively uniform, limiting the ability of parties to challenge the results of an arbitration and thus emphasising the importance of this tool in dispute resolution.[80]

Resources and Tips for Interested Students

Studying construction-specific subjects in law school is a useful, though not compulsory, start to an eventual career in construction law. The breadth of expertise required for construction law means interested students should seek opportunities for practical skill development.

Participation in moots will help in preparing for litigation by simulating a court experience and forcing participants to think on their feet and communicate a clear legal argument. Similarly, if your law society offers mock negotiations or mediations, it is advisable to participate in order to develop these skills.

Interested students should also look to gain work or volunteer experience in firms or organisations with a construction law practice. If looking for a graduate position in a construction-focused firm, consider that many firms will hire graduates from their pool of clerks; as such, it is worth considering clerking in the penultimate year of your law degree and looking carefully at which firm can offer you the specialty areas in which you are interested. Looking at networking opportunities through formal bodies, such as the National Association of Women in Construction, will also assist in the search for employment, experience and mentors.[81]

---

[80] Nouvelle Homes Pty Ltd. v G & M Smargiassi [2008] WASC 127.

[81] The National Association of Women in Construction, *Becme a Member Today* (2018). https://www.nawic.com.au/Web/Membership/Web/Membership/Become_a_Member.aspx?hkey=413085e8-5409-429e-85f5-e291fc8a8ac1

Career Pathway

As mentioned above, work and volunteer experience, as well as clerkships, are all invaluable steps students can take to kick-start a career in this area. Looking for firms with strong construction law practices and seeking graduate or junior positions in said firms is a means of best-placing yourself for exposure to this area of law.

If you have a background in the construction industry, for example a previous apprenticeship or engineering degree, you can use your experience to network, engage with clients and more thoroughly understand their needs and the nature of the projects. As such, it is important to emphasise your experience in the area to future and current employers, so they can help you play to your strengths. Having said this, a background in construction is not necessary to successfully practice construction law.

Although you are not required to become an accredited specialist to practice in construction law, a relevant specialisation may assist in career progression and skill-building. Relevant specialties in Victoria, for example, include but are not limited to: commercial litigation, environmental and planning law, property law and tax law.[82]

Corporate Governance Law

What is Corporate Governance Law?

Corporate governance law addresses both the external regulatory environment and internal system of management that exist within corporations. An accurate definition of corporate governance law is often contested, but an accepted description of the area is the 'control of corporations and to systems of accountability by those in control'.[83] Corporate governance is also primarily concerned with efficient management and strengthening the performance of the organisation.[84] The management of companies is regulated by the *Corporations Act 2001* (Cth), the listing rules of the Australian Securities Exchange (ASX) and oversight by ASIC. There are many differing types of company structures, such as publically-listed companies and proprietary companies, and each type of body requires different compliance regimes.[85] The content of the laws surrounding the regulation of corporations includes the constitution of a company, the compliance of meetings, balancing competing

[82] Law Institute of Victoria, *Become an Accredited Specialist* (2018). https://www.liv.asn.au/Learning-and-Networking/Become-an-Accredited-Specialist/Specialist-Areas-Key-Dates

[83] John Farrar & Pamela Hanrahan, *Corporate Governance*, LexisNexis Butterworths Australia 2017, 1st Edition, 3.

[84] Ibid, 4.

[85] *Corporations Act 2001* (Cth), s 113 and s 114

interests of shareholders and management and enforcing director's duties and their fidelity under the *Corporations Act*.[86]

What are the Challenges and Rewards of Working in This Area?

Corporate governance can be a very competitive sector and practitioners must be adequately informed of the complex system of rules and regulations under which they operate. Increasingly, the corporate environment is scrutinised for the cultural values and management practices that are utilised. Indeed, ASIC have recently noted their increased scrutiny into corporate culture as a preventative mechanism to enforce compliance.[87] Working in corporate governance can be demanding as it is a heavily-burdensome and regulatory area of law. Many challenges may arise for practitioners, including appropriately balancing client interests alongside competing management and shareholder interests.

Many practical skills gained in law school will be advantageous, including complex problem-solving, communicating effectively and placing strong arguments. Experience in this sector can deliver universal skills that can be transported into different industries and different jurisdictions. With a background in corporate governance law, it is possible to transpose your skills and experience into other management positions, the public or not-for-profit sector or to develop your own business.

Recent Developments in Corporate Governance Law

Following the collapse of major corporate bodies in the 2000s and the GFC in 2008, the law of corporate governance has shifted dramatically. The public responsibilities of these institutions has been heightened following corporate collapses and public scandals.[88] The result is an increased scope to the director's duties within the *Corporations Act* which include to act in the company's best interest, to exercise power for a proper purpose and to avoid conflicts of interest or profiting from one's position.[89] However, corporate culture has also been a highly critiqued element of corporate governance that has been tackled by a Royal Commission and revealed in

[86] Ibid, s 181 and s 183.

[87] ASIC Chairman, Greg Medcraft 'Corporate Culture, Corporate Values and Ethics', September 2016

[88] Jennifer Hill, 'Regulatory Responses to Global Corporate Scandals', Wisconsin International Law Journal 23 (2005), 367

[89] The Hon. Justice Berna Collier, 'Recent Developments in Australian Corporate Governance', *New Zealand Law Society's Corporate Governance Intensive in New Zealand*, 1 June 2017.

extensive litigation.[90] Corporate social responsibility is very topical, with many corporate institutions seeking to enhance their reputational standing in the community as a 'good corporate citizen'.[91] Some recent areas in which corporations have sought to assert this positive image has been in climate change, divesting in fossil fuels and advocating for social justice reform.

Resources and Tips for Interested Students

Candidates intent on a career in corporate governance should be aware of shifting methodologies in the industry. For example, the principles-based approach or the efficiency model are key but distinct approaches to corporate management of which students should keep abreast.[92] The professional landscape is always interested in management reform and changing societal sentiment on contemporary issues. It will always be helpful to develop opinions and insights into contemporary issues in this field of work. More recently, developments in public accountability and oversight are changing the way the sector perceives their overall responsibilities. It is important to engage with those presently in the industry to discover what specialised fields of corporate governance law are attractive.

Career Pathway

Candidates for commercial law would be adequately placed to apply for clerkships at major firms. In areas like corporate governance law, the larger firms will offer a greater level of experience and exposure given the scale of their work and high-profile clientele. Students should be researching firms that operate in their areas of particular interest. Specifically, many offer programs at an undergraduate or postgraduate level that could provide key insight into the daily work in the field. Alternatively, there are many smaller and mid-tier firms that also operate in this space as it is a field helpful to many areas of the law.

---

[90] Royal Commission into Misconduct in the Banking. Superannuation and Financial Services Industry, Terms of Reference, 14 December 2017, *ASIC v Adler; Bell Group*.

[91] Jennifer Hill, 'Regulatory Responses to Global Corporate Scandals', Wisconsin International Law Journal 23 (2005), 367.

[92] Lynne Dallas *Two Models of Corporate Governance: Beyond Berle and* Means in Thomas W. Joo, 'Corporate Governance: Law, Theory & Policy' Second Edition Carolina Academic Press 2010, 9.

Criminal Law

What is Criminal Law?

Criminal Law plays an important role in society and is often the subject of public debate and media coverage. It is also widely explored in popular culture through television and film, usually with a focus on adversarial court cases in the United States. In terms of legal practice in Australia, criminal law refers to the rules found in legislation, and in the common law which make certain acts illegal and therefore punishable by the state.[93] This means that criminal law is concerned with legal wrongs, and the resulting criminal proceedings and punishments that may be imposed.[94] The criminal justice system has evolved over time and is constantly in flux as Parliament responds to changing attitudes in the community, new technology, and as different cases come before the courts. Most criminal matters will be governed by the states, with only some crimes, such as certain types of fraud, being dealt with at a federal level.[95] In some states such as New South Wales, Victoria and South Australia, the criminal law is partially codified in legislation and is also found in cases based on the English common law. Other states have been influenced by the Model Criminal Code in an effort to ensure greater consistency of the criminal law throughout the nation.[96] Since the 1980s, there have been moves towards greater codification of the criminal law in Australia, with scholars and commentators suggesting that states should consolidate the criminal law into one single code or one act of Parliament.[97] However, common law principles would continue to apply to such statutes as the courts still need to interpret legislation. The fact that states have diverged and adopted different systems means that Australian criminal law is not uniform and varies from state to state, adding layers of complexity to any proposed changes.[98]

What are the Challenges and Rewards of Working in This Area?

Criminal law can certainly be a faced-paced and interesting area of law, with practitioners needing to stay on top of legislative changes. It can be rewarding to fight for justice and the rights of clients. The type of work that criminal lawyers engage with can depend on their location, with certain types of offences being more

[93] LexisNexis, *Encyclopaedic Australian Legal Dictionary* (at 29 December 2017) 'Criminal Law'.

[94] Ibid.

[95] Oxford University Press, *Australian Law Dictionary* (at 29 December 2017) 'Criminal Law'.

[96] Ibid.

[97] Virginia Bell, "Keeping The Criminal Law In 'Serviceable Condition': A Task For The Courts Or The Parliament?" (2017) 27(3) *Current Issues in Criminal Justice*.

[98] *Australian Law Dictionary*, above n 3.

prevalent in different areas.[99] Ensuring fairness for clients is a great motivating factor for lawyers in the field and is essential to criminal proceedings.[100] However, criminal law can also be an emotional and high-stress area of practice, particularly in complex cases where there is a lot at stake for clients.

Recent Developments in Criminal Law

As technology advances, the criminal law has to adapt as well. For example, recent improvements in DNA profiling and familial searching has enabled law enforcement to better identify suspects and draw links between cases and facts. DNA has now been used in cases to produce physical descriptions of suspects.[101] With such advancements, the law has had to adapt to ensure legal admissibility of new types of DNA evidence in criminal proceedings.[102] Greater community awareness of issues such as family violence has also led to changes in the criminal law. For example, in jurisdictions such as Queensland Parliament has introduced partial defenses to murder for defendants who have suffered family violence and abuse.[103] Australian courts have also allowed evidence of 'battered woman syndrome' to be admissible in court, allowing for expert evidence on the psychological and mental health impacts of prolonged abuse.[104] There have been many other recent developments in criminal law – such issues are often the subject of important debate in the community.

Resources and Tips for Interested Students

Criminal lawyers can be barristers or solicitors working either in prosecution, or defending clients. Some firms and barristers will specialise in certain types of criminal matters, working in more niche areas of the law. Other firms may be more generalist in the types of cases they take on. Starting out as a graduate in criminal law will involve a great deal of close supervision and often a lot of contact with clients

---

[99] Lawyers Weekly and Staff Reporter, *Practice Profile: Criminal Lawyers Say Real Life Practice Is Far From Prime Time* (2017). Lawyersweekly.com.au. https://www.lawyersweekly.com.au/features/9050-practice-profile-criminal-lawyers-say-real-life-pr

[100] Ibid.

[101] See generally, Marcus Smith and Monique Mann, "Recent Developments In DNA Evidence" [2015] (506) *Trends and Issues in Crime and Criminal Justice*.

[102] Ibid.

[103] Kerstin Braun, ""Till Death Us Do Part": Homicide Defenses For Women In Abusive Relationships—Similar Problems—Different Responses In Germany And Australia" (2016) 23(10) *Violence Against Women* 1178.

[104] Ibid.

for defence lawyers.[105] Many firms will engage in pro bono work, helping clients with less resources to achieve the best outcome possible. Lawyers also have the opportunity to engage in legal aid work and work with community legal centres. Volunteer experience at a community legal centre is a great way for aspiring law students to gain exposure to criminal law. Law students can also look for part-time work as research assistants to criminal law barristers, or as paralegals in criminal law firms which is also a great way to gain experience. Shadowing a barrister can also be an excellent way to understand how criminal proceedings work. Your university may also offer externships with opportunities to gain practical experience the courtroom, government departments or even in areas of criminal law policy research.

Dispute Resolution

What is Dispute Resolution?

Dispute resolution, also known as appropriate dispute resolution (ADR), encompasses a number of justice-based processes for resolving disputes outside of the traditional court system.[106] Dealing with disputes and conflicts through framed discussion and negotiation reduces the strain on court systems, can be substantially less expensive and more accessible for parties, and can often allow for continued relationships between disputing parties. For these reasons, dispute resolution has become popular across a number of settings, beyond the legal and commercial to the social, environmental, international and political.[107] Types of dispute resolution which are commonplace internationally, nationally and locally include negotiation, mediation, facilitation, evaluation, case appraisal, arbitration, and conciliation. Courts will sometimes require parties to reach an agreement using dispute resolution before hearing a case.[108]

Dispute resolution processes usually involve an impartial practitioner who either helps parties reach an agreement or recommends their own decision. In a mediation, for example, the 'mediator' is the relevant practitioner; their role is to facilitate the mediation process, ideally encouraging maximum cooperation and productive dialogue. In an arbitration, the arbitrator investigates the dispute by way of submissions, witness testimonies, expert reports and other evidence before making a determination in an 'award'; arbitration awards are often binding on parties,

---

[105] *Criminal Law Area Of Practice* (2017) GradAustralia. https://gradaustralia.com.au/law/criminal-law-area-of-practice

[106] Tania Sourdin, Alternative Dispute Resolution (Thomson Reuters Professional Australia, 4th ed., 2012) 2 [1.10].

[107] Tania Sourdin, *Alternative Dispute Resolution* (Thomson Reuters Professional Australia, 4th ed., 2012) 2 [1.10].

[108] *Dispute Resolution* (31 October 2017) Victoria Legal Aid. https://www.legalaid.vic.gov.au/find-legal-answers/courts-and-legal-system/dispute-resolution

similar to a court's judgment. Where a practitioner makes a determination, it may be binding or non-binding, depending on the type of dispute resolution agreed upon by the parties and the legislative requirements of the process.

What are the Challenges and Rewards of Working in This Area?

Dispute resolution practitioners must have an extremely diverse skill set which includes not only sound legal reasoning and logic but also strong emotional intelligence. Conciliation, for example, may largely require mediation skills where the practitioner encourages cooperation and active participation from parties; by the same token, a conciliator may be required to make a determination, which calls for a more clinical examination of the law and relevant facts.

Dispute resolution processes can also involve extremely complex client needs, requiring parties' lawyers and dispute resolution practitioners to remain flexible in their approach. For example, clients that are less tech-savvy may be more irritable or anxious when conducting dispute resolution via video-conferencing or other technology-based options. Clients with a history of violence, on the other hand, may need to be communicated with remotely. The responsiveness of clients is often crucial to the success of dispute resolution and therefore will be a primary consideration in determining which method is adopted. Each dispute will present its own sensitivities and will require sound problem-solving skills.

Best practice in dispute resolution is still yet to be clearly defined, leaving practitioners with a mountain of dispute-resolution theories to examine and possibly implement. There are no strict rules on how to approach many of the established and still developing areas of dispute resolution; thus, practitioners have the flexibility to use their own research, experience and judgment.

Recent Developments in Dispute Resolution

Until recently, ADR stood for 'alternative dispute resolution', a term still commonly used in the legal profession. However, as ADR has evolved into a preferred and common element of legal proceedings, the word 'alternative' has become less appropriate. Mandatory forms of dispute resolution have been gradually integrated into legal systems, reducing the burden of litigious services. It is a worldwide trend that dispute resolution systems be built alongside judicial systems, becoming a crucial element of civil society.

The evolution of dispute resolution has also moved toward blending traditional processes to create newer models which better suit the needs of participating parties. Lawyers in this space act as advocates, peacemakers and negotiators, often discouraging litigation in favour of discursive conflict resolution through facilitative processes. Dispute resolution aligns with the shift of the legal profession towards doing what is best for the client, involving not just advice but collaboration.

Resources and Tips for Interested Students

Dispute resolution is a growing area requiring advanced communication and problem-solving skills for dealing with changing, dynamic client-centric situations. Thus, students interested in a career in dispute resolution are encouraged to gain as much experience as possible in negotiation and other relevant contexts. Your university is likely to offer mock mediations and negotiations where you can practice dispute resolution skills. However, look also for broader opportunities to see negotiation at work, such as within student unions, committees and communication roles.

Career Pathway

Lawyers in disputes will almost inevitably find themselves representing parties in a dispute resolution process at various points throughout their career, with no further training required beyond admission to practice. To become a dispute resolution practitioner, there are many different accreditation requirements.[109] For example, mediators need to undertake training with a recognised mediator accreditation body, and do not require a law degree to conduct mediations.[110] Arbitrators, who must be legal professionals, are also required to go through an accreditation process to acquire professional certification.[111]

Drug Control Law

What is Drug Control Law?

Drug control law is a sub-area of criminal law. This area relates to drug offences where the government regulates the use, possession, trafficking or sale of certain drugs.[112] Drugs are grouped into various classes, with some drugs being controlled,

---

[109] *Confidence in Alternative Dispute Resolution,* (28 December 2017) Australian Disputes Centre. https://www.disputescentre.com.au/

[110] *Training* (21 September 2017) Dispute Settlement Centre of Victoria. https://www.disputes.vic.gov.au/training

[111] *CIArb Australia* (2014) Chartered Institute of Arbitrators. https://www.ciarb.net.au/

[112] LexisNexis, *Encyclopaedic Australian Legal Dictionary* (at 4 January 2018) 'Drug Offence'.

dangerous or prohibited altogether. State legislation covers offences relating to possession or trafficking.[113] However, offences relating to the importation or exportation of prohibited or controlled drugs is dealt with by federal legislation and is enforced by federal police and border security officers.[114] Drug control law is an area which will often overlap with other criminal offences, and is of great importance to the community as it is used to combat the misuse and trafficking of dangerous drugs. There are also strict regulations around the manufacture of narcotics. In some states, such as Victoria and Queensland, the manufacture or production of a drug of dependence is considered to be a form of trafficking.[115] Laws relating to narcotics and drugs also have an impact on family law, as the use of drugs by a parent is a relevant consideration for the court in an application for a parenting order, particularly if the welfare of the child is affected as a result.[116] Most Australian states have specialised drug courts which usually operate to place drug users into treatment and rehabilitation programs and avoid terms of imprisonment.[117]

What are the Challenges and Rewards of Working in This Area?

Working as a criminal lawyer in this area can be intensive and highly rewarding. Most lawyers in the area of drug law would work as defence lawyers, helping clients who have been charged with a drug-related offence. In each state, drug offences and penalties vary depending on factors such as the amount of drugs involved, the reason for offending, and also the steps the defendant takes towards rehabilitation and changing their behaviour.[118] This can be a challenging area of law as legal professionals work to navigate the often complex circumstances surrounding drug offending and recidivism. Clients can be facing tough situations emotionally and financially. Some clients may be repeat offenders and others may be innocent. However, it can be incredibly rewarding to help clients achieve a better outcome that may lead to a path of recovery.

---

[113] Ibid.

[114] Ibid.

[115] LexisNexis, *Encyclopaedic Australian Legal Dictionary* (at 4 January 2018) 'Drug Manufacture'.

[116] Oxford University Press, *Australian Law Dictionary* (at 29 December 2017), 'Drug'.

[117] *Australian Institute Of Criminology – Drug Courts* (2018) Aic.gov.au. http://www.aic.gov.au/criminal_justice_system/courts/specialist/drugcourts.html

[118] *Drug Charges – Melbourne Criminal Lawyers | Doogue + George* (2017) Doogue + George. https://www.criminal-lawyers.com.au/criminal-law/offences/drug-charges

Recent Developments in Drug Control Law

In 2017, the Victorian Parliament passed new penalties banning synthetic drugs and also introducing more severe penalties for those dealing in the drug 'ice'.[119] This is particularly relevant in the midst of increasing ice use in the community and the detrimental impact of the drug on families, individuals and society as a whole. There has also been increased use of synthetic drugs that mimic the effects of illegal drugs in an effort by offenders to evade drug control measures.[120] Such psychoactive synthetic drugs have been linked to hospital admissions and, tragically, drug-related deaths.[121] Over the past few years, the Commonwealth, States and Territories have also responded to community attitudes and advances in medical research to legislate for the manufacture and prescription of cannabis for medicinal use.[122] The boundaries and uses of cannabis continue to be the subject of debate in Australia and the international community.[123] Drug control laws are frequently revised due to fluctuations in how drugs are utilised in the community, as well as new developments such as synthetic drugs.

Career Pathway

Students who are interested in this area should consider visiting one of the specialised drug courts in their state. This can be a very informative experience and will give you a real insight into how the legal system tackles drug offences. It will also give you a glimpse into how lawyers argue cases for their clients, and the often emotional and difficult situations that people face. There are a wide spectrum of cases that lawyers can encounter, from more minor offences of possession to more serious trafficking offences. It can also be a good idea to research firms or barristers who have a criminal or drug offence focus in their work to find out more about what they do. For more information about becoming a criminal lawyer, see the "Criminal Law" section in this chapter.

---

119 *Cracking Down On Synthetic Drugs And Drug Dealing* (2017) Premier of Victoria. https://www.premier.vic.gov.au/cracking-down-on-synthetic-drugs-and-drug-dealing/

120 Ibid.

121 Ibid.

122 "Medicinal Cannabis Law Reform In Australia" (2016) 23(3) *Journal of Law and Medicine*.

123 *Guidance For The Use Of Medicinal Cannabis In Australia: Overview* (2017) Therapeutic Goods Administration (TGA). https://www.tga.gov.au/publication/guidance-use-medicinal-cannabis-australia-overview

Employment or Labour Law

What is Employment Law?

In the broadest sense, employment law (sometimes synonymously referred to as labour law) is the area of law governing the legal relationship between the employee and the employer.[124] Though there are some incidental pieces of state legislation, employment law is largely dominated by federal legislation; most importantly, the *Fair Work Act*.[125]

Employment law is by no means a standalone area of law; other areas of law will influence the work a practitioner undertakes. The most obvious, but by no means the only, example is the importance of contract law. Employment contracts are of central importance to any dispute arising between and employer and employee, and any employment law practitioner will have a strong understanding of contractual concepts such as implied and explicit terms.[126]

Typically, a lawyer specialising in employment law will find that most of their work involves constructing and interpreting employment contracts, as well as managing disputes arising from the employee-employer relationships such as conflict over remuneration, benefits and unfair dismissal.

What are the Challenges and Rewards of Working in This Area?

Employment law can be both a challenging and rewarding area in which to work. Particularly if you specialise in representing individual employees and/or small businesses, their disputes can be at the forefront of their priorities, and in many cases the livelihood of individuals and businesses can depend on the outcome of disputes.

Employment law is a highly politicised area of law, with frequent legislative changes occurring after shifts in political sentiment.[127] As such, practitioners need to be able to adapt to change and keep up with recent developments in law even more so than other areas.

---

[124] Natalie van der Waarden, *Understanding Employment Law: Concepts and Cases* (LexisNexis, 3rd ed., 2014) 1–2.

[125] *2009* (Cth).

[126] See, e.g., *Tibaldi Smallgoods (Australasia) Pty Ltd v Rinaldi* (2008) 172 IR 86; *Goldman Sachs JB Were Services v Nikolich* [2009] NSWSC 979.

[127] See *Workplace Relations Amendment (Work Choices) Act 2005* (Cth); *Fair Work Act 2009* (Cth).

Recent Developments in Employment Law

As with many other areas of law, employment law underwent (and is still undergoing) vast changes in response to the development and utilisation of the Internet by both employees and employers. Widespread usage of the Internet has led to various legal questions arising which are by no means definitively answered. For example, the ability of employers to access and hold employees responsible for sentiments expressed on the employee's private social media accounts is ill-defined and the subject of much public debate.[128]

The Fair Work Commission's decision regarding penalty rates in some modern awards was extremely publicised and politicised; the decision affects an enormous number of workers and highlights the importance of employment standards to a large portion of the community, as well as the tension inherent in the employee/employer relationship.[129]

Resources and Tips for Interested Students

As with all areas of law, it is of utmost importance that if you have an interest in working in employment law, you stay abreast of developments in this area. Being able to demonstrate an interest in employment law beyond merely what you learned at university will help set you apart from your contemporaries. The Fair Work Ombudsman frequently publishes articles discussing points of interest in reference to developing legislation and case law,[130] while the Fair Work Commission maintains a database of employment law cases decided before the Commission,[131] as well as a weekly bulletin drawing attention to cases of particular consequence.[132]

Further to demonstrating an interest in employment law beyond academia, sitting in on hearings can be a great way to get a first-hand appreciation for the area and is of particular importance if you have aspirations of working in litigation. The Fair Work Commission's hearings are usually open to the public (unless the Commission orders that the hearing be held in private)[133] and the Federal Court maintains a list for employment and industrial relations. Mooting can help you

---

[128] Australian Broadcasting Corporation, '*SSM: Fair Work Australia to investigate after Canberra contractor fired for backing No vote*', (20 September 2017). http://www.abc.net.au/news/2017-09-20/fair-work-to-probe-sacking-over-same-sex-marriage-survey/8964558

[129] *4 yearly review of modern awards – Penalty rates* [2017] FWCFB 1001 (23 February 2017).

[130] Fair Work Ombudsman, *News and Media releases*. https://www.fairwork.gov.au/about-us/news-and-media-releases

[131] Fair Work Commission, *Cases, decisions & orders*. https://www.fwc.gov.au/cases-decisions-and-orders

[132] Fair Work Commission, *FWC Bulletin*. https://www.fwc.gov.au/cases-decisions-and-orders/fwc-bulletin

[133] *Fair Work Act 2009* (Cth) s 593(3).

develop your practical advocacy skills and is another factor that will help you stand out from your fellow students.

An aptitude for alternate dispute resolution and negotiation will be of particular benefit for a lawyer practising in employment law as there is a strong push (similar to many other areas of civil law) to have the vast majority of disputes resolved before resorting to litigation.[134]

Energy Law

What is Energy Law?

The legal realities of managing energy resources can collectively be referred to as 'energy law'.[135] Energy law and environmental law both relate to the management of natural resources, however the former focuses solely on the resources that can yield energy.[136] In Australia, energy resources have profound impacts on our economy, making it an important area of the law for both the government and private enterprises.[137] Energy law interacts closely with other specialty areas such as politics, economics, geography, environmental sciences and engineering.[138] Separating energy law from energy policy is near impossible, with the two being substantially intertwined.[139] The importance of energy law cannot be understated, with its expansive impact on the environment, jobs, the economy, trade and our lifestyles.

Energy policy and laws are often influenced by analytical, scientific and lobbyist organisations. There are three levels of interaction in legislating energy law: local, national and international.[140] International law usually stems from United Nations agreements, such as the United Nations Conference on the Human Environment,[141] or other agreements from international or supranational organisations. The Kyoto

[134] Fair Work Ombudsman, *Best Practice Guide: Effective dispute resolution* (December 2013). https://www.fairwork.gov.au/how-we-will-help/templates-and-guides/best-practice-guides/effective-dispute-resolution

[135] Raphael J Heffron, *Energy law: an Introduction* (Springerlink, 1st ed., 2015), 3.

[136] Ibid 7.

[137] Michael Crommelin, *Energy and Resources Law*, University of Melbourne. http://law.unimelb.edu.au/study/masters/specialist-legal-areas/energy-and-resources-law?utm_source=2017_mlm_adwords_energy_resources_law&utm_medium=sem&utm_campaign=mlsmlm_20160415_adwords&utm_content=register_now&gclid=CjwKCAiA4vbSBRBNEiwAMorER8e17UjSGkeNENS3ddd9FDeYKTCCL9CCRMRqtQ18FyjMywSxGZh5ExoCoTAQAvD_BwE

[138] Heffron, above n 1, 1–2.

[139] Ibid 3.

[140] Ibid 4.

[141] Adopted in Stockholm on 16 June 1972.

Protocol, which specifically addressed greenhouse gas emissions,[142] is an example of an international agreement which has heavily influenced energy policy and infrastructure in signature countries. Of course, international agreements need the support of national legislation to be implemented, and are often supplemented by national legislative schemes. In addition, local governments will sometimes have their own schemes to incentivise or reward the development of energy infrastructure.[143]

What are the Challenges and Rewards of Working in This Area?

Energy law often concerns long-term goals, founded in international agreements and treaties. As such, the implementation and practice of energy law is challenged by the evolving nature of politics (such as policy changes which allow or prevent one country selling their expertise), societies' expectations and technological advancements.[144]

As such, those working in energy law need to be abreast of international standards and best-practice; infrastructure and policies put in place in the near future will ultimately determine the success or failure of goals set for 2025–2050.[145] Practitioners need to have a mind for steadfast rules to ensure goals are not forgotten, whilst also allowing for flexibility where technology and priorities may change over the coming decades.

Recent Developments in Energy Law

As mentioned above, the area of energy law is constantly developing for a variety of reasons. Recently, for example, the Australian Government has implemented a National Energy Guarantee which requires energy retailers to deliver energy which is increasingly reliable and producing lower emissions.[146]

---

[142] Heffron, above n 1, 4–5.

[143] Ibid 5.

[144] Heffron, above n 1, 9.

[145] Ibid.

[146] *We're Powering Forward* (16 January 2018) Australian Government: Department of the Environment and Energy. https://poweringforward.energy.gov.au/

Resources and Tips for Interested Students

It is important to use law school as an opportunity to develop strong communication skills, for a key area of energy law is being able to communicate with clients in terms they understand. Look for opportunities to perform mock client interviews, or actual client interviews if your university offers in-practice experience.

Finding work or volunteer experience in a firm, agency or company which deals with energy law is also invaluable in ascertaining whether this area truly interests you and how to best start specialising. In looking for work experience in the relevant field, it is beneficial to have good basic knowledge of industry trends, such as the price of oil and the effect this has on oil and gas companies.[147] This will show you have an interest in the area and also assist you to better understand matters you may be working on, or policy you are advising on or helping to develop. The kind of knowledge you need is often easily found in mainstream media: news reports and newspapers, for example.

Career Pathway

There are many different pathways available for those seeking a career in energy law. Private resource companies (for example gas and oil companies, nuclear producers or renewable energy providers), as well as banks, investors and governments are just some examples of possible employers.[148]

If working in a commercial firm, specialist areas such as corporate, mergers and acquisitions, projects, construction or similar are generally going to provide the best opportunity to work in energy law if there isn't a more specific practice.[149] To successfully specialise in energy law in an in-house position, it is advisable to get as much commercial experience as possible and develop specific knowledge of the energy industry.[150]

[147] Julia Derrick, *Energy and Natural Resources*, LawCareers.Net. https://www.lawcareers.net/Solicitors/SolicitorPracticeAreas/Energy-natural-resources

[148] *So You Want to be an Energy Lawyer*, Robert Walters. https://www.robertwalters.co.uk/career-advice/energy-legal-jobs-market.html

[149] Ibid.

[150] Ibid.

Entertainment Law

What is Entertainment Law?

Entertainment law involves working with artists, musicians and creators in a variety of areas of law including intellectual property, contract law, employment law, and litigation.[151] Clients may come from areas such as film and television, music, radio, theatre, and video games, to name a few. The predominant role of lawyers in this field is to ensure that their clients reach fair agreements and partnerships with industry professionals, such as record labels or publishers, as well as with each other. However, their work may cross into many different realms, depending on the nature of the clients managed. For example, clients may want a creative logo trade marked, be seeking advice on a management agreement, have an internal dispute amongst band members threatening litigation, or claim to have been defamed online. Importantly, entertainment lawyers must have an industry-level understanding of their clients' area of expertise in order to provide the best possible service. As such, it is uncommon for any one lawyer to work across all areas of entertainment law; rather, they are likely to specialise in one space, such as just music, or specifically film.

What are the Challenges and Rewards of Working in This Area?

Working in entertainment law can be highly rewarding as it provides lawyers with the opportunity to assist artists who may otherwise have a limited understanding of their rights, or who may have been pressured into unfavourable agreements with industry professionals. This too though is one of the area's challenges. That creators are typically unfamiliar with the law can lead to disappointment if they are unable to obtain the result they are seeking, such as when trade mark applications are refused. As a consequence, it is important to explain possible roadblocks in the process before commencement of work. Similarly, fee structure ought to be set out early, for many pre-breakthrough artists face necessary budgeting in respect of their creative career pursuits. When a client does 'blow up', this is most rewarding. A client's success is also their lawyers', and reflective of a job well done.

[151] Kirk Schroder, *Entertainment and Sports Industries*, American Bar Association. https://www.americanbar.org/newsletter/publications/gp_solo_magazine_home/gp_solo_magazine_index/schroder.html

Recent Developments in Entertainment Law

As with other subsidiaries of media law, entertainment law has expanded and developed since the advent of the Internet, as well as other technological advancements in the movement towards an online industry. Of particular noteworthiness are online services such as YouTube and Twitch, which have opened an array of jurisdictional issues, copyright questions, and challenges due to ongoing changes in partnership agreements. Despite the arrival of these new platforms, the role of entertainment lawyers has, in essence, stayed the same; to ensure this avenue is fair and productive, and that their client's rights are heard and acknowledged.

Resources and Tips for Interested Students

Students interested in pursuing a career in entertainment law ought to be aware, as already mentioned, that the most reliable entertainment lawyers are often those who hail from a strong background in their relevant area, whether this be music, television, or similar.[152] For example, bands and artists benefit most from a lawyer familiar with the workings of the music industry, for they can relate to and understand the position of the artist and act in their best interest. As such, this area of law is intrinsically linked to a love of the arts, in one form or another, and is best suited to those with existing networks in and passion for entertainment.

It is also worth noting that, though entertainment law sounds like a glamorous area of practice, it is not necessarily so.[153] Working with artists can be stressful, and deadlines may be short. Clients may also be demanding, particularly if they see themselves as of celebrity-level status and hence deserving of your full and immediate attention. This being said, working in this field can be highly rewarding, and comes well recommended for those who believe they are up for the challenge.

Career Pathway

The best way to begin your career in entertainment law is to research relevant firms in your city and enquire as to possible internships. Though entertainment law firms may not advertise volunteer positions, there are often such opportunities available to those who seek them out.

---

[152] Ibid.

[153] Gordon Firemark, *What Does An Entertainment Lawyer Do?* (20 July 2012) Law Offices of Gordon P. Firemark. https://firemark.com/2012/07/20/what-does-an-entertainment-lawyer-do-part-i/

As mentioned, most entertainment lawyers hail from a background in entertainment generally; gaining industry knowledge before or during the commencement of your career in this field is sure to open doors, as is networking with potential future clients. A background in commercial law is also highly beneficial – hence, a beginning in this area may lead to later opportunities in the field of entertainment.

Environmental Law

What is Environmental Law?

Environmental law is a broad term generally referring to laws regulating how humans interact with the environment,[154] including the management and protection of natural resources.[155] In earnest, a separate book could be written just on specialist areas within environmental law. This area of the law is an example of a strong intersection between policy and the law, with lawyers working not just to interpret the law, but to influence policy.

Closely linked to planning and construction law, environmental law impacts large-scale projects which will often require comprehensive consideration of their environmental impact.[156] In addition, environmental law is closely linked to clean technologies. Due to its intersection with innovation and project development, many large companies employ lawyers to consult on planning and environmental awareness.

Approval for large projects is often required by ministerial departments. Environmental law also stretches to local governments, who are responsible for things such as planning approvals, waste collection/disposal, water management and supply, coastal management, sewage, pollution, conservation and maintenance of existing ecosystems.[157] These are just some examples of the spectrum of work environmental lawyers may deal with or specialise in.

What are the Challenges and Rewards of Working in This Area?

Environmental law often requires striking a balance between potential economic activity with environmental impacts.[158] This can be a tricky balancing act, with many elements and interest groups competing for primary consideration. Despite

---

[154] Rachael J Baird, *Environmental Law* (Thomson Reuters, 1st ed., 2012), 3.

[155] Raphael J Heffron, *Energy law: an Introduction* (Springerlink, 1st ed., 2015), 6.

[156] Baird, above n 1, 7.

[157] Ibid, 1.

[158] Ibid, 3.

these complexities, environmental law can be truly rewarding and serve to enrich communities: from protecting national parks to allowing beneficial projects executed sustainably and responsibly.

Recent Developments in Environmental Law

Over the past two decades, one of the most prominent areas of progress in environmental law in terms of media coverage and policy development has been climate change law.[159] In Australia, this has included Commonwealth law requiring annual reports from corporations on their greenhouse gas emissions and energy use.[160] Lawyers make up a large number of the specialists employed to consult on policy development and implementation in this area.

Resources and Tips for Interested Students

Remaining aware and informed about the environmental consequences of activities – whether they be the building of government highways, mining ventures or the implementation of local recycling promotions – will assist students in developing an understanding of where jobs or volunteer opportunities may arise. Much of the work completed in this area involves being aware of assessment processes for new projects and streamlining them where possible; as such, demonstrating awareness of the impact of projects and the nature of assessment criteria will make you stand out when applying for experience-building positions. Many organisations welcome volunteers and interns seeking experience in environmental law.

Whilst at law school, look to join environmental awareness groups. Most universities have student-run environmental/conservation groups which can assist you in finding meaningful conservation projects and remaining alive to environmental issues. Also look to implement environmentally-conscious agendas in other groups in which you participate. Becoming an advocate for minimising waste or an environmentally-aware approach to a university construction project can be rewarding for the community as well as for you, both personally and professionally. Professionally, you gain valuable experience which will help you determine if you are best-suited to this area, but you also demonstrate a commitment that may catch the eye of future employers.

As environmental law can often involve large-scale litigation, mooting is a great way to improve your advocacy skills and prepare you for court appearances later in your career.

---

[159] Baird, above n 1, 2.

[160] See the *National Greenhouse and Energy Reporting Act 2007.*

Career Pathway

There is no one career pathway for environmental law; instead, look to the area you are most passionate about and work toward developing networks, skills and experience there. Broadly, careers in private firms or corporations, government or academia can accommodate a meaningful career in environmental law.[161] Starting your career in one of these streams will not prevent you later changing course and, in fact, a diverse range of experiences is often beneficial for professional development.

Local governments and government bodies such as the Department of the Environment and Energy play a huge role in policy development and project approval.[162] For those interested in environmental law, graduate or junior positions in these bodies are an ideal way to start a career in this area. Look at the dates for graduate role applications early in your law degree to avoid missing deadlines in your final year; the Department for Environment and Energy graduate position applications, for example, close around February/March.[163]

Equipment Finance Law

What is Equipment Finance Law?

Equipment financing is a distinct industry that involves the provision of infrastructure and goods for business. This area is dominated by contractual relationships and proprietary interests. There are multiple methods of obtaining finance which include private leasing or hiring agreements, pre-pay of equipment, equipment pools, bridge financing and guarantees on work and credit.[164]

A major area of equipment finance law includes the leases and contracting of corporate and commercial aircraft, marine vessels, railcars and locomotives, trucks and other transportation, agricultural machinery and mining equipment, office and information technology equipment, medical technology and even alternative energy products like wind turbines and solar technology. There are many parties to commercial leasing transactions including buyers, sellers, lessors, lessees, owners, lenders, trustees and creditors.

---

[161] *What is an Environmental Lawyer,* Environmental Science.org. https://www.environmental-science.org/career/environmental-lawyer

[162] Baird, above n 1, 12.

[163] *Graduate Program*, The Department of Environment and Energy. http://www.environment.gov.au/about-us/employment/graduate-program

[164] Linda Deelen and Kwaky Osei Bonsu, 'Equipment finance for small contractors in public work programmes', March 2002, Published by Social Finance Programme Employment-intensive Investment Branch, Working Paper No 8.

What are the Challenges and Rewards of Working in This Area?

A commercial background of some inclination will be useful in this area. This area of law is heavily dependent on business acumen and can present numerous challenges during economic downturn. Whilst there is a lot of transactional work, it is also a heavily litigated field. It is a rewarding industry to be involved in due to the variety of subject matter and case law that is involved. There is also the opportunity to develop one's skills in this industry and to increase the capacity of one's workload based on the calibre of the clients involved.

Recent Developments in Equipment Finance Law

Due to the relative bargaining status of parties involved in equipment financing, unfair contract terms are always an area of interest. The New South Wales Supreme Court has recently dispensed with a leasing dispute over the rental of computer technology. Adams J noted that whilst the strict terms of the contract may have amounted to unjust enrichment or an unfair advantage, he was bound to uphold a strict construction. This decision arguably represents the extension of the rights of consumers under the *Competition and Consumer Act 2009* (Cth).[165]

Another key area of equipment financing that has seen recent progress is aviation financing and leasing. Aviation law has an intrinsically international character and is primarily dictated by the Chicago Convention.[166] The International Civil Aviation Organization has recently published Circular 295 which seeks to address responsibility and accountability for states in the transfer of aviation equipment between jurisdictions.[167] This provides an insight into the varying issues one may encounter in the domestic and international sphere.

Resources and Tips for Interested Students

Equipment financing traverses many different subject areas within the law. The scale and degree of the particular projects one works on will depend on the size of clientele. Some firms will represent large companies and others will assist with relatively small transactions. Many legal disciplines are involved in this area of law including banking, tax, property, contract and litigation. Students would be best

[165] *Unison Finance Group Pty Ltd v Electric Life Pty Limited* [2015] NSWSC 170.

[166] Convention on International Civil Aviation Doc 7300, 4 April 1947.

[167] Ruwantissa Abeyratne, 'Rulemaking in Air Transport: A Deconstructive Analysis', Springer International Publishing 2016, 19.

advised to undertake some preliminary research or to enrol in construction law or commercial leasing electives at university.

Career Pathway

A background in commercial law will almost be essential in this field. However, any commercial or business experience will be advantageous to students embarking on a career in equipment finance law. A variety of employment options are available, including working at a firm that specialises in equipment financing or leasing, working as in-house counsel for a company directly, or administering public works projects. Further tertiary education in the format of a Master's of Law in Banking and Finance Law may be advantageous to students who are intent on pursuing a career in this area.

Family Law

What is Family Law?

Family law is an area of law covering personal, domestic and family relationships and the legal ramifications of such relationships. Usually, this includes matters such as property disputes, the wellbeing and care of children, divorce, annulments and disputes over maintenance.[168] Beyond separations, family law also covers issues relating to adoption and fostering children, surrogacy and artificial insemination, and children travelling overseas. In Australia, family law is an area of concurrent jurisdiction, meaning that both state and federal laws can apply.[169] Under ss 51(xxi) and (xxii) of the Constitution, the power to make laws relating to marriage and divorce rests with the Federal Parliament.[170] However, the scope of federal family law has gradually expanded, including not just marriage, but also matters relating to property and finances – except in Western Australia.[171] State legislation continues to operate for some aspects of family law, such as the welfare of children.[172]

---

[168] LexisNexis, *Encyclopaedic Australian Legal Dictionary* (at 29 November 2017) 'Family Law'.

[169] Ibid.

[170] Oxford University Press, *Australian Law Dictionary* (at 29 November 2017), 'Family Law'; *Australian Constitution.*

[171] Above n 1.

[172] Ibid.

What are the Challenges and Rewards of Working in This Area?

Family law is regarded as an emotionally charged area of law which affects clients and lawyers alike. Often in family law proceedings clients are at their most vulnerable, especially where it concerns children. A career in family law can be truly rewarding, helping these clients amidst relationship breakdowns, family violence and child abuse. An effective family lawyer exercises empathy and is able to handle the vast gamut of emotions that the parties bring to their case. Cases are unique and can involve property, superannuation, contract, succession, trust and criminal laws. Negotiation and mediation are also familiar territories to family lawyers who typically prefer a conciliatory approach over the combative adversarial nature of court. Indeed, the introduction of compulsory mediation prior to litigation is intended to promote an open dialogue between the parties and reduce post-separation traumas.

Recent Developments in Family Law

The adversarial nature of litigation is considerably more problematic in family law than with other areas. Zealous advocacy, for instance, is inappropriate when the court is required to determine matters in the child's best interests – for example, when deciding where children will live and who they will spend time with. Likewise, the rules of litigation disempower the parents, who are the traditional decision makers, from determining their children's futures.[173]

As a result, there has been a push to reduce the role of courts in family law disputes and encourage out-of-court settlement via compulsory family dispute resolution,[174] government-funded family relationship centres, a 12-month limitation period for property division applications,[175] and an administrative (rather than judicial) body to handle child support assessments.[176] In *Re Kelvin*,[177] the Full Court of the Family Court, overturning previous authority, held that a minor seeking hormone-therapy treatment for gender dysphoria was not required to seek the court's approval – a process that resulted in an average delay of eight months and a cost between $8,000 and $30,000.[178] These developments illustrate that

[173] Firestone & Weinstein "In the Best Interests of the Children: A Proposal to Transform the Adversarial System" (2004) 42(2) *Family Court Review* 203, 204.

[174] See *Family Law Act 1975 (Cth)* ss 13C, 60I.

[175] *Family Law Act 1975 (Cth)* s 44(3).

[176] See Australian Government Department of Human Services, "Child Support". https://www.humanservices.gov.au/individuals/child-support

[177] [2017] FamCAFC 258.

[178] Fiona Kelly, "'The Court Process Is Slow but Biology Is Fast': Assessing the Impact of the Family Court Approval Process on Transgender Children and Their Families" (2016) *La Trobe Law School – Law & Justice Research Paper Series*, Paper No. 16–4 as cited in *Re Kelvin* [2017] FamCAFC 258 at [54] (Thackray, Strickland & Murphy JJ).

therapeutic jurisprudence is becoming an increasingly important consideration in the way family lawyers act for their clients.

Resources and Tips for Interested Students

Student involvement in community legal centres, many of which provide assistance in family law, is likely to provide an excellent insight into the area. For students lucky enough to have first-hand involvement with clients whilst volunteering, it is important to bring an open mind and ear. Clients will often be seeking assistance on matters of a highly personal and emotional nature.

Local magistrates' courts can also provide students with practical family law experiences. While some family issues are heard at a federal level, many popular matters, such as those concerning intervention orders, are undertaken at local courts. Further, local courts often give rise to nearby law firms practising in areas relevant to the court, which typically includes family law. Visiting your local magistrates court or speaking with a surrounding family lawyer or barrister is a great way to learn more about this area of the legal profession. For even greater benefit, students may wish to seek out an internship at a family law firm, or shadow a family law barrister.

Lastly, there are a number of organisations that employ students on a voluntary basis to deliver educational seminars in family law to prisoners.[179] These opportunities are best suited to students who seek to 'dive in at the deep end' of family law. If selected, students are guaranteed an in-depth and unequivocal family law experience.

Students are advised to avoid restricting their experiences if interested in this area of law. As family law is highly diverse, it is beneficial to obtain knowledge of a broad range of legal specialities, including but not limited to; property and contract law, company law, criminal law, tax and trusts.

Career Pathway

Family law is a subject you can elect to study in your law degree, though it is not compulsory to have studied the subject before practising. Studying family law and practising it are very different.[180]

As with any legal specialty, you can become an 'accredited specialist' in family law by sitting the exam set by the Accredited Specialisation Board. However, you must first show the Board that you have worked a certain number of hours in this

[179] See, e.g., The Prison Legal Education and Assistance Project (PLEA) at http://pleaproject.org.au/

[180] See tips from a practicing Accredited Specialist on the Law Institute of Victoria's "LIV Young LawyersBlog".https://www.liv.asn.au/younglawyersblog/april-2014/why-choose-to-specialise-in-family-law-

area. Studying for accreditation will fill gaps in your knowledge and serves as public validation of your skills in the area of family law.

Firearm Law

What is Firearm Law?

This is an area of law covering use of and access to guns and firearms. Firearms are regulated to varying degrees all over the world. In Australia each state has its own gun laws. However, federal laws govern the importation of firearms into Australia. The current approach to gun laws can be traced to the reforming influence of former Prime Minister John Howard after the tragic 1996 Port Arthur massacre.[181] Mr Howard and his government worked closely with states to convince them of the need to create more uniformity in gun license laws and regulations governing storage and registration of weapons.[182] A firearms license is required in order to legally possess or use a registered firearm, and are governed by state acts such as the *Firearms Act 1996* (Vic).[183] A firearms licence can only be issued where the applicant has satisfied the Commissioner of Police that they have a 'genuine reason for possession or using the firearm'.[184] This generally includes reasons such as recreational hunting or pest control.[185] However, protecting yourself or your property is not considered a genuine reason for issuing a firearms licence.[186] Firearm law can also be an interesting area in terms of international and human rights law. Various international and regional treaties, protocols and conventions cover the field of firearm use, importation, and classification of weapons, as well as the use of force in conflicts.[187] The use of weapons is an area with great potential for policy considerations and continues to be a matter of public interest and academic debate.

---

[181] Anne Davies, *Seizing The Moment On Gun Control Changed Australia, Says John Howard* (2018) The Sydney Morning Herald. http://www.smh.com.au/national/seizing-the-moment-on-gun-control-changed-australia-john-howard-20160424-godwg6.html

[182] Ibid.

[183] *Firearms Act 1996* (Vic).

[184] LexisNexis, *Encyclopaedic Australian Legal Dictionary* (at 18 February 2018) "Firearms Licence".

[185] Ibid.

[186] Ibid.

[187] Stuart Casey-Maslen, *Weapons Under International Human Rights Law* (Cambridge University Press, 1st ed., 2014).

What are the Challenges and Rewards of Working in This Area?

Lawyers working in firearm law usually will not work exclusively in this area. This will generally mean that lawyers are barristers or solicitors who work in criminal law and may specialise in defending persons charged with weapons offences, or assist in appeals to the relevant tribunals and give advice in the issuing of licences. This can be an interesting area that will often touch on other areas of law including administrative law. For more information on the work conducted by a criminal barrister or solicitor see the "Criminal Law" section of this chapter.

This can also mean that solicitors or legal researchers can work in a policy capacity with government inquiries or other research into the use of firearms, both in Australia and internationally. If you are interested in human rights law, this can also be an interesting area of research and practice. There are a number of organisations that lobby for different sides of the firearms debate including human rights groups.

Recent Developments in Firearm Law

Firearm law continues to be an issue that is debated not only in Australia but around the world – particularly in the United States following continued gun violence tragedies and mass shootings.[188]

There have also been legislative responses to terrorism, in particular the 2014 Sydney siege, which have resulted in more restrictive laws around bail, firearm licences and possessing stolen firearms.[189] In 2017 there was a national firearms amnesty where all states and territories allowed any persons to surrender firearms or weapons without being prosecuted for possession of an unregistered firearm or ammunition.[190] This demonstrates that there have been continued efforts to reduce both unregistered firearms and gun violence in Australia.

---

[188] Katie Beck, *Would Australia's Gun Laws Help The US?* (2018) BBC News. http://www.bbc.com/news/world-australia-35048251

[189] *New NSW Bail And Firearms Laws Announced In Response To Lindt Cafe Sydney Siege* (2018) ABC News. http://www.abc.net.au/news/2015-08-28/mike-baird-announces-bail-and-illegal-firearms-reform/6732332

[190] *2017 National Firearms Amnesty | Victorian Government* (2018) Vic.gov.au. https://www.vic.gov.au/news/2017-national-firearms-amnesty.html

Franchise Law

What is Franchise Law?

Franchise law is the area of law governing the relationship between franchisors and franchisees who are bound together by franchise agreements. In simple terms, a franchise agreement exists where one party (the franchisor) grants another party (the franchisee) 'the right to carry on the business of offering, supplying or distributing goods or services in Australia under a system or marketing plan substantially determined, controlled or suggested by the franchisor'[191] where the carrying on of said business will be associated with a trade mark owned by the franchisor.[192]

Australian franchise law is governed specifically by the Franchising Code of Conduct (Code) found in Schedule 1 of the *Competition and Consumer Act 2010* (Cth),[193] which adds a statutory element to the generally common law area of contracts with regards to franchise agreements. The Code is notable in various regards; for example, the code specifies civil penalties for those who fail to act in good faith, over and above regular remedies that would usually be available at common law to restore an aggrieved party.[194] It is also of note that the Code provides that the obligation to act in good faith is an active, statutory duty, as opposed to merely an implied contractual term.[195]

Franchise law is involved in a large portion of the Australian economy, with total sales revenue for Australia's franchise sector estimated at $146 billion with 472,000 employees as of 2016.[196] As such, franchise agreements affect a significant number of individuals and businesses throughout Australia; lawyers practising in commercial law are likely to come across issues arising out of franchise agreements. A lawyer practising in this area could be tasked with advising franchisees and franchisors how to structure agreements, drafting franchising agreements and settling disputes arising out of franchising agreements.

[191] *Competition and Consumer (Industry Codes – Franchising) Regulation 2014* Sch 1 cl 5 (1)(b).

[192] Ibid 5 (1)(c).

[193] *2010* (Cth).

[194] *Competition and Consumer (Industry Codes – Franchising) Regulation 2014* Sch 1 cl 6.

[195] Ibid.

[196] The Franchise Centre, *2016 survey shows franchising on the rise in Australia*. https://www.franchise.edu.au/home/research/franchise-australia/2016-survey-shows-franchising-on-the-rise-in-australia

What are the Challenges and Rewards of Working in This Area?

The challenges and rewards of working in franchise law are similar to those of working in commercial law generally; namely, practitioners will require attention to detail and deep knowledge of relevant legislation, regulations and procedures.

Franchise law is by no means a standalone area of law; practitioners will benefit from keeping up to date in developments in contract and commercial law, but also intellectual property law, property law and others. A holistic knowledge of these areas will enable a practitioner to better further their client's interests.

Business ownership is an ambition of many individuals, and a practitioner skilled in franchise law can aid clients realise their goals while making what can be a convoluted and intimidating legal process more approachable. Similarly, disputes arising out of franchise agreements can be an extremely stressful process in which an understanding and diligent practitioner is indispensable. Litigation in particular has the ability to destroy the livelihoods of individuals and cause businesses to go bankrupt; a practitioner who pre-empts disputes through the thorough drafting of agreements and provision of quality advice is of immense benefit to their clients.

Recent Developments in Franchise Law

The recent, extremely well publicised case of 7-Eleven franchisees underpaying their workers has brought an enormous amount of public debate and scrutiny onto the franchise system as a whole.[197] 7-Eleven is the most widespread petrol retailer in Australia and certainly the most recognisable, however this did not prevent (and indeed may have contributed to) franchisees running afoul of the Code. The Fair Work Ombudsman, reporting on the underpayment of employees by 7-Eleven franchisees, noted that 7-Eleven had a 'culture of non-compliance'[198] with a system ostensibly in place to handle instances of non-compliance which was easily manipulated by franchisees.[199] 7-Eleven drew particular scorn from the public for its targeting of migrant workers who were in a vulnerable position due to having their visa statuses exploited by non-compliant franchisees.[200] This has given cause for some to strongly advocate for reforms to the franchise law system, with equally strong

[197] Alison Branley, *7-Eleven staff work twice as long at half pay rate, investigation reveals* (29 August 2015) Australian Broadcasting Corporation. http://www.abc.net.au/news/2015-08-29/7-eleven-half-pay-scam-exposed/6734174

[198] Fair Work Ombudsman, *Identifying and addressing the drivers of non-compliance in the 7-Eleven network* (April 2016). https://www.fairwork.gov.au/ArticleDocuments/763/7-eleven-inquiry-report.pdf.aspx. 7–11.

[199] Ibid 4.

[200] Ibid 14.

resistance being espoused from those who argue that said reforms would hurt businesses.[201]

Resources and Tips for Interested Students

As previously mentioned, franchise law overlaps with many different areas of law; primarily contract and commercial law but also property law, employment law, and intellectual property law, among others. Setting yourself up as a candidate with a holistic understanding of the needs of clients rather than just a strict theoretical knowledge of franchise law will aid you in providing quality legal service and setting you apart from other candidates.

As with many other areas of civil law, practitioners practising in franchise law will benefit from an aptitude for alternate dispute resolution; there is currently a push to have the vast majority of civil disputes decided out of court, and an appreciation for this along with relevant skills in areas such as negotiation and mediation will help set you apart as a candidate concerned with the overall needs of their clients rather than one preoccupied exclusively with legal considerations.

Gaming Law

What is Gaming Law?

Gaming law concerns the rules and regulations associated with the gambling industry, which includes activities undertaken in casinos, at racetracks and in lotteries.[202] Clients in this area may include gaming machine manufacturers, casino operators, gaming service providers, waging operators, and gambling industry associations.[203]

Gaming lawyers often find themselves advising businesses within the gambling sector of strategies, and how to approach these within the legal framework. Other common issues include licences, changes of control and breaches, commercial arrangements and transactions, intellectual property rights, and reviewing obligations.

---

201 Bruce McFarlane, *7-Eleven sparked reforms will bring franchising chaos* (18 April 2017) Sydney Morning Herald. http://www.smh.com.au/business/workplace-relations/7eleven-sparked-reforms-will-bring-franchising-chaos-20170417-gvm2qj.html

202 NSW Department of Industry, *Gaming & Wagering Law*, NSW Government. http://www.liquorandgaming.nsw.gov.au/Pages/gaming/law-and-policy/gaming-law.aspx

203 Addisons, *Gambling*, Addisons. http://www.addisonslawyers.com.au/service/Gambling/default.aspx

For legal work in the field of video games, please refer to the "Entertainment Law" section.

What are the Challenges and Rewards of Working in This Area?

Gaming law is particularly challenging in that the activities it involves are impactful on community welfare. Addiction is a constant concern in this industry, hence its firm and heavy regulation across the country. As a consequence, lawyers practising in this area may find themselves worrying about the ethical component of their work. However, this is not a challenge unique to gaming law. Often in other (and widespread) areas of law, lawyers will meet with situations that are ethically questionable and need to manage this accordingly.

This area is rewarding in that it is unusual and rather niche. It therefore presents otherwise unlikely situations and issues, the likes of which could not be experienced if practising in other areas of law.

Recent Developments in Gaming Law

Due to the introduction of new technologies, the gambling industry has recently become highly globalised. This has had significant implications for its regulation, revenue collection and community welfare, particularly as opportunities to gamble are now more readily available and often international.[204]

Traditionally, gaming services have been regulated at the state and territory level. However, since the introduction of new communication technologies, the Commonwealth government has faced required involvement, for these fall within their constitutional obligations and responsibilities. As a consequence, the gambling industry has become even more highly regulated, and federal legislation has been introduced to cater for these new issues.

Resources and Tips for Interested Students

Students interested in gaming law would be well advised of its similarity to other areas of law – gaming law is in many ways similar to commercial law, intellectual property, finance law and dispute resolution, to name a few. Therefore, those

---

[204] Kim Jackson, *Gambling Policy and Regulation* (September 2001) Parliament of Australia. https://www.aph.gov.au/About_Parliament/Parliamentary_Departments/Parliamentary_Library/Publications_Archive/archive/gamblingebrief

seeking to pursue a career in gaming law would benefit from studying subjects in these areas, or from completing some personal research into these topics.

As with any area of interest, the curious student would benefit from investigating and finding local firms with a gaming law specialisation. Making contact with said firms in respect of possible internship or shadowing opportunities cannot be more highly recommended as a means of commencing one's career in this area.

Career Pathway

As mentioned, gaming law is a blend of several other areas of law including, most prominently, commercial law. It is therefore feasible, and in some ways advisable, for a young lawyer to first practice in commercial law before finding their footing in gaming law. This will allow for a general grasp of commercial law to be gained, to the advantage and increased employability of the graduated student.

This being said, it is of course possible for graduate students to enter into gaming law directly out of law school. There are a number of firms that practice in this area who may be open to employing graduate students, should an appropriate enquiry be made.

Immigration Law

What is Immigration Law?

Immigration law refers to the body of law that provides the Australian government with control over who may enter the country, for temporary or permanent residence, and the terms of an individual's residence.[205] The most important pieces of legislation for lawyers practising in immigration law are the *Migration Act 1958* (Cth) and the *Migration Regulations 1994* (Cth), the latter document dealing with the types of visas that may be granted.[206] As decisions in immigration law are a form of government action, immigration law is an area of administrative law. Therefore, there may be both merits review and judicial review avenues open, depending on the particular case. Merits review is available for particular cases under the *Migration Act 1958* (Cth); for example, on-shore refugee claimants may seek merits review.[207]

Constitutional law may also has an impact on immigration law, such as High Court cases which review the constitutionality of the migration system. An example

[205] Ray Finkelstein and David Hamer (eds), *LexisNexis Concise Australian Legal Dictionary* (LexisNexis, 5th ed., 2015) 308.

[206] Ibid.

[207] Ibid 407.

of this was a case decided in February 2016 which challenged the constitutionality of funding offshore detention, *Plaintiff M68/2015 v Minister for Immigration and Border Protection & Ors* [2016] HCA 1.[208] The funding was upheld as constitutional.[209]

What are the Challenges and Rewards of Working in This Area?

Immigration law is a highly political area of the law as it involves refugees and asylum seekers. Due to the human rights issues surrounding refugee and asylum seeker policy, in particular the policies of mandatory detention, immigration law can have political consequences in the Australian and global community.[210] High-profile human rights lawyers often receive public attention for their work, such as Julian Burnside QC who has reported receiving hate mail from the public for his work and views on refugee and asylum seeker policy.[211] It may be emotional but rewarding work if you are passionate about the rights of asylum seekers and refugees.

There are many people who need immigration law advice other than refugees and asylum seekers. Any person who decides to move to Australia from another country is considered a migrant.[212] For example, people may require visas for work or study, or they may be seeking residence as a skilled migrant.

Recent Developments in Immigration Law

Stephen Gageler SC, writing in 2010, deemed it a 'trite' observation that migration law has been the most litigated area of administrative law in the last 25 years.[213] Gageler then notes that, as a consequence, migration law has provided the legislative framework for the greatest developments in administrative law, driven by the High Court, in those 25 years.[214] Recent developments in administrative law, with the *Migration Act 1958* (Cth) as the legislation in question, include the case of

[208] Julian Burnside, *Watching Out: Reflections on Justice and Injustice* (Scribe Publications, 2017) 200.

[209] Ibid 203.

[210] Ibid 200.

[211] Ibid 195; 211.

[212] Finkelstein and Hamer, above n 1, 407.

[213] Stephen Gageler, 'Impact of Migration Law on the Development of Australian Administrative law' (2010) 17 AJ Admin L 92, 92.

[214] Ibid 93.

Graham v Minister for Immigration and Border Protection.[215] The case concerned clauses in the *Migration Act 1958* (Cth) that limited the evidence available to the Court when it was confidential information. The High Court held that the clause was constitutionally invalid as it amounted 'to a substantial curtailment of the capacity of a Court exercising jurisdiction under or derived from s 75(v)'.[216]

Resources and Tips for Interested Students

There are community legal centres aimed towards providing legal assistance in immigration law. It may be possible to volunteer at a community legal centre in your state that offers immigration law. In particular, due to the human rights implications around asylum seekers and refugees, many general human rights law groups may provide legal assistance to refugees and asylum seekers.

Career Pathway

Immigration law is an area of administrative law, and administrative law is required to be studied in order to be admitted as a lawyer.[217] Therefore, it is likely that you will come across some of the important cases involving the *Migration Act 1958* (Cth) before being admitted.

In order to give 'immigration assistance' as defined by s 276 of the *Migration Act 1958* (Cth), you will need to become a migration agent, which requires a separate qualification outside of your law degree.[218] Immigration assistance includes work involved with migration procedure,[219] such as assisting clients in their application for a visa or preparing documentation required to sponsor a visa applicant.[220] However, a lawyer can provide 'immigration legal assistance' as defined by s 277 of *Migration Act 1958* (Cth).[221] A migration agent must be registered and pay a fee every year to the government.[222] You will need to be qualified as both a lawyer and a migration agent if you seek to practice in both areas of migration law.

---

[215] *Graham v Minister for Immigration and Border Protection; Te Puia v Minister for Immigration and Border Protection* [2017] HCA 33.

[216] Ibid [64].

[217] Law Council of Australia, *Prescribed Academic Areas of Knowledge* (December 2016) https://www.lawcouncil.asn.au/files/web-pdf/LACC%20docs/243473563_1_Prescribed_Academic_Areas_of_Knowledge.pdf

[218] Finkelstein and Hamer, above n 1, 407; *Migration Act 1958* (Cth), s 280(1).

[219] Finkelstein and Hamer, above n 1, 407.

[220] *Migration Act 1958* (Cth), s 276.

[221] *Migration Act 1958* (Cth), s 280(3).

[222] Finkelstein and Hamer, above n 1, 407.

Indigenous Law

What is Indigenous Law?

In the Australian legal system, the term 'indigenous' refers to any person or group of people that inhabited Australia prior to English colonisation.[223] This area of law involves the rights of Indigenous Australians, which includes native title claims; that is, a claim that native title interests and rights exist as governed by the *Native Title Act 1993* (Cth).[224] Native title was first recognised in the common law in the landmark case of *Mabo v Queensland [No 2]* (1992) 175 CLR 1 and was further recognised and regulated in legislation when the *Native Title Act 1993* (Cth) was passed.[225] The Native Title Registrar is responsible for managing native title applications, while the role of the National Native Title Tribunal, created under s 107 of the *Native Title Act 1993* (Cth), is to investigate and determine applications for native title.[226]

The term 'indigenous rights' also refers to legal rights of Indigenous Australians other than land claim rights.[227] The Indigenous Australian community face many inequalities in areas such as education, health and the protection of culture, languages, women and children.[228] The Indigenous Australian community also face higher rates of poverty and higher incarceration rates.[229] Consequently, promoting indigenous rights may involve practice and knowledge of areas of law other than native title law, such as criminal law, social security law, family law and human rights law.

What are the Challenges and Rewards of Working in This Area?

If you are passionate about human rights, then working in indigenous law may be highly rewarding, as many indigenous rights issues are also human rights issues.[230] The work can also be emotional due to the inequalities faced by Indigenous Australians.

---

[223] Ray Finkelstein and David Hamer (eds), *LexisNexis Concise Australian Legal Dictionary* (LexisNexis, 5th ed., 2015) 321.

[224] Ibid 422.

[225] Ibid.

[226] Ibid 420; 422.

[227] Ibid 321.

[228] Mick Gooda, 'Human Rights and Australia's Indigenous Peoples' in Paula Gerber and Melissa Castan (eds), *Contemporary Perspectives on Human Rights Law in Australia* (Lawbook, 2013) 302, 303.

[229] Ibid.

[230] Ibid.

Recent Developments in Indigenous Law

A current issue in indigenous law is that, presently, Indigenous Australians do not have constitutional recognition.[231] Sir Anthony Mason described the lack of recognition of Indigenous Australians as a 'glaring omission' in the Constitution.[232] On 30 June 2017, the Referendum Council released their Final Report on constitutional recognition of Indigenous Australians, recommending that the federal government hold a referendum on whether to include 'a body that gives Aboriginal and Torres Strait Islander peoples a Voice to the Commonwealth Parliament' in the Australian Constitution.[233] The government rejected this recommendation.[234]

Resources and Tips for Interested Students

Due to the human rights issues around indigenous rights, many human rights law groups provide assistance to Indigenous Australians. There may be volunteer positions available at a legal centre dedicated to promoting human rights law in your state. There are also internships available to students in indigenous law, for example the Aurora Project. The Aurora Project offers law internships to non-indigenous and indigenous students and graduates.[235] The placement may involve native title and land claims, social justice, policy development in relation to indigenous rights, constitutional law issues or local government regulation issues.[236] Further, writing on recent topics in indigenous law and reading articles on indigenous law may further your understanding of relevant issues. For example, keeping up to date with the *Australian Indigenous Law Review*, a peer-reviewed journal on current issues in indigenous law,[237] may assist in furthering you awareness and understanding.

---

[231] Commonwealth of Australia Referendum Council, *Final Report of the Referendum Council* (30 June 2017), iii. https://www.referendumcouncil.org.au/final-report

[232] Australian Human Rights Commission, *Constitutional reform: Creating a nation for all of us*, Social Justice Report 2010, 29. http://www.humanrights.gov.au/sites/default/files/content/social_justice/sj_report/sjreport10/pdf/sjr2010_CH2.pdf

[233] Commonwealth of Australia Referendum Council, *Final Report of the Referendum Council* (30 June 2017), 38. https://www.referendumcouncil.org.au/final-report

[234] Henry Bolt and Emily Laurence, *Malcolm Turnbull Defends Decision to Abandon Constitutional Recognition of Indigenous Australians* (5 November 2017) Australian Broadcasting Corporation. http://www.abc.net.au/news/2017-11-05/malcolm-turnbull-defends-decision-on-indigenous-recognition/9120252

[235] The Aurora Project, *Internship Streams: Legal* (January 2018). http://auroraproject.com.au/legal

[236] Ibid.

[237] University of New South Wales, *Australian Indigenous Law Review* (21 December 2017). http://www.ilc.unsw.edu.au/publications/australian-indigenous-law-review

Career Pathway

As noted above, work in indigenous law may require knowledge of native title law, criminal law, social security law, family law and human rights law. Students interested in practising in indigenous law may consider work in a community legal service in indigenous communities or work for legal aid organisations.

Currently, law reform and policy development is required in order to better address the human rights issues faced by Indigenous Australians.[238] Therefore, there is a large amount of work to be done in law reform with regard to the rights of Indigenous Australians. Work at a law reform agency may lead to researching and practising in indigenous law. The Univeristy of New South Wales Indigenous Law Centre is currently the only law centre dedicated to indigenous law in Australia.[239] However, other generalist human rights law centres also address issues in indigenous law.[240]

Insurance Law

What is Insurance Law?

Insurance can be said to be the agreement between two parties where one person, the insurer, undertakes, in return for some agreed consideration, to pay another person a sum of money or equivalent benefit, on the happening of a specified event, the occurrence or timing of which is uncertain.[241] As such, insurance law is the area of law governing agreements of this type and can be quite distinct from similar areas of contract law, with a noticeably higher level of statutory involvement than most comparable areas.

In terms of relevant legislation, insurance law is broadly governed on the federal level pursuant to the 'corporations power' of the Constitution.[242] The most important (but by no means the only) pieces of legislation are the *Insurance Act 1973*[243] and the *Insurance Contracts Act 1984*.[244] The former establishes (among other things) a statutory solvency test requiring insurers to maintain a margin of capital

[238] Gooda, above n 6, 330.

[239] University of New South Wales, *Indigenous Law Centre* (19 December 2017). http://www.ilc.unsw.edu.au

[240] See e.g. Monash University, *Castan Centre: Indigenous* (September 2017). https://www.monash.edu/law/research/centres/castancentre/our-areas-of-work/indigenous

[241] *Prudential Insurance Co v Inland Revenue Cmrs* [1904] 2 KB 658, 663.

[242] *Australian Constitution* s 51(xx).

[243] (Cth).

[244] (Cth).

beyond the commercial solvency threshold.[245] The latter requires those party to an insurance contract to act in *utmost* good faith, which is a legal standard above the regular contractual duty to act in good faith. Specific sub-areas of insurance law can have their own relevant legislation as well, for example the *Life Insurance Act 1995*[246] or the *Marine Insurance Act 1909*.[247]

What are the Challenges and Rewards of Working in This Area?

Insurance law is a particularly complicated sub-area of contract law and as such comes with all the challenges of contract law but with added complexities. Care has to be taken to ensure that the relevant contracts are drafted and executed in such a way that not only complies with the common law principles applicable to all contracts, but also the statutory requirements specific to the particular type of insurance. This applies not only to the drafting of contracts but all of the work a practitioner would be expected to undertake in insurance law generally.

With added challenge, for some, comes added reward; there can be inherent satisfaction in overcoming a particularly difficult problem and insurance law is not short of issues to be considered and solved. If you are the kind of individual with a penchant for detail and complexity you may well find insurance law extremely stimulating.

Recent Developments in Insurance Law

The Australian insurance industry underwent an intense crisis over the first few years of the twenty-first century, leading to a number of reactionary reports and reforms being implemented which quite drastically shifted the state of not only insurance law but other areas of law as well, particularly torts law. While the nature of the crisis is itself quite complex, perhaps the most well-known cause of the crisis was unpredictability in the outcome of negligence disputes, which had a severe impact on many types of insurance, but in particular public liability insurance and

[245] Palmer J, *Review of the Role Played by the Australian Prudential Authority and the Insurance and Superannuation Commission in the Collapse of the HIH Group of Companies* (15 July 2002) Australian Prudential Regulatory Authority. http://www.apra.gov.au/mediareleases/documents/the-palmer-report.pdf. 16.

[246] (Cth).

[247] (Cth).

professional indemnity insurance,[248] which saw premiums increase to the point where many community and professional groups could no longer afford them.[249]

This led to the commissioning of a number of reports on insurance law and related areas of law, including the now very well known 'Ipp Report' (named after its chairman, the Honourable David Ipp), which made a number of recommendations on how the relevant tort law should be reformed to relieve pressure on the insurance industry.[250] In the broadest possible terms, the recommendations of the Ipp Report were largely implemented and increased certainty for all parties operating in the insurance industry by limiting the scope of various kinds of liability.[251]

Resources and Tips for Interested Students

The Australian insurance industry is strongly consolidated, with a relatively small number of companies maintaining a majority of the market share.[252] Most of these companies maintain large legal teams and some even run their own graduate programs. If a particular company seems like a good fit for you, endeavour to research what they look for in candidates; companies find candidates who want to work for *them* in particular much more attractive than a candidate who wants to work for *anyone*.

As mentioned previously, insurance law is, at its core, a sub-area of contract law, albeit a more complicated and much more statutorily involved sub-area. As such, a strong foundation in contract law will be a necessity, as well as a strong knowledge in the various other kinds of law affecting insurance companies, such as corporations law and securities law. With contract law being so central to insurance law, strong analytical and legal writing skills will of course be of benefit to any candidate, as will skills in negotiation and alternate dispute resolution since the majority of disputes (across all of civil law) are settled before or during litigation.

Finally, if you consider yourself more concerned with policy making, bodies such as ASIC and APRA are heavily involved in regulating the insurance industry, with many other government departments (such as the Department of the Treasury) being incidentally involved as well.

[248] Department of the Treasury, *Available and Affordable – Improvements in Liability Insurance Following Tort Law Reform In Australia* (12 December 2006). http://archive.treasury.gov.au/contentitem.asp?ContentID=1200. 6–11.

[249] Ibid.

[250] Department of the Treasury, *Review of the Law of Negligence Final Report* (September 2002) https://treasury.gov.au/review/review-of-the-law-of-negligence

[251] See, e.g., *Wrongs and Other Acts (Public Liability Insurance Reform) Act 2002* (Vic).

[252] Above n 5, 66.

Intellectual Property Law

What is Intellectual Property Law?

Intellectual property law concerns intangible creations such as inventions, designs, artistic works, and names, symbols and artwork used in commerce.[253] Intellectual property is protected by the laws of patents, trade marks and copyright, amongst others, all which ensure initiators benefit financially and otherwise from their creations, and that their ideas are not stolen and used by others.[254] An intellectual property lawyer may work in one, two, or even all three of these key sub-areas of law.

Patents are exclusive rights granted for inventions – processes and products that are innovative and offer something new to the market. In order to acquire a patent, a patent application must be filed, wherein the creator discloses technical information about the information to the public.[255]

Trade marks may be distinctive words, symbols or images that identify products or services as belonging to a certain company, such as a logo. However, they are not limited to this. Trade marks may also encompass letters, numbers, phrases, sounds, smells, shapes, movements, aspects of packaging, or any such combination of these.[256] Trade marks are registered by filing applications with the intellectual property body of the respective country or countries in which a creator wishes to register their property.

Copyright laws grant protection to artistic works such as film, music, or literature, provided these works are expressed in material form – written down or recorded, as examples. In Australia, copyright is applied automatically once material form has taken shape. Copyright endures for 70 years after the death of the creator.[257]

In principle, owners of patents, trade marks and copyright have the exclusive right to prevent others from using or exploiting their creations. Therefore, they can only be used, replicated, distributed or similar with the permission of the holder of the relevant intellectual property registration. In practice, this can be more difficult than it appears. It is in situation such as this where the role of the intellectual property lawyer is most crucial.

---

[253] World Intellectual Property Organisation, *What is Intellectual Property?* World Intellectual Property Organisation. http://www.wipo.int/edocs/pubdocs/en/intproperty/450/wipo_pub_450.pdf

[254] Ibid.

[255] Ibid.

[256] IP Australia, *Trade Mark Basics* (10 March 2016) Australian Government. https://www.ipaustralia.gov.au/trade-marks/understanding-trade-marks

[257] The University of Melbourne, *What is Copyright?* The University of Melbourne. http://copyright.unimelb.edu.au/information/what-is-copyright

What are the Challenges and Rewards of Working in This Area?

Intellectual property is a highly rewarding field in which to work. When a lawyer files an application for a trade mark, for example, and the application is successful, the client will likely be very appreciative and pleased with the outcome. Similarly, if a copyright case is brought and the result is that it is either won or settled, a great sense of satisfaction will usually accompany the win.

Conversely, an undesirable result can be challenging. When a sought outcome is not achieved, this can be difficult for clients and result in them having to change their branding or similar to gain registration. This can prove frustrating for clients and lawyers alike, but is not insurmountable.

Another key challenge of working in intellectual property is the difficulties that arise through online sharing, and the vast expanse of the Internet. Piracy has long been problematic in the world of intellectual property, as has been finding a means by which to identify and punish culprits. Despite regulated 'take-downs' of perpetuating websites, that the Internet is so large poses extensive problems – for where one site is removed, another copycat site takes its place. This challenge will be an ongoing issue for intellectual property lawyers, possibly into the distant future.

Recent Developments in Intellectual Property Law

A particularly interesting development in intellectual property pertains to copyright, and the significance of Disney in determining its date of expiration. In the *Copyright Act*, the duration of copyright in original works was initially '50 years after the end of the calendar year in which the author of the work died'.[258] Given that Walt Disney passed away in 1966, this would have resulted in staple, highly popular characters, such as Mickey Mouse, becoming public property in Australia at the end of 2016. Following Disney's copyright amendment plight in the US and elsewhere, the 2004 amendments to the *Copyright Act* have since altered the copyright period from 50 to 70 years following death.[259] However, the new deadline of 2036 is likely to generate a similar response, posing challenges for intellectual property lawyers in future.

More recently, the Federal Court gained the power to block websites that facilitate copyright infringement, as granted by section 115A of the *Copyright Act*. The outcome of the *Dallas Buyers Club Case* is also prominent, as it affirmed that internet service providers are not obligated to provide copyright owners with contact information in respect of potential pirates.[260]

---

[258] *Copyright Act 1968* (Cth) s33.

[259] Josh Escovedo, *Disney's Influence on United States Copyright Law* (17 February 2016) The IP Law Blog. https://www.theiplawblog.com/2016/02/articles/copyright-law/disneys-influence-on-united-states-copyright-law/

[260] Felicity Sheppard, *The Dallas Buyers Club Case has Been Abandoned But Illegal Downloaders May Still Face Trouble* (12 February 2016) ABC. http://www.abc.net.au/news/2016-02-12/dallas-buyers-club-case-abandoned-illegal-dowloads-pirate/7162180

Resources and Tips for Interested Students

Students interested in a career in intellectual property law ought to be aware that it is a vast area in which to practice. As is clear from the above description, the term 'intellectual property' encompasses a wide range of subcategories, any combination of which one may or may not undertake in the course of employment. As a consequence of this, students ought to consider whether they prefer any one component of intellectual property, so that they may pursue a career that is best suited to them. It is advisable that interested students do their own research or studies to assert this.

Those interested in a career in intellectual property would do well to seek out internships or shadowing opportunities where possible. Ideally, students should look to expose themselves to as many subcategories of intellectual property as possible through these experiences. This will help students to determine whether they have a particular, narrowed interest – or, conversely, whether there is an area with which they are less concerned.

Career Pathway

Many universities offer post-graduate studies that provide for specialisation in intellectual property – for example, a Master of Intellectual Property, or a Master of Laws (Intellectual Property). These are wonderful avenues into practice as an intellectual property lawyer, as they greatly increase knowledge and employability.

Immediate employment following the conclusion of studies is also available to graduate lawyers. There are a large number of firms that practice intellectual property in some capacity, for intellectual property is such a broad area of law. Interested students ought to apply for graduate programs and positions with relevant firms if they are seeking to gain employment in this field.

International Trade and Finance Law

What is International Trade and Finance Law?

International trade refers to the body of law created through bilateral and multilateral agreements between nation-states and derived from international institutions. The regulation of international trade was developed through the General Agreement on Tariffs and Trade and then formally through the World Trade Organisation

(WTO).[261] The WTO predominantly serves as a negotiating forum with the aim of free trade and a single market economy.[262]

International finance law refers to the lending mechanism or exchange of financial assets that cross national borders.[263] The International Monetary Fund (IMF) also operates as an international institution in the international finance space. There are many subject areas that are covered by international trade, and some unique ones including international shipping, aviation law, and the system of tariffs that currently operates between nation-states.

What are the Challenges and Rewards of Working in This Area?

International trade and finance can be a very fluid field. Whilst a lot of major firms practice in international finance, there are many governmental or publically-oriented jobs that aim to facilitate the rules around international trade. An international trade career can manifest in very diverse ways. However, some universal attributes to such a career may include travel, opportunities to engage with colleagues from different jurisdictions, and a rapidly changing commercial landscape. Working in this space can include very exciting areas like cross-border litigation, international trade deals and international dispute resolution. A multitude of skills are required, as well as preferential skills in commerce. It is also a requirement to have knowledge of foreign law in multiple jurisdictions, especially regarding contract, equity and torts.

Recent Developments in International Trade and Finance Law

Many of the contemporary issues surrounding international trade and finance relate to jurisdiction, and the Singapore International Commercial Court (SICC) has recently contributed to the jurisprudence of this area. There have been several recent decisions in the SICC from a broad range of jurisdictions which indicate that the utility of these international commercial courts has increased.[264]

International trade in particular is subject to the political will of nation-states and their policy objectives. Change in this area is always contingent on the negotiation

[261] John H Barton, Judith L Goldstein, Timothy E. Josling, Richard H Steinberg, 'The Evolution of the Trade Regime: Politics, Law and Economics of the GATT and WTO', 1 January 2006, Princeton University Press, 61.

[262] Joost Pauwelyn, Andrew Guzman, Jennifer Hillman, *International Trade Law*, Wolters Kluwer Third Edition 2016

[263] Phillip R. Wood, 'Law and Practice of International Finance: Law & Practice of International Finance' University Edition, Thomson Reuters 2008, 3.

[264] *BNP Paribas 2016* [2017] 3 SLR 27, 34 [17]; *Telemedia Pacific Group Ltd v Yuanta Asset Management International Ltd* [2016] SGHC(I) 03 (30 June 2016) [159]

of bilateral trade agreements and recent discussion has centered around the North American Free Trade Agreement. Some issues that have been presented in these negotiations relate to domestic agricultural protections, modernisation in less developed states, and the inclusion of indigenous and gender chapters into the agreement.[265] It is also worth keeping informed of global events and trends regarding international trade as this can be largely influential.

Resources and Tips for Interested Students

Most universities should offer courses with some practical elements that pertain to the international trade and finance sector. Prospective students should be encouraged to conduct their own research into particular subject areas that are attractive to them. Some sought-after attributes in the industry include skills in writing, statutory interpretation, and negotiation, and some understanding of economics or banking/finance. However, lacking these skills is not prohibitive and any academic work into international law will also be advantageous. A broader geopolitical understanding of how the current international system was developed would also be useful, which could be conducted at either an undergraduate or post-graduate level.

Career Pathway

There are a number of ways that prospective students can engage with this sector. There is advocacy work to be conducted in the WTO and IMF, as well as transactional work. Due to the international nature of this field, any bilingual skills would be advantageous. Commercial aptitude may also be required to work in spaces like the International Commercial Courts established in Singapore, Qatar, Dubai and Abu Dhabi.[266]

There is both a public and private law path to be followed in international trade and finance law. Pursuing the private sector can include work in export-import banks, overseas private investment corporations, and international finance corporations. Alternatively, governmental work is available in multiple fields including at a multinational level through bodies such as the WTO, World Bank and IMF.[267]

[265] Simon Lester, International Economic Law and Policy Blog, 'Finishing the NAFTA Renegotiation: Some Outstanding Issues' 24 April 2018 http://worldtradelaw.typepad.com/ielp-blog/2018/04/finishing-up-nafta.html

[266] Andrew Godwin, Ian Ramsay & Miranda Webster, 'International Commercial Court: The Singapore Experience', 31 January 2018, Melbourne University International Law Journal Vol 18(2)

[267] Georgetown Law (Georgetown University), 'International Trade Law', accessed: https://www.law.georgetown.edu/careers/career-planning/practice-areas/international-corporate-arbitration-trade.cfm

Prospective candidates should research internship programs at the aforementioned institutions. Another avenue to explore international finance and trade is to begin a career in finance or banking at a domestic level. There are many outreach programs sponsored by large banking and finance institutions that students should research in order to gain access to this resource.

Investment Law

What is Investment Law?

Mutual Funds

Mutual funds are a type of investment vehicle where shareholders pool their money and typically entrust it to a financial firm to manage and invest the money in a portfolio of investments such as company stocks, bonds and treasury notes.[268] The shareholders hope that by pooling their contributions with other people and utilising the skills, resources and purchasing power of the investor firm, they can obtain better outcomes than, for instance, investing alone in a single company's stocks. The financial firm investor, in turn, derives income from professional service fees, which are often based on the fund's performance.

Hedge Funds

Hedge funds are a similar, but distinct, investment vehicle to mutual funds. Like mutual funds, investors (typically high net-wealth individuals) pool their money into the fund, which is invested into a diverse portfolio by a manager or financial firm. Similarly, this means that investors buying into these funds have the benefit of an instantly diversified, managed range of investments. The difference, however, is in the fund's approach to investing. Hedge funds aim to obtain the highest investment returns as quickly as possible, which often involves speculative, leveraged and thus highly risky investments. Short-selling is common and means that the fund is able to earn money even when markets and company stocks are falling.[269] Mutual funds, in contrast, do not engage in short-selling or highly speculative investments, which make them less risky for investors.

---

[268] Investopedia, *Mutual Fund.* https://www.investopedia.com/terms/m/mutualfund.asp

[269] Investopedia, *Hedge Fund.* https://www.investopedia.com/terms/h/hedgefund.asp

Private Equity

Private equity funds are likewise a similar but distinct creature. These funds also involve a pooling of resources (as opposed to a sole investor) with a firm managing the investment portfolio. Where hedge funds typically involve short-term, highly liquid investments that can be bought and sold quickly, private equity involves longer-term investments. A common investment is the purchase of financially distressed or poor-performing private companies. The fund engages in a leveraged buyout of the company – using a large portion of bank debt to buy out the company, using the targeted company's own assets as security for the loan – and aims to improve the company's performance by, for example, changing senior management or improving efficiency. If successful, the fund sells off the company at a profit which is returned to the investors.[270] Another major activity in this area is initial public offerings (IPOs), where the private equity fund has purchased a private company and has grown it to a stage where it is able to become a public company. The amount of work involved is enormous, with a plethora of legal issues from many different areas of law on which to consider, research and advise.

Venture Capital

Venture capital funds can be seen as a subset of private equity. The portfolio's focus is on investing in start-up, entrepreneurial companies or small businesses with the hope to grow the target companies to a point where they can be sold off to a private equity firm for continued growth, or be taken to a public offering stage on a stock exchange. The professional investors managing the venture capital funds are highly sophisticated businesspersons and typically provide mentorship support and lend their business expertise to the start-ups.[271] The idea of investing in the next Facebook, Snapchat or Uber might sound alluring. However, venture capital investment is highly risky – it is very possible that for every ten start-ups the fund invests in, all but one will fail.

Working in Investment Law

Across each type of investment vehicle, there are various stages where lawyers become involved. In the establishment stage, lawyers may advise the client on how to best structure the fund (e.g. via a limited partnership) and on the contractual

---

[270] Marvin Dumon, *What is private equity?* (3 November 2017) Investopedia. https://www.investopedia.com/articles/financial-careers/09/private-equity.asp

[271] Stephen Barkoczy et al., *Innovation and Venture Capital Law and Policy* (The Federation Press, 2016) 52–5.

terms by which investors will contribute their money. Then, when the fund decides to buy or sell an investment, lawyers are also needed with the transactional side.

Much of the law of mutual funds relates to regulation which includes, for example: an ASIC Australian Financial Services licensing regime, which controls who can operate a mutual fund; a registration scheme, which imposes governance regimes on mutual funds; and various reporting and disclosure requirements. In addition, because mutual funds in Australia are constituted as unit trusts (as opposed to corporations), there are also a suite of trustee and fiduciary duties sourced in the general law, in conjunction with duties under Part 5C of the *Corporations Act 2001* (Cth).[272]

In private equity and venture capital, lawyers may be engaged to advise the investee company on improving the business; for example, a start-up might require legal advice on intellectual property law, employment law, or insurance law.

What are the Challenges and Rewards of Working in This Area?

Lawyers practising in these investment vehicles have the opportunity to gain experience in a wide variety of commercial laws, ranging from contract, corporate, equity, trusts, taxation, banking, competition, corporate governance and domestic and international regulatory law. When advising clients on the transactional side – when the client is buying or selling investments – the work has similarities to a mergers and acquisitions legal team.

Clients are also highly sophisticated financial investors and businesspeople, which offers the prospect of significantly expanding the lawyer's personal network. Further, because these funds typically aim to have a diversified portfolio of investments, there is also constant exposure to a vast range of industries.

Being in a commercial industry, lawyers have the opportunity to earn significantly larger incomes compared to those practising in non-commercial areas of law. However, this area also frequently requires practitioners to work long hours under tight deadlines with periods of intense stress. It is also important to note that these investment vehicles are economically cyclical. This means that, with the exception of hedge funds which can still earn money through short-selling when the market is falling, the availability of legal jobs will rise and fall with economic booms and recessions.

[272] Pamela Hanrahan and Ian Ramsay, 'Regulation of mutual funds in Australia' in William Birdthistle and John Morley (eds), *Research Handbook on Mutual Funds* (Edward Elgar Publishing, 2017) (forthcoming). https://poseidon01.ssrn.com/delivery.php?ID=741072022102024090065117126097083026016056000029024069069123111076083091009066088108016120111006027011049007074028112099003102123042042011081092091105014016006064024021054127102121093083125102004006105114030006074004086090088118125095070068005099025&EXT=pdf

Recent Developments in Investment Law

Following the GFC, governments and financial service regulatory bodies around the world have pushed for greater scrutiny and regulation of the investment industry. In the United States, the 2010 Dodd Frank Act[273] had a significant effect on hedge funds, implementing a broad suite of financial regulatory processes to enhance transparency and accountability.[274]

Due to Australia's compulsory superannuation scheme, Australia has one of the world's largest pools of managed funds. Following the global trend of increased regulation, the federal government introduced draft legislation in late-2017 seeking to increase accountability in the financial services industries to retail investors.[275] Draft legislation for the Asia Region Funds Passport (ARFP) regime in Australia was also released in late 2017, which will allow for regulated managed funds to be marketed internationally with participating countries in Asia.[276]

Within the private equity and venture capital sphere, there were significant recent tax reforms as part of the Turnbull government's National Innovation and Science Agenda. In 2016, tax incentives in the form of a tax offset and modified capital gains tax treatment were introduced to encourage investment in small, innovative, unlisted Australian start-up companies with high growth potential. These early stage innovation companies (ESICs) traditionally struggle to raise capital finance and are therefore unable to undertake the research and development which is necessary for their growth.[277]

Resources and Tips for Interested Students

In this area of commercial law, financial literacy and awareness are perhaps the most important skills. Students interested in a career in any of these investment law areas should be aware of current trends in the economy and financial markets, in Australia and internationally, and be able to discuss these in detail with a potential employer. This means that it is almost mandatory to read the business and finance sections of multiple newspapers, such as the Australian Financial Review, the Australian, the Wall Street Journal, Bloomberg, the International Business Times, Business Insider, Reuters, the BBC, or the Economist.

---

[273] See *Dodd–Frank Wall Street Reform and Consumer Protection Act*, Pub L No 111–203 § 929-Z, 124 Stat. 1376, 1871 (2010).

[274] Margaret Rouse, *Dodd-Frank Act* (February 2017) Tech Target. http://searchfinancialsecurity.techtarget.com/definition/Dodd-Frank-Act

[275] Susan Hilliard, Glenda Hanson, Scott Heezen, *Retail investment funds in Australia: regulatory overview* (January 2018) Thomson Reuters. https://uk.practicallaw.thomsonreuters.com/2-501-3497?transitionType=Default&contextData=(sc.Default)#co_anchor_a899216

[276] See Asia-Pacific Economic Cooperation (APEC), *Asia Region Funds Passport*. http://fundspassport.apec.org/

[277] Stephen Barkoczy, *Foundations of Taxation Law* (Oxford University Press, 9th ed., 2017) 822–3.

When applying for jobs in these areas, students should familiarise themselves with various deals, clients and investments in which the employer has been involved and be able to demonstrate an understanding of the commercial context, the work involved, and the reason for interest. Students should also avoid restricting themselves too early into a niche area of law, and instead become knowledgeable on a broad range of commercial laws. Students interested in venture capital law may also become involved in innovative start-up companies to gain experience of working in a future potential client.

Juvenile or Youth Law

What is Juvenile Law?

Juvenile law is a general term which usually refers to the way that youths are treated in the legal system and at law. The justice system recognises that minors and young people who commit crimes ought to be treated differently for their protection and rehabilitation than those in the adult criminal justice system.[278] Often the focus with young offenders is strongly on their prospects of rehabilitation, acknowledging not only a threat to their safety in adult facilities, but also preventing recidivism and providing constructive pathways for young people to avoid being pulled back into the system later in life. However, where the offences committed are of a very serious nature, such as murder, youth may not be considered sufficient to override a punitive sentence.[279]

Youth law can also cover family law proceedings and child protection. An example of how the justice system has special regard to children or youth is in the existence of specialist children's courts, which have been adopted in some states such as Victoria and Queensland. These courts function both in criminal and family law contexts.[280] The Children's Court of Victoria hears applications about the protection and care of children and young people, as well as criminal offences by children and youth. There is also a Victorian Children's Koori Court which specifically addresses the needs of young Koori people by including Elders and Respected Persons in the criminal law process.[281]

Australia is a signatory to various international treaties concerning the rights of children, which are binding in terms of international law.[282] Arguably the most

---

[278] Oxford University Press, *Australian Law Dictionary* (at 29 November 2017), "Youth".

[279] Ibid.

[280] *Role Of The Court | Children's Court Of Victoria* (2018) Childrenscourt.vic.gov.au. http://www.childrenscourt.vic.gov.au/about-us/role-court

[281] *Koori Court | Children's Court Of Victoria* (2018) Childrenscourt.vic.gov.au. http://www.childrenscourt.vic.gov.au/jurisdictions/koori-court

[282] Children's Rights: Australia | Law Library Of Congress (2018). https://www.loc.gov/law/help/child-rights/australia.php

significant of these treaties is the Convention on the Rights of the Child (CRC).[283] The CRC aims to ensure that the best interests of the child is the 'primary consideration', along with establishing the rights of children to survival and development, freedom of expression in matters which concern them, and freedom from discrimination in enjoying such rights.[284] Australia's domestic legislation has enshrined many aspects of these protections. However, ongoing debates exist as to the extent of such implementations. See below in "Recent Developments in Juvenile Law" for more information.

What are the Challenges and Rewards of Working in This Area?

There are many ways that lawyers can get involved in the area of youth and the law. There are non-government and other organisations that seek to promote the rights and interests of children and youth in the legal system where volunteers and practitioners alike are able to help young people. Some criminal law practitioners may also specialise in representing minors who have been charged with criminal offences. Family law firms may also have specific expertise in Children's Court matters. Working in this area generally results as a part of practising other areas of law, and can be emotionally challenging. For example, lawyers in family law matters involving children may help families achieve an outcome that is in the best interests of the child. In criminal law matters there can also be complexities around the role of family members in the lives of young people who have been charged with criminal offences, especially for first-time offenders where the emphasis is on helping them to get back on track. The severity of the offences in question can also vary, and so the kinds of cases taken on may depend on the particular areas of expertise of criminal law solicitors and barristers. There are several support services available in the youth justice system, which can vary from state to state, which focus on case management, advice, health and rehabilitation, as well as education and vocational programs.[285]

Recent Developments in Juvenile Law

Recently there has been cause to look at a number of human rights considerations for youth law. In particular, following the publication of shocking images and video of abuse of children in youth detention centres in the Northern Territory, former

[283] About Children's Rights | Australian Human Rights Commission. https://www.humanrights.gov.au/our-work/childrens-rights/about-childrens-rights; *Convention on the Rights of the Child*, opened for signature 20 November 1989, 1577 UNTS 3 (entered into force 2 September 1990).

[284] About Children's Rights | Australian Human Rights Commission. https://www.humanrights.gov.au/our-work/childrens-rights/about-childrens-rights

[285] *Support Services In The Youth Justice System – Department Of Justice And Regulation, Victoria* (2018) Justice.vic.gov.au

Prime Minister Malcolm Turnbull announced that there would be a Royal Commission into the territory's child protection and youth detention system.[286] Other states have also expressed major concerns and have launched their own investigations and inquiries into their youth detention centres.[287] Commentators have raised concerns over Australia's obligations under the Convention on the Rights of the Child and other international agreements.[288] This is an interesting area of human rights law in Australia and is very important to our community.

Maritime or Admiralty Law

What is Maritime Law?

Maritime law is the body of law governing the activities related to the sea, such as shipping and sailors and the carriage of people and property by sea.[289] Admiralty law is governed by the *Admiralty Act 1988* (Cth)[290] and came into force following an Australian Law Reform Commission report.[291] The aim of this act is to make admiralty jurisdiction complete, comprehensible and adherent with Australia's international obligations.[292] A Court of Admiralty, as defined under Part II of the *Admiralty Act 1988* (Cth), has jurisdiction to hear and decide maritime law claims.[293] Some of the many other statutes that are relevant to maritime law include the *Crimes at Sea Act 2000* (Cth), the *Carriage of Goods by Sea 1991* (Cth), the *Navigation Act 2012* (Cth) and the *Historic Shipwrecks Act 1976* (Cth).[294] Some Australian maritime law comes from international law, such as the *Admiralty Act 1988* (Cth).[295] This act was modelled on a United Kingdom act, where Part I was based on both the International Convention Relating to the Arrest of Sea-Going Ships, and the International Convention on Certain Rules Concerning Civil Jurisdiction in Matters of Collision.[296] Further, the areas of sea around Australia are also the subject of other

[286] Chris Cunneen, Barry Goldson and Sophie Russel, "Juvenile Justice, Young People And Human Rights In Australia" (2016) 28(2) *Current Issues in Criminal Justice*, 173.

[287] Ibid, 174.

[288] Ibid, 174.

[289] Ray Finkelstein and David Hamer (eds), *LexisNexis Concise Australian Legal Dictionary* (LexisNexis, 5th ed., 2015) 397.

[290] Ibid 19.

[291] Michael White, *Australian Maritime Law* (Federation Press, 3rd ed., 2014) 40.

[292] Ibid 40; Explanatory Memorandum to the Admirality Bill 1988, "Outline", reproduced in D Cremean, *Admiralty Jurisdiction: Law and Practice in Australia* (Federation Press 1997) 156.

[293] Finkelstein and Hamer, above n 1, 152.

[294] Ibid 397.

[295] Damien J. Cremean, *Admiralty Jurisdiction: Law and Practice in Australia, New Zealand, Singapore and Hong Kong* (Federation Press, 3rd ed., 2008) 8.

[296] Ibid.

law, such as international law and the law of surrounding countries. Therefore, practising in maritime law will require a practitioner to also have an understanding of international law, and perhaps even the laws of nearby countries.

What are the Challenges and Rewards of Working in This Area?

Maritime law can be very political, especially in the current Australian climate regarding refugee and asylum seeker policy and people arriving in Australia by boat. Australia's international obligations and rights are primarily found in the United Nations Convention on the Law of the Sea.[297]

Recent Developments in Maritime Law

The case of *CPCF v MIBP* (2015) 255 CLR 514 required the High Court to interpret particular provisions in the *Maritime Powers Act 2013* (Cth).[298] These provisions were the law that enacted the government's policy of turning back the boats.[299] The High Court held that the detention was lawful pursuant to provisions of the *Maritime Powers Act 2013* (Cth).[300] The decision fuelled debate and discussion regarding the length and conditions of detention, and further whether the detention of asylum seekers attempting to arrive in Australia by boat was legal.[301]

Resources and Tips for Interested Students

If a student is interested in practising in maritime law, they should read broadly on the topic and stay updated on current developments in maritime law. For example, a student may look to journals such as the *Australian and New Zealand Maritime Law*

[297] Australian Government Attorney-General's Department, *Law of the Sea and Maritime Law* (Web Page). https://www.ag.gov.au/Internationalrelations/InternationalLaw/Pages/LawoftheSeaandMaritimeLaw.aspx

[298] Amanda Sapienza, *Chief Justice French on Non-Statutory Executive Power: A Timely Reflection* (20 December 2016). https://auspublaw.org/2016/12/chief-justice-french-a-timely-reflection/

[299] Ibid.

[300] Patrick Emerton And Maria O'Sullivan, 'Rethinking Asylum Seeker Detention At Sea: The Power To Detain Asylum Seekers At Sea Under the *Maritime Powers Act 2013* (Cth)' (2015) 38 *UNSW Law Journal* 695, 697.

[301] Ibid.

Journal.[302] This journal publishes academic writing on maritime law and commerce. A student interested in maritime law may consider joining clubs and organisations dedicated to this area, such as the Maritime Law Association of Australian and New Zealand (MLAANZ).[303] It is possible to obtain a student membership.[304] The MLAANZ holds conferences each year, including the national conference held in October.[305] You may also consider writing on the topic of maritime law and submitting it to the *Australian and New Zealand Maritime Law Journal*.

Career Pathway

An associateship position in the Federal Court would be an excellent start to a legal career practising in maritime law, as the Federal Court has jurisdiction to hear admiralty/maritime law claims; however, it must be noted that associateship positions are highly competitive.

Media and Communications Law

What is Media and Communications Law?

Media and communications law is a broad area that encompasses the regulation of subjects such as journalism, authorship, radio, television, advertising and marketing. As a consequence of this, its concerns are far-reaching. Prominent issues include freedom of speech, defamation, copyright and censorship.[306] This area of law also raises questions related to privacy infringement, as information to be published, broadcast or aired must be accordingly regulated.

Advertising and marketing law is a pertinent subcategory of this area and is regulated largely by the Australian Consumer Law (ACL). Under the ACL, advertising is not to be false, misleading or deceptive,[307] a regulation which is commonly

---

[302] Australian And New Zealand Maritime Law Journal, *Australian And New Zealand Maritime Law Journal*, (2009–2012). http://Ssl.Law.Uq.Edu.Au/Journals/Index.Php/Maritimejournal/

[303] Australian And New Zealand Maritime Law Journal, *Membership*, (2009–2012). http://Www.Mlaanz.Org/Membership/0,2715,11532,00.html

[304] Australian And New Zealand Maritime Law Journal, *Membership*, (2009–2012). http://Www.Mlaanz.Org/Membership/0,2715,11532,00.html

[305] Australian and New Zealand Maritime Law Journal, *MLAANZ National Conference 2017*, (2009–2012). http://www.mlaanz.org/Page-Preview/0,2793,19332,00.html

[306] Thomson Reuters, *What is Media and Communications Law?*, FindLaw. http://hirealawyer.findlaw.com/choosing-the-right-lawyer/communications-and-media-law.html

[307] *Competition and Consumer Act 2010 (Cth)* sch 2 s18.

enforced under law.[308] This sub-area of law also frequently involves matters such as defamation, consumer protection, packaging, labelling, intellectual property, privacy, censorship and broadcasting matters.[309]

For more information on intellectual property and copyright specifically, please refer to the "Intellectual Property Law" section.

What are the Challenges and Rewards of Working in This Area?

The biggest challenge in this field of work is intrinsically linked to the ever-expanding nature of communications. People are now communicating in more modes and more frequently than ever previously experienced. Consequentially, media and communications law must develop in an equally rapid and diverse manner. Some examples of recent changes include wearable communication devices, such as smartwatches and fitness monitors, and the increasing popularity of online services for socialisation, entertainment, and news.[310] Hence, the challenge in media and communications law is to adapt existing law to new concepts and experiences, endeavouring to find the most appropriate solutions available.

As is often the case, this challenge is also a key reward of working in this area. Media and communications law is highly diverse and constantly developing, leading to work that is interesting, fresh, and ever-enhanced.

In the sub-category of advertising and marketing law, it is easy to identify that there are many new modes by which companies and individuals can market themselves or their brand. While the ACL is broadly responsible for a large portion of regulation in this area, it must be interpreted in accordance with constantly evolving manners of communication and media. This is a particular issue in respect of online mediums, as platforms are almost always trans-national.

---

308 See, e.g., The Australian Competition and Consumer Commission, *ACCC Cracks Down on Fine Print Advertising* (9 July 2001) The Australian Competition and Consumer Commission. https://www.accc.gov.au/media-release/accc-cracks-down-on-fine-print-advertising

309 Studio Legal, *Media, Advertising and Marketing Law*, Studio Legal. http://studiolegal.com.au/media-advertising-and-markting-law/

310 Australian Communications and Media Authority, *Six Emerging Trends in Media and Communications* (November 2014) Australian Communications and Media Authority. https://www.acma.gov.au/~/media/Research%20and%20Analysis/Research/pdf/Six%20emerging%20trends%20in%20media%20and%20communications_Final%20pdf.pdf

Recent Developments in Media and Communications Law

In previous times, this area predominantly concerned media outlets such as television channels and radio stations.[311] Since the advent of the Internet, however, even the average person now faces subjection to these laws. For example, a casual blogger or self-claimed reviewer may risk defamation claims over their online publications.

Similarly, in the case of advertising and marketing, there are now many different and relatively novel means by which one can display a product. The recent YouTube 'adpocalypse' widely demonstrated the need for changes in online marketing and advertising regulations after many companies sought to pull their ads from YouTube videos that were unknowingly offensive, crude, or obscene.[312] YouTube were forced to amend their policy to permit such action by advertisers, and have since set about installing a system of machine learning that identifies when a video is unsuitable, and hence worthy of 'demonetisation'. Through a combination of general advertising and contract law, this unheard-of situation has piqued both legal and non-legal interest across the globe.

Career Pathway

As is much the same for any area of law in which one wants to practice, the best means of wriggling into media and communications law is to research and become acquainted with firms and workplaces that practice in this space. Networking is the young lawyer's greatest tool; reach out to firms that practice in this area for volunteer opportunities and internships or ask to meet with practising lawyers to discuss their work if possible. Demonstrating an interest not only brings your name to the attention of the right people, but may also result in opportunities that you would never otherwise have come across.

There are also post-graduate options available which, if undertaken, will increase a student's ability to gain employment in this field. Completing an LL.M specialising in media and communications law demonstrates a keen sense of interest and dedication to relevant firms, and also allows graduates to gain a leg-up in respect of both employment prospects and practice.

---

[311] Above n 1.

[312] Erik Kain, *YouTube Wants Content Creators to Appeal Demonetisation, But it's Not Always That Easy* (18 September 2017) Forbes. https://www.forbes.com/sites/erikkain/2017/09/18/adpocalypse-2017-heres-what-you-need-to-know-about-youtubes-demonetization-troubles/#1c8e08cd6c26

Mergers and Acquisitions Law

What is Mergers and Acquisitions Law?

While corporations engage daily in various transactions, mergers and acquisitions law concerns exchanges that involve a large shift in the control or direction of a company.[313] Typically, these transactions involve investment, disposition or purchase of ownership in a corporation. Mergers and acquisitions describes various types of large scale commercial interactions including private equity, venture capital, corporate development and takeovers.[314] In its most simple form, these exchanges involve a buyer and seller. However, some transactions may involve negotiation with numerous parties, corporations and their subsidiaries.[315]

What are the Challenges and Rewards of Working in This Area?

While mergers and acquisitions is an area of law, it is also a market in which transactions are made. Like any market, it is subject to peaks and troughs. Poor economic conditions may cause a downturn in the market. Such downturns may be unpredictable and difficult to navigate.

Recent Developments in Mergers and Acquisitions Law

There has been a policy and legislative focus on enhancing transparency in mergers and acquisition law. In recent years, there has been a shift to ensure that dealing is conducted in a way that is fair and open.

To exemplify, in mid-2002, ASIC published Regulatory Guide 25, coined the 'Truth in Takeovers'.[316] This policy sought to provide guidance to market participants engaging in negotiation.[317] Notably, it stressed the importance of transparency and honesty in the negotiation process. One focus of the guide was 'last and final statements'. Last and final statements serve as an endmost indication of a party's position during negotiation of a deal.[318] ASIC stressed the importance of viewing

---

[313] Michael E. S. Frankel, *Mergers and Acquisitions Basics* (John Wiley & Sons, 2005) 1.

[314] Ibid.

[315] Ibid, 7.

[316] Australian Securities and Investment Commission, *Regulatory Guide 25* (2002), 1.

[317] Ibid.

[318] Ibid, 2.

these statements as promises and reiterated the severity of penalties associated with making a wrongful last and final statement.[319]

Similarly, there have been efforts made to ensure that foreign investment is transparent. Amendments have been made to the *Foreign Acquisitions and Takeovers Act 1975* (Cth) (FATA).[320] This act regulates foreign investment through a screening process administered by the Foreign Investment Review Board (FIRB).[321] FIRB considers investment proposals on a case by case basis.[322] However, this board does not have the power to reject or accept proposals, it merely advises potential investors.[323] The power to enforce FATA rests with the treasurer, who has the power pass or reject applications in consideration of our national interests or identity.[324] The 2015 changes to FATA sought to ensure that legislation was in line with the government's policy platforms.[325] There has been strong political debate around foreign investment in sectors that are specific to our economy or national identity.[326] Notably, the changes singled out Australia's agribusiness sector. The amendments established a more onerous threshold for foreign investment in this sector as it is often viewed as both a cultural and economic treasure.[327] Further, FATA placed similar restraints on foreign investment pertaining to other forms of land, such as pre-existing residential property.[328]

Resources and Tips for Interested Students

Mergers and acquisitions is a competitive area of law in which to be become involved. Given the nature of the work, it is at times not an area in which students are able to gain experience at early stages of their degree. However, various Australian law student societies offer competitions in negotiations and mergers and acquisitions. Participating in these competitions is a good way to gain experience and show future employers a genuine interest in this area.

---

[319] Ibid, 4.

[320] Department of Treasury (Cth), 'Government Strengthens the Foreign Investment Framework' (Media Release, 21 September 2015) http://jbh.ministers.treasury.gov.au/media-release/034-2015/

[321] Mallesons Stephen Jaques, *Australian Finance Law* (Thompson Reuters, 6th ed., 2008), 11.

[322] Ibid.

[323] Ibid.

[324] Ibid, 12.

[325] Department of Treasury (Cth), 'Government Strengthens the Foreign Investment Framework' (Media Release, 21 September 2015). http://jbh.ministers.treasury.gov.au/media-release/034-2015/

[326] Ibid.

[327] Ibid.

[328] Ibid.

Further, there are numerous Australian firms with extensive mergers and acquisitions practice areas. If you wish to explore this area of law you might choose to direct your clerkship applications to such firms.

If you are not yet in your penultimate year, some firms offer 1–3 day programs that aim to give insight into commercial law for pre-penultimate students. Often these programs allow students to interact and build connections with lawyers and partners at the firm.

Military Law

What is Military Law?

Military law is a body of national law, made up of rules and regulations, that governs the military service and armed forces.[329] There are a number of statutes that are relevant to this practice. For example, the *Defence Force Discipline Act 1982* (Cth), which seeks to uphold military discipline, and the *Defence Act 1903* (Cth). Military law requires an understanding of military discipline law, military administrative law and military operations law.[330]

What are the Challenges and Rewards of Working in This Area?

Military law may be a rewarding area to work in, and may be particularly suited to individuals who are interested in law beyond Australian domestic law. Practice in military law, especially if an individual is involved in reform of military law, may require that a practitioner have a good understanding of international law, for example, conventions governing international humanitarian law such as the Hague Conventions and the Geneva Conventions.

[329] Ray Finkelstein and David Hamer (eds), *LexisNexis Concise Australian Legal Dictionary* (LexisNexis, 5th ed., 2015) 408.

[330] Defence Legal, *Military Law Centre* (2018) Australian Government Department of Defence. http://www.defence.gov.au/legal/mlc.asp

Recent Developments in Military Law

In 2009, the High Court handed down the case of *Lane v Morrison* [2009] HCA 29 which lead to substantial reforms that changed the shape of military discipline law.[331] In this case, the High Court held that the Australian Military Court was constitutionally invalid as it was exercising the judicial power of the Commonwealth contrary to Chapter III of the Constitution.[332] Now, the Defence Force Discipline Appeals Tribunal (DFDAT) hears appeals, such as appeals of convictions.[333] DFDAT hears matters in the buildings of federal courts and their registry is the Federal Court Registry.[334] The President and Deputy President of DFDAT must be a Federal Court or a state or territory Supreme Court judge.[335]

Resources and Tips for Interested Students

Any student interested in military law should keep up to date with current reforms and read broadly on military law. Military law may require an understanding of law beyond Australia, such as international law and domestic military law of countries surrounding Australia. Students may wish to keep up to date through publications of organisations dedicated to military law, such as the Asia Pacific Centre for Military Law, an organisation that seeks to uphold respect for the rule of law in military law matters in Australia and throughout the Asia-Pacific region.[336]

---

[331] Defence Legal, *Military Law Centre* (2018) Australian Government Department of Defence. http://www.defence.gov.au/legal/mlc.asp

[332] *Lane v Morrison* [2009] HCA 29.

[333] John Alexander Logan, *What now for Defence Force Discipline Appeals?* (16 April 2016) Federal Court of Australia. http://www.fedcourt.gov.au/digital-law-library/judges-speeches/justice-logan/logan-j-20160416

[334] John Alexander Logan, *What now for Defence Force Discipline Appeals?* (16 April 2016) Federal Court of Australia. http://www.fedcourt.gov.au/digital-law-library/judges-speeches/justice-logan/logan-j-20160416

[335] John Alexander Logan, *What now for Defence Force Discipline Appeals?* (16 April 2016) Federal Court of Australia. http://www.fedcourt.gov.au/digital-law-library/judges-speeches/justice-logan/logan-j-20160416; *Defence Force Discipline Appeals Act 1995* (Cth), s 8(1).

[336] Asia Pacific Centre for Military Law. http://www.apcml.org

Career Pathway

Students interested in military law should consider applying for jobs in government. For example, there are jobs in the Australian Defence Force in military law and justice.[337] As part of the Australian Defence Force, lawyers are required to undertake legal training and professional development through the Military Law Centre.[338] This involves completion of core legal training module units, completed through the Australian National University or the University of Adelaide, leading to receipt of a Graduate Diploma in Military Law.[339] The Defence Force also offers a university graduate program within the Capability Acquisition and Sustainment Group.[340] Although applicants are not required to have a law degree such a degree is well regarded.

Mining Law

What is Mining Law?

Mining law has been an important part of Australian law since before federation, as the first mining laws in Australia were passed in 1851.[341] In contrast to other common law countries, Australian mining law developed so that the Crown owned most natural resources.[342] This means that today, most minerals are owned by the Crown in right of the State.[343] The Warden's Court is the name given to a court established under mining statute in particular states, for example the *Mining Act 1971* (SA) s 64.[344] Mining is mostly governed by state law, so a practitioner may be required to understand the different laws of mining of other states if the person intends to work in more than one state or territory.

---

[337] Graduate Careers Australia, *Careers for Law Graduates* (2008) GradAustralia. http://www.graduatecareers.com.au/wp-content/uploads/2011/12/careers_for_law_graduates.pdf

[338] Defence Legal, *Military Law Centre* (2018) Australian Government Department of Defence. http://www.defence.gov.au/legal/mlc.asp

[339] Defence Legal, *Military Law Centre* (2018) Australian Government Department of Defence. http://www.defence.gov.au/legal/mlc.asp

[340] Department of Defence, *Defence Graduate Program (Capability Pathway)*. http://www.defence.gov.au/casg/Careers/StudentsandGraduates/Graduates/Default.aspx

[341] Michael Hunt, *Mining Law in Western Australia* (Federation Press, 4th ed., 2009) 1.

[342] Ibid.

[343] Ibid 2.

[344] Ray Finkelstein and David Hamer (eds), *LexisNexis Concise Australian Legal Dictionary* (LexisNexis, 5th ed., 2015) 661.

What are the Challenges and Rewards of Working in This Area?

As mining is very important to Australia's economy, mining law can be highly political. Mining in Australia contributes to approximately 7% of Australia's gross domestic product.[345] Mining law may hereby be challenging to work in due to the political repercussions. On the other hand, a practitioner may be drawn to mining law for this very reason, and find that mining law can be very rewarding to work in due to the important role mining has for Australia's economy. Australia exports the most coal in the world, and also mines and contributes to exportation of aluminium, copper, iron ore and tin, just to name some of the other minerals that Australia produces.[346]

Recent Developments in Mining Law

Mining law has a large impact on the environment, and therefore policy and environmental groups often seek to be involved in reforming mining law. The granting of mining permits is an executive function and is therefore subject to judicial review. Environmental groups may involve themselves through judicial review applications. For example, in 2015 an application for judicial review was brought in the Federal Court, seeking review of the Commonwealth Environment Minister's decision to approve the Adani-Carmichael coal mine.[347] However, the parties agreed before the Court delivered judgment that the Minister had made the decision without considering the animal species that were threatened, which was contrary to a provision in the *Environment Protection and Biodiversity Conservation Act 1999* (Cth).[348] The Minister has now made the decision to approve the mine again, with consideration to these threatened species. However, environmental groups are still outraged and are attempting to halt the mine at all costs. The Australian Climate Council has reported that the mine will, among other things, be a hazard to human health, lead to disaster for the Great Barrier Reef, and create a risk to agriculture due to extreme weather events that will be aggravated by coal pollution.[349]

---

[345] James Carr, *Careers for Law Graduates in Mining and Resources*, GradAustralia. https://gradaustralia.com.au/law/careers-for-law-graduates-in-mining-and-resources

[346] James Carr, *Careers for Law Graduates in Mining and Resources*, GradAustralia. https://gradaustralia.com.au/law/careers-for-law-graduates-in-mining-and-resources

[347] Environmental Law Australia, *Carmichael Coal Mine cases in the Federal Court*. http://envlaw.com.au/carmichael-coal-mine-federal-court/

[348] Environmental Law Australia, *Carmichael Coal Mine cases in the Federal Court*. http://envlaw.com.au/carmichael-coal-mine-federal-court/

[349] The Climate Council, *New Report: Adani Monster Mine could Damage Climate, Health, Tourism* (17 May 2017). https://www.climatecouncil.org.au/carmichaelmediarelease

Resources and Tips for Interested Students

If a student is interesting in mining law, they should seek to stay updated on the latest political developments. Mining law may require an individual to have good knowledge of property law, contract law, employment law and potentially government law, depending on the type of work the practitioner is undertaking, and hereby students should strive to excel in these subjects.

Career Pathway

Many large mining companies have in-house counsel and students may consider applying for graduate positions as part of these teams.[350] Further, law firms that have a general practice may also employ individuals in mining law.[351] There may be opportunities to be employed near the mines themselves, which are mostly located in South Australia and Western Australia.[352]

Privacy Law

What is Privacy Law?

Privacy has been broadly described as 'the right of individuals to protect their personal life from intrusion and to control the flow of personal information about themselves'.[353] However, no conclusive definition of privacy has been reached and debate continues around whether a rights approach to privacy should be implemented. The High Court of Australia has thus far steered clear of creating a tort of privacy similar to that of other jurisdictions.[354] In the United States, for example, individuals can bring an action or a suit against an entity or an individual who unlawfully 'intrudes' into a person's 'private affairs or concerns'.[355] Whilst defamation laws exist in

[350] James Carr, *Careers for Law Graduates in Mining and Resources*, GradAustralia. https://gradaustralia.com.au/law/careers-for-law-graduates-in-mining-and-resources

[351] James Carr, *Careers for Law Graduates in Mining and Resources*, GradAustralia. https://gradaustralia.com.au/law/careers-for-law-graduates-in-mining-and-resources

[352] James Carr, *Careers for Law Graduates in Mining and Resources*, GradAustralia. https://gradaustralia.com.au/law/careers-for-law-graduates-in-mining-and-resources

[353] LexisNexis, *Encyclopaedic Australian Legal Dictionary* (at 18 April 2018) 'Privacy".

[354] Ibid.

[355] *Right To Personal Privacy—Developments In Australia And Elsewhere* | *ALRC* (2018) Alrc.gov.au. https://www.alrc.gov.au/publications/74.%20Protecting%20a%20Right%20to%20Personal%20Privacy%20/right-personal-privacy%E2%80%94developments-austral

Australia, we do not have any cause of action which allows you to claim damages for breaches of privacy.

Legislation in Australia does protect privacy in specific contexts, such as that of personal information and health information. For example, at a federal level, the *Privacy Act 1988* (Cth) was drafted to regulate the management of individuals' personal information.[356] The *Privacy Act* obliges businesses with a turnover of more than $3 million per year, health service providers, federal government agencies, not-for-profit organisations and others to comply with several responsibilities in terms of maintaining privacy and dealing with information.[357] The act aims to help people know why and how personal information is collected, to whom it will be disclosed, and the various protection mechanisms available, including complaints procedures.[358] There are also relevant state and territory statutes which may apply, depending on the case and the applicable jurisdiction.[359] For example, states and territories generally have their own health record laws.[360] The *Privacy Act* also created the Office of the Australian Information Commissioner (OAIC) which has power to conduct privacy assessments of entities that fall under the act. The OAIC also hears complaints about privacy if direct complaints to agencies or organisations are made, or if conciliation fails to adequately resolve the issue.[361] Additionally, the act provides for compensation of financial and non-financial loss, along with other non-monetary remedies such as apologies, staff training or changes to an organisation's procedures.[362]

What are the Challenges and Rewards of Working in This Area?

Firms may specialise in assisting clients with navigating the complex and often fluctuating regulatory landscape of privacy law obligations, helping them to ensure compliance with all their requirements. This can involve dealing with organisations and service providers in many different sectors such as health, education, energy and many more. There can be quite a lot at stake for businesses, as the *Privacy Amendment (Enhancing Privacy Protection) Act 2012* (Cth) introduced stronger

---

[356] *Privacy Law| Office Of The Australian Information Commissioner – OAIC* (2018) Oaic.gov.au. https://www.oaic.gov.au/privacy-law/

[357] Ibid.

[358] Ibid.

[359] Ibid.

[360] *Overview Of Privacy Law In Australia* (2018) Hall & Wilcox. https://hallandwilcox.com.au/overview-of-privacy-law-in-australia/

[361] *How Do I Make A Privacy Complaint?| Office Of The Australian Information Commissioner – OAIC* (2018) Oaic.gov.au. https://www.oaic.gov.au/individuals/how-do-i-make-a-privacy-complaint

[362] *Privacy Law| Office Of The Australian Information Commissioner – OAIC* (2018) Oaic.gov.au. https://www.oaic.gov.au/privacy-law/

powers for the OIAC to impose hefty fines of over $1 million where there have been serious breaches of privacy.[363] Several of the larger Australian law firms have teams dedicated to privacy law issues, and help businesses draft terms and conditions and manage compliance.

Individuals making complaints about privacy may also seek independent legal advice through the OIAC complaints process discussed above.[364] If they are still dissatisfied with the decision of the OIAC and have gone through a merits review process, applicants may be able to seek judicial review of the decision under administrative law.

This can be a challenging and interesting area of law, where practitioners have the opportunity to liaise with a variety of stakeholders and use their skills to help prevent issues down the track.

Recent Developments in Privacy Law

Privacy law is an area that is constantly under revision as the way information is distributed continues to develop. As the flow of information is now a globalised process due to the increasing prevalence of the Internet and social media, the impact of other states' laws on Australian businesses, individuals and organisations is also changing. For example, in March 2018 the United States passed the *Clarifying Lawful Overseas Use of Data (CLOUD) Act 2018*, which is aimed at modernising data protection laws and regulating cross-border data use in the digital age.[365] This may not only have an impact on Australian businesses with operations in the United States, but also influence future reform in international agreements and in Australia's own domestic laws. Privacy law is an area of great community concern and is relatively recent is in its development, so it is likely that the coming years will bring new laws and amendments, particularly as technology continues to evolve.[366]

---

[363] *Data & Privacy – Holding Redlich Lawyers – Law Firm Melbourne Sydney Brisbane Australia* (2018) Holdingredlich.com. https://www.holdingredlich.com/practice-group/privacy

[364] *Privacy Act Compliance Guide – Law Institute Of Victoria* (2018) Liv.asn.au. https://www.liv.asn.au/For-Lawyers/LIV-Privileges-Member-Savings/Practice-Resources/Privacy-Act-Compliance-Guide

[365] *What New US CLOUD Laws Mean For Australian Businesses* (2018) Financial Review. http://www.afr.com/technology/cloud-computing/what-new-us-cloud-laws-mean-for-australian-businesses-20180413-h0ypuu#ixzz5CzysCEtX; *Clarifying Lawful Overseas Use of Data (CLOUD) Act* of 2018 (H.R. 4943 and S. 2383).

[366] Ibid.

Private International Law

What is Private International Law?

Private international law, also commonly known as 'conflict of laws', is the area of law which 'governs the choice of law or forum in cases of private rights arising under business contracts or marriage'.[367] The role of practitioners in this area includes determining the answers to questions in matters dealing in 'foreign elements' such as 'which court has jurisdiction in the matter; what is the applicable law; and whether the court can recognise and enforce the judgement of another law area'.[368] For example, what happens when a Victorian business buys goods from a French business which later turn out to be bankrupt?[369] Should the matter be heard in a French or Victorian court? Which of the two conflicting laws should apply? If an order is made for compensation, does the court have any ability to affect enforcement?

Private international law is famous (or perhaps infamous) for its complexity and existence on the periphery of mainstream legal practice and scholarship. It is as an extremely nebulous area of law, both in theory and practice.[370] One commentator famously described it as 'a dismal swamp, filled with quaking quagmires, and inhabited by learned but eccentric professors who theorize [sic] about mysterious matters in a strange and incomprehensible jargon'.[371]

What are the Challenges and Rewards of Working in This Area?

As previously stated, the complexity of this practice area acts as a barrier to entry for many; it requires a particularly thorough and analytical individual to thrive in private international law. This is owing to the fact that it not only requires a strong understanding of domestic court procedural rules, as well as the relevant areas of legislation, but also the domestic laws of other nations. These can vary wildly from those of Australia. With that being said, the challenge inherent in practising in private international law can be extremely rewarding to individuals who revel in the web of complexity. If you excel at using your analytical skills to deconstruct complicated legal problems and enjoy doing so, private international law may be for you.

---

367 LexisNexis, *Encyclopaedic Australian Legal Dictionary* (at 12 February 2018) 'Private International Law'.

368 Ibid.

369 *Lewis Construction Co Pty Ltd v M Tichauer Societe Anonyme* [1966] VR 341.

370 Michael Tilbury, Gary Davis and Brian Opeskin, *Conflict of Laws in Australia* (Oxford University Press, 2002) v.

371 William Prosser, 'Interstate Publication' (1953) 51 *Michigan Law Review* 959, 971.

In addition to the legal complexity inherent in private international law, many matters can have a distinctly human element. For example, the Attorney-General's department recognises that in family law, particularly cases concerning the guardianship of children, an already extremely distressing dispute can be made worse by the added challenges brought on by parties split across international borders.[372] While private international law has the ability to challenge practitioners, it can also be extremely rewarding as it provides positive outcomes for distressed and otherwise vulnerable clients.

Recent Developments in Private International Law

As with many other areas of law, the mainstream usage of the Internet has brought forward a number of novel challenges for those working within this practice area. For example, where can an 'act' be said to have occurred in cyberspace? Does it occur at the location in which a final action occurs (such as a mouse click), or when and where a server receives the resulting flow of data? What implications does this have for deciding which laws are applicable, and what is the most appropriate forum in which to hear the matter? These are questions which have been examined by the court in cases such as *K & S Corporation Ltd v Number 1 Betting Shop Ltd*.[373] Here the Supreme Court of South Australia granted leave for summons to be served outside of Australia where the defendants had no physical presence in Australia, and the only connection was the occurrence of electronic bank transfers in the Australian Capital Territory.[374]

Resources and Tips for Interested Students

As mentioned previously, a strong set of analytical skills and knowledge of applicable domestic and foreign laws will greatly benefit anyone seeking to practice in private international law.

If you are interested in a career in the public sector, the Attorney-General's department maintains responsibility for various functions important to the processes of private international law, such as providing general advice for the service of documents from overseas jurisdictions. If you are more interested in private practice, be sure to do your research and seek out firms that actively take on private

[372] Attorney-General's Department, *International family law and children*. https://www.ag.gov.au/FamiliesAndMarriage/Families/InternationalFamilyLaw/

[373] [2005] SASC 228 (24 June 2005).

[374] Ibid 131.

international law matters, as some can be hesitant about taking on said matters due to their complexity relative to their domestic counterparts.

Property Law

What is Property Law?

Property law concerns relationships to lands, goods or ideas.[375] It involves deciphering who has the right to exclude others from using, profiting from or dealing with property. 'Real property' (land) is at the centre of most property lawyers' practice, outside of intellectual property. As such, most property lawyers work primarily to assist clients in buying, selling, leasing and developing land. Lawyers are likely to be involved in the negotiation of property transactions and the subsequent drafting of the relevant contracts. Whilst much of the work is transactional, property lawyers may also be involved in litigation in the event of a dispute related to property.[376]

Property law is a broad area, allowing practising lawyers to develop a range of skills and gain a variety of experiences.[377] For example, property law has a strong overlap with equity, trusts, contract law, planning law, environmental law, construction law and dispute resolution.[378] Lawyers can be involved in residential and commercial property matters, though may specialise in one or the other. Graduates working in property law may find themselves doing any number of tasks, from drafting and preparing reports on the title of the property to liaising with local councils and housing authorities.[379] Oftentimes, junior lawyers and graduates will be given a degree of autonomy in drafting contracts related to property transactions and will later move on to greater involvement in the negotiation of deals.

What are the Challenges and Rewards of Working in This Area?

Property law in Australia can vary depending on a practitioner's jurisdiction. As such, lawyers dealing with interstate property need to be abreast of what may be different laws, or how similar laws are expressed differently. For graduates, the complexities and required diligence of property law creates a steep learning curve,

---

[375] Anthony Moore, Scott Grattan and Lynden Griggs, *Bradbrook, MacCallum and Moore's Australian Real Property Law* (Thomson Reuters, 6th ed., 2015), V. See the 'Intellectual Property' section for further information on 'ideas' as property.

[376] Jaymes Carr, *Real Estate and Property Law Area of Practice*, GradAustralia. https://gradaustralia.com.au/law/real-estate-and-property-law-area-of-practice

[377] Ibid.

[378] Ibid.

[379] Ibid.

especially for matters involving a deep understanding of real estate law from multiple jurisdictions.[380] For this reason, property law is an area that will demand patience from those who are learning, as well as their mentors. However, successfully completing transactions or litigation is rewarding from both a problem-solving and client satisfaction perspective.

Recent Developments in Property Law

Technology has enabled the computerisation of land transactions and title records, forever changing the way these important and complex documents are stored and accessed.[381] The shift to computerised records and systems, such as PEXA, has made masses of information available at the click of a button, in many ways simplifying much of the necessary conveyancing, research and paperwork. However, the move toward technology dependence has been accompanied by its own challenges. For example, verifying the identity of those seeking to look and deal with the relevant records can be difficult; fraudulently stealing an identity could lead to inappropriate dealings similar to that of someone stealing a PIN to access another person's bank account.[382] For this reason, professionals such as property lawyers may be held to a higher standard of accountability in ascertaining identities as we move forward with these systems.[383]

Resources and Tips for Interested Students

Drafting skills and a strong familiarity with the relevant laws and regulations is what makes a successful property lawyer; as such, familiarising yourself with drafting and research throughout law school are ideal ways to prepare yourself for a career in property law. Studying property law and contracts is a necessary foundation. However, work or volunteer experience in a firm which deals in property law is also invaluable.

Communication and negotiation skills are also important for property lawyers. To help develop these skills, consider participating in moots, mock-negotiations and mock client interviews in law school. This will also give you experience and a skills base to draw upon when you do enter a professional setting.

---

[380] Ibid.

[381] Moore, Grattan and Griggs, above n 1, 3.

[382] Moore, Grattan and Griggs, above n 1, 3.

[383] Ibid, 4.

Career Pathway

When seeking a graduate position, look for firms dealing in property law or in-house positions within organisations that frequently deal with property law (such as a large corporation or government body).[384]

Beginning in a firm with a strong property practice is one way of commencing a career in property law whilst also affording yourself the opportunity to work with a range of clients. When considering which firms with whom to apply for graduate positions, keep in mind that many firms will only hire graduates from their field of vacation clerks. As such, applying for clerkships with firms that interest you may be a useful career step during your penultimate year.

As you gain more experience, becoming an accredited specialist in property law may be valuable. To become an accredited specialist in Victoria, one must be a member of the Law Institute of Victoria, hold a current practising certificate, have at least five years' experience in the practice in which they seek to specialise, and have substantial involvement in that area of practice over the past three years.[385] The Law Society of New South Wales has similar requirements, with the additional prerequisite of needing to have practiced in the area for not less than 25% of your full-time practice in the three years preceding the application.[386] If accreditation is something that interests you later in your career, look at the requirements in the state where you seek to earn your accreditation, remembering that requirements may vary.

Public Health Law

What is Public Health Law?

Public health law concerns the legal powers and duties of the state to assure the conditions for people to be healthy; identifying, preventing, and ameliorating risks to health in the population. It also considers the limitations on the power of the state to constrain the autonomy, privacy, liberty, proprietary or other legally protected interests of individuals for the common good.[387]

Public health law has the ability to intersect with an extremely diverse range of practice areas and as such practitioners from many different areas of law may find themselves incidentally confronted with public health law considerations.

[384] Jaymes Carr, *Real Estate and Property Law Area of Practice*, GradAustralia. https://gradaustralia.com.au/law/real-estate-and-property-law-area-of-practice

[385] Law Institute of Victoria, *Become an Accredited Specialist* (2018). https://www.liv.asn.au/Learning-and-Networking/Become-an-Accredited-Specialist/Specialist-Areas-Key-Dates

[386] Law Society of New South Wales, *Professional Development: Specialist Accreditation* (2018). http://www.lawsociety.com.au/ForSolictors/Education/specialists/Howtoapply/index.htm

[387] Lawrence Lawrence O. Gostin, Lindsay F. Wiley, *Public Health Law: Power, Duty Restraint* (University of California Press, 3rd ed., 2016) 4.

For example, a specialist in intellectual property law might represent a tobacco company disputing plain packaging legislation (discussed below in "Recent developments in Public Health Law"). Similarly, a practitioner specialising in administrative law may represent a client disputing the government's ability to withhold social benefits on the basis of their unwillingness to immunise their children.

What are the Challenges and Rewards of Working in This Area?

As mentioned above, practitioners from many different areas of law will come across public health law in the course of their practice. As such, the challenges and rewards that come with working in public health law will depend on which (if any) area of law is intersecting. In the example given above of a specialist in administrative law, challenges would include working in an extremely politicised subject matter, as well as the potential for extremely distressed clients. However, the same matter could be rewarding as the practitioner is assisting the client to challenge what they view to be an overreach in government authority, providing a sense of resolution.

A policy officer working for a body responsible for public health law faces an extremely difficult task in balancing the interests of the individual and the interests of the broader community. Opponents of expansive public health law argue that its paternalistic character restricts individual autonomy as sacrosanct,[388] while proponents argue that the potential for societal good far outweighs the harm caused by restriction of individual liberties.[389]

Recent Developments in Public Health Law

The *Tobacco Plain Packaging Act 2011*,[390] commonly known as the 'plain packaging legislation', has been the subject of much public debate. The act requires that all tobacco products sold conform to a strict list of requirements,[391] with the aim of, among other things, reducing the attractiveness and appeal of tobacco products to consumers, particularly young people.[392] At the time the legislation was announced, tobacco smoking was calculated to be responsible for 15,000 deaths annually and total social costs of more than $31.5 billion.[393] Many large tobacco companies voiced their displeasure with the legislation, culminating in a constitutional

---

388 Ibid, 45.

389 Ibid 48.

390 (Cth).

391 Ibid, Pt 2.

392 Explanatory Memorandum, *Tobacco Plain Packaging Bill 2011* (Cth) 1.

393 Tania Voon et al., *Public Health and Plain Packaging of Cigarettes: Legal Issues* (Edward Elgar Publishing, 2012).

challenge in the High Court.[394] This claimed that the legislation amounted to an acquisition of property and as such was required to be made 'on just terms' according to the Constitution.[395] The application was dismissed on the grounds that the legislation did not amount to an 'acquisition' or property, and the plaintiffs were ordered to pay the defendants' costs.[396]

Resources and Tips for Interested Students

An extremely diverse range of practice areas will intersect with public health law to some degree. As such, the skills beneficial to practitioners will vary accordingly. Generally speaking, keeping up to date with developments in the broader field of public health, such as new research carried out and technologies developed, will aid practitioners in responding appropriately when confronted with public health law concerns.

While few practitioners will work *exclusively* in public health law (outside of certain government departments such as the Department of Health), it should be kept in mind that, as many areas intersect with public health law, opportunities to work in this area will sometimes present themselves in unorthodox ways. As such, an open mind should be kept; think about other areas of law you might enjoy practising in and how they could potentially intersect with public health law.

Public International Law

What is Public International Law?

Public international law is the area of law which 'regulates relations (i) among States and public international organisations per se; (ii) between States and individuals in the field of international human rights; and (iii) between the international society and individuals who have committed international crimes'.[397] The format of public international law as we know it today, with the United Nations serving as the preeminent supranational body in international politics and law, was solidly established in 1945 during the waning months[398] of World War II.[399]

394 *JT International SA v Commonwealth of Australia* [2012] HCA 43.

395 *Australian Constitution* s 51(xxxi).

396 *JT International SA v Commonwealth of Australia* [2012] HCA 43.

397 Stephen Hall, *Principles of International Law* (LexisNexis, 4th ed., 2008) xlvi.

398 The *Charter of the United Nations* was opened for signature on the 26th of June 1945 and came into force on the 26th of October 1945.

399 *Charter of the United Nations* Preamble.

Public international law is an extremely diverse area covering a number of practices, and has been the stage for some of the most important developments in recent history. For example, the Nuremberg Trials were perhaps the most widely publicised and consequential judicial set pieces in history, with the later developed International Criminal Court taking inspiration from the tribunals to prosecute axis war crimes.[400] However, prosecuting individuals for war crimes is by no means the only area of law under the umbrella of public international law. The United Nations are responsible for a range of functions including settling disputes between states and ensuring the observance of human rights.

What are the Challenges and Rewards of Working in This Area?

Public international law is unique in the challenges and rewards it can offer; few areas of law can match it in terms of complexity or difficulty of entry. The complexity of working in public international law stems from the fact that it occupies a nebulous quagmire between law and politics; political considerations and legal considerations intersect seamlessly. In addition, the usual tensions which exist in a domestic legal system between parties in civil disputes, between the prosecution and the defence in criminal matters and between the courts and society generally are amplified by orders of magnitude due to the scale and implications of the proceedings. Public international law is also notorious as one of the, if not *the* hardest area of law in which to practice, at least initially.

If you are able to practise in public international law, the complexity of the subject matter you deal with will be intrinsically rewarding and will offer a level of prestige. The subject matter itself is also extremely interesting and professionally stimulating; the area is extremely competitive for this reason.

Recent Developments in Public International Law

Many bodies of public international law have been criticised for their ineffectiveness, particularly in relation to powerful member-states.[401] Despite this, the Special Court for Sierra Leone, a judicial body created specifically by the United Nations,

---

[400] Judge Philippe Kirsch, 'Applying the Principles of Nuremberg in the ICC' (Speech delivered at the 'Judgement at Nuremberg' Conference, Washington University, 30 September 2006). https://www.icc-cpi.int/NR/rdonlyres/ED2F5177-9F9B-4D66-9386-5C5BF45D052C/146323/PK_20060930_English.pdf

[401] See, e.g., Kevin Sieff, Krista Mahr, *South Africa says it will quit the International Criminal Court* (22 October 2016) The Sydney Morning Herald. https://www.smh.com.au/world/south-africa-says-it-will-quit-the-international-criminal-court-20161022-gs8aiy.html

sentenced Charles Taylor, former president of Liberia, to 50 years' imprisonment for his role in planning, aiding and abetting war crimes against the Sierra Leonean people.[402] The sentencing of Taylor represents the first time since the Nuremberg Trials that a former head-of-state has been convicted of war crimes,[403] and the first time ever for a former African head-of-state.[404]

Resources and Tips for Interested Students

It bears repeating that public international law is an extremely competitive field to enter, with relatively low-level positions requiring multiple years of relevant industry experience and/or advanced degrees such as a Master's. For example, a Legal Officer role at the New York based Office of the Under-Secretary-General for Management of the United Nations is expected to have a Master's Degree (or a Bachelor's Degree from a 'first-rate' university) and five years' relevant industry experience.[405] As such, it is important to identify the area of public international law in which you want to work and take every opportunity to accrue experience in that area.

While programs such as internships are available through organisations such as the United Nation, places are, again, extremely competitive, with the majority being offered in locations far removed from Australia. This compounds the inherent difficulty of entry, as interns are expected to bear their own costs. These could be extreme in locations with a high cost of living, such as New York.

Some large private firms have a public international law practice.[406] If you want to practise through large private firms, then on top of academic excellence in relevant subjects and extra-curricular activities such as volunteering, a genuine, demonstrable interest and thorough knowledge of current events in public international law will help set you apart from other candidates.

---

[402] *Prosecutor v Taylor (Sentencing Judgement)* (Special Court for Sierra Leone, Trial Chamber II, Case No SCSL-03-01-T, 30 May 2012).

[403] Human Rights Watch, *Sierra Leone: Landmark Conviction of Liberian Ex-President* (26 April 2012). https://www.hrw.org/news/2012/04/26/sierra-leone-landmark-conviction-liberian ex-president

[404] Al Jazeera, *War crimes court finds Charles Taylor guilty* (27 April 2012). https://www.aljazeera.com/news/africa/2012/04/201242693846498785

[405] Legal Officer role advertised on *United Nations Careers*. https://careers.un.org/lbw/home.aspx. accessed 05 March 2018.

[406] Herbert Smith Freehills, *Public International Law* (accessed 05 March 2018). https://www.herbertsmithfreehills.com/our-expertise/services/public-international-law

Social Security Law

What is Social Security Law?

Social security law refers to the law of government payments (either a pension, a benefit or an allowance) to individuals under the *Social Security Act 1991* (Cth).[407] Social security law plays an important role in other practice areas, such as family law, homelessness law and refugee law. When practising in social security law, individuals may come to you seeking advice on how to appeal decisions, problems relating to overpayment or underpayment of their benefit, debt recovery problems, an issue with their allowance, or a benefit or pension reduction or cancellation.[408] The Social Security Appeals Tribunal (SSAT) is responsible for reviewing decisions made under social security law.[409] This is a specialist division under the Administrative Appeals Tribunal which can review most child support and Centrelink decisions,[410] as since 1 July 2015 (pursuant to the 1971 Kerr Committee Report) many different administrative law tribunals including the SSAT were merged into one body, the Administrative Appeals Tribunal.[411] As a decision regarding whether to grant payments is government action, this is an area of administrative law where merits review and judicial review may be available.

What are the Challenges and Rewards of Working in This Area?

Social security law may be a very challenging and rewarding area in which to work, as clients in financial hardship often have other legal and non-legal matters with which they also require assistance, such as problems with obtaining housing and basic living necessities. There is also an overlap between social security law and human rights law, as people need some sort of income in order to obtain basic economic human rights. Assisting people to obtain their basic human rights may be very rewarding. Social security law may also overlap with family law. For example, one of the primary reasons that victims of family violence become homeless is insufficient independent finance.[412] This can be addressed through social security law.

---

407 Ray Finkelstein and David Hamer (eds), *LexisNexis Concise Australian Legal Dictionary* (LexisNexis, 5th ed., 2015), 584.

408 Canberra Community Law, *Social Security Law* (2017). http://www.canberracommunitylaw.org.au/social-security-law.html

409 Finkelstein, Ray and David Hamer (eds), *LexisNexis Concise Australian Legal Dictionary* (LexisNexis, 5th ed., 2015), 584.

410 Administrative Appeals Tribunal, Social Services & Child Support Division (23 January 2018). http://www.aat.gov.au/social-services-child-support-division

411 Social Security Appeals Tribunal, *Annual Report 2014/2015* (28 September 2015). http://www.aat.gov.au/AAT/media/AAT/Files/SSCSD%20documents/Reports/SSAT-Annual-Report-2014-15.pdf

412 Australian Law Reform Commission, *Family Violence and Commonwealth Laws – Improving Legal Frameworks*, Final Report 117 (November 2011) 51 [1.17]; 135 [5.23].

Recent Developments in Social Security Law

In mid-2016, the federal government started using the Online Compliance Intervention (OCI) program to oversee the Centrelink system and report overpayments of Centrelink recipients, also referred to as the 'robo-debt' program.[413] The program led to approximately 20% of Centrelink recipients who did not owe any debt to Centrelink receiving an initial letter stating that they did owe a debt.[414] The Victorian Council of Social Service have expressed their concern that there may be more individuals that this 20% that do not owe a debt, however these other Centrelink recipients were unable to explain that they did not owe any debt and hereby have paid or are currently paying debts that they do not owe.[415] The situation of the other 80% of individuals who received an initial debt letter is not known.[416] The Community Affairs Reference Committee recommended that the government should stop using the OCI system until they were able to fix these issues regarding the procedural fairness of the system.[417]

Resources and Tips for Interested Students

There are many community legal services that practise in social security law. There may be a position available for law students to volunteer, under the supervision of a lawyer. Individuals who are eligible for a government benefit, pension or allowance often will not have the funds to seek legal advice from a private lawyer. Therefore, there are many clients who require assistance from volunteer students, pro bono lawyers and community legal services.

Career Pathway

As social security law is vital in other practice areas, such as family law, homelessness law, indigenous rights law and refugee law, an individual may practise in all these areas of law rather than specialising only in social security law. Another avenue that a student may consider is policy development in social security law. For example, the Australian Law Reform Commission released a report in 2011 that

---

[413] Community Affairs Reference Committee, Commonwealth Parliament, *Design, scope, cost-benefit analysis, contracts awarded and implementation associated with the Better Management of the Social Welfare System initiative* (June 2018) 1–2.

[414] Ibid 33.

[415] Ibid 33.

[416] Ibid 34.

[417] Ibid 108.

addressed how social security law may assist victims of family violence,[418] which further demonstrates the overlap between social security law and other areas of law, i.e. family law in this context.

Space Law

What is Space Law?

Space law refers to the laws, agreements and treaties that govern outer space.[419] This can include laws regarding the exploration of space, damage and liability for space-related incidents, use of weapons, rescuing distressed astronauts, environmental regulations and other activities in space.[420] A career in space law may be attractive for people interested in space, science, politics and diplomacy.[421]

A career in space law is likely to involve the drafting of international treaties or their translation into national law. It may involve consulting space agencies or other bodies on relevant regulations and liabilities related to space. It will involve intimate knowledge of the treaties from the United Nations' Committee on the Peaceful Uses of Outer Space, the main international body for discussing space-related agreements.[422] Treaties cover a broad range of topics, from the decision that no state can claim sovereignty over celestial bodies, to banning the use of nuclear weapons in space.[423] Remaining abreast of NASA's updates and policies is also likely to be an important part of a career in space law, as the agency coordinates activities on the International Space Station.

What are the Challenges and Rewards of Working in This Area?

As with any international agreement, there is reticence amongst some states to become signatories and curb their autonomy. For instance, the 1979 Moon Treaty only has 17 signatories; this limits its overall effectiveness in regulating moon-related activities. It is a general trend that international agreements with broader language are more successful in attracting signatories; though in terms of their

---

[418] Australian Law Reform Commission, *Family Violence and Commonwealth Laws – Improving Legal Frameworks*, Final Report 117 (November 2011).

[419] *What is Space Law*, Legal Career Path. http://legalcareerpath.com/space-law/

[420] Ibid.

[421] Ibid.

[422] Ibid.

[423] Ibid.

enforceability, the value of broadly drafted agreements decreases with vagueness.[424] As such, space lawyers are required to have strong negotiation and diplomacy skills to ensure maximum signatories for meaningful agreements.

Recent Developments in Space Law

On 25 September 2017 the Australian Government announced the establishment of a national space agency in Australia.[425] The announcement was largely in response to a growing international space industry on the back of cheaper satellite technology and increased private space industry funding. The agency is intended to help the growth of the Australian space industry and promote international engagement. The space industry in Australia is of growing importance to our lifestyles and economy: earth observation data assists in weather and fire predictions, satellite communications are of the utmost importance to individuals and companies, whilst navigation data has become part of our everyday lives.[426] The expansion of Australia's space industry may represent an exciting opening for young lawyers passionate about space and/or the international cooperation it represents.

Resources and Tips for Interested Students

Space lawyers will generally be expected to have a strong understanding of the science involved in space explorations, so they can draft accurate legislation and provide educated advice.[427] As such, undertaking some educational training in science either before, after or alongside your law degree will assist in building a career in space law. At law school, consider studying commercial law and international law. Undertaking work or volunteer experience in aviation or space-related bodies would provide a valuable start to a career in this area. Similarly, seeking out a position which involves advising on, drafting or implementing legislation based on international agreements would provide relevant experience.

[424] Ibid.

[425] Department of Industry, Innovation and Science (Cth), 'Turnbull Government to Establish National Space Agency' (Media Release, 25 September 2017).

[426] *Australian Civil Space,* Australian Government: Department of Industry, Innovation and Science. https://industry.gov.au/INDUSTRY/IndustrySectors/SPACE/Pages/default.aspx

[427] *What is Space Law,* Legal Career Path. http://legalcareerpath.com/space-law/

Career Pathway

Space law is an incredibly competitive area to break into, though the demand for specialists in this area is increasing.[428] Studying space-specific or physics-related subjects will put you in a strong position for relevant volunteer or work experience in space law.[429] Similarly, finding positions in companies involved in the private space industry is a way of beginning a career in this speciality area; there are a growing number of space start-up companies in Australia, as well as a number of established companies, who require specialised space lawyers.[430] For example, major telecommunications companies require advice on contract negotiation and liability in relation to satellites. Alternatively, looking for positions in government or international bodies who are responsible for advising on, drafting, negotiating or interpreting international treaties will help you build on the necessary credentials and experience for a career in space law. Working in aviation may also provide a pathway into space law as the industry grows.

Sports Law

What is Sports Law?

Sports law is as it sounds – it concerns the regulation of athletes, sporting matches, and related competitive activities. Sports law is not only about policy and procedure, but also concerns a wider breadth of subjects such as commercial contract negotiation, intellectual property, personal injury and defamation.

Sports lawyers do not, as may be commonly misconceived, work only with amateur and professional athletes. Other clients may include coaches, referees, officials, sporting clubs, governing bodies, educational institutions, sports broadcasters or equipment manufacturers.[431] It is therefore important that sports lawyers not only have a firm understanding of the sports in which their clients compete, but also the underpinnings of said sport, from beginning to end.

---

[428] Anna Salleh, *Out-of-this-world space careers you can have without leaving Earth* (5 December 2017) ABC News. http://www.abc.net.au/news/science/2017-11-27/space-careers:-theres-more-to-being-an-astronaut/9157980

[429] Ibid.

[430] Sallleh, above n 10.

[431] Matthew Mitten, *What is Sports Law and Who is a Sports Lawyer?* American Bar Association. https://www.americanbar.org/groups/young_lawyers/publications/tyl/topics/professional-development/what-is-sports-law-who-is-sports-lawyer.html

What are the Challenges and Rewards of Working in This Area?

Sports law is rewarding as it provides a broad range of topics on which sports lawyers may give advice to their clients. Both the type of client and the scope of inquiries are almost endlessly wide, providing for an occupation that is ever changing and engaging.

However this is, in a complementary sense, also a challenge of sports law. Sports lawyers may wish to become specialised in a particular area of sports law, rather than allowing themselves to operate for many different people in many different capacities. This would encourage sports lawyers to become experts in particular sections of sports law, rather than forcing them to be flexible and knowledgeable in a wide array of matters.

Recent Developments in Sports Law

The most exciting recent development in sports law is the rise of e-sports. E-sports are online sporting events between professional video-game players.[432] Though not yet as radically popular in Australia as in other countries, such as South Korea, China and North America, their continued growth is imminent.[433] E-sport events are not only watched online, but also achieve high attendance rates at packed stadiums across the globe – for example, at the League of Legends 2014 World Finals, 45,000 fans filled the Sang-am World Cup Stadium in Seoul.[434]

E-sports are a creature unlike anything sports lawyers have had to deal with before. Essentially, they are a new breed of sports that require their own set of regulations and standards. Rules vary from game to game, and from genre to genre – while some tournaments are team based, others are entered in an individual capacity, and the aim of the game can differ widely.

Differences aside, for the lawyer's purposes, many principles of e-sports are the same as for regular sports. Sports lawyers will still be relied upon to negotiate contracts between competitors, teams, and associated bodies, for one. However, they are less likely to be involved in personal injury claims, due to the reduced capacity in which competitors are physically involved.

[432] Hannah Dwan, *What Are Esports? A Beginner's Guide* (18 October 2017) The Telegraph. https://www.telegraph.co.uk/gaming/guides/esports-beginners-guide/

[433] Peter Warman, *Esports Revenue Will Reach $696 Million This Year and Grow to $1.5 Billion by 2020 as Brand Investment Doubles* (14 February 2017) Newzoo. https://newzoo.com/insights/articles/esports-revenues-will-reach-696-million-in-2017/

[434] Joshua Nino De Guzman, *The World's Biggest and Best eSports Arenas* (27 February 2015) Red Bull. https://www.redbull.com/gb-en/the-biggest-and-best-esports-stadiums-in-the-world

Resources and Tips for Interested Students

Those strongly interested in becoming a sports lawyer ought to research relevant law firms in their vicinity, and reach out for internship or shadowing opportunities. While these may not always be available, any expression of interest is beneficial as it demonstrates desire and dedication to work in the specified area. For similar reasons, any opportunity to network with applicable figures ought to be accepted and undertaken, so that interested students can separate themselves out from the crowd.

It is important to remember that sports lawyers must be familiar with the sports in which they work. Therefore, it is advisable that students who are passionate in this area also remain passionate in their preferred sports, and ensure they are aware of the regulations in all their complexity. This is particularly advised for those interested in e-sports, as rules are diverse, unique, and often very new.

Career Pathway

As above, reaching out to firms early, and completing an internship or other work experience if possible, is key to making and maintaining connections. It is through opportunities such as this that graduates are most likely to be able to move into this specific area of law shortly after completing their studies.

However, this area of law is niche and may be difficult to enter immediately. It is thus worth acknowledging the components relevant to a career as a sports lawyer – contract negotiation, intellectual property, and so forth. It is not uncommon for sports lawyers to first practise elsewhere, developing their skills in one or more of the constituents of sports law before transitioning into this area at a later stage of their career. This is because, particularly in respect of clients that are high-level athletes, it is imperative that a good sports lawyer be able to, in particular, draft and negotiate a solid contract in order to meet their clients' needs.[435]

Taxation Law

What is Taxation Law?

Benjamin Franklin once said that '[i]n this world nothing is certain but death and taxes.' The statutes and common law governing an entity's liability to pay taxes to the government is known as taxation law. Taxes have always been an integral part of a functioning society and records of taxation date back even to ancient Egyptian and Greek civilisations. The famous Rosetta Stone, a key decipherer of Egyptian

[435] Above n 1.

hieroglyphics, uncovered a decree by King Ptolemy V granting taxation immunity to the priesthood.

Being the government's primary source of revenue, taxation enables government expenditure that benefits society as a whole, such as public infrastructure, social welfare benefits, hospitals, defence and educational institutions. The taxation system has an important social and political engineering function, influencing for example the purchasing decisions of consumers and businesses. It also plays important roles in redistributing wealth and speeding up or slowing down the economy. The ubiquity of tax in practically every aspect of commercial life is reflected in the vastness of taxation law and its many specialities. Major specialities include corporate tax, employment tax, indirect tax, global tax, research and development, and superannuation.

What are the Challenges and Rewards of Working in This Area?

Taxation law is both an incredibly challenging and an extremely rewarding area in which to work. In general, tax law practitioners enjoy more comparatively stable working hours than other legal disciplines. However, opportunities for travel and a change of scenery are less available. Lawyers are typically fixed to the same office.

Tax law is voluminous, highly technical and constantly changing every year at the state, federal and global level. However, the constant reform happens to make taxation law very topical and an important point of discussion for those interested in political debate. The personal utility of understanding tax law to plan your personal finances is, of course, already noteworthy, but its enormous practical commercial relevance also makes taxation a particularly worthwhile study. Almost every transaction has some link to taxation law, its principles or policies. These principles are influenced by many ethical and philosophical issues which can make the discipline also academically interesting.

The work of a tax lawyer may include tax advice, tax compliance, tax law reform submissions, negotiations or litigation. Because tax law is a crucial component in practically every transaction, there is significant scope for practitioners to join other commercial legal teams and gain diverse experience in, for instance, mergers and acquisitions, property transfers, family law, criminal law, or trusts and estates. Similarly, a background in tax opens up employment opportunities in other commercial fields such as accounting, business management, and finance.

Recent Developments in Taxation Law

One does not have to look far and wide to find recent developments in taxation law, which is continually changing with new statutes, judicial decisions and (non-binding) rulings by the Australian Taxation Office. The Turnbull Government heralded the National Innovation and Science Agenda, hoping to boost economic growth in Australia by supporting innovation in STEM-related businesses. As part of the agenda, the government introduced significant tax reforms designed to encourage investment in ESICs. These tax incentives included a 20% tax offset to investors for shares purchased in ESICs, as well as a 10 year exemption on any capital gains made from these shares.[436]

Superannuation also underwent significant changes in 2017. According to the 2016 Tax Expenditures Statement, concessional taxation of superannuation is the second most expensive tax expenditure in Australia.[437] In response, the government tightened access to the heavily concessional tax rates. For example, the non-concessional (after-tax) contributions cap has been lowered from $180,000 per year to $100,000.[438] One of the main reasons for this suite of reforms is to prevent superannuation from being a tax shelter for high-net-wealth individuals, which in turn ultimately aims to preserve the long-term sustainability of the superannuation scheme in light of the ageing population.

Resources and Tips for Interested Students

It is not necessary to have an accounting, finance or business background to practise taxation law, although they certainly do help in honing your financial literary skills. It goes without saying that students interested in a tax law career should also undertake a taxation law unit at university. Many Australian universities also offer a further advanced taxation law unit, which is highly recommended. Students should also focus on the core law units of company, contract, property and trusts, which are important foundational units for tax.

As with all commercial law specialities, students should also maintain an awareness of the current commercial and economic climate by reading the Australian Financial Review, or the business section of any reputable newspaper. Many developments in tax law are also highly political and reported in detail in the news.

The Australian Taxation Office (ATO) website is an excellent source of information about tax laws, often written in plain English and accompanied by example scenarios. The ATO also has many videos on YouTube which explain key tax topics in an even more simplified format. Law students seeking additional work experience should also consider joining the ATO's Tax Help Program, which assists low-income earners with their taxes. No prior tax knowledge is required to volunteer.

---

[436] Income Tax Assessment Act 1997 (Cth) pt. 3–45 div 360.

[437] The Treasury, Australian Government, *2016 Tax Expenditures Statement* (2017) 9.

[438] Income Tax Assessment Act 1997 (Cth) pt. 3–30 divs 291–292.

Career Pathway

In tax law, there is always more to learn. Almost every tax practitioner continuously seeks to expand their knowledge through further university study, continuing professional development (CPD) courses, research, and tax newsletter updates. Australian universities offer diplomas in accounting and finance, Master's of Taxation, or Master's of Commercial Laws. The Tax Institute is Australia's leading professional body of tax practitioners and provides many educational courses which can also count towards mandatory CPD requirements.

Technology Law

What is Technology Law?

Technology law is a broad, parent category of law that encompasses technological concerns, including but not limited to artificial intelligence, online services, smart devices and ongoing advancements. Due to its wide birth it is often subdivided into smaller categories, and commonly practised in part, rather than in whole. It is very common for technology lawyers to deal frequently in intellectual property and consumer protection.

Cyber or internet law is a subsidiary of technology law, and encapsulates rules and regulations relating to the Internet and its use. As the Internet only continues to broaden in content and scope, this is a very wide area of law that faces endless expansion. Typical issues managed include copyright, freedom of speech, defamation, privacy, and access to and use of the Internet and its resources. Most of the subcategories of cyber law predate the Internet, and as such have been, and continue to be, adapted in accordance with technological advancement.[439]

What are the Challenges and Rewards of Working in This Area?

A large challenge in this area is working through the limits that result from the Internet's ethereal nature, as the Internet is so critical to technological advancements. Technology law, and hence cyber law, is unique in that it concerns platforms that are internationally accessible, and as such cannot be bound by national laws. Consequently, some claim that the Internet is 'unable to be regulated' at all. It is true that applicable laws are limited, at least geographically, but it is also evident that laws can and do apply to online conduct – take recent changes to sexting law in

[439] Carlos Leyva, *What is Cyberlaw?* Digital Business Law Group. http://www.digitalbusinesslaw-group.com/what-is-cyberlaw.html

Victoria, for example.[440] Hence, lawyers that work in this area must ensure the relevant law applies in the given circumstances.

This area can also be highly rewarding as it is so incredibly diverse, and hence there the workload is less repetitive than in other specialisations. As a result of this diversity, lawyers who work in other areas of law often find themselves dabbling in different areas of technology law, for example media lawyers working through a defamation case involving an online media outlet.

Recent Developments in Technology Law

Net neutrality is the current hot-topic in technology and cyber law. This concept ensures that all online content is treated equally, with internet-service providers unable to privilege data flow to one website over another.[441] In the United States, there have been moves to abandon net neutrality, such that service providers can potentially control what users see and do online.[442] While this is unlikely to affect the Australian public directly, it may well affect Australian companies. Therefore, it is of critical importance that technology lawyers understand how to manage the new laws coming into play, so that their clients may be advised accordingly.

Resources and Tips for Interested Students

Interested students ought to be aware that technology law is niche to specialise in, but common to practise. Most lawyers are likely to come across technology law at some point in their career, and perhaps on a regular basis. However, to specialise in this area one must aptly research Australian firms in related areas, and enquire as to whether they have specialised technology or internet lawyers on hand. Those who wish to specialise would be best advised to seek out internships in such firms, in the hopes to gain employment or find similar connections for graduate opportunities.

---

[440] Tom Maddocks, *New Sexting Laws to Exempt Young People from Child Pornography Charges* (21 August 2014) ABC. http://www.abc.net.au/news/2014-08-21/australian-first-sexting-laws-to-be-introduced-in-victoria/5686166

[441] Stefan Kostarelis, *What is Net Neutrality and How Will Its Death Affect Australians?* (17 December 2017) Techly. https://www.techly.com.au/2017/12/18/net-neutrality-will-death-affect-australians/

[442] Ibid.

Career Pathway

Unlike many other areas, technology law is not necessarily its own specialised sector. In fact, most areas of practice will delve into aspects of technology law from time to time, whether this be through banking or financial cases concerning online transactions, contracts signed online and electronically, or cases of harassment that include communications via social media. Technology law is, for the most part, absorbed into and accessible from other areas of practice.

For those specifically looking to specialise in technology law, one ought to look to firms that specialise in internet law, intellectual property, and communications law. These companies are more likely to practice technology law on a regular basis, and may have or be seeking lawyers to specialise specifically in the cyber division.

Torts Law

What is Torts Law?

Torts are civil wrongs such as defamation, negligence, and trespass.[443] These are civil cases where a person can bring a claim because they have suffered a legal wrong (such as someone trespassing on their property), and can claim compensation for the injury that has been caused as a result of the wrong.[444] The law takes into account physical injury or bodily harm suffered, as well as emotional or mental harm. All of these factors depend on the law in each area, along with the nature and facts of the case.[445] Courts will also look at damage to property, monetary loss, and damage to one's reputation.[446] A right to sue in this area arises even if you have no contract with the party who caused the injury, and no crime needs to have occurred for a claim to be brought.[447] However, sometimes civil claims and criminal proceedings can overlap, such as where there has been assault or battery which can result in the plaintiff having a right to sue, and the defendant is being prosecuted for a crime relating to the same facts. This area covers practice specialisations such as health law, which involves dealing with medical negligence and other similar claims. This provides an interesting intersection between medicine and the law. Torts law also covers defamation law, which allows plaintiffs to bring a claim where a party has damaged the plaintiff's good reputation by publishing information or distributing defamatory information through other means.[448]

---

[443] LexisNexis, *Encyclopaedic Australian Legal Dictionary* (at 29 December 2017) 'Torts Law''.

[444] Ibid.

[445] Ibid.

[446] Ibid.

[447] Ibid.

[448] Oxford University Press, *Australian Law Dictionary* (at 29 December 2017), 'Defamation'.

What are the Challenges and Rewards of Working in This Area?

Torts law can be a diverse area, and some firms or lawyers may specialise in particular areas. Often lawyers will be working to try and reach an agreement between the parties outside of court. Court proceedings can be very costly and lengthy, so it is often in the parties' best interests to reach an agreement or come to a settlement without taking the case to court. This involves use of excellent advocacy and interpersonal skills in helping clients achieve the best outcome. Sometimes lawyers will need to act quickly in order to try and prevent further irreparable damage to a client's reputation in defamation cases. Lawyers may also encounter high profile cases involving wide media coverage, or class actions with large numbers of plaintiffs bringing a claim for damages.

Recent Developments in Torts Law

There has been recent debate regarding the area of privacy and its place within our legal system. In an increasingly digital era where our information is being stored in online locations, and where the Internet has enabled far greater access to personal information, privacy is a growing concern. The Australian Law Reform Commission (ALRC) considered whether a new tort of privacy should be enacted in 2014, noting that other countries such as New Zealand have accepted a common law tort of misuse of private information and of intrusion.[449] The ALRC noted that privacy should be considered a 'fundamental value' which is 'worthy of legal protection'.[450] The United States, in particular, is a strong example of a country which has provided protection of privacy through torts law for several decades.[451] The ALRC also highlighted the need for privacy laws to adapt to technological change to ensure laws do not rapidly become obsolete.[452] This is an interesting area of policy debate, both in academia and in the community, as we adjust and adapt to changing technology.

Resources and Tips for Interested Students

It is important to note that lawyers do not generally specialise in torts law. This is a broad area that covers many sub-areas, such as medical negligence and defamation law, as explained above. With this in mind, gaining exposure to different types of civil cases can be a good way to find out if this could be the right area for you. Even

---

[449] *Serious Invasions Of Privacy In The Digital Era (ALRC Report 123)* | *ALRC* (2014) Alrc.gov.au. https://www.alrc.gov.au/publications/serious-invasions-privacy-digital-era-alrc-report-123

[450] Ibid, 29.

[451] Ibid.

[452] Ibid, 36.

attending court to listen to some interesting cases or going to seminars on topics such as health law can help you learn more about different areas of torts law. Get involved wherever you can, either at your law school, through law associations or by gaining practical legal experience through a part-time job or volunteer position. Firms and legal associations in this area will often have excellent blogs and websites that can help you learn about the kind of work that they do.

Many firms and lawyers work in 'plaintiff law' or 'personal injury' law, which involves working to obtain compensation for negligence claims and related matters. Often larger firms will take on class actions involving areas such as medical negligence. Working in plaintiff law can be extremely rewarding and diverse with a lot of client contact and the opportunity to obtain justice for people who have suffered injuries or damage to property or reputation.[453] More specific information on other areas of torts law can be found throughout this chapter.

Transport Law

What is Transport Law?

Transport law is not a standalone area of law per se; rather, it is a practice area incidental to a large number of areas of law such as (but not limited to) aviation law, maritime law, international trade law and contract law. For example, the negotiation and subsequent procurement of goods across international borders will inevitably require a discussion of which international commercial terms (commonly referred to as 'incoterms')[454] will apply to the transaction. As a result, what rights and responsibilities the vendor and purchaser will have in regards to the transportation of the goods can be regarded as transport law. However the term transport law can equally be used to describe the laws and regulations surrounding transport services such as trains and taxis. In essence, transport law is an incredibly diverse umbrella term for many different kinds of laws.

What are the Challenges and Rewards of Working in This Area?

As mentioned above, transport law is an extremely diverse category, and as such the challenges and rewards can be equally diverse. Taking the examples used above, a practitioner specialising in international trade law will need a sound understanding

453 *Beyond Law | Legal Jobs, News And Resources For Australian Law Students, Graduates And Young Lawyers* (2018) Beyondlaw.com.au. https://beyondlaw.com.au/news/91-tort-story-4-reasons-to-think-about-working-in-plaintiff-law

454 International Chamber of Commerce, *Incoterms® Rules 2010* (accessed 21 February 2017). https://iccwbo.org/resources-for-business/incoterms-rules/incoterms-rules-2010/

of contract law in the broader context of international trade law, while also dealing with parties across national borders. While initiatives such as incoterms have been developed for the express reason of reducing uncertainty and encouraging uniformity,[455] international trade law and the relevant transport law considerations remain relatively complex. With complexity, however, comes the opportunity for the professional satisfaction inherent in overcoming a difficult task; individuals who thrive amongst complexity may well find themselves suited to this particular area of transport law.

In contrast, a policy officer working to reform areas of domestic transport law may come across problems more conceptual in nature, such as how best to balance the competing interests of particular classes of road users including drivers and cyclists. In being tasked with developing and reforming policy, an individual can engage with creative problem solving more so than in other areas. As such, individuals with strong lateral thinking skills may find themselves suited to roles developing and reforming the laws and regulations governing domestic transport law.

Recent Developments in Transport Law

The recent, meteoric rise in the availability and popularity of commercial 'ridesharing' services such as Uber have sparked an extremely polarised and, at times, bitter debate as to the liability of such companies to pay duties and fees associated with the longstanding taxi industry, such as licensing fees and police background checks, both overseas[456] and in Australia.[457] The resulting legal battle led to a number of separate actions being taken, widely different across state lines. For example, while the Victorian Government moved to legalise ridesharing services such as Uber, a class-action lawsuit against Uber alleged that the service had caused 'severe financial losses' to taxi drivers by circumventing Victorian transport law.[458] In Queensland, laws were introduced to obligate Uber drivers to become licensed and pay annual fees in a manner analogous to traditional taxis.[459]

[455] International Chamber of Commerce, *Incoterms® Rules History* (accessed 21 February 2017).

[456] Katie French, *Transport chiefs tell Uber drivers they must apply for new criminal record checks*, Daily Mail Australia (4 September 2017). http://www.dailymail.co.uk/news/article-4848046/Uber-drivers-apply-new-criminal-record-checks.html

[457] Melissa Cunningham, *Delays for passengers at Melbourne Airport taxi drivers stage Uber protest*, The Age (16 August 2017). https://www.theage.com.au/national/victoria/delays-for-passengers-as-melbourne-airport-taxi-drivers-stage-uber-protest-20170815-gxwzlf.html

[458] Ebony Bowden, *Victorian taxi drivers planning multimillion-dollar class action against Uber*, The Age (21 November 2017). https://www.theage.com.au/national/victoria/victorian-taxi-drivers-planning-multimilliondollar-class-action-against-uber-20171121-gzpfjz.html

[459] *Transport and Other Legislation (Personalised Transport Reform) Amendment Bill 2017* (Qld).

The Victorian Government passed the *Transport Integration Act 2010*[460] with the intention of moving towards 'an integrated and sustainable transport system that contributes to an inclusive, prosperous and environmentally responsible State'.[461] The act requires that decision makers concerned within the transport system must have regard to the objectives and principles set out within the act when carrying out their duties.[462] The act broadly sets out the framework in which the Victorian transportation system will be developed into the future and is an example of forward-looking policy drafting.

Resources and Tips for Interested Students

Depending on which area of transport law you want to enter, the skills and knowledge you will want to focus on developing will vary wildly. As a policy officer, written communication and creative problem solving will be skills most sought after in applicants. If you come across any opportunities in the course of your studies to develop these, take them. As with all areas of law, a *demonstrable* interest in the area of law will make you stand out amongst other candidates.

For further information, resources and tips on other areas of transport law, see the relevant sections of "Admirality Law", "Aviation Law" and "International Trade Law".

Trusts and Estates Law

What is Trusts and Estates Law?

Trusts and estates is a very interesting area of law with a complex history dating all the way back to the medieval period.[463] Today, trusts are used for a variety of purposes such as commercial arrangements, joint ventures, investments, superannuation, and wills. Trusts are used by solicitors for holding client money in designated accounts.[464] Trusts are often used as mechanisms to manage taxation and assets where property is held on trust for beneficiaries by a trustee.[465] Trusts are found both

---

[460] (Vic).

[461] Ibid s 6.

[462] Victoria State Government, *Transport Integration Act* (14 August 2015). http://economicdevelopment.vic.gov.au/transport/legislation/transport-integration-act

[463] The Honourable Justice Margaret A McMurdo AC, "Faith Hope And Charity: The Resilience Of The Charitable Trust From The Middle Ages To The 21St Century. The WA Lee Lecture 2011" (2013) 13(1) *QUT Law Review* 5.

[464] Ibid.

[465] "Tax Tips: Discretionary Trusts: Beneficiary Issues" (2017) 51(7) *Taxation in Australia*, 353.

in family contexts and for business, with many businesses being set up as trusts. Trusts may also be utilised to advance benefits to the public or a section of the public through a charitable purpose trust.[466]

However, this particular section is going to focus specifically on estates and wills as a very common area of legal practice. A will only comes into force where a person has died, and can include the creation of testamentary trusts.[467] Wills and estates issues will often arise in a family law setting, where a family member passes away and leaves a will behind that dictates what should happen to the deceased person's estate. A person's estate, in the context of trusts, consists of all the property that the person owned, which will be distributed by an executor.[468] Wills need to be properly drafted and executed in order to be valid, so much of the law in this area is concerned with their validity.[469] This includes various formalities, along with ensuring that the way the will is drafted is clear and unambiguous. The deceased person who made the will is called the testator.[470] The testator makes gifts in their will to essentially distribute their estate among chosen beneficiaries. For example, if a relative passes away, they might leave you a sum of money, or perhaps they may leave you property such as land, or a collection of books in their will. This would make you a beneficiary of your relative's will.

What are the Challenges and Rewards of Working in This Area?

Practising in the area of wills and estates can be challenging, particularly where there are family dynamics and relationships to take into account. Wills and estates matters may frequently lead to conflicts and disputes between family members, which is something for which practitioners need to be prepared.[471] Lawyers will often need to exercise their negotiation skills in these situations and maintain a professional distance from disputes between beneficiaries.[472] There can also be conflicting instructions from different family members which can add to the complexity of these matters.[473] The possibility of disputes between executors, where

[466] The Honourable Justice Margaret A McMurdo AC, "Faith Hope And Charity: The Resilience Of The Charitable Trust From The Middle Ages To The 21St Century. The WA Lee Lecture 2011" (2013) 13(1) *QUT Law Review* 5–6.

[467] Oxford University Press, *Australian Law Dictionary* (at 29 November 2017), 'trust estate'.

[468] Oxford University Press, *Australian Law Dictionary* (at 29 November 2017), 'will'.

[469] G. E. Dal Pont, *Equity And Trusts In Australia* (Lawbook Co., 6th ed., 2015) 565–568.

[470] *Australian Law Dictionary,* above n 6.

[471] "Stay On The Estate: Practitioners Handling Estate Matters Should Not Get Involved In Family Disputes" (2017) 91(6) *Law Institute Journal.*

[472] Ibid.

[473] Ibid.

co-executors exist, and disputes between beneficiaries and executors is also something for practitioners to bear in mind and to assist in anticipating for any conflicts of interests.[474]

However, it can be rewarding to help clients achieve satisfactory outcomes where a dispute arises. Whilst wills and estates can be an emotional or difficult issue for families, being able to act for clients, whether it be in drafting a will or helping them settle disputes, can be a fulfilling experience in helping them achieve the best result possible.

Recent Developments in Trusts and Estates Law

Succession laws and laws relating to wills are subject to change, just like any area of law. In Victoria, for example, there have been a number of amendments to the *Administration and Probate Act 1958* (Vic), the *Guardianship and Administration Act 1986* (Vic) and the *Powers of Attorney Act 2014* (Vic).[475] Reforms include improvements for situations where a person has died, but their partner and children survive them.[476] The reforms provide for higher amounts to be paid to the deceased person's partner in such cases under the statute.[477] There have also been measures taken to reduce excessive fees being charged by executors (who administer the will and distribute the assets).[478] It is hoped that these reforms will improve the position of beneficiaries under a will and provide stronger protections against unduly high fees charged by executors.

Often reforms in this area will be focussed on preventing financial abuse or undue pressure or influence on both testators and trustees, along with broader social issues such as elder abuse.[479] These are issues which have been identified by the Australian Law Reform Commission and the Financial Ombudsman Service Australia as areas which require change and improvements.[480]

[474] Ibid.

[475] "Changes To Succession Laws: Latest Amendments Address Matters Including What Happens When A Person Dies Intestate" (2018) 91(12) *Law Institute Journal*.

[476] Ibid.

[477] Ibid.

[478] Ibid.

[479] *Wills: The Law's Response* (2018) Alrc.gov.au. https://www.alrc.gov.au/sites/default/files/pdfs/publications/fr131_08_wills.pdf

[480] Ibid.

Resources and Tips for Interested Students

Many firms will have a team devoted to wills and estates. There are also several specialist boutique law firms which focus exclusively on trusts, wills and estates. The work can be diverse as practitioners may be involved in drafting wills and estate planning, taxation and trusts disputes, establishing powers of attorney and helping executors administer estates, or managing the entire process of administration of estates themselves. The area will inevitably overlap with other areas such as transfer and sale of property, dealing with guardianship, superannuation succession matters and family law issues.

For students, gaining practical legal experience in this area can help you decide if this is an area which interests you. For example, community legal centres will sometimes help clients draft simple wills or help with probate matters.

Utilities Regulation Law

What is Utilities Regulation Law?

The law surrounding public utility regulation includes the regulation of gas companies, electricity companies, phone companies, toll companies, water companies and other companies that provide public goods to the community. Many utilities that were previously controlled by government bodies have now been contracted to private companies, which means that much of the law that governs the regulation of public utilities is the Australian Competition and Consumer Law.[481] In the mid-1990s, public utility regulation in Australia underwent major changes with the implementation of the National Competition Policy reforms.[482] In this way, much of public utility regulation law is contract law, the focus being on particular contracts i.e. contracts regulating public utilities. The functions of the ACCC and the Australian Energy Regulator include acting as an appeal body for disputes in utilities regulation law.[483]

[481]Australian Competition and Consumer Commission, *Public Utility Regulation in Australia*, Working Paper No. 4 (July 2011).

[482]Australian Competition and Consumer Commission, *Public Utility Regulation in Australia*, Working Paper No. 4 (July 2011) 10; 52.

[483]Australian Competition and Consumer Commission, *Public Utility Regulation in Australia*, Working Paper No. 4 (July 2011) 44.

What are the Challenges and Rewards of Working in This Area?

Utilities regulation law can be demanding as it requires individuals working in the area to make ongoing decisions in response to the substantial resources required by our ever-growing population. As noted by the ACCC, the decisions are becoming substantially longer as time goes on – for example, decisions regarding the distribution of Victorian electricity have increased from a 433-page document in the year 2000 to a 1833-page document in 2010.[484] However, if you have a passion for contract law then public utilities regulation law may be an avenue for pursuit, as it is highly relevant and affects most people in Australia. The services of public utilities, such as water and electricity, are fundamental to healthy living in modern day society. If public utilities are unaffordable or inaccessible, then the impact is felt most by disadvantaged individuals in society.[485] Working in public utilities regulation and policy development may be extremely rewarding as it can have a large impact on people's lives.

Recent Developments in Utilities Regulation Law

As much of public utility regulation law is contract law, the problems facing public utilities regulation are also problems in other areas of contract law. For example, in 2011 the ACCC released a report that recommended that the law should create a greater role for consumers in public utility regulation.[486] Linked to this problem is the long-standing issue of monopolies in public utilities and the consequent imbalance of power between the consumer and the provider.[487]

Resources and Tips for Interested Students

Interested students may consider taking up all opportunities involving practice in contract law. Although the contracts may not be specific to public utilities regulation, a firm grasp of contract law will be useful for future practice in public utilities regulation. For example, students may consider applying for the Honourable

---

[484] Australian Competition and Consumer Commission, *Public Utility Regulation in Australia*, Working Paper No. 4 (July 2011).

[485] Consumer and Utilities Advocacy Centre, *Welcome to CUAC* (2011). https://www.cuac.org.au/contact-us/welcome-to-cuac

[486] Australian Competition and Consumer Commission, *Public Utility Regulation in Australia*, Working Paper No. 4 (July 2011), 42.

[487] Australian Competition and Consumer Commission, *Public Utility Regulation in Australia*, Working Paper No. 4 (July 2011), 52.

Michael Kirby Contract Law Moot through their university. This competition is open to Australian law students and runs for four days.[488] Another mooting experience involving consumer law and contract law is the Annual Willem C. Vis International Commercial Arbitration Moot, the contracts in this instance relating to transactions falling under the United Nations Convention on Contracts for the International Sale of Goods.[489]

Career Pathways

Interested students may consider applying to work for the ACCC, or to work at firms practising in contract law as a pathway to more specific work in contracts relating to public utilities regulation. Another pathway to practising in public utilities regulation may be through policy development bodies. Students may also consider future work in an advocacy centre, for example the Consumer Utilities Advocacy Centre (CUAC). CUAC upholds the interests of Victorian consumers, specifically energy and water consumers, through the avenues of policy and regulation.[490]

References

References for Section "Animal Law"

A. Articles/Websites/Books

Cao, D., & White, S. W. (2016). *Animal law and welfare*. New York: Springer.
Domestic Animals Amendment (Puppy Farm and Pet Shops) Bill 2016.
Oxford University Press. *Australian Law Dictionary* (at 29 November 2017).
What is the Australian *Legislation Governing Animal Welfare? – RSPCA Australia Knowledgebase* (2017). Kb.rspca.org.au. http://kb.rspca.org.au/what-is-the-australian-legislation-governing-animal-welfare_264.html
Your Legal Calling*: Considering a Future in Animal Law?* (2017). Liv.asn.au. https://www.liv.asn.au/younglawyersblog/april-2013-(1)/your-legal-calling%2D%2Dconsidering-a-future-in-animal

[488] College of Law and Justice, Victoria University, *The 7th Annual Michael Kirby Contract Law Moot Melbourne, Australia* (2017). https://www.vu.edu.au/sites/default/files/kirby-moot-2017.pdf

[489] Annual Willem C. Vis International Commercial Arbitration Moot, *Annual Willem C. Vis International Commercial Arbitration Moot: About the Moot* (2018). https://vismoot.pace.edu/site/about-the-moot

[490] Consumer and Utilities Advocacy Centre, *Welcome to CUAC* (2011). https://www.cuac.org.au/contact-us/welcome-to-cuac

B. Bills/Legislative Materials

Domestic Animals Amendment (Puppy Farm and Pet Shops) Bill 2016 (Vic).

References for Section "Aviation Law"

Griffin, K. (2013). Aviation law. *GPSolo, 30*(2), 46–50.

Havel, B. F. (2014). *The principles and practice of international aviation law*. Cambridge: Cambridge University Press.

Kyoto Protocol to the United Nations Framework Convention on Climate Change, art. 2(2), opened for signature Dec. 11, 1997, 2303 U.N.T.S.

Reference for Section "Bankruptcy Law/Insolvency Law"

Symes, C. F., & Duns, J. (2015). *Australian insolvency law* (3rd ed.). Chatswood: LexisNexis Butterworths Australia.

References for Section "Capital Markets/Securities Law"

Carter, A., Natesh, S., & West, T. (Eds.). *Financial services disputes – What's new?* (2017, June). Ashurst Australia. https://www.ashurst.com/en/news-and-insights/insights/financial-services-disputes-whats-new-federal-budget/

Cunningham, M., Pollari, I., & Trinci, M. *10 key banking and capital markets regulatory challenges in 2017* (2017, March 3). KPMG. https://assets.kpmg.com/content/dam/kpmg/au/pdf/2017/banking-capital-markets-regulatory-challenges-2017.pdf

Chambers Associate. *Capital Markets*. http://www.chambers-associate.com/practice-areas/capital-markets

Hossack, M. Capital markets. Globe Business Media Group https://www.lawcareers.net/Solicitors/SolicitorPracticeAreas/Capital-markets

Investopedia. *Capital Markets*. https://www.investopedia.com/terms/c/capitalmarkets.asp

Langworth, H. *Capital markets law*. The Gateway. http://thegatewayonline.com/law/types-of-work/clifford-chance-capital-markets-law

References for Section "Competition and Consumer Law"

Books

Coorey, A. (2015). *Australian consumer law* (1st ed.). Chatswood: LexisNexis Butterworths.

Websites

Carr, J. (2018). *Consumer law area of practice*. GradAustralia. https://gradaustralia.com.au/law/consumer-law-area-of-practice

References for Section "Constitutional Law"

AUSPUBLAW. (2017, July 3). *Public law events roundup July 2017*. https://auspublaw.org/2017/07/public-law-events-roundup-july-2017/

Blackshield, T. (2017, October 30). *Seven little Australians*. AUSPUBLAW. https://auspublaw.org/2017/10/seven-little-australians/

Constitution Education Fund Australia. *Governor-General's Prize*. http://www.cefa.org.au/governor-generals-prize

Finkelstein, R., & Hamer, D (Eds.). (2015). *LexisNexis concise Australian legal dictionary* (5th ed.). Chatswood: LexisNexis.

Joseph, S., & Castan, M. (2014). *Federal constitutional law: A contemporary view* (4th ed.). Pyrmont: Lawbook.

Law Society of New South Wales. (2009, October 1). *Young lawyers: Careers guide to public law and government*, 9. https://www.lawsociety.com.au/cs/groups/public/documents/internetyounglawyers/064359.pdf

Melbourne University Law Students' Society. (2017). *Sir Harry Gibbs Constitutional Law Moot*. http://mulss.com/competitions/2015_sir_harry_gibbs_constitutional_law_moot

New South Wales v Commonwealth (2006) 229 CLR 1.

Quick, J., & Garran, R. R. (2015). *The annotated constitution of the Australian Commonwealth* (Rev ed.). Chatswood: LexisNexis.

Re Canavan*; Re Ludlam; Re Waters; Re Roberts [No 2]; Re Joyce; Re Nash; Re Xenophon* [2017] HCA 45.

Twomey, A. (2017, November 27). *Wilkie v Commonwealth: A retreat to Combat over the Bones of Pape, Williams, and responsible government*. AUSPUBLAW. https://auspublaw.org/2017/11/wilkie-v-commonwealth/

References for Section "Construction Law"

Books

Bailey, I., & Bell, M. (2011). *Construction law in Australia* (3rd ed.). Pyrmont: Thomson Reuters.

Cases

Nouvelle *Homes Pty Ltd v G & M Smargiassi* [2008] WASC 127.

Websites

Law Institute of Victoria. *Become an Accredited Specialist* (2018). https://www.liv.asn.au/Learning-and-Networking/Become-an-Accredited-Specialist/Specialist-Areas-Key-Dates

Law Society of New South Wales. *Professional Development: Specialist Accreditation* (2018). http://www.lawsociety.com.au/ForSolictors/Education/specialists/Howtoapply/index.htm

The National Association of Women in Construction. *Becme a Member Today* (2018). https://www.nawic.com.au/Web/Membership/Web/Membership/Become_a_Member.aspx?hkey=413085e8-5409-429e-85f5-e291fc8a8ac1

References for Section "Criminal Law"

A. Articles/Books/Websites

Bell, V. (2017). Keeping the criminal law in 'serviceable condition': A task for the courts or the parliament? *Current Issues in Criminal Justice, 27*(3), 335–344.

Criminal Law Area of Practice (2017). GradAustralia. https://gradaustralia.com.au/law/criminal-law-area-of-practice

LexisNexis. *Encyclopaedic Australian Legal Dictionary* (at 29 December 2017).

Oxford University Press. *Australian Law Dictionary* (at 29 December 2017).

Smith, M., & Mann, M. (2015). Recent developments in DNA evidence. *Trends and Issues in Crime and Criminal Justice, 506*, 1–7.

Weekly, Lawyers and Staff Reporter. *Practice Profile: Criminal Lawyers Say Real Life Practice Is Far From Prime Time* (2017). Lawyersweekly.com.au. https://www.lawyersweekly.com.au/features/9050-practice-profile-criminal-lawyers-say-real-life-pr

References for Section "Dispute Resolution"

CIArb Australia (2014). Chartered Institute of Arbitrators. https://www.ciarb.net.au/

Confidence in Alternative Dispute Resolution (2017, December 28). Australian Disputes Centre. https://www.disputescentre.com.au/

Dispute Resolution (2017, October 31). Victoria Legal Aid. https://www.legalaid.vic.gov.au/find-legal-answers/courts-and-legal-system/dispute-resolution

Training (2017, September 21). Dispute Settlement Centre of Victoria. https://www.disputes.vic.gov.au/training

Training (2017, September 21). Dispute Settlement Centre of Victoria. https://www.disputes.vic.gov.au/training

Sourdin, T. (2012). *Alternative dispute resolution* (4th ed.). Pyrmont: Thomson Reuters Professional Australia.

References for Section "Drug Control Law"

A. Articles/Books/Websites

Australian Institute of Criminology – Drug Courts (2018). Aic.gov.au. http://www.aic.gov.au/criminal_justice_system/courts/specialist/drugcourts.html

Cracking Down on Synthetic Drugs and Drug Dealing (2017). Premier of Victoria. https://www.premier.vic.gov.au/cracking-down-on-synthetic-drugs-and-drug-dealing/

Drug Charges – Melbourne Criminal Lawyers | Doogue + George (2017). Doogue + George. https://www.criminal-lawyers.com.au/criminal-law/offences/drug-charges

Guidance for the Use of Medicinal Cannabis in Australia: Overview (2017). Therapeutic Goods Administration (TGA). https://www.tga.gov.au/publication/guidance-use-medicinal-cannabis-australia-overview

LexisNexis. *Encyclopaedic Australian Legal Dictionary* (at 29 December 2017).

Medicinal Cannabis Law Reform in Australia. (2016). *Journal of Law and Medicine, 23*(3).

Oxford University Press. *Australian Law Dictionary* (at 29 December 2017).

References for Section "Energy Law"

Books

Heffron, R. J. (2015). *Energy law: An introduction* (1st ed.). Heidelberg: Springer.

Websites

Crommelin, M. *Energy and Resources Law*. University of Melbourne. http://law.unimelb.edu.au/study/masters/specialist-legal-areas/energy-and-resources-law?utm_source=2017_mlm_adwords_energy_resources_law&utm_medium=sem&utm_campaign=mlsmlm_20160415_adwords&utm_content=register_now&gclid=CjwKCAiA4vbSBRBNEiwAMorER8e17UjSGkeNENS3ddd9FDeYKTCCL9CCRMRqtQ18FyjMywSxGZh5ExoCoTAQAvD_BwE

Derrick, J. *Energy and Natural Resources*. LawCareers.Net. https://www.lawcareers.net/Solicitors/SolicitorPracticeAreas/Energy-natural-resources

So You Want to be an Energy Lawyer. Robert Walters. https://www.robertwalters.co.uk/career-advice/energy-legal-jobs-market.html

We're Powering Forward (2018, January 16). Australian Government: Department of the Environment and Energy. https://poweringforward.energy.gov.au/

References for Section "Entertainment Law"

Firemark, G. *What Does an Entertainment Lawyer Do?* (2012, July 20). Law Offices of Gordon P. Firemark. https://firemark.com/2012/07/20/what-does-an-entertainment-lawyer-do-part-i/

Schroder, K. *Entertainment and sports industries*. American Bar Association. https://www.americanbar.org/newsletter/publications/gp_solo_magazine_home/gp_solo_magazine_index/schroder.html

References for Section "Environmental Law"

Books

Baird, R. J. (2012). *Environmental law* (1st ed.). Pyrmont: Thomson Reuters.

Heffron, R. J. (2015). *Energy law: An introduction* (1st ed.). Heidelberg: Springer.

Websites

Graduate Program. The Department of Environment and Energy. http://www.environment.gov.au/about-us/employment/graduate-program

What is an Environmental Lawyer. Environmental Science.org. https://www.environmentalscience.org/career/environmental-lawyer

References for Section "Family Law"

A. Articles/Websites

Australian Government Department of Human Services, "Child Support". https://www.humanservices.gov.au/individuals/child-support

Firestone, G., & Weinstein, J. (2004). In the best interests of the children: A proposal to transform the adversarial system. *Family Court Review, 42*(2), 203.

LexisNexis. *Encyclopaedic Australian Legal Dictionary* (at 29 November 2017).

Oxford University Press. *Australian Law Dictionary* (at 29 November 2017).

Pillai, S., & Williams, G. (2017). The High Court, the constitution and family law. *Australian Journal of Family Law, 2*(29).

B. Legislation

Australian Constitution.

Family *Law Act 1975 (Cth).*

C. Cases

Re Kelvin [2017] FamCAFC 258.

References for Section "Firearm Law"

A. Articles/Books/Websites

Beck, K. *Would Australia's Gun Laws Help The US?* (2018). BBC News. http://www.bbc.com/news/world-australia-35048251

Casey-Maslen, S. (2014). *Weapons under international human rights law* (1st ed.). Cambridge: Cambridge University Press.

Davies, A. *Seizing the moment on gun control changed Australia, Says John Howard* (2018). The Sydney Morning Herald. http://www.smh.com.au/national/seizing-the-moment-on-gun-control-changed-australia-john-howard-20160424-godwg6.html

LexisNexis. *Encyclopaedic Australian Legal Dictionary* (at 29 December 2017).

New NSW Bail and Firearms Laws Announced in Response to Lindt Cafe Sydney Siege (2018). ABC News. http://www.abc.net.au/news/2015-08-28/mike-baird-announces-bail-and-illegal-firearms-reform/6732332

2017 National Firearms Amnesty | Victorian Government (2018). Vic.gov.au. https://www.vic.gov.au/news/2017-national-firearms-amnesty.html

B. Legislation

Firearms Act 1996 (Vic).

References for Section "Gaming Law"

Addisons. *Gambling*. Addisons. http://www.addisonslawyers.com.au/service/Gambling/default.aspx

Jackson, K. *Gambling policy and regulation* (2001, September). Parliament of Australia. https://www.aph.gov.au/About_Parliament/Parliamentary_Departments/Parliamentary_Library/Publications_Archive/archive/gamblingebrief

NSW Department of Industry. *Gaming & wagering law*. NSW Government. http://www.liquorandgaming.nsw.gov.au/Pages/gaming/law-and-policy/gaming-law.aspx

References for Section "Immigration Law"

Burnside, J. (2017). *Watching out: Reflections on justice and injustice* (p. 200). Brunswick: Scribe Publications.

Finkelstein, R. (2015). In D. Hamer (Ed.), *LexisNexis concise Australian legal dictionary* (5th ed.). Chatswood: LexisNexis.

Gageler, S. (2010). Impact of migration law on the development of Australian administrative law. *Australian Journal of Administrative Law, 17*, 92.

Graham v Minister for Immigration and Border Protection; Te Puia v Minister for Immigration and Border Protection [2017] HCA 33.

Law Council of Australia. *Prescribed Academic Areas of Knowledge*. (2016, December). https://www.lawcouncil.asn.au/files/web-pdf/LACC%20docs/243473563_1_Prescribed_Academic_Areas_of_Knowledge.pdf

Migration Act 1958 (Cth).

References for Section "Indigenous Law"

Australian Human Rights Commission. *Constitutional reform: Creating a nation for all of us*. Social Justice Report 2010. http://www.humanrights.gov.au/sites/default/files/content/social_justice/sj_report/sjreport10/pdf/sjr2010_CH2.pdf

Commonwealth of Australia Referendum Council. *Final Report of the Referendum Council* (2017, June 30). https://www.referendumcouncil.org.au/final-report

Finkelstein, R., & Hamer, D. (Eds.). (2015). *LexisNexis concise Australian legal dictionary* (5th ed.). Chatswood: LexisNexis.

Gooda, M. (2013). Human rights and Australia's indigenous peoples. In P. Gerber & M. Castan (Eds.), *Contemporary perspectives on human rights law in Australia* (p. 302). Rozelle: Lawbook.

Henry Bolt and Emily Laurence. *Malcolm Turnbull Defends Decision to Abandon Constitutional Recognition of Indigenous Australians* (2017, November 5). Australian Broadcasting Corporation. http://www.abc.net.au/news/2017-11-05/malcolm-turnbull-defends-decision-on-indigenous-recognition/9120252

Monash University. *Castan Centre: Indigenous* (2017, September). https://www.monash.edu/law/research/centres/castancentre/our-areas-of-work/indigenous

The Aurora Project. *Internship Streams: Legal* (2018, January). http://auroraproject.com.au/legal

University of New South Wales. *Australian Indigenous Law Review* (2017, December 21). http://www.ilc.unsw.edu.au/publications/australian-indigenous-law-review

University of New South Wales. *Indigenous Law Centre* (2017, December 19). http://www.ilc.unsw.edu.au

References for Section "Intellectual Property Law"

Copyright Act 1968 (Cth).

Escovedo, J. *Disney's Influence on United States Copyright Law* (2016, February 17). The IP Law Blog. https://www.theiplawblog.com/2016/02/articles/copyright-law/disneys-influence-on-united-states-copyright-law/

IP Australia. *Trade Mark Basics* (2016, March 10). Australian Government. https://www.ipaustralia.gov.au/trade-marks/understanding-trade-marks

Sheppard, F. *The Dallas Buyers Club Case has Been Abandoned But Illegal Downloaders May Still Face Trouble* (2016, February 12). ABC. http://www.abc.net.au/news/2016-02-12/dallas-buyers-club-case-abandoned-illegal-dowloads-pirate/7162180

The University of Melbourne. *What is copyright?* The University of Melbourne. http://copyright.unimelb.edu.au/information/what-is-copyright

World Intellectual Property Organisation. *What is Intellectual Property?* World Intellectual Property Organisation. http://www.wipo.int/edocs/pubdocs/en/intproperty/450/wipo_pub_450.pdf

Reference for Section "Investment Law"

Perry, B. *Private equity law: Area of practice*. Target Jobs. https://targetjobs.co.uk/career-sectors/law-solicitors/advice/290555-private-equity-law-area-of-practice

References for Section "Juvenile or Youth Law"

A. Articles/Websites/Books

About Children's Rights | Australian Human Rights Commission. https://www.humanrights.gov.au/our-work/childrens-rights/about-childrens-rights

Children*'s Rights: Australia | Law Library of Congress* (2018). https://www.loc.gov/law/help/child-rights/australia.php

Cunneen, C., Goldson, B., & Russel, S. (2016). Juvenile justice, young people and human rights in Australia. *Current Issues in Criminal Justice, 28*(2), 173–189.

Koori *Court | Children's Court Of Victoria* (2018). Childrenscourt.vic.gov.au. http://www.childrenscourt.vic.gov.au/jurisdictions/koori-court

LexisNexis. *Encyclopaedic Australian Legal Dictionary* (at 14 April 2018).

Oxford University Press. *Australian Law Dictionary* (at 29 November 2017).

Role of the Court I Children's Court of Victoria (2018). Childrenscourt.vic.gov.au. http://www.childrenscourt.vic.gov.au/about-us/role-court

Support Services in the Youth Justice System – Department of Justice and Regulation, Victoria (2018). Justice.vic.gov.au. http://www.justice.vic.gov.au/home/justice+system/youth+justice/support+services

B. Treaties

Convention on the Rights of the Child. opened for signature 20 November 1989, 1577 UNTS 3 (entered into force 2 September 1990).

References for Section "Maritime (Admiralty) Law"

Australian and New Zealand Maritime Law Journal. *Membership*. (2009–2012). http://www.mlaanz.org/Membership/0,2715,11532,00.html

Australian and New Zealand Maritime Law Journal (2009–2013). http://ssl.law.uq.edu.au/journals/index.php/maritimejournal/

Australian and New Zealand Maritime Law Journal. *MLAANZ National Conference 2017* (2009–2012). http://www.mlaanz.org/Page-Preview/0,2793,19332,00.html

Cremean, D. J. (2008). *Admiralty jurisdiction: Law and practice in Australia, New Zealand, Singapore and Hong Kong* (3rd ed.). Annandale: Federation Press.

Emerton, P., & O'Sullivan, M. (2015). Rethinking asylum seeker detention at sea: The power to detain asylum seekers at sea under the *Maritime Powers Act 2013* (Cth). *University of New South Wales Law Journal, 38*(2), 695.

Finkelstein, R., & Hamer, D (Eds.). (2015). *LexisNexis concise Australian legal dictionary* (5th ed.). Chatswood: LexisNexis.

Sapienza, A. *Chief Justice French on Non-Statutory Executive Power: A Timely Reflection* (2016, December 20). https://auspublaw.org/2016/12/chief-justice-french-a-timely-reflection/

White, M. (2014). *Australian maritime law* (3rd ed.). Annendale: Federation Press.

References for Section "Media and Communications Law"

Australian Communications and Media Authority. *Six Emerging Trends in Media and Communications* (2014, November). Australian Communications and Media Authority. https://www.acma.gov.au/~/media/Research%20and%20Analysis/Research/pdf/Six%20emerging%20trends%20in%20media%20and%20communications_Final%20pdf.pdf

Competition *and Consumer Act 2010 (Cth).*

Kain, E. *YouTube Wants Content Creators to Appeal Demonetisation, But it's Not Always That Easy* (2017, September 18). Forbes. https://www.forbes.com/sites/erikkain/2017/09/18/adpocalypse-2017-heres-what-you-need-to-know-about-youtubes-demonetization-troubles/#1c8e08cd6c26

Studio Legal. *Media, Advertising and Marketing Law. Studio Legal.* http://studiolegal.com.au/media-advertising-and-markting-law/.

The Australian Competition and Consumer Commission. *ACCC Cracks Down on Fine Print Advertising* (2001, July 9). The Australian Competition and Consumer Commission. https://www.accc.gov.au/media-release/accc-cracks-down-on-fine-print-advertising

Thomson Reuters. *What is Media and Communications Law? FindLaw.* http://hirealawyer.findlaw.com/choosing-the-right-lawyer/communications-and-media-law.html.

References for Section "Military Law"

Defence Force Discipline Appeals Act 1995 (Cth), s 8(1).

Defence Legal. *Military Law Centre* (2018). Australian Government Department of Defence. http://www.defence.gov.au/legal/mlc.asp

Finkelstein, R., & Hamer, D. (Eds.). (2015). *LexisNexis concise Australian legal dictionary* (5th ed.). Chatswood: LexisNexis.

Graduate Careers Australia. *Careers for Law Graduates* (2008). GradAustralia. http://www.graduatecareers.com.au/wp-content/uploads/2011/12/careers_for_law_graduates.pdf

Lane v Morrison [2009] HCA 29.

Logan, J. A. *What Now for Defence Force Discipline Appeals?* (2016, April 16). Federal Court of Australia. http://www.fedcourt.gov.au/digital-law-library/judges-speeches/justice-logan/logan-j-20160416

References for Section "Mining Law"

Carr, J. *Careers for Law Graduates in Mining and Resources*. GradAustralia. https://gradaustralia.com.au/law/careers-for-law-graduates-in-mining-and-resources

Environmental Law Australia. *Carmichael Coal Mine cases in the Federal Court*. http://envlaw.com.au/carmichael-coal-mine-federal-court/

Finkelstein, R., & Hamer, D. (Eds.) (2015). *LexisNexis concise Australian legal dictionary* (5th ed.). Chatswood: LexisNexis.

Hunt, M. (2009). *Mining law in Western Australia* (4th ed.). Annandale: Federation Press.

The Climate Council. *New Report: Adani Monster Mine could Damage Climate, Health, Tourism* (2017, May 17). https://www.climatecouncil.org.au/carmichaelmediarelease

References for Section "Privacy Law"

A. Articles/Websites/Books

Data *& Privacy – Holding Redlich Lawyers – Law Firm Melbourne Sydney Brisbane Australia* (2018). Holdingredlich.com. https://www.holdingredlich.com/practice-group/privacy

How *Do I Make A Privacy Complaint?| Office of the Australian Information Commissioner – OAIC* (2018). Oaic.gov.au. https://www.oaic.gov.au/individuals/how-do-i-make-a-privacy-complaint

LexisNexis. *Encyclopaedic Australian Legal Dictionary* (at 18 April 2018) 'Privacy".

Overview of Privacy Law in Australia (2018). Hall & Wilcox. https://hallandwilcox.com.au/overview-of-privacy-law-in-australia/

Privacy Act Compliance Guide – Law Institute of Victoria (2018). Liv.asn.au. https://www.liv.asn.au/For-Lawyers/LIV-Privileges-Member-Savings/Practice-Resources/Privacy-Act-Compliance-Guide

Privacy Law| *Office of the Australian Information Commissioner – OAIC* (2018). Oaic.gov.au. https://www.oaic.gov.au/privacy-law/

Right *to Personal Privacy—Developments in Australia and Elsewhere | ALRC* (2018). Alrc.gov.au. https://www.alrc.gov.au/publications/74.%20Protecting%20a%20Right%20to%20Personal%20Privacy%20/right-personal-privacy%E2%80%94developments-austral

What *Happens to My Complaint| Office of the Australian Information Commissioner – OAIC* (2018). Oaic.gov.au. https://www.oaic.gov.au/individuals/what-happens-to-my-complaint

What New US CLOUD Laws Mean for Australian Businesses (2018). Financial Review. http://www.afr.com/technology/cloud-computing/what-new-us-cloud-laws-mean-for-australian-businesses-20180413-h0ypuu#ixzz5CzysCEtX

B. Legislative Materials

Clarifying Lawful Overseas Use of Data (CLOUD) Act of 2018 (H.R. 4943 and S. 2383).

Privacy Act 1988 (Cth).

References for Section "Property Law"

Books

Moore, A., Grattan, S., & Griggs, L. (2015). *Bradbrook, MacCallum and Moore's Australian real property law* (6th ed.). Pyrmont: Thomson Reuters.

Websites

Carr, J. *Real Estate and Property Law Area of Practice*. GradAustralia. https://gradaustralia.com.au/law/real-estate-and-property-law-area-of-practice

Law Institute of Victoria. *Become an Accredited Specialist* (2018). https://www.liv.asn.au/Learning-and-Networking/Become-an-Accredited-Specialist/Specialist-Areas-Key-Dates

Law Society of New South Wales. *Professional Development: Specialist Accreditation* (2018). http://www.lawsociety.com.au/ForSolictors/Education/specialists/Howtoapply/index.htm

References for Section "Social Security Law"

Administrative Appeals Tribunal, Social Services & Child Support Division. (2018, January 23). http://www.aat.gov.au/social-services-child-support-division

Australian Law Reform Commission. *Family Violence and Commonwealth Laws – Improving Legal Frameworks* (Final Report 117) (2011, November).

Canberra Community Law. *Social Security Law* (2017). http://www.canberracommunitylaw.org.au/social-security-law.html

Community Affairs Reference Committee, Commonwealth Parliament. *Design, scope, cost-benefit analysis, contracts awarded and implementation associated with the Better Management of the Social Welfare System initiative* (2018, June).

Finkelstein, R., & Hamer, D. (Eds.). (2015). *LexisNexis concise Australian legal dictionary* (5th ed.). Chatswood: LexisNexis.

Social Security Appeals Tribunal. *Annual Report 2014/2015* (2015, September 28). http://www.aat.gov.au/AAT/media/AAT/Files/SSCSD%20documents/Reports/SSAT-Annual-Report-2014-15.pdf

References for Section "Space Law"

Websites

Australian Civil Space. Australian Government: Department of Industry, Innovation and Science. https://industry.gov.au/INDUSTRY/IndustrySectors/SPACE/Pages/default.aspx

Salleh, A. *Out-of-this-world space careers you can have without leaving Earth* (2017, December 5). ABC News. http://www.abc.net.au/news/science/2017-11-27/space-careers:-theres-more-to-being-an-astronaut/9157980

What is Space Law. Legal Career Path. http://legalcareerpath.com/space-law/

Other

Department of Industry, Innovation and Science (Cth). 'Turnbull Government to Establish National Space Agency' (Media Release, 25 September 2017).

References for Section "Sports Law"

De Guzman, J. N. *The World's Biggest and Best eSports Arenas* (2015, February 27). Red Bull. https://www.redbull.com/gb-en/the-biggest-and-best-esports-stadiums-in-the-world

Dwan, H. *What Are Esports? A Beginner's Guide* (2017, October 18). The Telegraph. https://www.telegraph.co.uk/gaming/guides/esports-beginners-guide/

Mitten, M. *What is Sports Law and Who is a Sports Lawyer?* American Bar Association. https://www.americanbar.org/groups/young_lawyers/publications/tyl/topics/professional-development/what-is-sports-law-who-is-sports-lawyer.html

Warman, P. *Esports Revenue Will Reach $696 Miilion This Year and Grow to $1.5 Billion by 2020 as Brand Investment Doubles* (2017, February 14). Newzoo. https://newzoo.com/insights/articles/esports-revenues-will-reach-696-million-in-2017/

References for Section "Taxation Law"

Barkoczy, S. (2017). *Foundations of taxation law* (9th ed.). Docklands: Oxford University Press.

Barkoczy, S., et al. (2016). *Innovation and venture capital law and policy*. Sydney: The Federation Press.

References for Section "Technology Law"

Kostarelis, S. *What is Net Neutrality and How Will Its Death Affect Australians?* (2017, December 17). Techly. https://www.techly.com.au/2017/12/18/net-neutrality-will-death-affect-australians/

Leyva, C. *What is Cyberlaw?*. Digital Business Law Group. http://www.digitalbusinesslawgroup.com/what-is-cyberlaw.html

Maddocks, T. *New Sexting Laws to Exempt Young People from Child Pornography Charges* (2014, August 21). ABC. http://www.abc.net.au/news/2014-08-21/australian-first-sexting-laws-to-be-introduced-in-victoria/5686166

References for Section "Torts Law"

A. Articles/Books

Beyond Law | *Legal Jobs, News and Resources for Australian Law Students, Graduates and Young Lawyers* (2018). Beyondlaw.com.au. https://beyondlaw.com.au/news/91-tort-story-4-reasons-to-think-about-working-in-plaintiff-law

LexisNexis. *Encyclopaedic Australian Legal Dictionary* (at 3 January 2017).

Oxford University Press. *Australian Law Dictionary* (at 3 January 2017).

Should *a New Tort Be Enacted?* | *ALRC* (2011). Alrc.gov.au. https://www.alrc.gov.au/publications/1-executive-summary/should-new-tort-be-enacted

References for Section "Trusts and Estates Law"

A. Articles and Websites

Changes to Succession Laws: Latest Amendments Address Matters Including What Happens When a Person Dies Intestate (2018). *Law Institute Journal, 91*(12).

Dal Pont, G. E. (2015). *Equity and Trusts in Australia* (6th ed.). Pyrmont: Lawbook Co.

McMurdo, A. C., & The Honourable Justice Margaret, A. (2013). Faith Hope and Charity: The Resilience of the Charitable Trust from the Middle Ages to the 21St Century. The WA Lee Lecture 2011. *QUT Law Review, 13*(1).

Oxford University Press. *Australian Law Dictionary* (at 29 November 2017).

Stay on the Estate: Practitioners Handling Estate Matters Should Not Get Involved in Family Disputes (2017). *Law Institute Journal, 91*(6).

Tax Tips: Discretionary Trusts: Beneficiary Issues (2017). *Taxation in Australia, 51*(7).

Wills*: The Law's Response* (2018). Alrc.gov.au. https://www.alrc.gov.au/sites/default/files/pdfs/publications/fr131_08_wills.pdf

B. Legislation

Administration and Probate Act 1958 (Vic).

Guardianship *and Administration Act 1986 (Vic).*

Powers of Attorney Act 2014 (Vic).

References for Section "Utilities Regulation Law"

Annual Willem C. *Vis International Commercial Arbitration Moot: About the Moot* (2018). https://vismoot.pace.edu/site/about-the-moot

Australian Competition and Consumer Law. *Public Utility Regulation in Australia* (Working Paper No. 4) (2011, July).

College of Law and Justice, Victoria University. *The 7th Annual Michael Kirby Contract Law Moot Melbourne, Australia* (2017). https://www.vu.edu.au/sites/default/files/kirby-moot-2017.pdf

Consumer and Utilities Advocacy Centre. *Welcome to CUAC* (2011). https://www.cuac.org.au/contact-us/welcome-to-cuac

Chapter 8
The Future of the Law Profession

John Devereux

The Future of Law: An Australian Perspective

There are as many visions for the future of law, as there are for the future of any professional practice – be it medicine, dentistry or law. A careful review of the literature and public enquiries reveals certain key themes which permeate the different visions. This chapter will summarise key predictions as to the future of law, and of legal practice in particular. The chapter draws heavily upon two Australian reports – The Commission of Inquiry into the Future of Law and Innovation in the Profession,[1] and a Report entitled The Future of the Legal Profession.[2]

Law or Laws?

As technology, society and business progress, the law moves, grows and adapts with it. Law is often reactive – that is, requires a change or dispute to have arisen first, before reacting to it. As Justice Windeyer remarked "law marches with medicine – but to the rear, and limping a little".[3] New technologies – the internet, smart phones, genetic tests all demand regulation and control. How should the law prevent

[1] Law Society of New South Wales Commission of Inquiry The Future of Law and Innovation in the Profession, Sydney, 2017.

[2] Law Society of Western Australia The Future of the Legal Profession, Perth, 2017.

[3] Mt Isa Mines v Pusey (1970) 125 CLR 383 per Windeyer J at 395.

J. Devereux (✉)
Faculty of Law, The University of Queensland, Brisbane, QLD, Australia
e-mail: j.devereux@law.uq.edu.au

M. Raz et al. (eds.), *Careers in Law: A Guide for Students, Graduates and Professionals*, https://doi.org/10.1007/978-981-15-3627-4_8

bullying on social media?[4] Should the law restrict access to genetic information lodged by a person, if access to that information would identify a relative as the perpetrator of a crime?[5] Inevitably, the number and complexity of laws increases.to cope with developments. Not just proliferation of legislation or court judgments – but legal debate, law review discussions and blogs. It is not, however, just technological developments which drive change. What the media refer to as "loopholes in the law" become closed by legal review. New loopholes are discovered. New fact scenarios challenge the applicability of existing laws. So the law is reconfigured, re-considered and re-made. Double jeopardy laws traditionally prevented an accused from being re-tried, following an acquittal.[6] The modern availability of DNA evidence has seen these laws relaxed.[7] Re-trials are becoming more common.

Some areas of the law have always been subject to substantial amendment. These areas will continue to be the source of change. It was common in Australian law schools in the 1980s to advise students they would be examined on tax law which existed at the date it was taught to them, and not at the date at which the examination would be sat. The pace at which laws are developed seems unlikely to slow anytime soon. This places demands on lawyers to ensure they keep up to date. It also drives a process of specialisation of lawyers as the sheer number of laws challenges the profession's ability to keep pace. As the Law Society of Western Australia puts it "the success of a future profession will depend on an openness to change, and on a willingness to embrace the challenges and opportunities afforded by new and emerging technologies and methods of working. Above all, it will depend on the profession's capacity to adapt."[8]

Turbulent Times

The immediate future of law is driven by turbulence in the broader society. The Commission of Inquiry into the Future of Law and Innovation in Legal Practice notes the waves of change and contradiction that are apparent in modern society.[9]

[4] There are existing laws such as Criminal Code Act 1995 (Cth) s 474.17 which makes it an offence to use a carriage service to menace, harass or cause offence. Each state also has anti stalking legislations – see, for example, Criminal Code (Qld) s 359E. There have been calls in the media for stronger laws, see for example https://www.sunshinecoastdaily.com.au/news/laws-needed-to-crack-down-on-cyberbullying/3357090/; https://www.kidspot.com.au/parenting/real-life/in-the-news/parents-outraged-about-joke-new-antibullying-laws/news-story/85d280bf81a2a97c6a4427b2fcf4c1ff

[5] The issue arose in California in the so called Golden State Killer case, see generally "The Ethics of Catching Criminals using their Family's DNA. (2018) *Nature* 2018 557.

[6] See for example, Criminal Code (Qld) s. 17.

[7] See for example, Criminal Code (Qld) s. 678B.

[8] Note 2 op cit at 11.

[9] Law Society of New South Wales op cit note 1 at 10.

Britain, contrary to expectations, voted in 2015 to leave the European Union. This decision "reflected an immense public distrust of existing institutions, a hostility that had evidently been growing over time."[10] During the same period, by contrast, the "peer to peer" sharing economy continued to grow.[11] This latter economy "builds on trust and transparency".[12]

Globalisation

The above trends are, of course, overseas developments. But they feed into Australian law, as a consequence of one of the important trends already evident in the future of law. That of globalization. Australian law firms, once proudly city based, moved, in the 1980s to merge with one another into national firms.[13] In turn, some of these firms merged into multi national firms. Inevitably, cross fertilization of ideas, experience and staff have followed. Broadly speaking the phenomena is called "increased connectivity".[14]

Globalisation is, of course, not new. But what is new is the sheer speed of the process.. The focus of change is less on the movement of people, as the movement of ideas: "ideas, or small bits of data, can now move through unstructured networks wherever they need to go, moving very quickly across time and space, and disrupting today's knowledge hierarchies (as the professions are sometimes termed)."[15] Implications for practitioners are threefold.[16] Firstly, transaction planning and dispute resolution raise questions of the skills that practitioners need, and how law reform should be conducted .It may, for example be advantageous for tax reasons for a contract to be entered into in country x, rather than country y. Alternatively, the burden of business reporting and associated costs might be reduced if a company were incorporated in country z, rather than in country a. Secondly, a thorough knowledge of the conflict of laws rules- those laws which govern disputes between parties who have different connections in different countries, becomes important. This is not just the specifics of, say, contract law or corporations law in different countries. Equally important is a knowledge of when an Australian court has

---

[10] Ibid.

[11] Ibid.

[12] Ibid.

[13] See generally, Dan Boyd, *Globalisation changes the legal service business* (3 June 2011) The Australia Business Review http://www.theaustralian.com.au/business/legal-affairs/globalisation-changes-the-legal-service-business/news-story/0cd6c60bb158de6ac2e473cf096d8e07., cited in Law Society of Western Australia, op cit note 2 at 5.

[14] Law Society of New South Wales op cit note 1 at 95.

[15] David Abrahams, testimony 19 October 2016, cited in Law Society of New South Wales op cit note 1 at 95.

[16] See generally on the new skills and knowledge required of Australian lawyers outlined in this paragraph, Law Society of New South Wales op cit note one at Chapter 9.

jurisdiction over a foreign defendant that is, in what circumstances can a foreign person be forced to comply with an Australian court order. Lastly, also important will be in what circumstances will a foreign court order be enforceable in Australia, how to enforce foreign judgments in Australia (and vice versa) and how to gather evidence abroad.

Use of Technology in the Profession

Allied to globalization is the push for greater use of technology in the profession. The Law Society of New South suggests that the use of the correct technology makes the job of being a lawyer more efficient, effective and enjoyable.[17] Competition and client expectation also play a part. This is reflected in a number of developments. Lost cost on-line provision of legal services, on-line provision of free documents by law firms to start-up companies, remote storage of documents (such as cloud computing).[18]

Cloud computing is defined by the Office of the Legal Services Commissioner (WA) as "the delivery of hosted services over the internet".[19] The advantages include "instant accessibility anywhere and anytime and the reduced costs firms otherwise would pay on hardware and software to store the material".[20]

The most exciting (and written about) trend is the use of Artificial Intelligence – computer programs which can read, collate and interpret data to produce solutions. There is considerable debate as to how much "lawyer time" can be saved by the use of AI – anywhere from 13% to 23%.[21] Although AI may retrieve the information, will lawyers still be required to interpret the data, correct errors arising from nuances or the like.[22] The use of AI by non lawyers also raises the spectre of non lawyers providing legal advice – and the extent to which doing so is permitted under current laws.[23]

Technology, particularly, on-line services and remote data storage raise serious liability and cybercrime issues. Risks and challenges include "data security affected by viruses, identity theft; IP issues; maintenance of confidentiality, the question of when and whether lawyer-client relationship is created".[24]

---

[17] Law Society of New South Wales op cit note 1 at 31.

[18] See generally, Law Society of New South Wales op cit note 1 at chapter 2.

[19] The Office of the Legal Services Commissioner, *Cloud Computing Practice Note* (14 August 2015) http://www.olsc.nsw.gov.au at 1, cited in Law Society of Western Australia op cit note 2 at 6.

[20] Law Society of Western Australia op cit note 2 at 6.

[21] Kingsley Martin, *Artificial Intelligence: How will it affect legal practice – and when?* (27 April 2016) Thomson Reuters https://blogs.thomsonreuters.com/answerson/artifical-intelligence-legal-practice/. Cited in Law Society of Western Australia op cite note 2 at7.

[22] Law Society of Western Australia op cit note 2 at 8.

[23] Ibid.

[24] Law Society of Western Australia op cit note 2 at 10.

It is yet to be seen whether Australia will follow the lead of the US and make lawyers observe a duty of "technological competence".[25] The American Bar Association Model Rules of Professional Conduct state "to maintain the requisite knowledge and skill, a lawyer should keep abreast of changes in the law and its practice, including the benefits and risks associated with relevant technology, engage in continuing study and education and comply with all requirements to which the lawyer is subject."

New Ways of Working

Legal practice has been the subject of growth and change over centuries. Originally set up as trade-based, learning in a firm ("articles of clerkship"), there was a move to University based training, supplemented by articles. Now University training in law, followed by legal practice training (which includes an element of work experience) is the norm. Legal practice, too, has changed and emerged. From days where lawyers could expect to be paid by the word. Documents created by hand. Documents lodged in large, government run central paper based registries. Now documents are computer generated. Some transactions (such as searches and conveyances) can be conducted on-line.

Feeding on the two developments of globalization and technology, there have been developments in what is described as "new ways of working".[26] Lawyers traditionally jealously guarded their independence. This was reflected in a prohibition on lawyers sharing work offices with non lawyers. These is now a move to multidisciplinary practices (such as joint lawyer and accountants offices). Online and virtual firms are also starting to emerge – with consequent savings in costs from a lack of physical offices. Another trend is likely to be "insourcing"[27] – where, instead of employing a large law firm to undertake legal work, a consumer of legal services would appoint an in-house counsel. Lawyers Weekly in July 2017 asked Australian lawyers "in the next 12 months, which of the following economic/market disruptors will have the biggest impact on the legal industry?" Nearly 40% said it would be in house counsel doing more of their own legal work. The Law Society of Western Australia suggests this trend is because in house lawyers are becoming more specialist in the roles, able to offer business advice – not just final legal sign off. "In house counsel are becoming expert in their own company's commercial drivers, goals, strategy and risk".[28]

[25] Law Society of Western Australia op cit note 2 at 11.

[26] Law Society of New South Wales op cit note 1 at chapter 3, Law Society of Western Australia op cit note 2 at 2–5, 8.

[27] Law Society of New South wales op cit note 1 at 53, Law Society of Western Australia op cit note 2 at 2.

[28] Quoted in Law Society of Western Australia ibid.

Time billing, dating back to 1919, has been criticized as "perpetuating unfair stereotypes about lawyers, has the potential to disrupt work-life balance, deprioritise pro bono work, strain the lawyer/client relationship. It may also increase mental health stress on practitioners".[29]

Alternatives to time based billing abound.[30]

The Western Australia law society has suggested that "unbundling" of legal tasks – "where, instead of paying for an entire task, the transaction is broken down to individual parts, in which an expert works on each separate part" – is a potential solution. Other solutions include a flat fee plus an incentive structure based on outcome, or flat fees (which offer predictability for client and predictable profit for the firms). A final alternative is blended rates – "a fixed fee agreed in advance which acknowledges that different lawyers, of different experience will be working on a file".

Courts, too, are not immune from the winds of change. Driven by community expectations, and limits on government spending, on-line dispute resolution is likely to be prominent, together with paperless trials.[31]

Legal Education

The above developments will, of course, put pressure on legal education. It has been suggested that, in addition to the traditional skills of legal knowledge, critical thinking and communication; lawyers will need to increasingly be "tech savvy".[32] Additionally, it has been argued that the changes may force educators to provide instructions on corporate finance, or learning another language.[33]

A Way Forward for Lawyers?

It should not be forgotten that, at the centre of this change, are lawyers. Though they will be buffeted by winds of change, their responses to impetus for change will affect the rate of change and the continuation of the change.

[29] Law Society of Western Australia op ci note 2 at 5.

[30] The alternatives are discussed in Law Society of Western Australia op cit note 2 at 6.

[31] Law Society of New South Wales op cit note 1 at 67.

[32] Law Society of New South wales op cit note 1 at 77.

[33] Law Society of Western Australia op cit at 1.

According to the Law Institute of Victoria,[34] lawyers can adapt to change by:

- Specializing in their legal services
- Collaborating with other professionals
- Starting and ending with the client by delivering the services that the client needs
- Providing access to justice
- Considering billing practices
- Using technology to work virtually, remotely or in a different environment
- Looking for job opportunities that use their legal and non legal skills
- Using failure as a mechanism to improve their practice and
- Using technology

[34] Katie Miller, 'Forecasting the Future: What will lawyers be doing in 5 years?'(2016) 38(5) The Bulletin 28 at 28, 29. Cited in Law Society of Western Australia op cit note 2 at 11.

The manufacturer's authorised representative in the EU is Springer Nature Customer Service Centre GmbH, Europaplatz 3, 69115 Heidelberg, Germany. If you have any concerns regarding our products, please contact ProductSafety@springernature.com

Printed and bound by CPI Group (UK) Ltd, Croydon, CR0 4YY
30/09/2026
02225505-0011